GW01465156

What Can Parents Do?

What Can Parents Do?
New Insights into the Role of Parents in Adolescent Problem Behavior

Edited by

Margaret Kerr
Center for Developmental Research, Örebro University, Sweden

Håkan Stattin
Center for Developmental Research, Örebro University, Sweden

Rutger C. M. E. Engels
Behavioural Science Institute, Radboud University, Netherlands

John Wiley & Sons, Ltd

Copyright © 2008 John Wiley & Sons Ltd, The Atrium, Southern Gate, Chichester, West Sussex PO19 8SQ, England

Telephone (+44) 1243 779777

Email (for orders and customer service enquiries): cs-books@wiley.co.uk
Visit our Home Page on www.wiley.com

Other Wiley Editorial Offices

John Wiley & Sons Inc., 111 River Street, Hoboken, NJ 07030, USA

Jossey-Bass, 989 Market Street, San Francisco, CA 94103-1741, USA

Wiley-VCH Verlag GmbH, Boschstr. 12, D-69469 Weinheim, Germany

John Wiley & Sons Australia Ltd, 42 McDougall Street, Milton, Queensland 4064, Australia

John Wiley & Sons (Asia) Pte Ltd, 2 Clementi Loop #02-01, Jin Xing Distripark, Singapore 129809

John Wiley & Sons Canada Ltd, 6045 Freemont Blvd, Mississauga, ONT, L5R 4J3, Canada

Wiley also publishes its books in a variety of electronic formats. Some content that appears in print may not be available in electronic books.

Library of Congress Cataloging in Publication Data

What can parents do? : new insights into the role of parents in adolescent problem behavior / edited by Margaret Kerr, Håkan Stattin, and Rutger C. M. E. Engels.
p. cm.
Includes bibliographical references and index.
ISBN 978-0-470-72363-0 (alk. paper)
1. Parent and teenager. 2. Parenting 3. Adolescence. 4. Adolescent psychology. I. Kerr, Margaret, 1915– II. Stattin, Håkan. III. Engels, Rutger C. M. E.
HQ799.15.W43 2008
306.874—dc22

2007043593

British Library Cataloguing in Publication Data

A catalogue record for this book is available from the British Library

ISBN 978-0-470-72363-0

Typeset in 10/12pt Palatino by Integra Software Services Pvt. Ltd, Pondicherry, India.
Printed and bound in Great Britain by Antony Rowe Ltd, Chippenham, Wiltshire.
This book is printed on acid-free paper responsibly manufactured from sustainable forestry in which at least two trees are planted for each one used for paper production.

Contents

About the Editors

Margaret Kerr is Professor of Psychology at Örebro University, Sweden, and Co-director of the Center for Developmental Research. She earned her PhD at Cornell University, USA, and then completed a postdoctoral research fellowship with Richard Tremblay at the University of Montreal, Canada. She is an associate editor of the *Journal of Research on Adolescence*. Her research focuses on internal and external adjustment in adolescents and their roles in the life course. Her current research interests include adolescents' choices of developmental contexts and parent–child relationships and their role in the development of delinquency.

Håkan Stattin is Professor of Psychology at Uppsala and Örebro Universities, Sweden. He earned his PhD at Stockholm University. He directs the Center for Developmental Research at Örebro University and has served as President of the European Association for Research on Adolescence and associate editor for the *British Journal of Developmental Psychology*. He is probably best known for his research in three areas: delinquency development, pubertal maturation in adolescent girls, and parental monitoring. His works include an authored book (with David Magnusson in 1990), *Pubertal Maturation in Female Development*. In addition to his continued basic research in these areas he is conducting prevention trials to reduce alcohol drinking and delinquency among adolescents.

Rutger C. M. E. Engels is Professor in Family Psychology at the Behavioural Science Institute, Radboud University Nijmegen, Netherlands, since 2001. He obtained his PhD at the Department of Medical Sociology, Maastricht University in 1998. Since then he has worked for three years as a post-doctoral researcher and assistant professor at the Department of Child and Adolescent Studies, Utrecht University. He is involved in fundamental research on the link between (social) environmental influences on adolescent and young adult substance use and delinquency.

List of Contributors

Krista L. Beiswenger, Department of Psychology, Clark University, 950 Main Street, Worcester, Massachusetts 01610, USA.

Zintars G. Beldavs, Oregon Social Learning Center, 10 Shelton McMurphey Blvd, Eugene, OR 97401, USA.

Marc H. Bornstein, Child and Family Research, National Institute of Child Health and Human Development, Suite 8030, 705 Rockledge Drive, Bethesda MD 20892-7971, USA.

Susan J. T. Branje, Research Centre Adolescent Development, Utrecht University, Postbox 80140, 3508TC Utrecht, Netherlands.

Bernadette Marie Bullock, University of Oregon Child and Family Center, 195 West 12th Avenue, Eugene, OR 97401-3408, USA.

David S. DeGarmo, Oregon Social Learning Center, 10 Shelton McMurphey Blvd, Eugene, OR 97401, USA.

Thomas J. Dishion, University of Oregon Child and Family Center, 195 W 12th Avenue, Eugene, OR 97401, USA.

Rutger C. M. E. Engels, Radboud University Nijmegen, PO Box 9102, 6500 HE Nijmegen, Netherlands.

Catrin Finkenauer, Department of Social Psychology, Vrije Universiteit, Van der Boechorststraat 1, 1081 BT Amsterdam, The Netherlands.

Marion S. Forgatch, Oregon Social Learning Center, 160 East 4th Street, Eugene, OR 97401, USA.

Wendy S. Grolnick, Department of Psychology, Clark University, Worcester, MA 01610-1477, USA.

Joan E. Grusec, Sidney Smith Hall, 4th Floor, University of Toronto, 100 St George Street, Toronto, Ontario, Canada M5S 3G3.

William W. Hale III, Utrecht University, PO Box 80140, 3508 TC Utrecht, Netherlands.

Margaret Kerr, Örebro University, Center for Developmental Research, BSR: Psychology, 701 82 Örebro, Sweden.

Jeff Kiesner, Dipartimento di Psicologia DPSS, Università di Padova, Via Venezia 8, 35131 Padova, Italy.

Kaska E. Kubacka, Department of Social Psychology, Vrije Universiteit, Van der Boechorststraat 1, 1081 BT Amsterdam, Netherlands.

Sheila K. Marshall, Associate Professor, Family Studies, School of Social Work and Family Studies, 2080 West Mall, Vancouver, BC V6T 1Z2, Canada.

Wim H. J. Meeus, Utrecht University, PO Box 80140, 3508 TC Utrecht, Netherlands.

Aaron Metzger, Department of Clinical and Social Sciences in Psychology, Meliora Hall, RC 270266, University of Rochester, Rochester NY 14627, USA.

Nina S. Mounts, Department of Psychology, Northern Illinois University, DeKalb, IL, 60115, USA.

Vilmante Pakalniskiene, Örebro University, Center for Developmental Research, BSR: Psychology, 701 82 Örebro, Sweden.

Gerald R. Patterson, Oregon Social Learning Center, 10 Shelton McMurphey Blvd, Eugene OR 97401.

Carrie E. Price, Department of Psychology, Clark University, 950 Main Street, Worcester MA 01610, USA.

Judith G. Smetana, Department of Clinical and Social Sciences in Psychology, Meliora Hall, RC 270266, University of Rochester, Rochester NY 14627, USA.

Håkan Stattin, Örebro University, Center for Developmental Research, BSR: Psychology, 701 82 Örebro, Sweden.

Lauree C. Tilton-Weaver, Arts and Sciences Hall, 347, University of Nebraska at Omaha, Omaha NE 68182-0274, USA.

Acknowledgements

We wish to thank Tara Lindén for editorial assistance. We are grateful to The Swedish Foundation for International Cooperation in Research and Higher Education for supporting the collaborative project between the editors that resulted in the Hot Topics book series.

Introduction: What's Changed in Research on Parenting and Adolescent Problem Behavior and What Needs to Change?

Margaret Kerr
Örebro University, Sweden
Håkan Stattin
Uppsala University and Örebro University, Sweden
Rutger C. M. E. Engels
Radboud University Nijmegen, Netherlands

In a review of research on parenting in 1992, Eleanor Maccoby described early theory and research as having a top-down orientation in which parents were thought to shape children's outcomes. She went on to explain that the view had changed, by the time of that writing, to an interactive perspective where parents were no longer thought to influence children unilaterally but were recognized as being influenced by them as well (Maccoby, 1992). Conceptually and theoretically, this is probably true when it comes to parenting research generally. Few researchers would disagree with the idea that parenting is an interactive process in which the child plays a large and active role. Many refer to transactional and interactional theories, such as those of Sameroff, Kuczynski, and Patterson (e.g., Kuczynski, 2003; Kuczynski & Parkin, 2007; Patterson, 1982; Sameroff, 1975, 2000; Sameroff & Mackenzie, 2003). In many areas of parenting research, the interactive view might be represented in the empirical models that are tested, but in the area of adolescent problem behavior this perspective has seldom been represented conceptually or empirically.

What Can Parents Do? New Insights into the Role of Parents in Adolescent Problem Behavior
Edited by Margaret Kerr, Håkan Stattin and Rutger C. M. E. Engels.

The ideas that have dominated research on parenting and adolescent problem behavior since the late 1970s focus on parents' direct supervision and control of adolescents' whereabouts and associations as deterrents to deviant peer affiliation and involvement in problem behaviors such as delinquency and drug use. This focus can be seen in research on parenting styles and in investigations of parents' roles in preventing delinquency and other problem behaviors in the developmental psychology, criminology, and adolescent health literatures. All these lines of research have primarily taken the conceptual approach that Maccoby referred to—that parents shape adolescents' outcomes through their actions or failures to act. The conclusions have been that if parents monitor or supervise their adolescents they can steer them away from problems. These lines of research have their limitations (for a critique, see Kerr *et al.*, 2003) but they have been influential and the conclusions widely accepted. In fact, the research landscape was so homogeneous at the turn of the millennium that in his 2001 presidential address to the Society for Research on Adolescence Laurence Steinberg said, "We can stop asking what type of parenting most positively affects adolescent development. We know the answer to this question."

WHAT'S CHANGED?

By that time, the research landscape had already begun to change, and the changes would become more obvious a few years later. The critical changes were a recognition of youth agency and an interest in examining bidirectional effects.

Recognition of Youth Agency

By the early 2000s, a few researchers had begun looking into and discussing at conferences adolescents' withholding or disclosing information to their parents. Their work, which would come out a few years later, revealed that adolescents are consciously aware of their parents' desires for information and their own willingness to disclose some things and to keep other things to themselves (Finkenauer, Engels, & Meeus, 2002; Frijns *et al.*, 2005; Marshall, Tilton-Weaver, & Bosdet, 2005; Smetana *et al.*, 2006). Although the connection to adolescent problem behavior was not a focus in this work, the work had implications for research on problem behavior because items assessing parents' knowledge of youths' daily activities were being used in measures of supervision, monitoring, behavioral control, and authoritative parenting. The assumption behind the use of these items was that if parents have knowledge it is primarily because they took active steps to get it. Research on youths' reasons for disclosure and secrecy, and the impact of individual differences in adolescent disclosure on how much parents know and subsequently might do made clear that youths play active roles in determining how much their parents know about their daily activities. Consequently, because it is at least partly determined by teenagers acting out of their own interests, parental knowledge cannot be seen as a measure of parenting. At about the same time, Stattin and Kerr (Stattin & Kerr, 2000; Kerr & Stattin, 2000) tackled this issue empirically, showing that knowledge was much more closely linked to adolescent disclosure of information than to parents' efforts to get information. Parental knowledge seemed to represent youth agency more than parental action, so they argued for a reinterpretation of the findings in the literature involving parental knowledge as the operationalization of parental monitoring, supervision, behavioral control, or authoritative parenting. Obviously, this has created significant debate, and because of the implications that research on youth disclosure and secrecy has for this argument we see it as a hot area of developmental research.

Interest in Examining Bidirectional Effects

Another recent change in research on parenting and adolescent problem behavior is the emergence of empirical studies testing bidirectional effects. Until very recently, virtually all of the research in this area, whether cross-sectional or longitudinal, has proceeded from the perspective that parents affect adolescent problem behaviors but are affected by them little, if at all. The possibility of bidirectional effects has almost always been mentioned in discussion sections, but only in passing. Before 2002 there were only a few exceptions to this. There were some studies in the behavioral genetic tradition (e.g., Ge *et al.*, 1996; Neiderhiser *et al.*, 1995) and at least two longitudinal studies (Patterson, Bank, & Stoolmiller, 1990; Stice & Barerra, 1995). In the literature on younger children, in contrast, a small but impressive literature has amassed showing that conduct problems and externalizing behaviors can and do influence the behaviors of parents and other adults toward children (Anderson, Lytton, & Romney, 1986; Bell, 1968; Bell & Chapman, 1986; Buss, 1981; Dix *et al.*, 1986; Huh *et al.*, 2006; Lytton, 1990, 2000; Mulhern & Passman, 1981; Passman & Blackwelder, 1981). These "child effects" findings, however, have not been integrated into the corpus of knowledge on "parenting." On the contrary, they seem to have been viewed as separate or even competing ideas that conceptually threaten the role of parents in socialization. In our view, one of the most positive recent developments in research on parenting and adolescent problem behavior is the growing acceptance of the idea that parenting might be both action and reaction, and the desire to understand it as such. Although some have expressed concern that this movement will shift the focus too far away from how parenting affects youths (e.g., Fletcher,

Steinberg, & Williams-Wheeler, 2004), a growing number of researchers are now striving to understand parenting of adolescents as part of a bidirectional process in which parents and adolescents both act on their own agendas and react to each other. In short, for some, the question has changed. It is no longer "what type of parenting *affects* adolescent development?" It is "what roles do adolescents and parents play in the interactive, dynamic family processes through which adolescents develop?" The interactive perspective that Maccoby described in 1992 in parenting research broadly is beginning to take hold in the area of parenting and adolescent problem behavior. This is a hot area of developmental research today.

WHAT NEEDS TO CHANGE?

There are several additional changes that in our minds would be positive for this area of enquiry. One is a clarification of constructs used—particularly when it comes to parental management of youth behavior. Grolnick and colleagues (this volume) grapple with this issue concerning parental control. Regarding monitoring or supervision, measures as diverse as parents' efforts to get information about youths' activities (Kerr, Stattin, & Pakalniskiene, this volume) and the amount of time youths spend with their peers away from adults (Dishion, Bullock, & Kiesner, this volume) are considered to capture parental monitoring or supervision. It is likely that these measures are actually tapping very different phenomena. Arriving at agreement about constructs and measures will require some period of debate in the literature, but for the progress of the field it will be worthwhile. Another positive change in research on parenting and adolescent problem behavior would be the use of new research methods. The most commonly used methods are observational studies, longitudinal survey or interview studies, qualitative interviews, and intervention studies. They all have their advantages and limitations. When the question is "what can parents do?" however, what is implied is that an answer to this would say what they can *best* do. Observations, interviews, and surveys of behavior cross-sectionally or longitudinally can tell us what parents do in the normal course of events, but not necessarily what they might *best* do. Intervention studies are most able to show what would happen if the normal course of events were changed, but for various reasons they seldom test one alternative against another. Thus, they seldom reveal what parents could *best* do. Creativity will be required to fill this need but one thing that seems essential is to find ways to test different theoretically based interventions against each other. A third welcome change would be the emergence of new theoretical perspectives. As mentioned above, the dominant theoretical focus has been on direct control of behavior but the new awareness of youth agency opens up alternative perspectives. The chapters in this volume by Bornstein (positive parenting) and Grolnick (self-determination theory) give some possible starting points.

THIS VOLUME

In this volume, we highlight new views in research on parenting adolescents. The book is divided into three sections. The first comprises three chapters focusing on *adolescents as active agents* in managing the information that their parents have about their whereabouts and associations. Tilton-Weaver and Marshall illustrate with qualitative interviews that adolescents can articulate well thought-out and purposeful reasons for disclosing or withholding information. Finkenauer and colleagues examine youth disclosure and secretiveness in a social psychological perspective, looking at the implications for parent-adolescent relationships. Smetana and Metzger bring in additional features of adolescent agency—trust in parents and beliefs about obligations to disclose different types of information. They link these and disclosure to internal and external adjustment.

Second, we include a number of different attempts to conceptualize and empirically test more complex models of the role of parenting in the relationships and adjustment of agentic adolescents. Kerr and colleagues examine bidirectional relations between parenting and adolescents' problem behaviors at home and away from home and arrive at an integrative model describing how adolescent problem behavior interferes with effective parenting. Dishion and colleagues use a high-risk sample to examine daily events in the family, which they define as showing parent or adolescent agency, as predictors of increases in adolescent drug use and delinquency. Branje and colleagues test several bidirectional models of problem behavior and relationships, considering adolescents' relationships with both parents and romantic partners. Mounts proposes a theoretical model to describe the different ways that parents fit in to adolescents' peer relationships. Finally Forgatch and colleagues give a textbook example of how an intervention program can be systematically evaluated when it is thoroughly theory based. These studies do not always agree in their conclusions, which illustrates the "hot" nature of this area of research.

In the final section, we include three chapters by eminent parenting researchers whose work deals mainly with children rather than adolescents. They represent research traditions that offer lessons to the changing landscape of research on parenting adolescents. Grolnick and colleagues use self-determination theory to outline the major dimensions of parenting, and within this framework, they provide a way to come to terms with one of the most controversial concepts in the parenting literature: parental control. Grusec reviews the literature on parenting with an eye to changes in the ways that optimal parenting has been viewed. Finally, Bornstein discusses positive parenting, which up to now has not been a major area of research in parenting adolescents.

WHAT IS A HOT TOPIC?

A "hot" topic in research means any of the following. It:

- implies a new way of thinking in a particular domain
- is approached differently by different research groups
- cuts across disciplines and signals ways to conduct cross-discipline collaborative research
- integrates and systematizes ongoing research in different disciplines
- has important practical implications.

Because the issue of youth agency has recently come to the fore, bringing with it an urgency to understand bidirectional effects, what parents can do to prevent problem behavior and foster positive development in adolescence *is* a hot topic in developmental research today. Much has happened in this area in the past few years, and in this volume we bring together researchers who have made important theoretical and empirical advances.

This volume is the second in a book series on Hot Topics in Developmental Research. The first hot topic was peer relations in adolescence, and it dealt with issues such as behavioral genetic research on peer relationships, mechanisms of peer influence, romantic relationships, and peers in different contexts. The edited volume had the title *Friends, Lovers, and Groups: Key Relationships in Adolescence*.

This second volume summarizes and integrates important recent advances and draws implications for future work in the area of parenting adolescents. It gathers the freshest views on this issue. We have gone to great length to recruit some of the strongest researchers in this area to present their current thinking and research on this hot topic. We believe that the collection of chapters in this volume will convey the hot nature of this topic because they reveal some of the differences in assumptions and approaches among researchers, presently. These differences and the discussion they provoke are sure to help move this field forward.

REFERENCES

Anderson, K. E., Lytton, H., & Romney, D. M. (1986). Mothers' interactions with normal and conduct-disordered boys: Who affects whom? *Developmental Psychology*, *22*, 604–609.

Bell, R. (1968). A reinterpretation of the direction of effects in studies of socialization. *Psychological Review*, *75*, 81–95.

Bell, R. Q. & Chapman, M. (1986). Child effects in studies using experimental or brief longitudinal approaches to socialization. *Developmental Psychology, 22*, 595–603.

Buss, D. M. (1981) Predicting parent-child interactions from children's activity level. *Developmental Psychology, 17*, 59–65.

Dix, T., Ruble, D. N., Grusec, J. E., & Nixon, S. (1986). Social cognition in parents: Inferential and affective reactions to children of three age levels. *Child Development, 57*, 879–894.

Finkenauer, C., Engels, R. C. M. E., & Meeus, W. (2002). Keeping secrets from parents: advantages and disadvantages of secrecy in adolescence. *Journal of Youth and Adolescence, 31*, 123–136.

Fletcher, A. C., Steinberg, L., & Williams-Wheeler, M. (2004). Parental influences on adolescent problem behavior: Revisiting Stattin and Kerr. *Child Development, 75*, 781–796.

Frijns, T., Finkenauer, C., Vermulst, A., & Engels, R. C. M. E. (2005). Keeping secrets from parents: Longitudinal associations of secrecy in adolescence. *Journal of Youth and Adolescence, 34*, 137–148.

Ge, X., Conger, R. D., Cadoret, R. J. *et al.* (1996). The developmental interface between nature and nurture: A mutual influence model of child antisocial behavior and parent behaviors. *Developmental Psychology, 32*, 574–589.

Huh, D., Tristan, J., Wade, E., & Stice, E. (2006). Does problem behavior elicit poor parenting? A prospective study of adolescent girls. *Journal of Adolescent Research, 21*, 185–204.

Kerr, M. & Stattin, H. (2000). What parents know, how they know it, and several forms of adolescent adjustment: Further evidence for a reinterpretation of monitoring. *Developmental Psychology, 36*, 366–380.

Kerr, M., Stattin, H., Biesecker, G., & Ferrer-Wreder, L. (2003). Relationships with parents and peers in adolescence. In R. M. Lerner, M. A. Easterbrooks, & J. Mistry (eds) *Handbook of Psychology (Volume 6: Developmental Psychology)* (pp. 395–422). Hoboken, NJ: John Wiley & Sons.

Kuczynski, L. (2003). Beyond bidirectionality: Bilateral conceptual frameworks for understanding dynamics in parent-child relations. In L. Kuczynski (ed.), *Handbook of Dynamics in Parent-child Relations* (pp. 1–24). Thousand Oaks, CA: Sage.

Kuczynski, L. & Parkin, M. C. (2007). Agency and bidirectionality in socialization: interactions, transactions, and relational dialectics. In J. F. Grusec & P. D. Hastings (eds), *Handbook of Socialization: Theory and Research* (pp. 259–283). New York, NY: Guilford Press.

Lytton, H. (1990). Child and parent effects in boys' conduct disorder: A reinterpretation. *Developmental Psychology, 26*, 683–697.

Lytton, H. (2000). Toward a model of family-environmental and child-biological influences on development. *Developmental Review, 20*, 150–179.

Maccoby, E. E. (1992). The role of parents in the socialization of children: An historical overview. *Developmental Psychology, 28*, 1006–1017.

Marshall, S. K., Tilton-Weaver, L. C., & Bosdet, L. (2005). Information management: Considering adolescents' regulation of parental knowledge. *Journal of Adolescence*, 28, 633–647.

Mulhern, R. K. Jr. & Passman, R. H. (1981). Parental discipline as affected by the sex of the parent, the sex of the child, and the child's apparent responsiveness to discipline. *Developmental Psychology, 17*, 604–613.

Neiderhiser, J. M., Reiss, D., Hetherington, E. M., & Plomin, R. (1995). Relationships between parenting and adolescent adjustment over time: Genetic and environmental contributions. *Developmental Psychology, 35*, 680–692.

Passman, R. H. & Blackwelder, D. E. (1981). Rewarding and punishing by mothers: The influence of progressive changes in the quality of their sons' apparent behavior. *Developmental Psychology, 17*, 614–619.

Patterson, G. R. (1982). *Coercive Family Process: A Social Learning Approach, Vol. 3.* Eugene, OR: Castalia.

Patterson, G. R., Bank, L., & Stoolmiller, M. (1990). The preadolescent's contributions to disrupted family process. In R. Montemayor, G. R. Adams, & T. P. Gullotta (eds), *From childhood to Adolescence. A Transactional Period?* (pp. 107–133). Newbury Park: Sage.

Sameroff, A. J. (1975). Early influences on development: Fact or fancy? *Merrill-Palmer Quarterly, 21,* 267–294.

Sameroff, A. J. (2000). Developmental systems and psychopathology. *Development and Psychopathology, 12,* 297–312.

Sameroff, A. J. & Mackenzie, M. J. (2003). Research strategies for capturing transactional models of development: the limits of the possible. *Development and Psychopathology, 15,* 613–640.

Smetana, J. G., Metzger, A., Gettman, D. C., & Campione-Barr, N. (2006). Disclosure and secrecy in adolescent-parent relationships. *Child Development, 77,* 201–217.

Stattin, H. & Kerr, M. (2000). Parental monitoring: A reinterpretation. *Child Development, 71,* 1070–1083.

Stice, E., & Barrera, M. Jr. (1995). A longitudinal examination of the reciprocal relations between perceived parenting and adolescents' substance use and externalizing behaviors. *Developmental Psychology, 31,* 322–334.

Part 1
Adolescents as Active Agents

CHAPTER 1

Adolescents' Agency in Information Management

Lauree C. Tilton-Weaver
University of Nebraska at Omaha, USA
Sheila K. Marshall
University of British Columbia, Canada

INTRODUCTION

One of the primary tasks associated with childhood and adolescence is to shift from being regulated by others to self-regulation and self-control. Because adolescents in Western cultures tend to spend increasingly more time away from their parents (Larson *et al.*, 1996), much attention has been given to how parents continue to regulate their adolescents when the adolescents are not supervised by adults. The majority of research investigating this topic has focused on parents' attempts to monitor their adolescents' whereabouts and activities.

This body of research has been seriously flawed, however, assuming that parents' monitoring provides them with information about adolescents' whereabouts and activities. The use of invalid measures (e.g., measures of parental knowledge, rather than parents' monitoring behaviors) and unidirectional assumptions (i.e., parent effects) led researchers to conclude prematurely that parents who monitor not only know what their adolescents are doing, but are then able to protect their adolescents from engagement in problematic activities. Recent research revealed these flaws, showing that parents' knowledge of adolescents' friends and activities is derived more from adolescents' disclosure than from parents' monitoring efforts (Kerr & Stattin, 2000; Stattin & Kerr, 2000). In response, researchers have taken an interest in understanding the processes by which parental knowledge is generated.

What Can Parents Do? New Insights into the Role of Parents in Adolescent Problem Behavior
Edited by Margaret Kerr, Håkan Stattin and Rutger C. M. E. Engels.

In this chapter, we take the position that adolescents make strategic decisions about what information they provide to their parents about their friends and activities and act on those decisions, in a process we call *information management*. We began exploring this issue about the same time Stattin and Kerr were beginning to reinterpret the parental "monitoring" (knowledge) measures. In the main, these measures assess how much parents know about their adolescents' friends and activities (e.g., Brown *et al.*, 1993). From our perspective, the use of parents' knowledge as a measure of monitoring assumes (1) parents who monitor know what their adolescents are doing, because they try, and (2) parents who do not monitor do not know what their adolescents are doing, because they do not try to know. We saw this as problematic in two ways. First, these assumptions do not allow for parents who try, but fail to be able to monitor their adolescents, or for parents who, through little or no effort on their part, have adolescents who divulge information. Second, measures assessing parents' knowledge ignore what adolescents might do to preclude or enhance their parents' monitoring efforts. We concluded that it is important to understand the ways in which adolescents manage the information their parents obtain. In other words, we are interested in the processes of adolescents' disclosure and nondisclosure.

To make our case, we first review the existing literature, attending to the ways information management issues have been dealt with historically. We then review literature suggesting information management is indicative of a developmental progression involving social and cognitive processes. These processes include privacy boundary management and the development of autonomy. We then present evidence suggesting that adolescents' strategically enable or preclude parents' attempts to monitor them and some of the reasons why.

IMPORTANT TERMINOLOGY

The idea that individuals control information is not new and spans many areas of research. It is important, then, to establish common ground by reviewing the terminology used in the empirical literature.

Disclosure

Disclosure refers to the provision of information to parents, sharing of information either voluntarily or from prompting. Disclosure as an information management strategy is related to, but conceptually distinct from self-disclosure. Self-disclosure is the sharing of personal or private information that others are unable to discern (Pearce & Sharp, 1973), is part of the process through which intimacy is established, and is expected to be followed by reciprocated disclosure. None of these conditions necessarily apply to adolescents' disclosure to parents.

Nondisclosure

Nondisclosure is the conceptual opposite of disclosure, meaning information is not provided, voluntarily or otherwise. There are several means through which individuals may not disclose, including simply not providing information. This may be unintentional (e.g., an oversight) or it may be intentional. Researchers have referred to two ways in which individuals may *intentionally* not disclose or withhold information. They may actively choose not to provide information (in whole or in part) or deliberately provide misinformation. Intentionally providing no information or only partial information has traditionally been referred to as keeping secrets, concealing information, or lying by omission (Granhag & Strömwall, 2004). The deliberate provision of misinformation has been referred to as lying, specifically lying by commission. Lying can be further classified as falsifications (total fabrications where all information provided is untruthful) or distortions (altering the truth to fit a liar's goal). Further lies can be used to conceal the fact that information is being withheld (e.g., claiming one does not know or remember, when that is not the case) (Granhag & Strömwall, 2004).

Thus, both intentional withholding and providing misinformation can be construed as deception. Succinctly, Vrij (2000, p. 6) defined deception as "a successful or unsuccessful deliberate attempt, without forewarning, to create in another a belief which the communicator considers to be untrue." It is important to recognize that deception involves the intention to misrepresent the truth and that unsuccessful attempts are still considered deception.

The degree of maliciousness in intent is also an important consideration for understanding deception. Some intentions are to harm the listener (Sweetser, 1987) or take advantage of a specific situation (Van Manen & Levering, 1996). In contrast, "social lies" (i.e., "white lies") are defined as untruthful statements that are not accompanied by malicious intent (Bok, 1978). The intent of social lies may be to present self or others in a positive light, prevent speakers from hurting the feelings of the listener, or avoid receiving adverse reactions from the listener if the truth is hurtful (Talwar & Lee, 2002).

EXAMINING PRIOR RESEARCH

Research examining adolescents' information management is both sparse and scattered. However, at least three related areas of scholarship are concerned with the conditions under which adolescents provide or do not provide information to their parents. We briefly review each of these, examining the contribution of each in understanding information management.

Parenting and Behavioral Control

For decades, one of the primary messages coming from parenting research has been that in order to protect adolescents from embarking on antisocial or delinquent trajectories, parents must lay down guidelines and firmly enforce them. In research terminology, adolescents need to be behaviorally controlled (Barber, Olsen, & Shagle, 1994). Because adolescents spend increasingly more time out of sight and sound of their parents, an ancillary message has been that in order to control adolescents' behavior parents must know about their whereabouts and activities. In research terminology, adolescents need to be monitored (Steinberg, 1990).

In the body of research examining parents' behavioral control, which includes monitoring, the assumptions have generally been that (1) behavioral control is a parent-directed process, with parents "in control" of, or controlling adolescents, and (2) the relationships between behavioral control and adolescents' adjustment are largely linear. This suggests there are no upper limits as to how much a parent should or could monitor.

Recent empirical evidence has called the conclusions about monitoring into question. Stattin and Kerr, in a series of studies, have shown that (1) the previously used measures of monitoring were actually measuring parental knowledge (2) parental knowledge is more strongly related to adolescents' disclosure than it is to parents' monitoring or control efforts, and (3) when faced with delinquent and defiant adolescents, parents tend to decrease, rather than increase, their monitoring efforts (Kerr & Stattin, 2000; 2003; Stattin & Kerr, 2000).

It is clear from examining literature that has emerged since Stattin and Kerr's thought-provoking articles that some researchers have either ignored or dismissed the empirical evidence refuting both the construct of monitoring and its purportedly protective effects. We believe this is, in part, because the agency of the adolescents in the parenting process has not been fully recognized. This orientation is evident in reconfigurations of monitoring since the seminal articles questioning its measurement. Renaming parental knowledge (i.e., a cognitive state) "monitoring knowledge" or "monitoring-relevant knowledge" (e.g., Laird *et al.*, 2003) when it cannot be attributed to parents' monitoring behaviors simply shifts the logical errors to a different construct and level of analysis. The use of this terminology implies, as the original monitoring literature did, that parents know where adolescents are and what they are doing because of what *parents* do, rather than what adolescents do.

Advocates of this perspective have suggested that adolescents' disclosure is enhanced when parents are warm, supportive, and empathic (Fanzoi & Davis, 1985; Martin, Anderson, & Mottet, 1999; Norrell, 1984; Searight *et al.*,

1995), and undermined when parents are highly critical, rejecting, or unwilling to listen (Norrell, 1984, Rosenthal, Efklides, & Demetriou, 1988; Stouthamer-Loeber, 1986). Again, however, the emphasis is upon parents' behaviors and adolescents' disclosure or nondisclosure is considered the result of skillful or inept parenting.

Is the emphasis on parents' behaviors justified? Recent research suggests not. Stattin & Kerr (2000) found parents react to adolescents' delinquency by reducing their control and support. Additionally, parents who perceive their adolescents as warm and open maintain high levels of monitoring efforts (i.e., behavioral control and solicitation of information) whereas parents who perceive their adolescents are cold and closed to communication reduce their monitoring efforts over time (Kerr, Stattin, & Tilton-Weaver, 2007). Further, they have also found parents trust adolescents because they disclose, not the other way around (Kerr, Stattin, & Trost, 1999).

Summary

The evidence to date does not support an interpretation that parents who monitor more then know more. Instead, a picture emerges suggesting adolescents manage information to their parents and parents are knowledgeable about their adolescents' whereabouts and activities outside of their direct supervision because adolescents either do or do not divulge the information. Therefore, what adolescents do is at least as important as what parents do and parenting is likely as reactive to adolescents' behavior as adolescents' behaviors are to parenting. We turn now to a related body of research, examining the development of deception.

The Development of Deception

In developmental studies examining the concealment of information, the way in which deception is treated depends on the period of the lifespan. In childhood, the emphasis is on cognitive development, where it is recognized that the intentional presentation of misinformation requires individuals to be able to represent the beliefs of others (i.e., hold a theory of mind) and understand that beliefs can be altered (Chandler & Hala, 1991). The development of the ability to conceal information from others emerges around the ages of 4 to 5 years (Peskin, 1992) and is considered a normal and important progression in cognitive development, hailing the ability to distinguish between the mind of self and others as well as a nascent understanding of morality. This same body of research demonstrates that by adolescence individuals are able to regulate information through processes such as withholding information or engaging in deception because they realize they can have knowledge not accessible to others unless they tell them (Lee & Ross, 1997).

Likewise, the focus of much of the research on adults' deception in everyday life has been on its normative role in social relationships (e.g., DePaulo & Kashy, 1998; Metts, 1989). Adults report lying in one out of every five social interactions (DePaulo *et al.*, 1996). In close relationships, adults tend to report low rates of self-centered lies (e.g., for self-protection or material gain) and higher rates of other-oriented lies (e.g., pretending to agree, artificial compliment) (DePaulo & Kashy, 1998). Other-oriented lies play a significant role in close relationships (Metts, 1989). Other-oriented lies are used in close relationships to (a) indicate to a partner that the speaker is supportive and caring (e.g., fake agreements, false compliments); (b) gain or maintain control over resources or gain or maintain privacy, particularly from mothers; and (c) turn a humiliating or destructive interaction into a less tense experience (DePaulo & Kashy, 1998).

In contrast, the focus of most research on nondisclosure during adolescence has been on its linkages to maladjustment (e.g., Loeber, DeLamatre, & Keenan, 1998). In these bodies of research, deceiving others (such as parents) has generally involved the explicit provision of misinformation, which has been considered problematic when manifested in conjunction with other socially undesirable behaviors such as theft or aggression (Loeber, DeLamatre & Keenan, 1998).

There are, however, a few notable exceptions in the research literature. Finkenauer and colleagues (e.g., Finkenauer, Engels, & Meeus, 2002; Frijns *et al.*, 2005) examined secrecy during adolescence and its potential associations with adjustment. Using cross-sectional data, Finkenauer *et al.* (2002) found keeping secrets from parents was linked to somatic and depressive complaints, as well as emotional autonomy. However, in a short term (6 months) longitudinal study, Frijns *et al.* (2005) found only linkages to maladjustment suggesting that keeping secrets from parents is largely problematic.

However, this conclusion should be tempered because the secrecy measure used in both studies is primarily negative, "assessing (a) the tendency to keep things to oneself, (b) the possession of a secret or negative thoughts not shared with others, and (c) the apprehension of the revelation of concealed personal information" (Finkenauer *et al.*, 2002, p. 126; Frijns *et al.*, 2005, p. 141). This measure includes aspects of shyness (i.e., keeping to oneself) and does not recognize that secrets are also something about which people can feel positively (e.g., keeping a secret about a gift, pride in the ability to keep a secret).

Perhaps the reason researchers have tended to emphasize the negative in adolescence is because of attributions about nondisclosure. The most commonly attributed reason for adolescents' lying has been an attempt to avoid negative consequences (Ford, 1996; Stouthamer-Loeber, 1986), primarily from parents. It is not clear, however, whether adolescent lying is encouraged by certain types of parenting (e.g., extremely punitive) or whether parents cope with lying by responding punitively or by giving up.

Summary

Within the body of research on deception, there appears to be a strange developmental sequence in which the ability to deceive others has normative and important purposes in both childhood and adulthood but is primarily viewed as maladaptive in adolescence. This body of research, like the research on parental control, treats adolescents' nondisclosure as a sign or antecedent of maladaptive development. This view of adolescence does not allow us to examine the potential positive functions of nondisclosure, particularly the role information management has in normal communicative and relational processes located within important developmental trajectories. Recently, Furstenberg (2001, p. 120) argued that "learning what not to tell parents and how not to tell them" is a developmental task in adolescence. Research on the development of autonomy and maintenance of privacy boundaries within the family provides insight into why this might be the case.

Privacy Boundaries and Autonomy

From research on family dynamics and adolescent autonomy development, we gain another perspective on adolescents' management of information. Petronio & Caughlin (2006) suggest that privacy is an essential aspect of family functioning because it enables the development, maintenance, and coordination of boundaries between individuals and groups of family members. From a family systems theory perspective, boundaries help families organize the relationships between generations and between individuals (see White & Klein, 2002). Boundary violations, such as enmeshment or extreme symbiotic involvement (Bowen, 1978; Minuchin, 1974) between parents and adolescent children, are related to adolescents' emotional adjustment problems (e.g., Cohen, Vasey, & Gavazzi, 2003). Opportunities to practice keeping appropriate secrets and concealing information throughout childhood contribute to the establishment of autonomous identity in adolescence (Van Manen & Levering, 1996).

The establishment of privacy boundaries within families is understood as a normative developmental process within social domain theory (Smetana, 1988). According to this theory, the process of autonomy development entails parents and children negotiating and renegotiating behavioral control as children develop capacities for self-regulation. Negotiations over behavioral control determine whether the parents or the adolescents have the legitimate authority to make and enforce rules in a given area. In general, empirical accounts suggest in Western cultures, parents and children tend to agree with parents maintaining authority until late childhood or early adolescence, when adolescents expect some control over personal issues (e.g., Collins & Luebker, 1994). Parents generally begin to relinquish control during adolescence, first over personal issues, followed by other issues, but retaining control over situations in which the adolescents' safety or security could be compromised (Smetana & Asquith, 1994).

It is reasonable to expect that when adolescents perceive that they, not their parents, legitimately control a domain, privacy would be attained and maintained through management of information about that domain. Recent empirical studies have examined information management in relation to social domains. In a study examining the links between authority beliefs and information management, Smetana *et al.* (2006) found that adolescents feel less obligated to disclose information to their parents in domains in which they perceive they, not their parents, retain legitimate authority (e.g., less obligation to disclose personal issues than issues in other domains), suggesting adolescents make decisions about what they will and will not disclose.

In an examination of information management across social domains, Darling *et al.* (2006) found that most of the youth they interviewed reported some nondisclosure to their parents (97.5 %). When examining the reasons for disclosure, the adolescents reported they disclosed on 51 % of the issues examined because they felt obliged to, 34 % because they hoped their parents would change their minds, and 15 % because they felt they would not get away with nondisclosure. In contrast, the adolescents reported not disclosing for 37 % of the issues because of emotional reasons (i.e., their parents would worry, be disappointed, or wouldn't understand; or the adolescents would be embarrassed or uncomfortable), 39 % because of fear of consequences (i.e., parents would be angry, would lecture or hassle, would punish or stop the activity), and 24 % felt that the issue was not within their parents jurisdiction (i.e., the adolescents' private business or the adolescents' decision, not the parents).

Summary

The research on privacy boundaries and adolescents' information management points to the changes that both parents and children make to promote children's developing autonomy. In families where privacy boundaries do not accommodate children's development, adolescents may experience adjustment difficulties. When the regulation of behavior is slowly assigned to children, not only is autonomy promoted but communication strategies are altered to maintain privacy. Adolescents make decisions about what to disclose and what not to disclose to their parents as a part of normal development within the family.

Although research indicates that adolescents' management of information is linked to social domains as a normative developmental process, what is still missing is an account of the subtleties of information management as a normative as well as non-normative phenomenon. To expand on extant research, our research aims were twofold. First, we wanted to examine adolescents' information management strategies and decisions: How do adolescents manage information to their parents about their friends and whereabouts? What choices do they make? Are there implicit "rules" or conditions that guide their information management decisions? We also wanted to examine potential links between adolescents' strategies and decisions and information constructs such as parents' knowledge and adolescents' willingness to disclose.

We then aimed to determine if adolescents' strategies and decisions were linked to adjustment (e.g., types of peers, attachments to parents) or contextual issues (e.g., parental intrusiveness).

ADOLESCENTS' INFORMATION MANAGEMENT

Our first study examines the reasons why adolescents have friends their parents do not know. We chose to examine this area first, because of the degree to which the monitoring literature emphasizes parents' need to know with whom their adolescents are spending time. According to the monitoring literature, one of the avenues through which parents protect their adolescents from engaging in problem or delinquent behaviors is by intervening in their friendships and keeping adolescents away from problem peers (e.g., Fletcher, Steinberg, & Williams-Wheeler, 2005). In addition, domain theory suggests that friendships are a personal domain issue, and an area in which adolescents might withhold information from their parents (Smetana *et al.*, 2006).

In our second study, we chose to focus on adolescents' whereabouts, asking about their decisions to inform their parents about where they are going. We chose the topic of their whereabouts because *where* adolescents are, as well as *who* they are with are two of the topics consistently targeted by measures purportedly assessing monitoring.

To generate an understanding of adolescents' implicit rules for information management we used a qualitative analytic approach. It has been our experience that when qualitative approaches are used to examine adolescents' perspectives of themselves and contexts of their development, that adolescents provide us with information that has not been gained elsewhere.

Although the same qualitative approach was used in both studies, the two investigations varied in how the findings were used. Study 1 is focused on a specific issue, lending itself to a mixed methods approach. Specifically, the findings from the qualitative analysis were used in quantitative analyses in order to examine individual and contextual differences. Study 2 uses the qualitative findings to generate a model.

Qualitative Analytic Procedures

Adolescents' implicit rules regarding when to disclose information to parents were generated from respondents' written answers to questions about having friends whom their parents do not know (Study 1) and the conditions under which adolescents inform or do not inform their parents of their whereabouts and activities (Study 2). Extant information on adolescent information management was used to inform the qualitative analysis of the data. The use of prior research and theory helped to organize and assign meaning to the data in a process termed interpretive induction (Kuczynski & Daly, 2003).

The principles of open, axial, and selective coding (Strauss & Corbin, 1990) were followed during the cross-case analysis of the data. The first step in the analysis, open coding, involved an inductive approach of identifying key phrases or themes from across the written responses. Next, broader conceptual categories were identified from the recurring similarities across themes. This process is axial coding which involves stepping back from the data and looking at how themes are connected. For example, the category of "privacy and taking authority" was created in Study 1 because the privacy boundary also involves attempts to assert control over choices of friends. Similarly, the category of "assessing parental disapproval or sanctions" was created in Study 2 because it linked two types of potential parental responses (disapproval and sanctions) to engagement in prohibited behavior. Finally, the selective coding involved integrating and organizing the main categories into higher level concepts.

The sample size of Study 1 is large in order to employ quantitative analyses. The size of the sample made the use of consensus for reliability unwieldy. Therefore reliability was calculated on a subset of the data. The first author developed the categories and themes for the entire data set (using Wave 1 data) and provided the second author with the decision rules for coding. The second author coded a randomly selected 10 % of the 565 cases. Bakeman & Gottman (1986) suggest that a Cohen's kappa of 0.70 or higher reflects good interrater reliability. Interrater agreement was *kappa* = 0.82.

Study 2 examined a broader topic (rules for divulging information about whereabouts) with a smaller sample. For this study, open coding was conducted by both authors and any discrepancies in analyses were discussed and reconciled.

Study 1: Information About Friends—Who Tells and Who Doesn't?

For our first study, we were interested in determining the relative extent to which adolescents have friends their parents do not know. Previous data suggests that some adolescents have unknown friends (Tilton-Weaver & Galambos, 2003) but the reasons for which the friends are unknown has not been fully probed. We first explore adolescents' rationale using a qualitative approach, followed by quantitatively examining correlates of their explanations. We chose three sets of contextualizing correlates, reflecting both positive and negative aspects of adolescents' peers and parents, including measures of information management and parental knowledge, peers' social orientation, and parenting or parent–adolescent relationship variables.

Methods

Participants and Procedures

A sample of 565 adolescents (246 boys, 318 girls, 1 missing data) in grades 8 to 12 (age 12 to 19, $M = 14.16$ years, $SD = 1.22$) at an urban public school in western Canada participated in a computer-based survey. The students were ethnically mixed, with 53 % from European backgrounds, 30 % of East Asian heritage, 4 % from minority backgrounds (e.g., Native American, African), and 8 % from multiple ethnic backgrounds (5 % did not report their ethnicity). The majority of participants (64 %) lived with both parents, with an additional 35 % living with one parent/guardian or shared custody arrangements, and a small group (1 %) living in homestay arrangements (foreign students).

At the beginning of the school year, consent forms were distributed to parents by the school administration. Informed assent was explained to participants prior to completing the survey. No participants received remuneration for participation.

Measures

In order to reduce data, when mothers and fathers were reported on separately, we combined the reports into one mean score.

About friends. We assessed two types of information about friends: (1) if they had unknown friends and why, and (2) the prosocial or antisocial orientation of their friends. For *unknown friends,* we asked "Do you have any friends that your parents do not know about?" and if the response was yes, indicating unknown friends, we asked adolescents to elaborate with "Why don't your parents know about them?" For the *prosocial/antisocial orientation* of friends, the adolescents rated three items assessing their friends' prosocial orientation (e.g., "Most of my friends would jump in and help a stranger in trouble") and four items assessing their friends' antisocial orientation (e.g., "My friends often get into trouble with adults"). Adolescents endorsed the statements on a scale from 1 (*not true at all*) to 5 (*very true*), from which mean ratings were computed. These items have been used in previous studies (Galambos & Maggs, 1991; Tilton-Weaver & Galambos, 2003) and had good psychometric properties in this sample: Cronbach's alphas were 0.76 for prosocial orientation and 0.73 for antisocial orientation.

Information constructs. We used one of the most frequent measures of parental knowledge in the literature (previously known as monitoring, Brown *et al.*, 1993), and altered wording to assess how much parents *want* to know and adolescents' willingness to tell (Marshall, Tilton-Weaver, & Bosdet, 2005). We also added two items to evaluate Internet use and assessed reports on mothers and fathers separately. Thus, three scales composed of 6 items for each parent was created by asking "How much does your mother [father] *really* know about..." "How much does your mother [father] *want* to know about..." and "How much are you willing to tell your mother [father] about..." whereabouts at night, spare time and afternoon activities, spending money, who friends are, who is contacted and how much time is spent on the Internet. Mean responses to five-point Likert scales were used, with higher scores reflecting *mother/father knowledge, mother/father wanting to know,* and *adolescents' willingness to tell mother/father.* Cronbach's alphas for parental knowledge, parents wanting to know, and adolescents' willingness to tell were (respectively) 0.83, 0.85, and 0.86 for mothers and 0.84, 0.87, and 0.88 for fathers.

Parental psychological control. Barber's (1996) measure of parental psychological control is composed of eight items evaluating the adolescents' perception of parental behaviors that are intrusive (e.g., "My mother is a person...is always trying to change how I feel or think about things"). Adolescents provided responses for each parent separately using a five-point Likert-type scale ranging from 1 (not like her/him) to 5 = (a lot like her/him). Internal consistency was 0.90 for mothers and 0.89 for fathers.

Attachment security. The Adolescent Attachment Questionnaire (AAQ) (West *et al.*, 1998) was used to assess adolescents' perceptions of their attachment security to each parent separately. The AAQ consists of three questions for each of three subscales measuring availability (e.g., "I'm confident that my mother/father will listen to me"), anger ("I get annoyed at my mother/father because it seems I have to demand his/her caring and support"), and goal-corrected partnership (e.g., "I feel for my mother/father when he/she is upset"). Participants respond to items using a five-point Likert-type scale, ranging from *strongly agree* to *strongly disagree*. As recommended by the authors of the AAQ, the mean of all nine items was calculated to reflect adolescents' perception of attachment security (high scores portray greater security). Cronbach's alpha were 0.85 for mothers and 0.89 for fathers.

Results

Qualitative Results

The majority of the adolescents' responses could be classified into 12 categories. Some responses required more than one category to represent the response fully. A small percentage of the responses were too vague or ambiguous to code ($n = 6$; $< 1\%$). Table 1.1 provides a synopsis of the coded responses.

"Don't ask/don't tell." Some adolescents responded that their parents did not know about their unknown friends either because their parents did not ask, e.g., "Cause they never asked," or they did not provide information about their friends, e.g., "I just never bothered to tell them," without further elaboration. Some responses suggested that these may not have been an important topic

or just not part of everyday conversation. As two put it, "They normally don't bother asking" and "It never comes up in usual conversation."

"Parents don't care." Others indicated, without additional explanation, that their parents did not care to know about their friends or did not care about them in general. For example, one wrote, "Because they are not concerned about who I hang out with" whereas another suggested "They don't care about me or my friends."

Table 1.1 Categorical coding of adolescents' responses to being asked "do you have friends that your parents do not know about?"

			Percentage	
Category	**Description of code**	*n*	**Unknown**	**Total**
Don't ask/ don't tell	Adolescent indicates that they do not discuss with parents, either because adolescent does not tell, parent does not ask, or both. Not coded if additional explanations were provided	74	20	9
Parents don't care	Adolescent indicates that parents do not care about knowing.	14	4	2
Have not met	Adolescent suggests parent and friend have not met. Not coded if friends are not discussed.	36	10	4
Network issues:				
Too many friends	Adolescents' explanation is that his/her network of friends is too large.	18	5	2
Not close or regular friends	Explanation indicates that unknown friends are either new, not regular, or not close friends.	84	23	10
School only friends	Adolescent indicates friends are only seen at school. Not coded if also indicates that these friends are not close or regular friends.	26	7	3
Avoiding parents' reactions				
Unsuitable friend	Adolescents' justification includes indications that disapproval would be because of unsuitability or parental concerns.	39	11	5
Bad reactions	Adolescent indicates that parents would react in a manner that would be embarrassing, upsetting, or uncomfortable.	15	4	2

Table 1.1 (Continued)

Category	Description of code	*n*	Percentage	
			Unknown	Total
Privacy and authority	Includes justification that suggests consideration of authority or privacy issues			
Privacy/taking authority	Response indicates that adolescent is unwilling to cede authority over friendships to parents, or has a privacy need	25	7	3
Don't need every detail	Justification suggests that parents don't need to know all details (without additional explanation).	12	3	1
Parents ceded authority	Response indicates adolescent perceives that parent has ceded authority over friends to him/her	33	9	4
Parents retain if needed	Adolescent suggests that they have control over friendship issues, unless a potential prudential issue requires parental control	6	2	1

"Have not met." For some adolescents, their parents' lack of knowledge was attributable to not having met. As some suggested, this was because the friend had not been to their home, "Simply because they never come to the house so my mom never meets them" or otherwise been in contact with each other, "Because they have never seen them before."

Network issues. Several categories of responses reflected one of three network issues. *Too many friends* was coded when adolescents reported that their networks were too large to either remember all of their friends or to tell their parents about every friend. Several suggested that enumerating every friend would be unnecessary: "I have so many friends, I don't need to tell my parents about each of them. I think it's not necessary." Having a friend, then, that parents do not know is not only likely but also quite normal. As one 13 year old girl put it, "Because there isn't any reason to. Do you go to your parents and say I'm friends with _____ and _____ and _____ and _____ and ____ and _____ and _____ and _____ ...[etc.]...and so on and so forth?" The second category *not close or regular friends* were responses indicating that parents did not know about friends who were not central in their peer networks. Adolescents' responses suggested several ways of defining centrality, including closeness and regularity of contact. For example, one responded "It's not that those people are bad or anything it is just that they are not a big part of my life so I don't feel the need to share that I have a friendship with them." An unknown friend could also be too new to be considered central: "Because I don't tell my parents every time I become friends with someone new. It's not a big deal so they wouldn't actually care to know. My parents know all of my close friends." The last network issue category, *school only friends* was used when adolescents' responses implied the unknown friend was seen only at school. Many wrote that they felt that informing parents about school friends was unimportant or unnecessary because they did not spend time with them out of school. "Because it's just friends that I see at school, I don't hang out with them after school and it's mostly just in classes and at lunch. It's nothing they would need to know about and they probably don't care anyways." Like those with very large networks, not knowing about some friends was not only likely, but normal. "I don't know, I just don't tell my parents about everyone I met in school, it's no big deal... And I don't really see any obligation to tell my parents all the people I meet at school."

Avoiding parents' reactions. Another emergent theme arising from two categories was that adolescents were avoiding some type of reaction from their parents. One category *unsuitable friend* was used when adolescents suggested their friends would be considered unsuitable in one way or another: "Because they do drugs or drink a lot." "Because my parents sometimes don't want me to hang out with certain people because of their reputation or attitude." This category also included responses where adolescents suggested their parents would disapprove of their friend or prohibit contact: "Sometimes, I think my parents might not like them and prevent me from hanging out with them." For some, differences between their goals and parents' goals were indicated: "Because they don't want me to have any boyfriends." The second category in this theme, *bad reactions* was used when adolescents suggested their parents would have a bad reaction to their friend other than prohibiting contact. The expected reactions included "acting weird," being intrusive ("I don't feel like telling them because then they just hassle me and ask pointless questions about them."), becoming angry ("because if they knew then they would get pissed off"), and becoming overprotective ("they might get too protective"). For this theme, it was particularly evident that adolescents were evaluating their friends as well as their parents, at times disagreeing with their parents' opinions and deeming their parents' expected responses inappropriate. On the basis of these decisions, they would either provide no information ("They don't trust anyone, so I'm not about to give them information about people, because no matter how awesome they are my folks would never approve") or only partial information ("My mom may have heard me talk about her/him but not in detail, maybe because they smoke pot. I am afraid to know what my mom would think of that person from just that one detail, even though they may be extremely kind").

Authority and privacy issues. The final group of codes reflected adolescents' perceptions of parental authority and privacy issues. Two of the codes, *privacy and authority-taking* and *don't need every detail* fit into an emergent theme in which adolescents suggested friendships were an area where they drew boundaries themselves about privacy, suggesting that they deemed themselves the legitimate authority over friendship issues. *Privacy and authority-taking* was used when adolescents indicated that they had chosen not to inform their parents, either because they deemed it their prerogative (e.g., "Because I don't like telling my parents everything, and there are things I feel are none of their business, and I don't like other people deciding who my friend should be") or because they considered it a privacy issue (e.g., "I don't think I have to tell my parents about all of my friends. I believe it is some kind of privacy"). In contrast, we coded responses as *don't need every detail* when adolescents used these or very similarly worded responses, e.g., "I don't think I need to report them everything in my life." "Because they don't need to know everything." The last two categories were responses that suggested that the adolescents had assumed some authority over friendship choices but not because they disagreed with their parents. For the first of these categories, *parents ceded authority* the responses indicated they could make decisions about when to provide information and that their parents were not likely to be concerned. Their rationales were based on not having unsuitable friends (e.g., "My parents don't know about some of my friends because I have nothing about my friends that I feel need to be told. But none of my friends are bad/rule-breakers. They don't smoke, do graffiti, sexually harass someone, etc.") or parents already knowing about friends with similar characteristics (e.g., "I didn't tell them about it because those friends are similar to the friends that I have told my parents about"). These reflect an implicit rule for deciding which friends parents need to know about. Many of the responses coded in this category suggested that their parents had ceded authority, because of the adolescents' good judgment: "Because I didn't tell them and they didn't ask me since they trust me and I am a good child so they didn't worry about that." And "We don't talk much about my friends since my parents trust me." The other category, *parents retain if necessary* included responses where adolescents suggested that they willingly ceded authority to their parents where necessary. They alluded to established rules or agreed-upon conditions where parents needed to know, including going somewhere with their friends or otherwise interacting with them outside of their parents' supervisory abilities (e.g., "they don't know all my school friends and don't care unless I'm going to their house or chilling with them"). Others indicated that their parents only needed to know if there was reason for them to be concerned, e.g., "they won't really care as long I don't have any bad friends" and "they do not necessarily want to know, unless they feel suspicious."

Summary of qualitative results

The responses from the adolescents made it clear that many of the adolescents felt there were reasonable explanations for their parents not knowing about some of their friends. From their point of view, their parents did not need detailed information about their friendships, particularly if the parents indicated a trust in the adolescent. At times, the decision not to provide full information seemed reasonable because they were not interacting with them regularly or outside of an adult-controlled environment (e.g., school). Many indicated that if they regularly interacted with their friends, saw them outside of school, or met them away from their parents' supervision, their parents would know or they would inform them about their friends. There were times that adolescents indicated they were taking control of the information and not providing it, for reasons that their parents might not be happy with. These, however, were only about a fifth of all of the explanations.

Thus, from the perspective of many of adolescents, revealing everything to parents about friends is an unnecessary and cumbersome process. It is reasonable to expect, then, that some would feel that attempts to gain more information about their friends would be intrusive. We might therefore infer from these data that parents *could* monitor too much.

Quantitative results

Descriptive statistics for information constructs, friends' orientations, intrusiveness, and attachment security were first calculated. These are reported in Table 1.2.

Next, we examined gender and age differences in reasons for having unknown friends using logistic regression, and found none for most of the categories. However, for *parents ceded authority*, a significant interaction between gender and age was found ($\beta = -0.27$, Wald's $= 5.13$, $p < 0.05$). Probing suggested that younger girls were more likely than older girls to provide this as a reason for their parents not knowing their friends ($\beta = -0.44$, Wald's $= 7.05$, $p < 0.05$), with no age-related differences found for boys ($\beta = 0.11$, Wald's $= 0.39$, $p > 0.10$). We note that there were no gender differences for *too many friends* or for *unsuitable friends*. This was somewhat surprising, given that girls' peer networks are generally believed to be larger than boys (Urberg *et al.*, 1995), and that boys tend to be engaged in more delinquency and have more antisocial friends (Piquero *et al.*, 2005).

Table 1.2 Sample descriptive statistics

	Mean (*SD*)	**Minimum/maximum**
Information constructs		
Parental knowledge	3.23 (0.87)	1.00–5.00
Parents wanting to know	3.06 (0.94)	1.00–5.00
Adolescents' willingness to tell	3.04 (0.84)	1.00–5.00
Friends' orientation		
Prosocial friends	3.63 (0.80)	1.00–5.00
Antisocial friends	2.54 (1.03)	1.00–5.00
Parental intrusiveness	1.88 (0.79)	1.00–4.81
Adolescents' attachment security	3.87 (0.73)	1.50–5.00

We also examined group differences in information constructs, friends' orientation, parental intrusiveness, and adolescents' attachment security. One-way ANOVAs with Tukey's B *post hoc* probes were used to examine differences between adolescents with unknown friends, either with the explanation being examined or not, and those with known friends. The results are displayed in Table 1.3.

Many of the results have a similar pattern, where the main difference was between adolescents with unknown friends and adolescents with known friends. Where this pattern emerged, such as with all of the comparisons for "don't ask/don't tell" and "haven't met," adolescents who had an unknown friend reported having parents who knew less, parents who wanted to know less, were less willing to inform parents, had friends who were less prosocial and more antisocial, felt their parents were more intrusive, and felt less attachment security than adolescents who reported their friends were known to their parents.

When comparing codes for "Don't care," the pattern was different only for wanting to know prosocial friends and parental intrusiveness. For wanting to know, those with unknown friends who indicated their parents did not care reported their parents did not want to know as much as the other two categories. For prosocial friend and parent intrusiveness where those with unknown friends whose explanation was not that their parents do not care emerged as an intermediate group. Adolescents with unknown friends whose parents reportedly did not care had the least prosocial friends and most intrusive parents, whereas those with known friends had the most prosocial friends and least intrusive parents.

In contrast, the comparisons for "network issues" suggested that the adolescents with unknown friends with network issues were the intermediate group, with those with known friends having parents who knew the most, were themselves most willing to tell, reported the least antisocial friends, the least intrusive parents, and the most attachment security. Only the comparisons for wanting to know and prosocial friends had different patterns. In both cases, those reporting network issues were more similar to those with known friends than to the others with unknown friends, with parents who wanted to know more and reporting more prosocial friends than those who had unknown friends, but did not provide network issues as the reason.

The comparison for "avoiding reactions" suggested that adolescents who were avoiding their parents reactions had the parents who knew the least, were least willing to inform their parents, had the least prosocial and most antisocial friends, felt their parents were the most intrusive, and felt the least attachment security, with adolescents with known friends on the other extreme and adolescents with unknown friends who did not give this explanation in the middle.

Most of the comparisons for "privacy/authority-taking" and "parents retain if needed" had the first pattern (i.e., differences between those with and those without unknown friends). For "privacy-authority-taking" two comparisons

Table 1.3 Differences between adolescents with coded explanations, other code, and adolescents with known friends

	Parental knowledge	Wanting to know	Willing to inform	Prosocial friends	Antisocial friends	Parent intrusive	Attachment security
Don't ask/don't tell	2.95[a]	2.89[a]	2.72[a]	3.53[a]	2.82[a]	2.00[a]	3.63[a]
	3.00[a]	2.94[a]	2.86[a]	3.59[a]	2.75[a]	2.02[a]	3.78[a]
	3.71[b]	3.31[b]	3.48[b]	3.82[b]	2.10[b]	1.60[b]	4.13[b]
	50.63	10.09	43.59	8.10	28.25	17.69	19.40
Don't care	2.65[a]	2.25[a]	2.55[a]	3.20[a]	2.83[a]	2.42[a]	3.48[a]
	3.00[a]	2.96[b]	2.84[a]	3.55[ab]	2.76[a]	2.00[b]	3.76[a]
	3.71[b]	3.31[b]	3.48[b]	3.82[b]	2.10[b]	1.61[c]	4.13[b]
	52.07	13.94	43.56	9.33	28.10	19.90	19.10
Haven't met	2.85[a]	2.74[a]	2.74[a]	3.55[a]	2.91[a]	1.91[a]	3.85[a]
	3.01[a]	2.95[a]	2.84[a]	3.54[a]	2.75[a]	2.02[a]	3.74[a]
	3.71[b]	3.31[b]	3.48[b]	3.82[b]	2.10[a]	1.61[b]	4.13[b]
	51.25	10.84	42.78	7.90	28.54	18.05	18.40
Network issues	3.23[a]	3.11[a]	3.07[a]	3.73[a]	2.57[a]	1.87[a]	3.97[a]
	2.87[b]	2.85[b]	2.71[b]	3.45[b]	2.85[b]	2.08[b]	3.64[b]
	3.71[c]	3.31[a]	3.48[c]	3.82[a]	2.10[c]	1.61[c]	4.13[c]
	60.38	13.34	53.19	13.71	31.71	20.98	27.61

Table 1.3 (Continued)

	Parental knowledge	Wanting to know	Willing to inform	Prosocial friends	Antisocial friends	Parent intrusive	Attachment security
Avoiding reactions	2.68[a]	3.07[ab]	2.57[a]	3.28[a]	3.26[a]	2.45[a]	3.43[a]
	3.04[b]	2.91[a]	2.87[b]	3.58[b]	2.69[b]	1.95[b]	3.80[b]
	3.71[c]	3.30[b]	3.48[c]	3.82[c]	2.10[c]	1.61[c]	4.13[c]
	55.65	10.64	46.09	11.07	36.17	27.97	24.32
Privacy/authority taking	2.63[a]	2.90[a]	2.60[a]	3.22[a]	2.74[a]	2.01[a]	3.54[a]
	3.03[b]	2.94[a]	2.85[a]	3.57[b]	2.97[a]	2.08[a]	3.77[a]
	3.71[c]	3.31[b]	3.48[b]	3.82[b]	2.10[b]	1.61[b]	4.13[b]
	55.28	10.03	44.56	11.36	28.78	17.84	19.73
Parents cede authority	3.31[a]	3.33[a]	3.20[a]	3.71[a]	2.67[a]	2.06[a]	3.84[a]
	2.96[b]	2.89[b]	2.79[b]	3.52[b]	2.77[a]	2.01[a]	3.74[a]
	3.72[c]	3.32[a]	3.48[c]	3.82[a]	2.10[b]	1.61[b]	4.12[b]
	54.39	14.25	47.14	8.75	27.40	17.26	8.65
Parents retain if needed	2.46[a]	2.19[a]	2.29[a]	3.42	2.72	1.5833	3.7419
	3.00[a]	2.95[b]	2.84[a]	3.54	2.76	1.6074	4.0891
	3.71[b]	3.31[b]	3.48[b]	3.82	2.10	2.0202	4.1271
	52.03	12.06	26.83	7.89	28.06	18.73	18.75

Note Means are reported in the following order: coded category on top, followed by unknown but other category, and known friends, with the F value on the bottom. Means sharing subscripts are homogenous subsets. Sample sizes ranged between 555 and 561. All F values are significant at the 0.001 level.

differed, with differences between all three groups. Adolescents who used this explanation had the lowest scores on parental knowledge and prosocial peers, with adolescents with unknown peers and some other explanation in the middle, and adolescents with known peers having the highest scores on parental knowledge and prosocial peers. Similarly, for "parents retain if needed," adolescents with unknown friends who suggested their parents could retain authority reported their parents wanted to know the least, with the parents of the other two groups wanting more.

For "parents cede authority," antisocial friends, parents' intrusiveness, and attachment security evinced the pattern first noted (i.e., differences between those with and without unknown peers). The remaining variables had a different pattern. For parental knowledge and willingness to inform, adolescents with this explanation had intermediate scores, with adolescents with known friends having the highest, and the group with unknown friends and some other code having the lowest. For parents' wanting to know and prosocial friends, adolescents suggesting their parents had ceded authority were different only from others with unknown friends (but similar to those with known friends), with parents who wanted to know more and having more prosocial friends.

Summary of quantitative results

Scant evidence of gender or age differences in explanations for unknown friends were found, suggesting that the types of rationale and distinctions made in this study might be found across adolescents, at least in Western contexts.

In general, the comparisons between groups suggested that those with known peers were probably better adjusted than those with unknown peers. This did not apply as much, however, to those who indicated they had network issues or who felt their parents had ceded authority to them. Notably, there were several times that they did not differ from their peers with known friends, suggesting that their information management was more normative. Indeed, even when adolescents with network issues differed from adolescents with known friends, their scores were above the sample mean on positive indicators (i.e., parental knowledge, willingness to inform, and attachment security) and below the sample mean on negative indicators (i.e., antisocial friends and parental intrusiveness). The same was true for those who indicated their parents had ceded authority. We believe this suggests that although some forms of information management may not be particularly healthy, others may be more adaptive.

However, the questions used applied only to friends. We wondered then, what type of decisions, implicit rules, and information management strategies might we find if we asked about other issues?

Study 2: When Do Adolescents Disclose and Not Disclose?

Study 2 examined information management about whereabouts and activities to illuminate adolescents' rationale or explanations for divulging or withholding information.

Methods

Procedures

The administrative staff of two rural school districts in the northwestern USA assisted in contacting students of two senior high schools and their guardians for potential involvement in the study. Guardians were sent letters requesting indication of their consent or dissent for their adolescents' participation in the study. No parents withheld consent. Trained assistants administered surveys to students in the classrooms.

Sample

The sample consisted of 86 older adolescents (males, $n=47$; females, $n=39$) ranging in age from 16 to 19, with an average age of 17.33 ($SD=0.52$) years. The majority of participants (79 %) self-reported their cultural background as European but born in the USA. The remaining respondents reported themselves as Hispanic, North American Indian, or Asian. The adolescents in this sample lived with two biological parents (67.4 %), a biological parent and one step-parent (12.8 %), or with one parent or guardian (19.8 %).

Measures

Adolescents' rationale for telling. Adolescents' explanations for their decisions about divulging or withholding information from parents were generated from participants' written responses to four open-ended questions: (1) When do you feel it is important for your parents to really know where you are going? (2) When do you feel it is not important for your parents to really know where you are going? (3) Under what circumstances might you tell your parents exactly where you are going? and (4) Under what circumstances might you not tell your parents exactly where you are going?

Results

The results suggest that the participants use three broad types of assessments when considering whether or not to divulge information to parents. Adolescents report evaluating the *risk of activities and locations, costs and benefits of telling,* and *boundaries of privacy*. The three types of assessments are described below along with subcategories derived from the axial coding and examples from representative cases.

Assessing risk. Adolescents reported estimating the safety of situations when gauging whether or not to tell parents of their whereabouts and activities. Three types of assessments emerged from the data: (1) distance from home, (2) length of time away and (3) the perceived dangers associated with the location or activity. Because distance from home and length of time often co-occur (it takes time to travel long distances), we combine these two assessments in the examples.

Distance and time. Driving long distances, staying away from home for several hours, or spending the night at friends or relatives are reported by participants as reasons for telling parents where they will be. Shorter distances, such as going to the store, or brief absences are deemed as safe and therefore do not call for the need to tell parents. For example, a female participant describes: "When I'm going to be gone for more than a couple of hours I'll give [my parents] a buzz . . . or if I'm at a party or I'm going to stay after school. [But not] when I'm just out running errands." Similarly, a male participant said "[It is important to tell them] when it's night, when they don't know who I'm going with, or when I go somewhere I've never been before. [It is not necessary] when it's afternoon, when they know who I'm going with, when I'm going to do something I do every day."

Safety risk. Estimations of the risk of the situation also factor into telling parents about whereabouts and activities. A male participant reports that it is important for parents to know "when there is a potential for danger. For example, if I'm going hiking in the woods they should know exactly where I am in case I get hurt or something."

Parties are viewed by some adolescents as risky activities. A male participant notes "I feel it is important for my mom to know when I go to a party or when there's a chance I could get in trouble." Unlike the latter example, a portion of the sample does not judge parties as unsafe. These adolescents, while informing parents of most activities, judge themselves as able to handle parties or other such activities safely. Prohibited activities, in these cases, are not reported to parents. For example, a female participant reports how "I don't like to let them know if I go to party or something. But I do make sure I'll be safe. Partying doesn't always mean getting drunk or stoned."

The reticence to tell parents about engaging in prohibited activities does not mean that the adolescents are unaware of the importance of informing parents of whereabouts. A female participant reports that it is important to tell parents ". . . probably at all times because if something happened and I didn't come home they'd want to know where I was. They should know [where I am] almost all the time . . . [except] if I was going somewhere I didn't think they would approve of."

Assessing costs/benefits of telling. Although informing parents about whereabouts and activities may enhance a sense of safety, adolescents do weigh the costs and benefits of divulging information. Two types of costs and benefits of telling emerged from the data. Adolescents weigh the benefits of engaging in desired but prohibited behaviors against (a) the cost of parental disapproval or sanctions, or (b) worrying parents.

Cost of parental disapproval or sanctions. Adolescents estimate how their parents will respond to certain types of information. Although adolescents are well aware of the importance of parents knowing their whereabouts, there is a cost for parents knowing about engaging in prohibited activities. Adolescents estimate the cost of parental disapproval or sanctions for engaging in desired but prohibited behaviors and act accordingly. As such, adolescents elect to be selective about the information they provide to parents. For example, a female participant reports "They have the right as parents to know where I'm at... they have a right [to know] all the time. [I don't tell them] if I'm going somewhere I know they would freak out if they knew where I was." Another female participant said: "No, [I don't tell] because my mom would never approve of what I do. So I tell her I'm going to do homework and go out. It's none of her business what I do. For example, if I'm out with friends they don't need to know WHERE. At least they know I'm out and will be back later." Adolescents also consider the risk of withholding information from parents. Telling parents about activities and whereabouts, for some adolescents, is a matter of avoiding parental sanctions. One female participant reports "I am not allowed to do anything they don't know about and haven't previously approved. Under no circumstances [would I not tell]. The consequences are too high." Another adolescent concerned with parental sanctions follows her parents' rules very closely by telling them where she is going and what she is doing "... EVERY TIME I LEAVE THE HOUSE. I FEEL THAT IT IS IMPORTANT TO LET MY PARENTS KNOW WERE I AM GOING [caps in original]. There is not a place I go that I can't tell my parents. As long as I tell them the truth and follow the rules it is o.k."

Worrying parents. Adolescents are well aware that parents worry about the risks of certain behaviors. It is developmentally appropriate for adolescents to assess and interpret their parents' emotional responses, such as worrying. Indeed, empathic concern is an important prosocial characteristic. Raising parental concern is viewed as unnecessary under some circumstances. Adolescents assess when to withhold or divulge information to prevent what they deem as unwarranted parental worries or concerns. For example, a male participant reports "I'm open and honest with my parents. [I tell them where I am going] all of the time, because then they have that sense of security." Likewise, a female participant notes the importance of honesty for her relationship with her mother. However, she also notes the need to withhold information to prevent her mother from worrying. "I don't feel the need to lie to my mom about what I'm doing. Trust and honesty is important..... unless it's someplace where I think I will be safe, but my mom won't. Then I just save her worrying." Another female participant states: "I think it is courteous to tell my mom where I go (anytime) so she doesn't worry. [I tell her] whenever I feel comfortable doing so (almost always). Just not if I'm supposed to go to a class, but instead I go shopping instead ... things like that involving skipping of classes."

Assessing privacy boundaries. Learning when information is public or private is a social skill that is critically important for engaging in successful social relationships. Adolescents' awareness of privacy boundaries and the use of these boundaries are important for autonomy development (Van Manen & Levering, 1996; Petronio & Caughlin, 2006). Instances emerge from the data of adolescents not telling their parents about their whereabouts or activities because divulging information would cross privacy boundaries. Some boundaries involve keeping secrets such as gifts for family members. As one female participant notes "I feel it's important for my parents to really know where I'm going when I actually go somewhere. I feel it's not important for my parents to really know where I'm going when I go to get them a gift (Christmas, birthday, mother's day, father's day, anniversary etc.)" (underlining in original).

Other boundaries involve maintaining private information about the self such as sexual relations with a partner. A male participant explains that it is important for his mother to be able to contact him or know about prohibited activities. He assesses information about staying overnight at a girlfriend's house as less accessible to his parent: "Well I always tell my mother where I'm going. She trusts me, so if she needed to get a hold of me she could. Sometimes when you're doing something bad you don't want them to know where you are but I still tell her. Well, say I went to my girl friend's house and spent the night I might not tell her."

Summary

Taken together, the findings may be used to outline an initial model of how adolescents calculate when and what to tell parents about their whereabouts. Adolescents in this study assess (a) the context of activities, (b) relations with parents and (c) their sense of self within relationships with parents (boundaries). These assessments appear to be linked. For example, adolescents' understanding of safety risks are taken into account when evaluating their parents' likely responses to prohibited activities. The implicit rules underlying adolescents' calculations about what to tell are likely founded, in part, upon a history of interactions with their parents. Additionally, adolescents estimate the social benefits (e.g., time with peers) of experiences outside of the family.

Serendipitous Findings

In qualitative research, researchers often note findings that are unexpected because the information providing the revelations was not asked for directly or expected. These are called serendipitous findings and are important because they provide unique insight into the topic of interest. Across our data, we found three ways in which the qualitative data revealed aspects of adolescents' information management that may have been previously overlooked.

Joint processes

Although we expected information management to be a joint process between parents and adolescence, we also found evidence that it is a joint process involving peers. For example, a 17-year-old male responded that he would not tell "When they won't let me go, we don't explain exactly where I'm going." The "we" suggests that this is a friend or peer, with whom he is comanaging information. If information is comanaged with peers, particularly in deviant peer groups, information management could be a form of deviancy training.

Two other adolescents responded "If something was wrong with a friend and they didn't want me to tell anyone where we were" and "If I'm helping someone that doesn't want people to know" (respectively). These responses again suggest that the adolescents are not making the decisions on their own. However, in these cases, it is clear that they are trying to honor someone else's privacy boundaries and uphold the trust that the other has placed in them.

Opposite-sex issues

We fully expected that sexuality and contact with potential romantic partners would emerge as a reason why adolescents might withhold information about friends. What surprised us was finding that only girls reported having opposite sex friends that were unknown. Among the 196 girls who responded they had an unknown friend, 12 (6 %) responded that their "unknown" friends were boys. These girls also frequently communicated that the boys were not romantic partners but that their parents did make this distinction: "My parents don't like me to hang out with guys, they think [they're] all crazed sex maniacs! But I can't handle girls a lot of times. They're too fickle and backstabbing. Guys are just easier to hang with and they also do sports that make them very physically active so often I go skiing or such with guys. None of the girls will go with me." "Because they are guys and sometimes if I talk about guy friends they get all squealy and assume they're boyfriends."

In none of the cases reviewed in these studies (nor in two others studies with friendship data) did boys report having a similar issue that kept them from revealing information about a female friend. Although this might have been because parents do not bother their sons about having girls as friends, we may also not have seen it because boys do not disclose about topics involving the opposite sex. We suspect that the latter is unlikely, though, given other very personal information that boys have disclosed through these studies and others.

Internet friends

Given the rise in electronic media, it is not surprising that friends met over the Internet would be mentioned ($n = 9$, 4 boys and 5 girls, 3 % of adolescents indicating they had an unknown friend). This was noteworthy because some viewed these friends as something their parents did not need to be kept informed about: "They are on the internet and they are merely net friends that I play games with," "Because I don't bother to tell them, because I know them over the internet." This suggests that despite warnings in the media and elsewhere that many predators contact youth through chat rooms, some of these adolescents seem to be unaware of the dangers, or judge themselves capable of making judgments about Internet contacts. In some cases, it appears that this may be justified: "It's not necessary to let my parents know some of my friends who met me on the internet, cuz we won't meet each other alone. If my friends on the internet want to see me, I'll tell my parents then" (15-year-old boy).

SUMMARY AND CONCLUSIONS

Adolescents manage information. They choose at times to disclose and at other times to withhold information or lie to their parents. This was established before we started this project. The reasons adolescents managed information has been less understood. These results show that although engaging in undesirable or delinquent activities is part of the picture, there is much more to adolescents' information management. From the perspective of some of the adolescents, information management supports establishing boundaries of privacy and autonomy, as well as allowing them to preserve important relationships, all normative goals. Some indicate that they have to simultaneously consider these goals, attempting to strike a balance.

The adolescents' responses suggest that they use complex implicit rules when managing information. Many may be rules that are laid down or negotiated within the family. They weigh safety and security concerns, issues of trust, self-presentation matters, and possible reactions of others. They treat some information as important and other information as trivial. Indeed, many suggest their parents know the "important" information and they reveal much in their everyday interactions with parents. Their understanding of managing information includes not taxing others with minor details. In the view of many, this is what their parents prefer. Although these are the interpretations of adolescents, the quantitative comparisons suggest that at least some are likely consistent with their parents' views. However, because we did not ask *how* they manage information, it is not clear how adolescents retain control of information about their friends and whereabouts. We do not know when they use withholding or misinformation. It is also unclear how adolescents interpret nondisclosure. We cannot say, even from their perspective, when they are deceiving their parents. Future research needs to explore adolescents' subjective interpretations of withholding and lying, of disclosure and nondisclosure, of lies and white lies.

These results also suggest problems with quantitative measures of parental knowledge and information management. If parents' reports are used, both overestimation and underestimation occur. Conversely, if adolescents' reports are used, their interpretations color their responses. Neither tells researchers what they need to know—when "knowing a lot" means parents know enough and when "knowing nothing" is not a problem.

We acknowledge the limitations of these studies, including the lack of longitudinal data for examining causality. We also recognize the limitations for generalizing these results. Although our samples were ethnically diverse, they were still heavily weighted by European-based cultural contexts. Examining these issues in other cultures is important, particularly in cultures with less emphasis on individualism and with different interpretations of privacy and parental authority.

These issues acknowledged, we believe these results allow adolescents to speak to the debate on parental knowledge and information management. Their voices suggest that there are circumstances under which parents do not need to know, and perhaps should not know, everything about their peers and activities. Their voices demonstrate that they have a good deal of control over such information and that their agency should not be underestimated.

REFERENCES

Bakeman, R. & Gottman, J. M. (1986). *Observing Interaction: An Introduction to Sequential Analysis*. New York: Cambridge University Press.

Barber, B. K. (1996). Parental psychological control: revisiting a neglected construct. *Child Development, 67*, 3296–3319.

Barber, B. K., Olsen, J. A., & Shagle, S. (1994). Associations between parental psychological control and behavioral control and youth internalized and externalized behaviors. *Child Development, 65*, 1120–1136.

Bok, S. (1978). *Lying: Moral Choice in Public and Private Life*. New York: Random House.

Bowen, M. (1978). *Family Therapy in Clinical Practice*. New York: Jason Aronson.

Brown, B. B., Mounts, N., Lamborn, S. D., & Steinberg, L. (1993). Parenting practices and peer group affiliation in adolescence. *Child Development, 64*, 467–482.

Chandler, M. & Hala, S. (1991). Trust and children's developing theory of mind. In K. J. Rotenberg (ed.), *Children's Interpersonal Trust: Sensitivity to Lying, Deception, and Promise Violations* (pp. 135–159). New York: Springer-Verlag.

Cohen, E. A., Vasey, M. W., & Gavazzi, S. M. (2003). The dimensionality of family differentiation and the prediction of adolescent internalized distress. *Journal of Family Issues, 24*, 99–123.

Collins, W. A. & Luebker, C. (1994). Parent and adolescent expectancies: individual and relational significance. In J. G. Smetana (Ed.), *New Directions for Child Development*, Vol. 66 (pp. 65–80). San Francisco: Jossey-Bass.

Darling, N., Cumsille, P., Caldwell., L. L., & Dowdy, B. (2006). Predictors of adolescents' disclosure to parents and perceived parental knowledge: Between- and within-person differences. *Journal of Youth and Adolescence, 35,* 667–678.

DePaulo, B. M. & Kashy, D. A. (1998). Everyday lies in close and casual relationships. *Journal of Personality and Social Psychology, 74,* 63–79.

DePaulo, B. M., Kashy, D. A., Kirkendol, S. E. *et al.* (1996). Lying in everyday life. *Journal of Personality and Social Psychology, 70,* 979–995.

Fanzoi, S. L. & Davis, M. H. (1985). Adolescent self-disclosure and loneliness: Private self-consciousness and parental influences. *Journal of Personality and Social Psychology, 48,* 768–780.

Finkenauer, C., Engels, R., & Meeus, W. (2002). Keeping secrets from parents: Advantages and disadvantages of secrecy in adolescence. *Journal of Youth and Adolescence, 31,* 123–136.

Fletcher, A. C., Steinberg, L., & Williams-Wheeler, M. (2005). Parental influences on adolescent problem behavior: Revisiting Stattin and Kerr. *Child Development, 75,* 781–796.

Ford, C. V. (1996). *Lies! Lies!! Lies!!! The Psychology of Deceit.* Washington, DC: American Psychiatric Press.

Frijns, T., Finkenauer, C., Vermulst, A. A., & Engels, R. (2005). Keeping secrets from parents: longitudinal associations of secrecy in adolescence. *Journal of Youth and Adolescence, 34,* 137–148.

Furstenberg, F. F. (2001). The sociology of adolescence and youth in the 1990s: A critical commentary. In R. Milardo (ed.), *Understanding Families into the New Millennium: A Decade in Review* (pp. 115–129). Minneapolis, MN: National Council on Family Relations.

Galambos, N. L. & Maggs, J. L. (1991). Out-of-school care of young adolescents and self-reported behavior. *Developmental Psychology, 27,* 644–655.

Granhag, P. A. & Strömwall, L. A. (2004). Research on deception detection: Past and present. In P. A. Granhag & L. A. Strömwall (eds), *The Detection of Deception in Forensic Contexts* (pp. 3–14). Cambridge: Cambridge University Press.

Kerr, M. & Stattin, H. (2000). What parents know, how they know it, and several forms of adolescent adjustment: Further support for a reinterpretation of monitoring. *Developmental Psychology, 36,* 366–380.

Kerr, M. & Stattin, H. (2003). Parenting of adolescents: Action or reaction? In A. C. Crouter (ed.), *Children's Influence on Family Dynamics: The Neglected Side of Family Relationships* (pp. 121–151). Mahwah, NJ: Lawrence Erlbaum Associates.

Kerr, M., Stattin, H., & Tilton-Weaver, L. (2007). *Parental Monitoring: A Critical Examination of the Research.* Manuscript submitted for publication.

Kerr, M., Stattin, H., & Trost, K. (1999). To know you is to trust you: parents' trust is rooted in child disclosure of information. *Journal of Adolescence, 22,* 737–752.

Kuczynski, L. & Daly, K. (2003). Qualitative methods for inductive (theory-generating) research. In L. Kuczynski (ed.), *Handbook of Dynamics in Parent-Child Relations* (pp. 373–392). Thousand Oaks, CA: Sage.

Laird, R. D., Pettit, G. S., Bates, J. E., & Dodge, K. A. (2003). Parents' monitoring-relevant knowledge and adolescents' delinquent behavior: Evidence of correlated developmental changes in reciprocal influences. *Child Development, 74,* 752–768.

Larson, R. W., Richards, M. H., Moneta, G. *et al.* (1996). Changes in adolescents' daily interactions with their families from ages 10–18: Disengagement and transformation. *Developmental Psychology, 32,* 744–754.

Lee, K. & Ross, H. J. (1997). The concept of lying in adolescents and young adults: testing Sweetser's folkloristic model. *Merrill-Palmer Quarterly, 43,* 255–270.

Loeber, R., DeLamatre, M. S., & Keenan, K. (1998). A prospective replication of developmental pathways in disruptive and delinguent behavior. In R. B.

Cairns & L. R. Bergman (eds), *Methods and Models for Studying the Individual* (pp. 185–218). Thousand Oaks, CA: Sage.

Marshall, S. K., Tilton-Weaver, L., & Bosdet, L. (2005). Information management: considering adolescents' regulation of parental knowledge. *Journal of Adolescence, 28*, 633–647.

Martin, M. M., Anderson, C. M., & Mottet, T. P. (1999). Perceived understanding and self-disclosure in the stepparent-stepchild relationship. *Journal of Psychology, 133*, 281–290.

Metts, S. (1989). An exploratory investigation of deception in close relationships. *Journal of Social and Personal Relationships, 6*, 159–179.

Minuchin, S. (1974). *Families and Family Therapy*. Cambridge, MA: Harvard University Press.

Norrell, J. E. (1984). Self-disclosure: implications for the study of parent-adolescent interaction. *Journal of Youth and Adolescence, 13*, 163–178.

Pearce, W. B. & Sharp, S. M. (1973). Self-disclosing communication. *Journal of Communication, 23*, 409–425.

Peskin, J. (1992). Ruse and representations: on children's ability to conceal information. *Developmental Psychology, 28*, 84–89.

Petronio, S. & Caughlin, J. P. (2006). Communication privacy management theory: Understanding families. In D. O. Braithwaite & L. A. Baxter (eds), *Engaging Theories in Family Communication* (pp. 35–49). Thousand Oaks: Sage.

Piquero, N. L., Gover, A. R., MacDonald, J. M., & Piquero, A. R. (2005). The influence of delinquent peers on delinquency: does gender matter? *Youth and Society, 36*, 251–275.

Rosenthal, D. A., Efklides, A., & Demetriou, A. (1988). Parental criticism and young adolescent self-disclosure: a cross-cultural study. *Journal of Youth and Adolescence, 17*, 25–39.

Searight, H. R., Thomas, S. L., Manley, C. M., & Ketterson, T. U. (1995). Self-disclosure in adolescents: a family systems perspective. In K. J. Rotenberg (ed.), *Disclosure Processes in Children and Adolescents* (pp. 204–225). New York: Cambridge University Press.

Smetana, J. G. (1988). Adolescents' and parents' conceptions of parental authority. *Child Development, 59*, 321–335.

Smetana, J. G. & Asquith, P. (1994). Adolescents' and parents' conceptions of parental authority and personal autonomy. *Child Development, 65*, 1147–1162.

Smetana, J. G., Metzger, A., Gettman, D. C., & Campione-Barr, N. (2006). Disclosure and secrecy in adolescent-parent relationships. *Child Development, 77*, 201–207.

Stattin, H. & Kerr, M. (2000). Parental monitoring: A reinterpretation. *Child Development, 71*, 1072–1085.

Stattin, H. & Kerr, M. (2003). Parenting of adolescents: Action or reaction? In A. C. Crouter & A. Booth (eds.), *Children's influence on family dynamics: The neglected side of family relationships* (pp. 121–151). Mahwah, NJ: Lawrence Erlbaum Associates.

Steinberg, L. (1990). Autonomy, conflict, and harmony in the family relationship. In S. S. Feldman & G. R. Elliott (eds), *At the Threshold: The Developing Adolescent* (pp. 255–276). Cambridge, MA: Harvard University Press.

Stouthamer-Loeber, M. (1986). Lying as a problem behavior in children: a review. *Clinical Psychology Review, 6*, 267–289.

Strauss, A. & Corbin, J. M. (1990). *Basics of Qualitative Research: Grounded Theory Procedures and Techniques.* Thousand Oaks, CA: Sage.

Sweetser, E. E. (1987). The definition of lie: an examination of the folk models underlying a semantic prototype. In D. Holland (ed.), *Cultural Models in Language and Thought.* New York: Cambridge University Press.

Talwar, V. & Lee, K. (2002). Emergence of white-lie telling in children between 3 and 7 years of age. *Merrill-Palmer Quarterly, 48*, 160–181.

Tilton-Weaver, L. C. & Galambos, N. L. (2003). Parents' beliefs as predictors of parents' peer management behaviors. *Journal of Research on Adolescence,13,* 269–300.

Urberg, K. A., Degirmencioglu, S. M., Tolson, J. M., & Halliday-Scher, K. (1995). The structure of adolescent peer networks. *Developmental Psychology, 31,* 540–547.

Van Manen, M. & Levering, B. (1996). *Childhood's Secrets: Intimacy, Privacy, and the Self Reconsidered*. Williston, VT: Teachers College Press.

Vrij, A. (2000). *Detecting Lies and Deceit. The Psychology of Lying and the Implications for Professional Practice.* Chichester: Wiley.

West, M., Rose, M., Spreng, S. *et al.* (1998). Adolescent attachment questionnaire: a brief assessment of attachment in adolescence. *Journal of Youth and Adolescence, 27,* 661–673.

White, J. M. & Klein, D. M. (2002). *Family Theories* (2nd edn). Thousand Oaks, CA: Sage.

CHAPTER 2

Relational Implications of Secrecy and Concealment in Parent–Adolescent Relationships

Catrin Finkenauer
Vrije Universiteit, Amsterdam, Netherlands
Rutger C. M. E. Engels
Radboud University Nijmegen, Netherlands
Kaska E. Kubacka
Vrije Universiteit, Amsterdam, Netherlands

INTRODUCTION

Everybody has secrets of a kind: secrets kept to oneself, secrets shared with another person, or secrets shared with a group of people; secrets pertaining to possessions, feelings, beliefs, past or future behaviors, values, thoughts, or relationships. Secrecy is a common strategy in games, politics, economics, and interpersonal relationships. Any game requires players to use some secrecy as a strategy to mislead the partner and win the game. Politicians hide their past to get elected. Countries use their secret services and secret weapons to intimidate other countries. Chefs keep their recipes secret. Scientists protect their inventions and discoveries through secrecy. In relationships, people keep secrets to hide inadequacies, to avoid being punished, to protect others, to make themselves look more favorable or more interesting, to have power, or to prevent others from spoiling a special memory. On the other hand, people share secrets with others to demonstrate trust, to increase intimacy, or to define

What Can Parents Do? New Insights into the Role of Parents in Adolescent Problem Behavior
Edited by Margaret Kerr, Håkan Stattin and Rutger C. M. E. Engels.

the relationship as something special. To make a long story short, secrets are a fact of daily life.

Most of us experience a curious fascination about secrets. The very fact that they are secret and that we do not have access to them implies mystery and excitement. Yet our attraction to secrets quickly fades and changes into resentment when our partner or a friend persists in withholding certain information from us. Paradoxically, we also experience resentment when others intrude on our secrecy. It thus seems that secrets have important symbolic functions within relationships and that these functions go beyond the actual content of the secret. Secrets communicate separateness and distance if they are kept from another person and communicate closeness and intimacy if they are shared with others. Secrets happen between people and represent an important means whereby people regulate their relationships with others.

Despite the important role secrets and concealment play in everyday life and in relationships, empirical research knows little about secrets and secrecy. Our research is an attempt to fill some of the gaps in our knowledge about and understanding of secrecy and concealment in relationships. Specifically, our research focuses on the relational implications of secrecy and concealment in parent–adolescent relationships. Although communication, including both disclosure and secrecy, is at the heart of almost all relationships, it is particularly important and acute during adolescence, a period that for may put considerable strain on the relationship between some youngsters and their parents (Arnett, 1999; Kim *et al.*, 2001). In particular early adolescence is characterized by an increase in conflicts and family stress as compared to childhood and later on in the teenage years (Granic *et al.*, 2003). While the role of disclosure in parent–adolescent relationships has received considerable attention in research (e.g., Buhrmester & Prager, 1995; Finkenauer *et al.*, 2004; Kerr, Stattin, & Trost, 1999; see also Smetana & Metzger, this volume), research on secrecy is scarce.

This chapter aims to provide an overview of our research on secrecy and concealment in parent–adolescent child relationships. For a comprehensive understanding of the relational implications of secrecy in adolescence, it begins by briefly outlining developmental tasks in adolescence. Subsequently, the chapter will define secrecy and concealment, before highlighting how they can function to facilitate the accomplishment of developmental tasks in adolescence (Finkenauer, Engels, & Meeus, 2002). Although our research suggests that secrecy may be profitable for some aspects of adolescent development, these profits seem to come at a prize. Indeed, subsequent research suggests that this prize may entail considerable relational costs for both secret-keepers and people from whom a secret is kept, and for the relationship between these two (Finkenauer *et al.*, 2005; Frijns & Finkenauer, 2006; Frijns *et al.*, 2005). The chapter will conclude by portraying some of the theoretical and practical implications of secrecy and concealment for parent–child relationships and future research.

DEVELOPMENTAL TASKS IN ADOLESCENCE

Adolescence is a critical developmental transition (Petersen & Hamburg, 1986). Adolescents have to let go of the safety of childhood and parental protection and get a firm hold on the responsibilities and demands of adulthood. Self-related and social developmental tasks need to be accomplished to facilitate this transition. One task that is at the core of adolescence is an increase in independence from parents (e.g., behavioral, emotional, financial) and the formation and maintenance of own social networks outside the family (Grotevant & Cooper, 1986). This developmental task causes considerable social changes. Relationships with parents become more equal (Smetana, Campione-Barr, & Daddis, 2004) and romantic and sexual relationships gain importance (Furman & Shaffer, 2003). Adolescents spend more time with friends and peers and less time with their families, parents in particular (Larson *et al.*, 1996). Belonging to a popular group becomes an important goal for adolescents (Berndt, 1996). Having a friend to confide in becomes a social achievement for adolescents and an indicator of social competence (Hartup, 1996).

Developmental tasks in adolescence comprise seemingly contradictory goals. Adolescents have to develop intimate relationships, while striving for autonomy and independence. They have to develop a sense of who they are and what they want in various social domains, while trying to fit in (Finkenauer *et al.*, 2002). They have to become less dependent on their parents (Smetana, Campione-Barr & Daddis, 2004; Youniss & Smollar, 1985) but simultaneously they have to preserve a good relationship with them. After all parents remain important and influential throughout their children's lives (e.g., Whiston & Keller, 2004). We propose that secrecy and concealment may function to facilitate adolescents' accomplishment of these seemingly contradictory goals, because they allow adolescents to actively control information about the self. They thereby represent efficient strategies to balance independence and closeness, autonomy and connectedness, and stability and change. For a comprehensive understanding of this function of secrecy and concealment in adolescence, it is first necessary to define secrecy.

DEFINITION OF SECRECY AND CONCEALMENT

Defining Features of Secrecy and Concealment

According to our definition, secrets consist of information that (at least) one person conceals, withholds, or hides from (at least) one other person (Finkenauer, 1998; Finkenauer, Engels, & Meeus, 2002). Secrecy and concealment thereby draw a line between those who know and those who do not. They separate those who keep the secret, *the secret-keeper*(s), from those from whom the secret is kept, *the secret-target*(s). Thus secrecy is an inherently social phenomenon, happening between people rather than within them (Bok, 1989; Lane & Wegner, 1995). Moreover, secrecy and concealment involve purpose and intent (Bok, 1989). People do not flip a coin to decide whether or not to keep a secret. They have reasons to do so (Caughlin *et al.*, 2005). Although secrecy and concealment may in some cases not be a deliberate choice because some secret-keepers may believe they have no choice (e.g., when someone has to keep a secret to protect his or her life or that of others), in our definition secret-keepers are aware of their secret and know that they are concealing information form another person.

This definition of secrets as conscious phenomena excludes unconscious secrets (e.g., Schoicket, 1980). These secrets are inaccessible to consciousness and are theorized to result from the successful repression of intolerable or fearful experiences. In some cases, people may even have forgotten about their secrets altogether. Unconscious secrets are often the focus of psychoanalytic treatment that aims to uncover unconscious thoughts, desires or fantasies and help patients to work through them. In the present chapter we will not address unconscious secrets, however.

Given that secrecy is one aspect of communication, it is often considered as the mere opposite of disclosure (e.g., Buhrmester & Prager, 1995; Chelune *et al.*, 1984). However, purposefully concealing information from others is related to but different from disclosure (Finkenauer *et al.*, 2002; Smetana *et al.*, 2006). Secrecy and disclosure are not mutually exclusive. To illustrate, when telling her parents about her new boyfriend, an adolescent girl may disclose how and where they met, what they did, and what he said. At the same time, she may keep the fact that they already kissed a secret. Secrecy and disclosure may thus occur simultaneously. There is one exception, however. When one considers a specific piece of information, disclosure and secrecy are opposites of the same coin (e.g., she kept the kiss secret, hence did not disclose it). In our studies, results converge to suggest that disclosure and secrecy are related but distinct concepts that are simultaneously present in relationships (Finkenauer *et al.*, 2002; Frijns *et al.*, 2005; Smetana *et al.*, 2006). These results underline that secrecy is a unique concept that warrants research in its own right.

The scope of the information that is kept from others differentiates secrets from concealment. *Secrets* refer to a specific piece of information that can be placed in space and time, such as a particular behavior, thought, feeling, or event. *Concealment and secrecy* refer to a broader range of information, such as certain themes, personal dispositions, or preferences. Both secrecy and concealment, separate secret-keepers from secret-targets and involve intentional concealment from others. Given these commonalities in their definition, throughout this chapter, we will use both terms interchangeably.

Types of Secrets in Adolescence

In contrast to the implicit assumption that all secrets are equal, adolescents keep a variety of secrets (Frijns & Finkenauer, 2006). Across three studies, with more than 1000 Dutch adolescents ranging in age from 12–19 years, we found that about one-third of adolescents' secrets were *individual secrets*. These secrets are only known to the secret-keepers themselves and are kept from everybody else (e.g., "I want to be a topmodel but people would laugh about me if I told them"—adolescent girl, 14 years old). The large majority of adolescents (about 70 %) reported having *shared secrets*. These secrets are shared with others and kept only from one particular person or group of persons (e.g., "I went to see a prostitute and told all my friends, but not my parents. They'd kill me if they knew," adolescent boy 16 years old). Adolescents shared their secrets most frequently with best friends and friends, followed by parents and other family members (e.g., siblings, aunts). Other types of confidants were rarely mentioned, indicating that adolescents share their secrets with people close to them.

This finding indicates that adolescents have a sense of what is good for them. They reveal their secrets to appropriate confidants to protect themselves from harm and humiliation. Appropriate confidants are "(a) discreet and can be trusted not to reveal a secret, (b) perceived as nonjudgmental, and (c) able to offer the secret keeper new insights into the secret" (Kelly & McKillop, 1996, p. 458). The fact that adolescents share their secrets more frequently with friends than with parents may indicate that they perceive friends as more appropriate confidants than parents. Future studies should investigate this suggestion.

The existence of shared secrets can be considered as an indication that adolescents actively manage and control information about their selves and their lives and that strategically sharing and keeping secrets may help them to regulate their relationships with others. Shared secrets have a function that cannot be fulfilled by individual secrets. They may create and maintain intimacy and relatedness in the relationship between secret-keepers (Karpel, 1980; Simmel, 1950; Vangelisti, 1994; Van Manen & Levering, 1996). However, when secrets are shared there is the risk of betrayal. To share a secret the secret-keeper therefore has to trust the other with its protection. Shared secrets, by definition, are shared with a limited and selected number of insiders. To illustrate, telling someone "I'm going to tell you a secret" conveys a relational message that goes beyond what the secrets is about. Indeed, it communicates that the confidant is special and that one trusts him or her to protect my secret. Shared secrets thereby create a feeling of "we versus them," because they separate between "we who know about the secret" and "them who don't know about it" (Simmel, 1950). Sharing a secret with someone communicates trust in the other and may thereby lead to feelings of intimacy and feelings of relatedness among the secret-keepers. Conversely, keeping a secret from someone communicates separation and may thereby lead to feelings of social distance.

DEVELOPMENTAL FUNCTIONS OF SECRECY: INDEPENDENCE AND AUTONOMY

The defining features of secrecy, that it is a social phenomenon and that it is intentional, shed light on its developmental functions in adolescence. From a developmental perspective, being able to keep a secret can be considered as a necessary, although not sufficient, condition for an individual to develop a sense of the self (i.e., being different from others) and a feeling of autonomy (i.e., being independent from others) (Meares & Orlay, 1988; Peskin, 1992; Pipe & Goodman, 1991). As Tournier (1965) puts it: "One cannot become a person without first being an individual, without freeing oneself from the clan, from parental domination, without becoming aware of one's own individuality, which has the right to secrecy" (p. 29). Similarly, Jung (1961) suggests that there is no better means to become an independent individual than having a secret. Yet, he emphasizes that secrecy is a double-sided sword. "Nothing makes people more lonely, and more cut off from the fellowship of others, than the possession of an anxiously hidden and jealously guarded secret" (Jung, 1961, p. 192). Regarding the sense of self, secrecy may help to promote individuation and independence from others. Regarding social relationships, however, it also implies isolation and separation.

To have a secret the secret-keeper has to have secret knowledge that separates her/him from others and it is exactly because of this separation that the secret-keeper can feel independent from them. Hence, in secrecy independence and separation from others are inextricably intertwined. One cannot exist without the other. In this sense, secrecy may contribute to the development of autonomy and independence in adolescence (Margolis, 1966; Simmel, 1950; Van Manen & Levering, 1996). It involves skills and competences that are at the heart of independence and autonomy. First, secret-keepers need to exert self-control to prevent themselves from spilling the secret and to inhibit their impulse to confide their secret. Second, secret-keepers have to make personal choices and decide from whom they want to keep the secret and whom they want to confide in. Both self-control and personal choice are considered vital aspects of the development of autonomy and independence (e.g., Allen *et al.*, 1994; Larson *et al.*, 1996; Steinberg & Silverberg, 1986).

This exercise of self-control and personal choice inherent in secrecy may add to the development of independence and autonomy in adolescence in several ways. One possible way is that by keeping a secret adolescents may perceive themselves as separate, apart, and thus different from others. They may thereby be able to see themselves as an independent, self-determined, and unique individuals. Second, by keeping a secret adolescents may regulate and control others' access to the self (cf., Petronio, 1991). They thereby determine the extent to which they want to make themselves known and transparent to others and—at least partly—how they want others to view them (Kelly, 1998; Marshall, Tilton-Weaver, & Bosdet, 2005).

These correlates of secrecy and concealment bear particular importance to the relationship between the parent and the adolescent. By keeping secrets from their parents, adolescents may separate themselves from their parents and establish and consolidate their capacities of self-regulation and self-determination (e.g., Allen *et al.*, 1994; Larson *et al.*, 1996; Steinberg & Silverberg, 1986). Although parents do not become unimportant, adolescents increasingly rely on friends for advice and social support, they do not continue to see their parents as all-knowing or all-powerful and they become able to perceive and interact with their parents as people—not just as parents (Steinberg, 1990). Adolescents may hence use concealment and secrecy as strategic devices to control and regulate their relationship with their parents. Based on these theoretical assumptions, we expected that adolescents' concealment from parents would be related to adolescents' emotional autonomy from their parents.

To establish that secrecy from parents contributes to emotional autonomy in adolescence, one needs to control for the confounding influence of third variables, specifically disclosure, parent–child relationship quality, and frequency of contact with peers. Disclosure and concealment are related concepts (see above). To ensure that concealment from parents contributes to explaining variance in emotional autonomy, above and beyond mere "non-disclosure," one has to consider disclosure when investigating concealment from parents. Also, concealment from parents may result from a bad relationship with parents. Adolescents may not feel comfortable confiding in their parents when their relationship with them is negative. So, to ensure that concealment is not a mere by-product of a bad parent–adolescent relationship, one has to control for the quality of the parent–adolescent relationship. Finally, some adolescents may conceal information because they do not have friends to share their secrets with. To minimize the risk of this confound artificially inflating the link between concealment and emotional autonomy, we controlled for the frequency of contacts with peers.

INVESTIGATING THE LINK BETWEEN CONCEALMENT AND AUTONOMY: AN EMPIRICAL STUDY

To investigate the hypothesis that adolescent concealment and secrecy are positively related to emotional autonomy we conducted a cross-sectional study among adolescents (Finkenauer, Engels, & Meeus, 2002). Questionnaires were distributed among two groups of adolescents ($N = 110$ 12–13 year olds and $N = 117$ 16–18 year olds, respectively). The questionnaires assessed adolescents' concealment from parents, emotional autonomy in adolescents' relationships with parents, adolescents' disclosure towards parents, adolescents' satisfaction with their relationship with their parents, and frequency of contact with friends and peers. To assess emotional autonomy, which is defined as the extent adolescents relinquish dependence on parents and view themselves as independent agents, we used the Dutch version of the Emotional Autonomy Scale (original by Steinberg & Silverberg, 1986, translated and validated by Goossens, 1997). To assess disclosure to parents, adolescents rated to what extent they disclose information about themselves (e.g., personal habits, deepest feelings, what they like or dislike about themselves) to their parents.

Our descriptive findings showed that many adolescents reported keeping some secrets from their parents. The amount of concealment from parents did not vary across adolescent age or sex. Hierarchical regression analyses revealed that disclosure to parents and quality of the relationship with parents both contributed negatively to emotional autonomy. This finding indicates that adolescents who disclosed to their parents and who had a good relationship with their parents also had less developed feelings of emotional autonomy. Importantly, however, the analysis confirmed our prediction that concealment positively contributes to adolescents' feeling of autonomy, above and beyond disclosure and quality of the parent–child relationship. Thus, adolescents who concealed information from their parents perceived themselves as emotionally autonomous independent of the degree to which they disclosed information to them and independent of the quality of their relationship with their parents. Neither age nor sex affected these results.

These results provide first evidence for the suggestion that concealing information from parents may help adolescents to maximize the accomplishment of independence from their parents. Concealment from parents uniquely and strongly contributed to explaining variance in adolescents' feelings of emotional autonomy. A closer look at our definition of secrecy allows us to speculate about the mechanisms by which concealment may contribute to feelings of independence and autonomy. By actively concealing information from their parents, adolescents may establish a metaphoric boundary between themselves and their parents (cf. Petronio, 1991). They regulate this boundary by revealing or concealing information from their parents which controls parents' access to their self and their lives. This self-regulation may provide adolescents with a sense of self-determination (cf. Margolis, 1966). Also, concealment may provide them with an opportunity to free themselves from parental supervision and monitoring (Marshall *et al.*, 2005) and establish privacy (Buhrmester & Prager, 1995). Finally, by being selective about which aspects of themselves they reveal to their parents, adolescents may determine—in part—how parents view their self and thereby consolidate their identity (cf. Kelly, 1998; Marshall *et al.*, 2005). Thus, the defining features of concealment and secrecy can be assumed to promote important aspects of autonomy in adolescence and independence in the parent–adolescent relationship. These aspects include separation from parents, self-control and self-determination, personal choice, and identity formation (Allen *et al.*, 1994; Steinberg & Silverberg, 1986).

A note of caution in interpreting our findings is warranted. Although our findings may indicate that concealment from parents causes adolescents to develop emotional autonomy, and our hypotheses reflect such an assumption, they are inadequate to rule out alternative interpretations. The findings are based on adolescents' perceptions of their relationship with their parents and are correlational. They indicate that adolescents who report concealing information from their parents also tend to describe themselves as more emotionally autonomous and independent from them. In contrast, adolescents who report not concealing information from their parents tend to describe themselves as less autonomous and more dependent on their parents. Given the cross-sectional nature of our study, these findings can be interpreted both ways: adolescents' concealment from parents may increase emotional autonomy and independence, or high levels of autonomy may lead to concealment from parents. Longitudinal data in which cross-lagged paths between concealment and adolescent autonomy are examined, provide more insight into this problem of bidirectionality and facilitate to tease apart competing causal hypotheses.

Surprisingly, our results did not reveal effects for adolescents' age. One might expect that older adolescents are more skilled at and more used to secrecy from their parents and may therefore maximize their developmental profits from it more (e.g., autonomy, self-determination) than younger adolescents. From the age of five, most children are capable of keeping secrets (e.g., Pipe & Goodman, 1991) and possess the cognitive prerequisites for secrecy (e.g., Peskin, 1992). It is possible that the practice of secrecy and concealment yields most profits in late childhood and levels off before children enter adolescence. It is equally possible that age-related changes in the information that is kept secret attenuate the potential gains from secrecy-related skills (e.g., Last & Aharoni-Etzioni, 1995; Smetana *et al.*, 2006). To illustrate, Last & Aharoni-Etzioni (1995) asked third-, fifth-, and seventh-graders to write a short narrative about a very important secret that they were trying to keep from everybody. A clear developmental trend emerged. Secrets concerning heterosexual involvement and moral transgressions were frequent in early adolescence but rare among younger children. Possessions, on the contrary, were rare among early adolescents but were frequent among younger children. Thus, there seems to be a developmental shift from secrets about possessions to secrets about interpersonal relationships. It is possible that secrets about interpersonal relationships take a greater toll from the secret-keeper than secrets about possessions. More research is needed to systematically pit the costs and benefits of secrets against each other. Older adolescents' secrets may differ even more substantially from the those of younger adolescents as they are likely to concern prudential issues which pertain to their safety and health (e.g., Smetana, 2000), including secrets about drug and alcohol use, cigarette smoking, and sexual activity. It would be important in future research to examine the content of secrecy from parents to investigate how it affects secret-related developmental gains in self-control and self-determination, personal choice and identity formation.

The favorable view on secrecy in accomplishing developmental tasks is based on the fact that secrecy separates secret-keepers from secret-targets.

By keeping a secret from parents, the adolescent secret-keeper can feel autonomous and independent from them. However, one can look at this social separation induced by secrecy in two ways. As a metaphor, the glass can be viewed as half full or half empty depending on which perspective one takes. From a developmental perspective, one can look at secrecy in adolescence as promoting autonomy and independence. This perspective receives support by our findings. From a relational perspective, however, one can look at secrecy in adolescence as inducing separation and detachment from parents (Steinberg, 1990).

DEVELOPMENTAL TRADEOFFS OF SECRECY: RELATIONAL IMPLICATIONS OF CONCEALMENT

The suggestion that secrecy may be beneficial to adolescents' development of autonomy contrasts sharply with clinical views on secrecy in relationships which commonly consider secrets in relationships as destructive, dysfunctional and even pathological (e.g., Imber-Black, 1993; Karpel, 1980). Secrets interfere with values that are attributed to "good" relationships. They violate the other's "right to know" (cf. Smetana *et al.*, 2006). The suspicion or discovery that close relationship partners keep secrets may question and shatter secret-targets' beliefs that the relationship is based on honesty, trust, confidence, and/or fairness (e.g., Derlega *et al.*, 1993; Finkenauer & Hazam, 2000). Consequently, the clinical view considers secrets as "toxic" in that they may give rise to debilitating psychosocial problems and may question the reliability of relationships (Imber-Black, 1993).

The clinical view hence suggests that the social separation between secret-keeper(s) and secret-target(s) through secrecy may have adverse effects for both partners, and ultimately for their relationship with each other. In the following we will first focus on the relational implications for the adolescent secret-keeper before considering the relational implications for parents and the parent–child relationship.

Relational Implications of Secrecy for the Adolescent Secret-keeper

Because secrets separate secret-keepers from secret-targets, secrets may isolate secret-keepers from their social network (e.g., Imber-Black, 1993). Secrets about symptoms, illnesses, insecurities, or problems (e.g., incest, alcoholism, drug abuse, sexual relations, desires) may deprive secret-keepers from informational, instrumental, or emotional resources that are offered by social relationships and that would be needed to facilitate coping and adjustment. Secrets may cause social isolation or feelings of loneliness among secret-keepers (e.g., Imber-Black, 1993; Jung, 1961). In light of the different types of secrets we found in adolescence (Frijns & Finkenauer, 2006), this suggestion needs to be qualified. Specifically, we suggest that secrets' harmfulness for the secret-keeper varies across the types of secrets that are kept. As defined above, individual secrets are secrets that adolescents keep all by themselves. These types of secrets should be particularly harmful as they separate adolescents from their social network as a whole. Shared secrets, on the contrary, should be less harmful and perhaps even beneficial. They combine the best of both worlds. They allow adolescents to profit from the separation from certain people that results from keeping the secret from them, and, simultaneously, profit from the closeness with other people that results from sharing their secret with them.

To test the suggestion that the type of secret kept moderates the harmful relational effects of secrecy, we examined the relations of individual and shared secrets in adolescence with psychosocial problems (i.e., physical symptoms, depressed mood, self-esteem, loneliness) in a sample of 790 adolescents (Frijns & Finkenauer, 2006, Study 3). The results confirmed our expectations. We found that not having a confidant was strongly linked to all assessed psychosocial problems in adolescence, including physical complaints, low self-esteem, depressive mood, and loneliness. More importantly, above and beyond the availability of confidants, individual secrets contributed to explaining variance in all assessed psychosocial problems. Shared secrets, on the contrary, were unrelated to these problems. Rather these secrets were associated with an indicator of interpersonal competence. Specifically, shared secrets contributed to explaining variance in adolescents' competence in disclosure (e.g., "Knowing how to move a conversation with a date/acquaintance beyond superficial talk to really get to know each other," Buhrmester *et al.*, 1988).

These results suggest that social separation induced by secrecy in adolescence may affect secret-keepers differently depending on the type of secret that is kept. Not all secrets are equal. Individual secrets in adolescence may lead to feelings of isolation and loneliness. These secrets also seem to be linked to psychosocial problems commonly associated with loneliness, including low self-esteem, frequent depressed mood, and increased somatic symptoms (Ichiyama *et al.*, 1993) and may even contribute to the development of these problems in the long run (Frijns *et al.*, 2005). On the contrary, shared secrets may provide young people with a sense of belonging and control. These secrets may allow adolescents to feel securely embedded in social relationships and may even help to bolster relationships in a period in which they loosen their ties with their family (Larson *et al.*, 1996). Sharing secrets may be profitable in a variety of ways. First, by sharing their secrets adolescents may be able to form new relationships with confidants with whom the secret is shared while at the same time asserting their independence from people from whom the secret is kept. Second, sharing secrets may allow adolescents to "test the waters." Confidants may serve as a thermometer for what it would be like to reveal the secret to others and may help to verify (or falsify) one's expectations regarding the outcome of the revelation (Caughlin *et al.*, 2005).

Third, sharing secrets may allow adolescents to receive advice and feedback, that may help to reduce stress and uncertainties that are particularly acute during adolescence (Arnett, 1999; Larson *et al.*, 1996; Seiffge-Krenke, 1998). These suggestions bear further investigation in future research.

Although we discussed secrecy's relational implications for the secret-keeper independent from the secret content, there is little doubt that the secret content may contribute to these relational consequences. The secret content may vary considerably in terms of importance and severity. To illustrate, secrecy about incest is likely to affect adolescents' psychosocial wellbeing much more severely than secrecy about one's first kiss. However, to our knowledge, there is no empirical research investigating the effects of the content of a secret on psychological and relational wellbeing.

Relational Implications of Secrecy for the Parental Target

Because secrets are inherently social phenomena—without secret-targets there is no secrecy—they do not only concern secret-keepers but secret-targets as well. In fact, secrecy and concealment sever the relationship between these two. We already alluded to the fact that secrecy and disclosure, or in our case shared secrets, convey relational information that seems to go beyond the actual content of what is kept secret or shared (Finkenauer & Hazam, 2000; Frijns & Finkenauer, 2006). Openness through disclosure communicates intimacy, trust, and closeness between relationship partners, including romantic partners as well as parents and children (e.g., Dindia, Fitzpatick, & Kenny, 1997; Lippert & Prager, 2001; Finkenauer *et al.*, 2004). Conversely, secrecy seems to communicate lack of trust and seems to increase the distance between relationship partners (e.g., Bochner & Krueger, 1979; Finkenauer, 1998). A common statement of people who discovered that their partner had kept a secret is "I feel that I've been living a lie" (Imber-Black, 1993), reflecting the devastating impact the perception and/or discovery of secrecy can have on people's relationships and their beliefs about them.

These perceptions of secrecy by secret-targets are in sharp contrast to secret-keepers' perceptions of their secrets. Secret-keepers have good reasons for concealing information from others (Afifi & Guerrero, 2000; Caughlin *et al.*, 2005). They feel entitled to conceal the information from others and view their concealment as justified and important for the maintenance of the relationship (e.g., Finkenauer & Hazam, 2000; Smetana *et al.*, 2006; Vangelisti & Caughlin, 1997). In this regard, secrecy shares features with other aversive interpersonal behaviors, such as lying, cheating, criticizing, or teasing (Kowalski *et al.*, 2003). Like secrecy, these behaviors are characterized by considerable perceptual differences between victims (i.e., the person who is the target of the behavior) and perpetrators (i.e., the person who engages in the behavior). Specifically, perpetrators view their behavior as innocuous and often even tend to argue that they enacted the behavior for the "sake" of the victim (e.g., I didn't want to hurt her feelings). Victims have a very different view, however. They tend to perceive the behavior as more negative, more intentional and mean, and as more indicative of the perpetrator's personality than perpetrators themselves (e.g., Baumeister, Stillwell, & Wotman, 1990; Kowalski *et al.*, 2003).

Extending these findings to secrecy and concealment in adolescence led us to predict that adolescent concealment should have adverse implications for the adolescent–parent relationship. Because secret-targets perceive concealment as negative and as a sign of distrust, we expected that parents' perception of concealment from their adolescent children should negatively affect their behavior towards them. Specifically, we hypothesized that parents' perceptions of adolescent concealment should be associated with poorer parenting, including parental knowledge, responsiveness, and acceptance. In this study, we defined adolescent concealment from parents as adolescents' (a) tendency to keep things to themselves, (b) possession of a secret or negative thought not shared with parents, and (c) apprehension of the revelation of concealed personal information to their parents.

Does it matter whether adolescent children actually conceal information from their parents? The victim-perpetrator literature suggests that it may not make a difference whether children actually conceal information from their parents. Even suspecting concealment may serve as a clue for parents that the relationship with their adolescent child is not intact. Support for this suggestion is provided by a study by Caughlin & Golish (2002). They found that parents' perceptions of their child's concealment were strongly related to parental dissatisfaction with the relationship, even after controlling for the child's actual concealment. These findings suggest that parents' perceptions alone may have adverse implications for their behavior toward their child. It is also possible that actual child concealment amplifies the effects of parents' perception for their behavior toward their child. Support for this suggestion is provided by a study by Gable, Reis, & Downey (2003). These authors found that when both relationship partners agreed that one of them had enacted a particular behavior, the effects on wellbeing were much stronger than when partners disagreed (e.g., one partner reported having enacted a specific behavior, while the other reported the partner not having enacted the behavior). Extending these findings to our question implies that the degree to which parental perceptions of child concealment match actual child concealment relates to parenting behavior. Greater parent–child agreement should have stronger links with parenting. Lastly, actual child concealment may affect parenting above and beyond parental perceptions. Adolescents' concealment limits parents' access to their children's lives (Petronio, 1991) and may hence restrict parents' knowledge (Kerr & Stattin, 2000; Kerr, Stattin & Trost, 1999; Stattin & Kerr, 2000).

To investigate the adverse relational implications of parental perceptions of adolescent concealment and adolescents' actual concealment for parent–adolescent relationships, we conducted two large-scale studies involving both adolescent children and their parents (Finkenauer *et al.*, 2005). In both studies, mothers and fathers reported their perception of concealment from their adolescent child, their responsiveness to their child's needs, their acceptance of their child, and their knowledge about their child's whereabouts and activities. Additionally, adolescents reported their concealment from their parents.

A total of 105 families participated in the first study, 86 families provided data for an adolescent child and both father and mother and 19 families provided data for only one parent. Adolescents' age ranged from 10–18 years. The results provided support for our suggestion that parental perceptions of adolescent concealment have adverse implications for their behavior toward their child. For both mothers and fathers, we found that when they perceived their adolescent child to conceal information from them, they reported being less knowledgeable about their child's activities and whereabouts, less responsive to their child's needs, and less accepting of their child. Neither for mothers nor for fathers did actual concealment as reported by adolescents affect the relations found between parental perception of concealment and parenting behavior.

Although these findings confirm our predictions, they have to be interpreted with care. First, we failed to control for disclosure. Because parental knowledge is largely determined by child disclosure (Kerr, Stattin & Trost, 1999; Stattin & Kerr, 2000), the found link between parental perception of concealment and parenting may be due to parents' perception of a lack of disclosure, rather than a presence of parents' perception of concealment. Second, we did not examine whether parents engage in probing behavior as a response to perceived concealment (Kerr & Stattin, 2000). Indeed, upon perceiving concealment from their children, parents may try to counteract the perceived concealment by actively soliciting information from their children, rather than withdraw from the relationship.

To circumvent these shortcomings, we conducted a second study with 427 mother-adolescent pairs and 134 father-adolescent pairs. In this study adolescents' age ranged from 10 to 14 years. In addition to parents' perceptions of concealment and parenting and adolescents' actual concealment from parents, we assessed parents' perceived disclosure from their child. To this end, parents rated the extent to which they perceived their child to disclose information (e.g., personal habits, deepest feelings, what they like or dislike about themselves) about themselves to them (cf., Miller, Berg, & Archer, 1983). In the assessment of *parental solicitation*, parents rated the extent to which they actively solicit information about and are interested in their children's activities (Kerr & Stattin, 2000).

Even when controlling for parents' perception of disclosure from their child, parental perceptions of adolescent concealment were strongly negatively linked with parental responsiveness, knowledge, and acceptance. As in the first study these results held for both mothers and fathers. Parental perception of concealment was not linked to parental solicitation.

Perceived disclosure contributed positively to all parenting behaviors, even solicitation. This finding suggests that disclosure may instigate a cyclic process of communication in parent–child relationships. In a first step, children disclose information about their lives to their parents (Kerr & Stattin, 2000). This may signal to the parents that they are allowed to "enter" their children's lives (Smetana *et al.*, 2006), and consequently parents solicit more information from their children. Perceiving disclosure from one's child may increase parental trust (Kerr, Stattin and Trost, 1999), providing parents with confidence to actively solicit information from their children.

Actual child concealment did not affect the relations found, except for parental knowledge. Specifically, we found an interaction between parents' perceptions of concealment and adolescents' reported actual concealment. Parents who perceived much concealment had little knowledge of their children, whether their children actually concealed information from them or not. On the contrary, parents who perceived no concealment had significantly more knowledge about their child's whereabouts and activities when their children did not conceal information from them than when their child did conceal information from them. These findings are in line with our suggestion that actual child concealment may affect parenting above and beyond parental perceptions, because they indicate that actual child concealment may reduce parental knowledge even if parents do not suspect concealment.

Taken together, both studies corroborate our expectation that adolescent concealment has adverse implications for the adolescent–parent relationship. Mothers' and fathers' perception that their child intentionally concealed information from them contributed strongly and uniquely to explaining variance in indicators of poorer parenting. Parents who perceived their children to conceal information from them were less responsive to their children's needs, were less knowledgeable of their children's whereabouts and activities, and were less accepting of their children.

How can we explain the findings? First, it is possible that parents' perceptions affect their behavior. Just like other relationship partners, parents may resent their children's concealment and may react by withdrawing from the relationship with their children. This possibility is consistent with the suggestion that perceived concealment conveys a relational message of social separation (cf. Bochner & Krueger, 1979) and that it is an indication of a lack of trust or even betrayal (Kowalski *et al.*, 2003). Indeed, the pattern of parental reactions suggests that parents resent their child's secrecy, implying that secrecy in parent–child relationships carries relational messages. "This is none of your business." "I don't trust you enough to tell you about this." "You don't care anyway." "I don't like you anymore." These are only some examples for relational messages that may be conveyed through secrecy or strategies deployed to protect the secret from being discovered (e.g., lying, distraction, Finkenauer *et al.*, 2005). Not surprisingly, then, parents—and probably most of us—feel rejected and hurt when they perceive that their children conceal information from them. More research is needed to investigate the suggested mediating role of negative affect, such as distrust, feelings of hurt, and anger, in the link between targets' perception of concealment and their behavior toward the (presumed) secret-keeper.

Given the cross-sectional nature of our studies, it is equally possible that poor parent–child relationships may lead parents to expect more concealment from their adolescent children (cf. Guland & Grolnick, 2003; Jussim & Eccles, 1995). Future research should pit these possibilities against each other and examine the influence of third variables in the observed relations. To illustrate, it is possible that parents who are high self-concealers (Larson & Chastain, 1990) perceive more concealment in others, including their children. Longitudinal studies involving both parents and children need to investigate the causal relations between the perception of concealment and parenting and investigate the social mechanisms underlying the found link.

Actual child concealment had little effects on the found relations. It thus seems that the perception of concealment alone may affect parents' behavior toward their adolescent child. This finding reflects the subjective nature of concealment in interpersonal relationships and underlines that subjective perceptions of concealment may be more strongly colored by parents' experiences, beliefs, dispositions, or motives than by actual, "objective" adolescent concealment.

The question arises whether these findings extend to other types of relationships and hold when children perceive concealment from their parents. Parent–child relationships are special in a variety of ways. Most importantly, they are vertical because parents and children have unequal status, even in adolescence (Finkenauer *et al.*, 2004). Low concealment among parents may indicate that parents consider their children as equal partners and use them as emotional confidants. These parents keep few secrets from their children but share their secrets with them. Although low parental concealment may increase trust and closeness in the parent–child relationship (see above), it may put children at risk for psychosocial problems, because parents burden their children with their own worries and concerns (Lehman & Silverberg-Koerner, 2002).

Indirect support for the suggestion that the effects of concealment may vary across relationship types comes from a study by Finkenauer *et al.* (2004). They applied Kenny's social relations model (Kenny & La Voie, 1984) to identify the social mechanisms underling disclosure and its link with relationships satisfaction in a full family design (i.e., both parents and two adolescent children). They found that partners in horizontal relationships with similar family status (i.e., parents among each other, siblings) match their level of disclosure. In vertical relationships, however, parents' and children's disclosure was unrelated. Importantly, in horizontal relationships and in child-parent relationships, partners disclosed to those family members they liked and liked the family members to whom they disclosed. In parent–child relationships, however, this effect did not emerge. Parents' level of satisfaction with their relationship with their children was not related to their level of disclosure to their children.

These findings have important implications for the role of communication patterns in adolescent–parent relationships for the development of adjustment problems in children. They underline the differences between parent–child relationships and other types of relationships. Children turn to their parents for help, support, and guidance. Parents usually provide help, support, and guidance to their children but do not (and perhaps should not) in return, require help, support, and guidance from their children.

To examine these suggestions, research should examine secrecy and disclosure in different types of relationship. These studies need to involve both partners, secret-keepers and secret-target, to help us understand how communication processes shape interpersonal interactions and relationships. Ideally, these studies are longitudinal to monitor the influence of (the perception of concealment) on the secret-keeper, the secret-target, and the relationship between these two.

CONCLUDING REMARKS

Although our research does not offer a clear-cut answer to the question as to whether secrecy is beneficial or harmful to secret-keepers, secret-targets, and/or the relationship between these two, it suggests that secrecy and concealment represent powerful mechanisms in interpersonal relationships. Both secrecy and concealment have a negative connotation. As our research shows they have many drawbacks and may potentially harm relationships. However, we believe that our findings also emphasize the necessity of taking a closer look at secrecy. As an illustration, imagine a world without secrecy. A world in which we would be unable to hide and protect our weaknesses, vulnerabilities, and precious experiences. We would be unable to avoid hurting others, to control, at least in part, how they view us, to mark our privacy, or to be a loyal to a friend who asked us to keep a secret. Although it is hard to substantiate empirically, this illustration hints at the possibility that without secrecy our relationships with others may be less harmonious and more conflictive. In some scenarios, revealing a secret may cause more problems than it solves. For example, revealing that one suffers from a serious disease may cause others to show pity and treat one as an invalid. Similarly, revealing that one can imagine having sex with a same-sex partner may cause harassment or ridicule, especially in adolescence. More researchers should accept the challenge to investigate secrecy's "bright side." To do so, one of the most urgent tasks consists of using measures that allow for secrecy to have positive effects and that bypass people's reluctance to admit having and keeping secrets, in particular secrets from close relationship partners.

Another task consists of a systematic investigation of what kind of information adolescents keep secret. Perhaps because secrets are purposefully concealed, they are almost always associated with the proverbial skeleton in the closet or with "having something negative to hide": something shameful or undesirable, something stealthy or furtive (Bok, 1989). However, we do not know of any empirical research that tested this assumption. In fact, one can imagine situations where secrecy is maintained when the secret content is appraised as positive by the secret-keeper. To illustrate, an adolescent may be interested in magic. He astonishes his family and classmates with a trick that required a lot of time, practice, and creativity. He would love to tell others about the trick and how he does it, but giving away his secret would cost him and his admirers: He would lose (part of) their admiration and they would lose the capacity of being fascinated and mystified by magical tricks. Similarly, an adolescent girl may be in love with what her parents consider the "wrong" guy. To prevent her parents from spoiling her relationship, she keeps it a secret. These examples suggest that secrets can be kept not only because of their content, but also because they prevent undesired consequences that may accompany their revelation. The important implication is that one can be independent of the other. Future research should investigate both the secret content and the social consequences its revelation may have for the secret-keeper.

Another important task for research on secrecy in adolescence concerns the investigation of individual differences. In our studies, adolescents who reported having an individual secret commonly reported having shared secrets as well. These adolescents also scored higher on our measure of concealment from parents (e.g., Frijns & Finkenauer, 2006). Secret-keeping is associated with psychosocial problems, both cross-sectionally (Finkenauer *et al.*, 2002) and longitudinally (e.g., Frijns *et al.*, 2005). Although it has been acknowledged that individuals who tend to keep secrets also tend to be vulnerable to all sorts of physical and psychosocial problems, however, the mechanisms underlying these links remain unclear. More research is needed to investigate how adolescents' disposition for concealment and secrecy contributes to the development of psychosocial problems. This research should also consider other individual dispositions that may be associated with adolescents' tendency to keep secrets and concealment such as negative affectivity (e.g., Watson, Clark, & Tellegen, 1988) or neuroticism (e.g., Costa & McCrae, 1987).

We began this chapter by stating that secrecy is a fact of daily life. People frequently use secrecy to regulate interpersonal relationships. Despite their importance in everyday life, our knowledge about secrets and secrecy is limited. We hope that this chapter helps to draw a more complete picture of secrecy, enhancing our understanding of this intriguing everyday life phenomenon in parent–adolescent relationships. We provided ample evidence that secrecy is an important and pervasive phenomenon that impinges on virtually all dimensions of adolescents' and parents' lives. Almost all adolescents have secrets, secrets that can be positive and desirable (e.g., wanting to be a topmodel) and secrets that can be negative and harmful (e.g., incest). Sharing secrets may serve to enhance intimacy and belongingness. It may be an adaptive regulatory response to increases in independence from parents. In other words, secrecy may be a recommendable behavior. Yet, its benefits are bought at a prize. Secrecy is associated with and even contributes to psychosocial problems in adolescence in the long-run (Frijns *et al.*, 2005). Secrecy may have relational consequences. These consequences may be beneficial when secrecy is used selectively and appropriately (e.g., when adolescents share their secrets with their friends). However, they may be devastating when the perception of secrecy causes parents to withdraw from the relationship with their child. Given the importance of secrecy for adolescents' psychosocial wellbeing and development, it seems necessary to make a place for secrecy in research on close relationships—parent–child relationships in particular.

REFERENCES

Afifi, W. A. & Guerrero, L. K. (2000). Motivations underlying topic avoidance in close relationships. In S. Petronio (ed.), *Balancing the Secrets of Private Disclosures* (pp. 165–179). Mahwah, NJ: Erlbaum.

Allen, J. P., Hauser, S. T., Bell, K. L., & O'Connor, T. G. (1994). Longitudinal assessment of autonomy and relatedness in adolescent-family interactions as predictors of adolescent ego development and self-esteem. *Child Development, 65,* 179–194.

Arnett, J. J. (1999). Adolescent storm and stress, reconsidered. *American Psychologist, 54,* 317–326.

Baumeister, R. F., Stillwell, A., & Wotman, S. R (1990). Victim and perpetrator accounts of interpersonal conflict: Autobiographical narratives about anger. *Journal of Personality and Social Psychology, 59,* 994–1005.

Berndt, T. J. (1996). Transitions in friendship and friends' influence. In J. A. Graber, J. Brooks-Gunn, & A. C. Peterson (eds), *Transitions through Adolescence: Interpersonal Domains and Context* (pp. 57–84). Mahwah, NJ: Erlbaum.

Bochner, A. P. & Krueger, D. L. (1979). Interpersonal communication theory and research: An overview. In D. Nimmo (ed.), *Communication Yearbook 3* (pp. 197–212). New Brunswick, NJ: Transaction Books.

Bok, S. (1989). *Secrets: On the Ethics of Concealment and Revelation.* New York: Vintage Books.

Buhrmester, D., Furman, W., Wittenberg, M. T., & Reis, H. T. (1988). Five domains of interpersonal competence in peer relationships. *Journal of Personality and Social Psychology, 55,* 991–1008.

Buhrmester, D. & Prager, K. (1995). Patterns and functions of self-disclosure during childhood and adolescence. In K. Rotenberg (ed.), *Disclosure Processes in Children and Adolescents* (pp. 10–56). New York: Cambridge University Press.

Caughlin, J. P., Afifi, W. A., Carpenter-Theune, K. E., & Miller, C. E. (2005). Reasons for, and consequences of, revealing personal secrets in close relationships: A longitudinal study. *Personal Relationships, 12,* 43–59.

Caughlin, J. P. & Golish, T. D. (2002). An analysis of the association between topic avoidance and dissatisfaction: Comparing perceptual and interpersonal explanations. *Communication Monographs, 69,* 275–295.

Chelune, G. J., Waring, E. M., Vosk, B. N. *et al.* (1984). Self-disclosure and its relationship to marital intimacy. *Journal of Clinical Psychology, 40,* 216–219.

Costa, P. T. & McCrae, R. (1987). Neuroticism, somatic complaints, and disease: Is the bark worse than the bite? *Journal of Personality, 55,* 299–316.

Derlega, V. J., Metts, S., Petronio, S., & Margulis, S. T. (1993). *Self-disclosure*. London: Sage.

Dindia, K., Fitzpatrick, M. A., & Kenny, D. A. (1997). Self-disclosure in spouse and stranger dyads: A social relations analysis. *Human Communication Research, 23,* 388–412.

Finkenauer, C. (1998). *Secrets: Types, Determinants, Functions, and Consequences.* Unpublished doctoral dissertation, University of Louvain at Louvain-la-Neuve, Belgium.

Finkenauer, C. & Hazam, H. (2000). Disclosure and secrecy in marriage: Do both contribute to marital satisfaction? *Journal of Social and Personal Relationships, 17,* 245–263.

Finkenauer, C., Engels, R. C. M. E., & Meeus, W. (2002). Keeping secrets from parents: Advantages and disadvantages of secrecy in adolescence. *Journal of Youth and Adolescence, 31,* 123–136.

Finkenauer, C., Engels, R. C. M. E., Meeus, W., & Oosterwegel, A. (2002). Self and identity in early adolescence: The pains and gains of growing up. In T. M. Brinthaupt & R. P. Lipka (eds), *Understanding Early Adolescent Self and Identity: Applications and Interventions* (pp. 25–56). Albany, NY: State University of New York Press.

Finkenauer, C., Engels, R. C. M. E., Branje, S., & Meeus, W. (2004). Disclosure and relationship satisfaction in families. *Journal of Marriage and Family, 66,* 195–209.

Finkenauer, C., Frijns, T., Engels, R. C. M. E., & Kerkhof, P. (2005). Perceiving concealment in relationships between parents and adolescents: Links with parental behavior. *Personal Relationships, 12,* 387–406.

Frijns, T. & Finkenauer, C. (2006). When secrets are shared: Individual versus shared secrets and their links with well-being. Submitted for publication.

Frijns, T., Finkenauer, C., Vermulst, A., & Engels, R. C. M. E. (2005). Keeping secrets from parents: Longitudinal associations of secrecy in adolescence. *Journal of Youth and Adolescence, 34,* 137–148.

Furman, W. & Shaffer, L. (2003). The role of romantic relationships in adolescent development. In P. Florsheim (ed.), *Adolescent Romantic Relations and Sexual Behavior: Theory, Research, and Practical Implications* (pp. 3–22). Mahwah, NJ: Erlbaum.

Gable, S. L., Reis, H. T., & Downey, G. (2003). He said, she said: a quasi-signal detection analysis of spouses' perceptions of everyday interactions. *Psychological Science, 14,* 100–105.

Goossens, L. (1997). Emotionele autonomie, relationele steun en de perceptie van het gezinsfunctioneren door adolescenten. [Emotional autonomy, relational support, and the perception of family-functioning among adolescents.] In J. R. M. Gerris (ed.), *Jongerenproblematiek: hulpverlening en gezinsonderzoek* (pp. 92–103). Assen, The Netherlands: Van Gorcum.

Granic, I., Hollenstein, T., Dishion, T. J., & Patterson, G. R. (2003). Longitudinal analysis of flexibility and reorganization in early adolescence: A dynamic systems study of family interactions. *Developmental Psychology, 39,* 606–617.

Grotevant, H. D. & Cooper, C. R. (1986). Individuation in family relationships: A perspective on individual differences in the development of identity and role-taking skill in adolescence. *Human Development, 29,* 82–100.

Guland, S. T. & Grolnick, W. S. (2003). Children's expectancies and perceptions of adults: effects on rapport. *Child Development, 74,* 1212–1224.

Hartup, W. W. (1996). The company they keep: Friendships and their developmental significance. *Child Development, 67,* 1–13.

Ichiyama, M. A., Colbert, D., Laramore, H. *et al.* (1993). Self-concealment and correlates of adjustment in college students. *Journal of College Student Psychotherapy, 7,* 55–68.

Imber-Black, E. (1993). *Secrets in Families and Family Therapy*. New York: W. W. Norton & Company.

Jung, C. G. (1961). *Freud and Psychoanalysis* (translated by R. F. C. Hull). London: Routledge & Kegan Paul.

Jussim, L. & Eccles, J. (1995). Naturalistic studies of interpersonal expectancies. *Review of Personality and Social Psychology, 15*, 74–108.

Karpel, M. A. (1980). Family secrets. *Family Process, 19*, 295–306.

Kelly, A. E. (1998). Clients' secret keeping in outpatient therapy. *Journal of Counseling Psychology, 45*, 50–57.

Kelly, A. E. & McKillop, K. J. (1996). Consequences of revealing personal secrets. *Psychological Bulletin, 120*, 450–465.

Kenny, D. A. & La Voie, L. (1984). The social relations model. In L. Berkowitz (ed.), *Advances in Experimental Social Psychology*, Vol.18 (pp. 141–182). Orlando, FL: Academic Press.

Kerr, M. & Stattin, H. (2000). What parents know, how they know it, and several forms of adolescent adjustment: Further support for a reinterpretation of monitoring. *Developmental Psychology, 36*, 366–380.

Kerr, M., Stattin, H., & Trost, K. (1999). To know you is to trust you: Parent's trust is rooted in child disclosure of information. *Journal of Adolescence, 22*, 737–752.

Kim, K. J., Conger, R. D., Lorenz, F. O., & Elder, Jr., G. H. (2001). Parent-adolescent reciprocity in negative affect and its relation to early adult social development. *Developmental Psychology, 37*, 775–790.

Kowalski, R. M., Walker, S., Wilkinson, R. *et al.* (2003). Lying, cheating, complaining, and other aversive interpersonal behaviors: A narrative examination of the darker side of relationships. *Journal of Social and Personal Relationships, 20*, 471–490.

Lane, D. J. & Wegner, D. M. (1995). The cognitive consequences of secrecy. *Journal of Personality and Social Psychology, 69*, 237–253.

Larson, D. G. & Chastain, R. L. (1990). Self-concealment: Conceptualization, measurement, and health implications. *Journal of Social and Clinical Psychology, 9*, 439–455.

Larson, R. W., Richards, M. H., Moneta, G. *et al.* (1996). Changes in adolescents' daily interactions with their families from ages 10 to 18: Disengagement and transformation. *Developmental Psychology, 32*, 744–754.

Last, U. & Aharoni-Etzioni, A. (1995). Secrets and reasons for secrecy among school-aged children: Developmental trends and gender differences. *Journal of Genetic Psychology, 156*, 191–203.

Lehman, S. J. & Silverberg-Koerner, S. (2002). Family financial hardship and adolescent girls' adjustment: The role of maternal disclosure of financial concerns. *Merill-Palmer Quaterly, 48*, 1–24.

Lippert, T. & Prager, K. J. (2001). Daily experiences of intimacy: A study of couples. *Personal Relationships, 8*, 283–298.

Margolis, G. J. (1966). Secrecy and identity. *International Journal of Psycho-Analysis, 47*, 517–522.

Marshall, S. K., Tilton-Weaver, L., & Bosdet, L. (2005). Information management: Considering adolescents' regulation of parental knowledge. *Journal of Adolescence, 28*, 633–647.

Meares, R. & Orlay, W. (1988). On self boundary: A study of the development of the concept of secrecy. *British Journal of Medical Psychology, 61*, 305–316.

Miller, L. C., Berg, J. H., & Archer, R. L. (1983). Openers: Individuals who elicit intimate self-disclosure. *Journal of Personality and Social Psychology, 44*, 1234–1244.

Peskin, J. (1992). Ruse and representations: On children's ability to conceal information. *Developmental Psychology, 28*, 84–89.

Petersen, A. C., & Hamburg, B. A. (1986). Adolescence—a developmental approach to problems and psychotherapy. *Behavior Therapy, 17*, 480–499.

Petronio, S. (1991). Communication boundary management: A theoretical model of managing disclosure of private information between marital couples. *Communication Theory, 1*, 311–335.

Pipe, M. E., & Goodman, G. S. (1991). Elements of secrecy: Implications for children's testimony. *Behavioral Sciences and the Law, 9*, 33–41.

Schoicket, S. (1980). Secrets. *The American Journal of Psychoanalysis, 40*, 179–182.

Seiffge-Krenke, I. (1998). *Adolescents' Health: A Developmental Perspective*. Mahwah, NJ: Lawrence Erlbaum.

Simmel, G. (1950). The secret and the secret society. In K. W. Wolff (ed. and trans.), *The Sociology of Georg Simmel.* New York: Free Press.

Smetana, J. G. (2000). Middle-class African American adolescents' and parents' conceptions of parental authority and parenting practices: A longitudinal investigation. *Child Development, 71*, 1672–1686.

Smetana, J. G., Campione-Barr, N., & Daddis, C. (2004). Developmental and longitudinal antecedents of family decision-making: Defining health behavioral autonomy for African American adolescents. *Child Development, 75*, 1–17.

Smetana, J. G., Metzger, A., Gettman, D. C., & Campione-Barr, N. (2006). Disclosure and secrecy in adolescent-parent relationships. *Child Development, 77*, 201–217.

Stattin, H. & Kerr, M. (2000). Parental monitoring: A reinterpretation. *Child Development, 71*, 1070–1083.

Steinberg, L. (1990). Autonomy, conflict, and harmony in the family relationship. In S. Feldman & G. Elliott (eds), *At the Threshold: The Developing Adolescent* (pp. 255–276). Cambridge, MA: Harvard University Press.

Steinberg, L. & Silverberg, S. B. (1986). The vicissitudes of autonomy in early adolescence. *Child Development, 57*, 841–851.

Tournier, P. (1965). *Secrets.* (trans. J. Embry). London: SCM Press.

Vangelisti, A. L. (1994). Family secrets: Forms, functions, and correlates. *Journal of Social and Personal Relationships, 11*, 113–135.

Vangelisti, A. L. & Caughlin, J. P. (1997). Revealing family secrets: The influence of topic, function, and relationships. *Journal of Social and Personal Relationships, 14*, 679–705.

Van Manen, M. & Levering, B. (1996). *Childhood's Secrets: Intimacy, Privacy, and the Self Reconsidered*. New York: Teachers College Press.

Watson, D., Clark, L. A., & Tellegen, A. (1988). Development and validation of brief measures of positive and negative affect: The PANAS scales. *Journal of Personality and Social Psychology, 54*, 1063–1070.

Whiston, S. C. & Keller, B. K. (2004). The influences of the family of origin on career development: A review and analysis. *The Counseling Psychologist, 32*, 493–568.

Youniss, J. & Smollar, J. (1985). *Adolescent Relations with Mothers, Fathers, and Friends.* London: University of Chicago Press.

CHAPTER 3

Don't Ask, Don't Tell (Your Mom and Dad): Disclosure and Nondisclosure in Adolescent–parent Relationships

Judith G. Smetana and Aaron Metzger
University of Rochester, USA

INTRODUCTION

Much research has shown that adolescent–parent relationships are transformed during adolescence from unilateral to mutual forms of authority and from dependence to independence (Smetana, Campione-Barr, & Daddis, 2004; Youniss & Smollar, 1985). Although parents believe that it is important to facilitate teens' independence, they are also concerned with protecting their adolescents, keeping them safe, and ensuring that they follow social and moral norms (Smetana & Chuang, 2001). Therefore, parental monitoring, including knowing where children are, whom they are with, and what they are doing when they are away from home, becomes increasingly important during adolescence. Monitoring allows parents to supervise and protect their teens from a distance, thereby scaffolding their growing autonomy. A firmly established conclusion, based on a great deal of psychological research, is that parental supervision and monitoring during adolescence lead to reductions in externalizing behavior, including conduct disorders, juvenile delinquency, and drug and alcohol use (Barber, Olsen, & Shagle, 1994; Barnes & Farrell, 1992; Loeber & Stouthamer-Loeber, 1986, 1998).

What Can Parents Do? New Insights into the Role of Parents in Adolescent Problem Behavior
Edited by Margaret Kerr, Håkan Stattin and Rutger C. M. E. Engels.

This research has assumed that parental monitoring entails parents' active tracking and surveillance, but as has been noted recently (Crouter & Head, 2002; Kerr & Stattin, 2000; Stattin & Kerr, 2000), monitoring has been assessed primarily in terms of parents' *knowledge* of children's activities, and recent research has shown that parental knowledge can be obtained in different ways. Parents can seek information by asking the child directly, talking to the child's siblings, friends, or to other parents, listening in on conversations (for instance, while in the car or when the teen is on the phone), or even searching the teen's room. Parents also can attempt to control adolescents' behavior (for instance, by restricting their activities). On the other hand, adolescents may voluntarily disclose their behavior to their parents. Kerr & Stattin (2000; Kerr, Stattin, & Trost, 1999; Stattin & Kerr, 2000) investigated the influence of child disclosure, parental behavioral control, and parental solicitation of information on juvenile delinquency and found that only adolescents' voluntary disclosure predicted more positive outcomes. Moreover, by controlling for the influence of parents' trust in the adolescent, Kerr and Stattin ruled out the alternative hypothesis that these associations were due to higher quality parent–adolescent relationships.

Although current theoretical perspectives have emphasized the importance of transactive relationships between parents and adolescents and the contributions of adolescents' willingness to be socialized (e.g., Darling & Steinberg, 1993; Grusec & Goodnow, 1994; Kuczynski, 2003; Kuczynski & Navara, 2006), the strong presumption in much of the research on parenting is that the direction of effects is from parents to adolescents. Thus, Kerr and Stattin's findings underscore the need to focus on adolescents' and parents' reciprocal relationships and on adolescents' management of information. As adolescents spend less time with parents and more time with peers (Csikszentmihalyi & Larson, 1984; Larson *et al.*, 1996), they have increased opportunities to decide whether to disclose their activities or keep them secret. Furthermore, the findings raise interesting and unanswered questions about whether all (or how much) disclosure is healthy for adolescent development. In this chapter, we propose that identifying and theoretically specifying the conceptual domains of activities that are disclosed or kept secret can lead to a better understanding of these issues.

Consider the following example. Adolescents may feel differently about disclosing (and adults might respond differently to hearing) that teens were drinking alcohol at a party than disclosing (or parents learning) that adolescents have a new romantic interest to whom they have recently sent a love note. Adolescents may choose not to tell their parents about either of these events, but adolescents (and their parents) may differ in their beliefs about whether they are obligated to disclose in these different situations. Adolescents' decisions not to disclose may be motivated by different reasons, and their disclosure might elicit different parental responses. In the former instance, adolescents may believe that they are obligated to tell their parents but still conceal their behavior out of fear of punishment; if told, parents may react with alarm or anger. In the latter instance, adolescents feel that they do not have an obligation to disclose this information to parents and may choose not to disclose out of embarrassment or a belief that the acts are private matters. Revealing these feelings and actions to parents might lead to greater closeness, attachment, and intimacy.

As others (Marshall, Tilton-Weaver, & Bosdet, 2005; Searight *et al.*, 1995) have noted, however, we cannot assume that all disclosure to parents is appropriate or positive. Searight *et al.* (1995) have proposed that too much or inappropriate self-disclosure across intergenerational boundaries is more likely in enmeshed families, whereas too little adolescent self-disclosure characterizes disengaged families and that both too much or too little self-disclosure is associated with poorer adjustment. Likewise, Marshall *et al.* (2005) have suggested that knowing what to disclose may indicate better social skills and that as children move through adolescence, keeping some things private may index greater autonomy. However, this research has not specified what is considered "appropriate," "inappropriate," or "too much" disclosure.

In this chapter, we consider the recent findings on parental monitoring and child disclosure first in light of social-psychological and developmental research on intimacy and self-disclosure in interpersonal relationships and then in terms of social domain theory (Nucci, 2001; Smetana, 1995, 2002, 2006; Turiel, 1983, 1998, 2002), which, we assert, provides a potentially useful framework for understanding adolescent disclosure and its role in adolescent development. We review previous research on adolescent–parent relationships from the social domain perspective and then present some research employing this framework to examine adolescents' and parents' perceptions of disclosure and nondisclosure in their relationships.

SELF-DISCLOSURE AND INTIMACY IN INTERPERSONAL RELATIONSHIPS

Another body of literature, prominent in the 1980s, has examined self-disclosure during adolescence (see reviews by Berndt & Hanna, 1995; Buhrmester & Prager, 1995; Youniss & Smollar, 1985). In these studies, self-disclosure has been defined as disclosure of private thoughts and feelings and has been assessed through global questions, such as "How often do you share your private thoughts with your parents?" Thus, this literature differs from the current research on parental knowledge, which examines how much parents know and how they come to learn about adolescents' everyday activities. Drawing primarily on Sullivan's (1953) theory of interpersonal relationship development, this earlier research views self-disclosure as an aspect of intimacy development, although it is not equivalent to intimacy per se, as intimacy includes a broader range of qualities, including feeling validated, understood, and cared for (Reis & Shaver, 1988). However, self-disclosure may be one route towards achieving intimacy.

The vast majority of studies on adolescent self-disclosure of private thoughts and feelings have focused on normative developmental changes in the targets (recipients) of self-disclosure (Buhrmester & Prager, 1995). These studies have revealed that there is an increase with age across adolescence in self-disclosure to same-sex friends (and increasingly with age, romantic partners). Based on a review of 50 studies, Buhrmester and Prager (1995) concluded that there is a modest decline across adolescence in self-disclosure to parents and that disclosure is greatest between mothers and daughters, less between sons and parents, and least between fathers and daughters.

These latter findings are consistent with the studies of disclosure of daily activities, which also indicate that there are gender differences in disclosure. Across adolescence, both boys and girls, but especially girls, disclose more to mothers than to fathers, especially about personal issues (Noller & Callan, 1990; Youniss & Smollar, 1985). However, in families that included both early and middle adolescent boys and girls, Bumpus, Crouter & McHale (2001) found that fathers knew more about their sons' than daughters' daily experiences. Likewise, Noller and Callan (1990) found that adolescent males selectively disclose more (particularly about personal topics) to fathers than to mothers.

Although relatively few studies have examined parental knowledge of adolescents' activities separately for mothers and fathers, the available research has shown that mothers know more about their adolescents' lives than do fathers (Bumpus, Crouter, & McHale, 2001; Crouter *et al.*, 1999; Crouter & McHale, 1993; Crouter, McHale, & Bartko, 1993; Waizenhofer, Buchanan, & Jackson-Newsom, 2004), most likely because mothers are more involved in the everyday details and provide more emotional support than do fathers. Mothers also consistently know more about the activities of their second-born (pre- and early adolescent) than first-born early and middle adolescent offspring (Bumpus *et al.*, 2001; Crouter *et al.*, 1999). Furthermore, mothers and fathers of teenagers ranging in age from 10–17 appear to obtain their information in different ways. Waizenhofer *et al.* (2004) found that mothers relied more on asking the adolescent directly, asking informed others (like teachers or one's spouse) about what teens were doing, actively participating in activities with adolescents (such as driving the child to activities), and obtaining information voluntarily from their adolescent (e.g., child disclosure) than did fathers, while fathers relied more on obtaining information from their wives, particularly about their daughters. Crouter *et al.* (2005) have obtained similar findings in their sample of parents of 16 year olds, but they also conducted profile analyses; these revealed that there were three distinct groups of fathers and three somewhat different clusters of mothers. Some fathers relied primarily on their spouses for information, some relied on others inside (e.g., siblings) or outside the family, and others used relational methods (e.g., listened and observed, learned from their offspring's self-disclosure, or solicited information directly). Mothers likewise used relational methods, but they also questioned their teens or relied on others, including their spouses, for information. Longitudinal analyses revealed that relational methods in early adolescence led to greater parental knowledge when children were 16 years of age, which in turn negatively predicted risky behavior (such as alcohol, substance, and cigarette use and skipping school) one year later.

What do adolescents talk to their parents about and what do they keep secret? There has been little research addressing this issue. Youniss & Smollar (1985) found that middle and late adolescent males and females talk to both mothers and fathers about schoolwork, future plans, and social issues, but they do not communicate much about issues like dating (although they disclose more to mothers than to fathers). Research also has not considered how normative changes in disclosure might be linked with more general developmental processes of changing parental authority during adolescence.

SOCIAL DOMAIN THEORY AND ADOLESCENT–PARENT RELATIONSHIPS

Social domain theory focuses on identifying conceptual and developmental distinctions in children's social knowledge (for overviews, see Helwig & Turiel, 2003; Killen, McGlothlin, & Kim, 2002; Nucci, 1996, 2001; Smetana, 1995, 2006; Turiel, 1983, 1998, 2002). Social domain theory also has provided a theoretical framework for understanding transformations in adolescent–parent relationships and the development of adolescents' autonomy (Smetana, 1996, 2002). This research has shown that *moral judgments,* or prescriptive judgments regarding others' welfare, trust, or fairness, are conceptually and developmentally distinct from *social conventions*, or the arbitrary, consensually agreed on norms (like etiquette and manners) that provide individuals with expectations regarding appropriate behavior (Turiel, 1983, 1998).

In turn, morality and social convention have been distinguished from issues that are judged to be under the individual's jurisdiction and beyond the realm of societal regulation and moral concern (Nucci, 1996, 2001; Smetana, 1995, 2002). *Personal issues* comprise the private aspects of one's life and entail issues of preference and choice pertaining to friends, activities, the state of one's body, and privacy. Nucci (1996, 2001) has asserted that defining an arena of control over personal issues satisfies basic psychological needs for autonomy, personal agency, and effectance. Therefore, although there may be variations in the boundaries or content of the personal domain, as a substantial amount of research has shown (see Nucci, 2001; Smetana, 2002 for reviews), all cultures are thought to define a set of issues as up to the person to decide. *Prudential issues*, which pertain to safety, harm to the self, comfort, and health, also can be distinguished from moral issues (which have harmful consequences for others) and personal issues (which pertain to the self but do not have negative consequences—Nucci, Guerra, & Lee, 1991; Smetana & Asquith, 1994).

Research has demonstrated that these conceptual distinctions are useful in understanding parent–adolescent relationships. Several studies, including research with European-American (Smetana, 1988; Smetana & Asquith, 1994) and African-American middle-class families with teens ranging from 10 to 18 years of age (Smetana, 2000; Smetana, Crean, & Campione-Barr, 2005), Mexican American immigrant families (Lins-Dyer, 2003, described in Nucci, Hasebe, & Lins-Dyer, 2005), and middle- and lower-class children and adolescents in northeastern Brazil (Nucci, Camino, & Milnitsky-Sapiro, 1996) have shown that adolescents and parents agree that parents have the legitimate authority to regulate moral, conventional, and prudential issues. Although both adolescents and parents agree that adolescents should have some autonomy over personal issues (like choice of clothes or hairstyles or how to spend their allowance), adolescents usually want more control over personal issues than parents are willing to grant. Adolescents also assert autonomy over *multifaceted* issues, which entail overlaps between domains. (For instance, keeping the bedroom clean may be seen as a conventional issue of custom, authority, or social coordination by parents and a personal issue of identity, autonomy, or control by adolescents; likewise, some friendship issues may entail overlapping conventional, prudential, and personal concerns.) These studies demonstrate that adolescents and parents disagree as to the boundaries of adolescents' personal freedoms. Daddis (in press a, b) has proposed that adolescents' push for greater autonomy from parents may be partly influenced by close friends. His research demonstrates that reciprocally nominated close friends are more similar in how they define their personal domains than are nonfriends and that friends are important sources of information when making decisions about personal issues.

Furthermore, both cross-sectional and longitudinal studies have indicated that discrepancies between parents' and adolescents' interpretations of issues result in conflict and that conflict (in the context of warm, supportive parent–adolescent relationships) provides a context for parents and children to articulate, challenge, and negotiate their divergent perspectives (Smetana, 1989; Smetana & Asquith, 1994; Smetana & Gaines, 1999). These negotiations, in turn, lead to changes in the boundaries of parental authority and increases in adolescents' autonomy.

Conflict is only one route to independence, however. Adolescents' increasing involvement with peers provides many opportunities to disclose or conceal their activities, and decisions not to disclose to parents (at least over some issues) may provide another route to autonomy. Because personal issues are, by definition, private matters, adolescents and parents may view disclosure over personal issues as discretionary rather than obligatory, and disclosure over these issues may depend on the nature of the parent–adolescent relationship. Warm, trusting, and supportive relationships may entail voluntary disclosure over personal issues (as a way of enhancing the relationship or increasing intimacy), whereas relationships that are less supportive and warm or that are characterized by attempts to control psychologically or undermine autonomy may not. However, because parents consistently grant adolescents less autonomy over personal issues than adolescents feel they are due, adolescents and parents are likely to disagree over adolescents' obligations to disclose these issues, with parents viewing adolescents as more obligated to disclose to parents than adolescents view themselves.

RESEARCH ON DISCLOSURE AND NONDISCLOSURE IN ADOLESCENT–PARENT RELATIONSHIPS

We have conducted several studies using the framework of social domain theory to examine disclosure and secrecy in adolescent–parent relationships (Smetana *et al.*, 2006, 2007a,b). Given our interest in the underlying beliefs that structure behavior (Goodnow, 1988; Grusec & Goodnow, 1994), our first study (Smetana *et al.*, 2006) examined adolescents' and parents' perceptions of adolescents' obligations to disclose to parents their behavior in different social-cognitive domains, as well as their reports of actual disclosure, secrecy, and parental solicitation. Disclosure was defined in this study in terms of how much teenagers willingly disclosed different activities to parents, whereas secrecy was examined in terms of how often teens "keep secret or try to hide what they are doing" from their parents. Based on the prior research on concepts of legitimate parental authority, we expected that adolescents would be seen as more *obligated* to disclose moral, conventional, and prudential issues than personal issues, but we did not necessarily expect that similar distinctions would emerge in actual disclosure. Furthermore, the previous research led us to expect that there would be discrepancies in adolescents' and parents' perceptions, particularly over multifaceted and personal issues, and that parents would view adolescents as more obligated to disclose and more disclosing than adolescents perceived themselves to be. We included both middle (ninth graders) and late adolescents (twelfth graders) so that age differences could be examined, and we expected that disclosure (both obligations to disclose and actual disclosure) and parental solicitation would decrease with age. We also compared adolescents' ratings of disclosure and parental solicitation for mothers and fathers.

Finally, we examined the influence of domain-differentiated disclosure on adolescent adjustment. Our aim was to examine whether, including beliefs in our analyses, we obtained similar results to Kerr and Stattin (Kerr & Stattin, 2000; Stattin & Kerr, 2000). More specifically, we examined the influence of trust in the parent–adolescent relationship, beliefs about disclosure, actual disclosure, and parental solicitation on both internalizing symptoms (depression and anxiety) and adolescent problem behavior.

Sample and Procedures. The sample for our study consisted of a community sample of 276 lower middle class, ethnically diverse adolescents and parents drawn from a suburban high school near Rochester, NY. The sample included 154 ninth graders ($M = 14.62$ years of age, $SD = 0.51$, $n = 53$ males and 101 females) and 122 twelfth graders ($M = 17.40$ years, $SD = 0.47$, $n = 42$ males and 80 females) and their parents ($n = 249$; see Smetana *et al.*, 2006). The adolescents were 70% European American, 9% African American, 9% Asian, 7% biracial, 4% Hispanic, and 2% other, and most participating students (72%) lived in two-parent families with two biological parents. The students participating in the study closely matched the demographic characteristics (both race/ethnicity and socioeconomic status) of the school district from which they were recruited. Participation rates (33% for the ninth grade and 27% for the twelfth grade) were about average for community studies of this type.

Beliefs about Legitimate Parental Authority and Obligations to Disclose to Parents

We used procedures from previous research (Smetana, 1988, 2000; Smetana, Crean & Campione-Barr, 2005) to assess adolescents' and parents' beliefs about parents' legitimate authority to regulate moral (e.g., how friends are treated, hurting brothers and sisters), conventional (e.g., talking back or being rude to teachers, cursing or swearing), prudential (e.g., drinking alcohol when out with friends, smoking cigarettes, going to a party where alcohol is served), multifaceted (e.g., watching or listening to R-rated moves or CDs, if or who teens are dating, if a teen hangs out a friend's house when no adult is home), and personal issues (e.g., how teens spend their free time, how teens spend their own money, what teens talk about on the phone with friends, who teens like or have a crush on). Although a great deal of research has shown that morality and social convention are distinct forms of social knowledge (see Smetana, 2006; Turiel, 2006 for reviews), they are both socially regulated (albeit for different reasons). Thus, for the purposes of the present analyses, and consistent with a previous study (Smetana & Daddis, 2002), we combined moral and conventional issues to form a *socially regulated* category. We expected that there would be moderate to strong correspondence between judgments regarding the legitimacy of parental authority and beliefs about adolescents' obligations to disclose to parents, and thus we assessed beliefs about the legitimacy of parental authority to examine associations between these two sets of beliefs.

Beliefs about obligatory disclosure to parents were assessed by asking participants, "*Should* teens tell parents what they are doing, that is do they have a duty or obligation to tell parents about their behavior?" They rated the same set of issues used in the assessment of legitimate parental authority on a 5-point scale ranging from 1 (no, not at all) to 5 (definitely yes). Adolescents' and parents' ratings of adolescents' obligation to disclose their behavior to parents are shown in Figure 3.1. These responses were analyzed for differences in

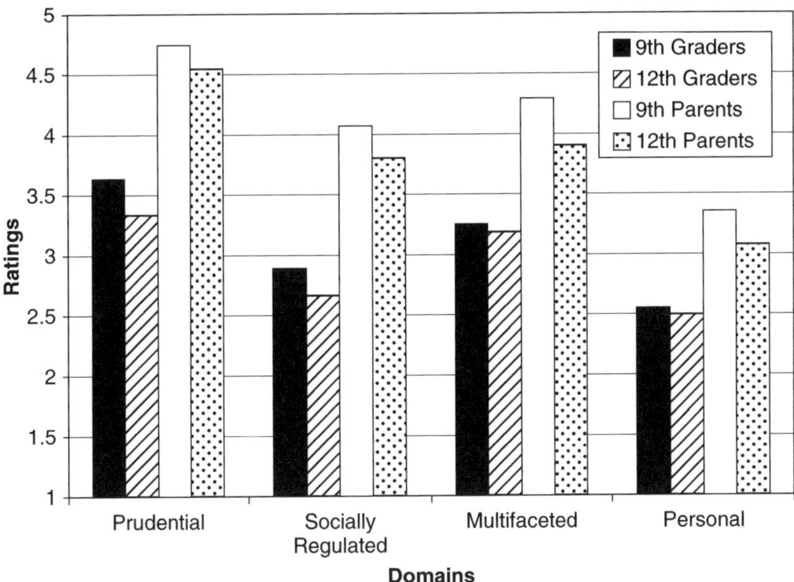

Figure 3.1 Adolescents' and parents' ratings of adolescents' obligations to disclose to parents

judgments according to adolescents' grade and sex, generation (parent versus adolescent), and conceptual domain.

As expected, and as found in the previous research on legitimate parental authority, parents' and adolescents' judgments consistently differed. Parents viewed adolescents as significantly more obligated to disclose all issues than adolescents perceived themselves to be. Furthermore, there were significant domain differences in obligations to disclose to parents. Parents and adolescents viewed adolescents as more obligated to tell parents about prudential (mis)behavior than anything else and about behavior regarding multifaceted issues than either socially regulated or personal issues. (Parental authority was seen as more legitimate, however, for socially regulated than multifaceted issues.) As expected, adolescents were seen as least obligated to disclose about personal issues. Indeed, consistent with our hypotheses, adolescents on average rated themselves as "probably not" obligated to disclose those issues.

Parents viewed their adolescents as less obligated to disclose all issues as they grew older, but differences between ninth and twelfth graders only approached statistical significance. Finally, we expected that beliefs about obligations to disclose to parents and beliefs about the legitimacy of parental authority would be highly correlated, and indeed, they were, $r(275) = 0.59$ for teens and $r(249) = 0.62$ for parents. Although these correlations are high, the strength of the correlations suggests that these two constructs are not identical.

Parental Solicitation of Information

Do parents who view their adolescents as more obligated to tell them about different types of issues try to find out more about those same behaviors? We also asked adolescents and parents to rate (on a five-point scale) how much parents "usually ask, try to find out about, or want to talk about" each issue. Parents' ratings of adolescents' obligations to disclose to parents were highly correlated with parents' reports of how much they sought information about those issues, $r(248) = 0.56$, $p < 0.001$, but adolescents' ratings were not, $r = 0.12$, n.s. Although the data are cross-sectional and thus, the causal direction cannot be determined, our hypothesis is that parents' information seeking is informed by beliefs. That is, parents are more likely to seek information about an activity or behavior when they believe their adolescents ought to disclose about it.

Because adolescents separately rated how much mothers and fathers sought information about each issue, we first examined differences in adolescents' judgments according to grade, gender, domain, and parent (mothers versus fathers). The findings were consistent with previous research (Bumpus, Crouter & McHale, 2001; Crouter *et al.*, 1999; Crouter & McHale, 1993; Crouter, McHale & Bartko, 1993; Noller & Callan, 1990; Waizenhofer, Buchanan & Jackson-Newsom, 2004; Youniss & Smollar, 1985) in indicating that adolescents perceived their mothers as trying to obtain more information about their behavior than did fathers. There also were more complex interactions that elaborated on this finding. More specifically, adolescent girls were more likely than adolescent boys to view mothers as trying to find out about personal and multifaceted issues.

Next, we examined differences (again, by grade, sex, and domain) across generations. Because most (84%) of participating parents were mothers, we compared adolescents' ratings of their disclosure to mothers with their mothers' reports. As hypothesized, and as can be seen in Figure 3.2, mothers reported seeking more information about their adolescents' behavior than adolescents reported their mothers seeking.

Furthermore, parental solicitation was greatest over multifaceted than all other issues. It might seem surprising that parents sought more information about multifaceted than prudential issues, as the prudential items included here were issues of risk during adolescence (drinking, smoking cigarettes, and trying illegal drugs). However, other studies have shown that parents solicit more information when their adolescents are more involved in problem behavior (Tilton-Weaver & Galambos, 2003); as this was a community sample (and as our data show), the rates of problem behavior were low. Furthermore, previous research has indicated that multifaceted issues are significant sources of disagreement and conflict in adolescent–parent relationships (Smetana, 1989, 2000; Smetana & Asquith, 1994) and that adolescents typically view these issues as personal whereas parents typically view them as social-conventional or prudential.

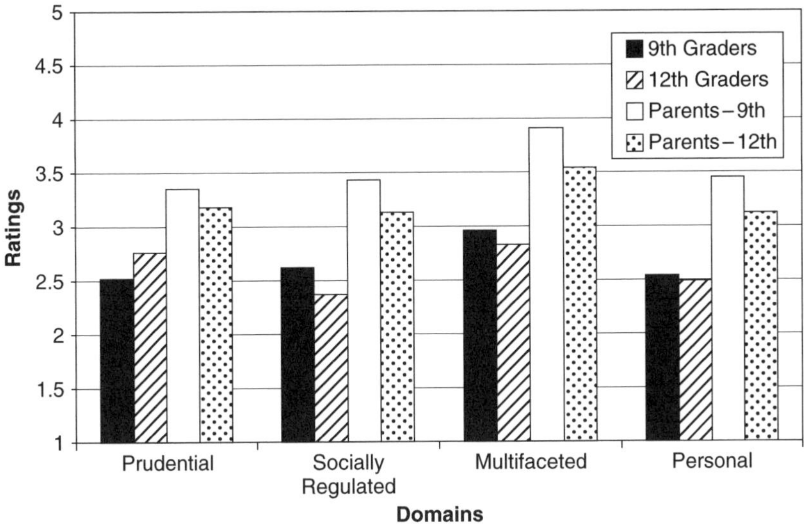

Figure 3.2 Adolescents' and mothers' ratings of parental solicitation of information

Mothers also reported soliciting more information about prudential and personal activities than about socially regulated behavior, most probably because the socially regulated (moral and conventional) behaviors examined in this study entailed routine expectations that are generally taken for granted by the time children transition to adolescence. Moreover, parents were seen as soliciting more information from their ninth graders than twelfth graders about socially regulated, multifaceted, and personal issues, but there were no age differences in how much mothers sought to find out about their adolescents' prudential behavior.

Disclosure

Next, we examined adolescents' and parents' perceptions of adolescent disclosure to parents, assessed in terms of how often the adolescent "usually tells or is willing to tell your mother (father) without them asking." We focused on disclosure regarding everyday issues (peers, personal, socially regulated, and schoolwork) to ensure that most teens would have opportunities to disclose (or conceal) their behavior. In assessing disclosure and secrecy, we focused our analysis of multifaceted issues to peer relationship issues (seeing someone parents don't like, going to someone else's house when no adult is at home, and whether and who the teen is dating). The socially regulated issues included teasing or saying something mean to someone you know, hurting (pushing, shoving, or hitting) a friend or sibling, lying to a friend, spreading rumors or saying something cruel about someone, talking back, not listening, or being rude to a teacher, and cursing or using swear words. The personal issues included how teens spend their free time, how teens spend their own money, who teens like or have a crush on, what teens talk about on the phone with friends, and what teens write in e-mails, letters, or journals. Rather than prudential issues of risk, we focused on schoolwork issues, including getting a bad grade or not doing well on an assignment, whether homework or assignments are completed, how teens are doing in different school subjects, and doing particularly well on an assignment.

We first compared adolescents' ratings of disclosure to mothers and fathers. Overall, and as shown in Figure 3.3, disclosure was moderate.

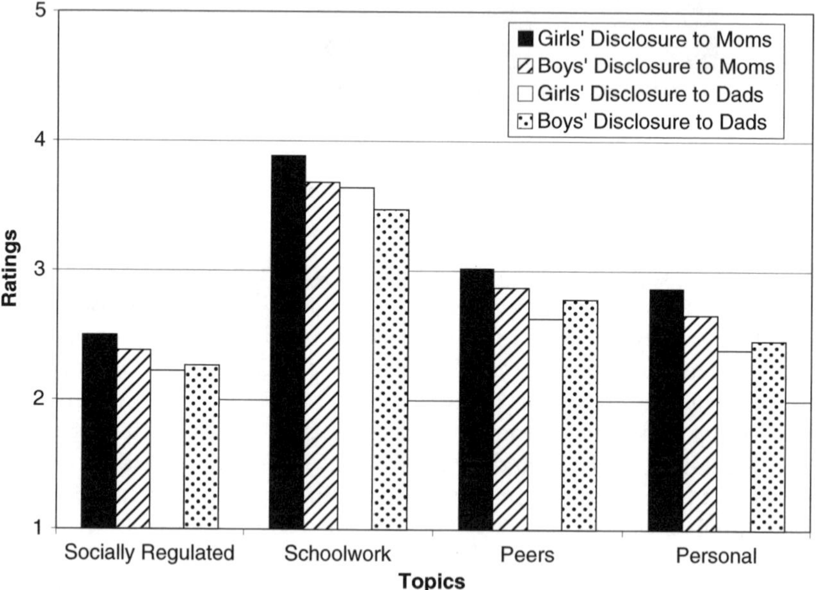

Figure 3.3 Adolescents' disclosure to mothers and fathers

Consistent with previous research (Noller & Callan, 1990; Waizenhofer *et al.*, 2004; Youniss & Smollar, 1985), however, there were interactions between adolescents' and parents' gender. Teenagers disclosed more to mothers than to fathers, and girls disclosed more to mothers than did boys. Adolescents disclosed more about schoolwork than about any other issue, and they voluntarily disclosed more about peer relations than about socially regulated and personal issues.

Finally, we compared mothers' and adolescents' ratings of adolescents' disclosure. The analyses revealed variations by age, gender, generation, and topic. Overall, mothers believed that their adolescents disclosed far more than adolescents reported disclosing. Although adolescents and parents both believed that adolescents' obligation to disclose to parents decreased from middle to late adolescence, adolescents' disclosure about peer issues showed a significant *increase* from ninth to twelfth grade (although parents' ratings about these issues did not show a corresponding increase). Previous research has shown that antisocial conformity to peers peaks at ninth grade, so it is possible that the older adolescents were more conforming to adult values (and thus, had less to hide) or at least, were more willing to be open. However, we also assessed adolescents' involvement in problem behaviors using a modified version of the Problem Behavior Survey (PBS) (Mason *et al.*, 1996), a 19-item report of problem behavior adapted from Jessor & Jessor (1977). The measure was modified slightly for this study to omit some of the more serious, violent behaviors, which we have found to be rare in community samples of adolescents, and to include more everyday instances of problem behavior. The 19 items used here were: drink beer or alcohol, use pot (marijuana), smoke cigarettes, take part in street-gang activity, cheat on school tests, steal at home, steal from places other than home, go to school high on drugs, get into fights, threaten to hurt people, go joy-riding, vandalize or trash property, cut classes or skip school, disobey at school, have unsafe sex, stay out past midnight, use drugs such as LSD or Ecstasy, and copy homework from others (alpha was 0.90). Contrary to the hypothesis that older adolescents had less to hide, however, problem behavior increased with age. Thus, adolescents may have engaged in more misbehavior, but they reported being more likely to voluntarily disclose to parents about their activities with peers than about their prudential misbehavior.

THE INFLUENCE OF BELIEFS, DISCLOSURE, AND PARENTAL SOLICITATION OF INFORMATION ABOUT MULTIFACETED AND PERSONAL ISSUES ON ADJUSTMENT

Finally, we examined the role of adolescents' domain-differentiated beliefs about obligations to disclose, actual disclosure, and parental solicitation on adolescent adjustment. For each of these assessments, the analyses included only personal and peer issues. Thus, our measure of disclosure included items that were similar to the ones used by Kerr and Stattin (Kerr & Stattin, 2000; Stattin & Kerr, 2000). We also selected these items because they focused on everyday activities and behaviors, and therefore, they were likely to be salient issues for the youth in our sample. Using structural equation modeling, we examined the path model presented in Figure 3.4.

As can be seen, we hypothesized that there would be a direct path from adolescents' disclosure to parents and their perceptions of parental solicitation of information to adolescent adjustment. We also examined whether adolescents' obligations to disclose to parents about personal and multifaceted issues and their trust in their parents would have both direct as well as indirect effects, as mediated by disclosure and parental solicitation, on adjustment.

Trust was assessed on the 10-item Trust subscale of the Parent–Peer Attachment Inventory (PPAI, Armsden & Greenberg, 1987). Adolescents

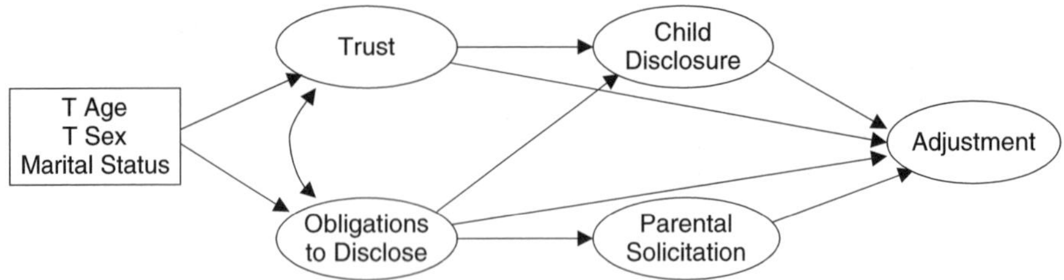

Figure 3.4 Hypothesized structural model

separately rated their relationships with mothers and fathers (alpha's = 0.74 and 0.77, respectively) on items such as, "I trust my mother," "my mother understands me," "my mother accepts me as I am," "I wish I had a different mother," and "when we discuss things, my mother considers my point of view." Adjustment was examined in terms of both externalizing behavior (as described previously) and internalizing symptoms, which were assessed using the Depression and Anxiety subscales (alpha = 0.89) of the Youth Self-Report—Child Behavior Checklist (YSL—CBC) (Achenbach, 1991). Finally, adolescents' age, gender, and family marital status (coded as two birth parents versus all else) were also incorporated into the model. The bivariate correlations among these variables are shown in Table 3.1. Trimming the model to include only significant and near-significant paths, the standardized structural coefficients and the goodness-of-fit indices suggested that this model provided an excellent fit of the model to the data, $\chi 2 = 12.74$, RMSEA = 0.044; CFI = 0.99. The results of the structural equation test of the model are presented in Figure 3.5.

Table 3.1 Correlations among variables

	1.	2.	3.	4.	5.	6.	7.	8.	9.
1. Teen sex (Female)	1.00	–0.04	–0.01	–0.12	–0.00	0.11	0.03	0.04	0.16**
2. Age		1.00	0.03	–0.01	0.07	–0.23**	0.06	–0.02	–0.07
3. Marital status			1.00	0.19**	0.28**	0.09	0.05	0.06	–0.18**
4. Teen trust				1.00	–0.52**	0.14*	0.48**	0.39**	–0.44**
5. Problem behavior					1.00	–0.14	–0.26**	–0.29**	0.58**
6. Parental solicitation						1.00	0.23*	0.26**	–0.11
7. Teen disclosure							1.00	0.56**	–0.26*
8. Obligations to disclose								1.00	–0.18**
9. Internalizing									1.00

Note All variables pertain to teen reports (for trust, parental solicitation, and disclosure, means are for ratings of mothers and fathers combined). Marital Status = married, two parent versus all else. $^*p < 0.05$, $^{**}p < 0.01$.

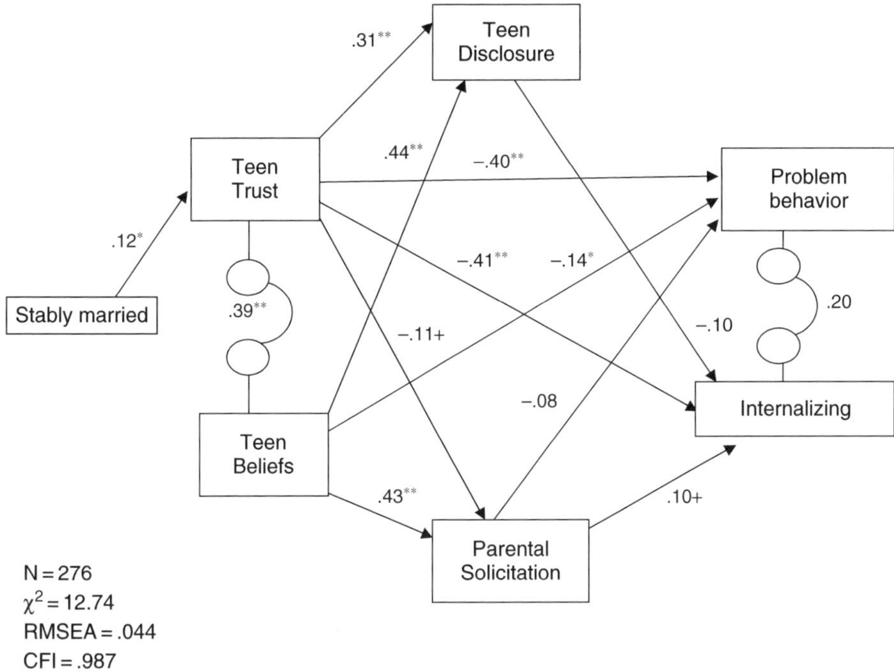

Figure 3.5 Standardized results of the structural model

As shown in Figure 3.5, trust and adolescents' obligations to disclose to parents about personal and peer issues strongly and significantly contributed to adolescents' disclosure about these issues. Although adolescents who believed they were more obligated to disclose these issues also rated their parents as trying to find out more about these issues, trust had only a marginally significant effect on adolescent-rated parental solicitation of information about personal and peer issues. However, in contrast to previous research (Kerr & Stattin, 2000; Stattin & Kerr, 2000) and although adolescents' voluntary disclosure to parents showed a modest bivariate association with problem behavior, disclosure *did not* contribute significantly to problem behavior in the model. Consistent with previous findings, however, the path between (adolescent-rated) parental solicitation of information about personal and peer issues and problem behavior also was not significant.

Adolescent-rated trust in parents and adolescents' perceptions of parents' attempts to solicit information about personal and peer issues had marginally significant effects on depression and anxiety, although for parental solicitation, the relationship was in the opposite direction from our predictions. Adolescents who perceived their parents as trying to find out more about these issues reported more internalizing distress. Previous research has shown that adolescents interpret parents' attempts to control their personal domains as overly intrusive and psychologically controlling (Smetana & Daddis, 2002) and research also has shown that overcontrol of the personal domain is associated with more internalizing problems (Hasebe, Nucci, & Nucci, 2004). The present findings are consistent with this research and suggest that parental solicitation of information about personal and peer issues may be perceived as intrusive, and thus is associated with more internalizing symptoms. Kerr & Stattin (2000) likewise have found that adolescents whose parents use high levels of behavioral control feel controlled and that feelings of control are related to poorer adjustment. (In their research, when adolescents' feelings of being controlled were partialed out, parental control was associated with better adjustment.) These results suggest that more research is needed on the ways that parents can seek information about their adolescents' activities without appearing overly intrusive. Given that parents appear to seek more information when they have indications that their adolescent is in trouble (Tilton-Weaver & Galambos, 2003), it is possible that the parents in the present study sought to find out more about their adolescents' behavior because they perceived that their adolescents were experiencing psychological distress.

The structural model also indicates that adolescents' beliefs about their obligations to disclose to parents and especially, adolescent trust, had strong, direct, and negative associations with problem behavior. That is, adolescents who had more trusting relationships with parents and who believed they were more obligated to disclose their behavior to their parents reported lower levels of problem behavior. Adolescent trust also was significantly, strongly, and negatively associated with internalizing disorders (indicating that higher levels of trust were associated with less depression and anxiety), although beliefs about obligations to disclose were not.

Our finding that adolescents' voluntary disclosure regarding personal and peer issues did not influence adjustment differed from Kerr and Stattin's research (Kerr & Stattin, 2000; Stattin & Kerr, 2000), although there were several important differences between the studies. First, our model did not include assessments of either parental knowledge or control, which were key measures in their research. In addition, our measure of trust assessed communication, trust, and understanding in the parent–teen relationship, whereas Kerr & Stattin (2000) focused explicitly on parents' trust in the adolescent. Kerr, Stattin & Trost (1999) assert that parents' trust in the teen and adolescents' trust in parents are profoundly different, due to their different developmental histories and trajectories and power inequalities in the parent–child relationship. In our study, we also obtained assessments of parents' perceptions of trust, communication, and understanding with their adolescents using a reworded version of the 10-item PPAI Trust scale (alpha was 0.69). Supporting Kerr and Stattin's assertion, we found that adolescents' and parents' perceptions of trust in the other were significantly but only moderately (0.39) correlated. In addition, our model expanded on the previous research by including beliefs about adolescents' obligations to disclose to parents, and adolescents' beliefs that they were less obligated to disclose to parents contributed significantly to problem behavior. Like others (e.g., Goodnow, 1988), our hypothesis is that beliefs influence behavior but as our data are cross-sectional, further longitudinal research would be needed to test the causal direction.

Finally, Kerr & Stattin (2000) found that adolescent disclosure had an independent effect on conduct problems over and above the effects of trust. Although they did not systematically examine the domain of the items included in their assessment, their items were similar to the items categorized here as personal and multifaceted. However, Kerr and Stattin assessed disclosure by asking whether adolescents spontaneously tell, like to tell, usually tell, keep a lot of secrets, or hide their everyday activities from their parents. Previous research has shown that disclosure and secrecy are only moderately (and inversely) correlated (Finkenauer, Engels, & Meeus, 2002; Finkenauer *et al.*, 2005) and that they have different implications for adjustment (Finkenauer, Engels, & Meeus, 2002) as well as parenting (Finkenauer *et al.*, 2005). As we have discussed in detail elsewhere (Smetana *et al.*, 2006), we also obtained parallel ratings of adolescents' secrecy regarding the same issues and found that these ratings were significantly but moderately and inversely related to voluntary disclosure (–0.46). Thus, it is possible that Kerr and Stattin's inclusion of secrecy along with their assessment of disclosure influenced their findings.

Our findings point to the centrality of trust, and more generally, the quality of the parent–child relationship in predicting lower levels of problem behavior and internalizing symptoms in a community sample of North American, ethnically diverse, lower middle-class middle and late adolescents. The findings are consistent with our hypothesis that disclosure over personal issues may contribute to the quality of parent–adolescent relationships but that such disclosure is discretionary rather than required. Indeed, our analyses indicated that disclosure over these issues was seen as less obligatory as adolescents got older.

Kerr, Stattin, & Trost (1999) have shown that adolescents who are more disclosing view their parents as more trusting of them, but we further hypothesized that adolescents' trust in parents would be more positively associated with disclosure in the personal domain than in other domains. To test this hypothesis, we examined associations between adolescents' ratings of trust and their self-rated disclosure in each domain. Adolescents' trust in their mothers was significantly associated with their self-reported disclosure to their mothers regarding social, multifaceted, and personal issues, $rs\,(275) = 0.33$, 0.45, and 0.47, respectively. Adolescents' trust in their fathers was likewise significantly associated with their disclosure to their fathers regarding social, multifaceted and personal issues, $rs\,(256) = 0.32$, 0.46, and 0.45, respectively. Using r to z transformations, we examined differences among these correlations and found that adolescents' trust in mothers was more strongly associated with disclosure regarding personal than social issues, $z = 1.948$, two-tailed test, and that adolescents' trust in fathers was more strongly associated with disclosure regarding personal and peer than social issues, $z = 1.85$, 1.98, respectively, two-tailed test. Thus, these findings show that trust in parents is strongly associated with adolescents' disclosure of personal issues (and for fathers, multifaceted peer issues). Adolescents who disclose more regarding personal issues have closer relationships with their parents (although the causal direction of these findings cannot be determined because our data are cross-sectional); we have recently replicated these findings in another sample (Smetana *et al.*, 2007a). The test of the structural model showed, however, that not disclosing these issues, at least in our sample, did not appear to have significant negative consequences for adjustment.

The findings also point to the potential importance of the conditions under which disclosure occurs. The results suggested that although beliefs about obligations to disclose personal and peer issues did not show a direct relationship with internalizing symptoms, they had indirect effects, as mediated by disclosure. In other words, adolescents who believed that they were obligated to disclose more about personal and peer issues disclosed more, which in turn, was significantly associated with less anxiety and depression. This suggests that adolescents' *voluntary* disclosure of personal issues is associated with better adjustment. In other analyses reported elsewhere (Smetana *et al.*, 2006), we found that more (parent-rated) psychological control was uniquely associated with more (adolescent-reported) disclosure over personal issues, but not other issues. Together with the present findings, this suggests that disclosure about personal issues that feels coerced may negatively influence adjustment. It should be noted that our results are consistent with Kerr & Stattin's (2000) findings, which also focused on *voluntary* disclosure, but our research examines the types of issues where voluntary disclosure may matter.

In future research, these findings should be compared with a similar model that focuses on prudential issues (like drug, alcohol, and cigarette use), particularly as adolescents and parents in the present study believed that adolescents are strongly obligated to disclose their prudential behavior. This is consistent with recent research indicating that adolescents believe that it is acceptable to lie to parents to circumvent their (what are seen as illegitimate) directives regarding moral or personal issues but that adolescents accepted the legitimacy of parental directives regarding prudential acts and considering lying regarding prudential behavior as wrong (Perkins & Turiel, 2007). Nevertheless, other studies suggest that adolescents do conceal these behaviors from their parents and that parents have a "parental personal fable" (Marshall, Tilton-Weaver, & Bosdet, 2005) that maintains an image of themselves as good parents while avoiding knowledge of their adolescents' potentially risky behavior. Unfortunately, in the study discussed here, we did not obtain an assessment of adolescents' disclosure over prudential issues because our methods were not sufficiently sensitive to distinguish between adolescents who engage in risky behavior but conceal their involvement and adolescents who have nothing to disclose (because they are not involved in these behaviors).

We have done this, however, in our more recent research (Smetana *et al.*, 2007a,b), using a procedure similar to the one employed in the Issues Checklist (Prinz *et al.*, 1979; Robin & Foster, 1989), a widely used measure of adolescent–parent conflict. Adolescents (seventh and tenth graders drawn from the same school district as the previous study) first identified which of 27 prudential, multifaceted, peer, and personal behaviors or activities they had engaged in at least once and then rated their disclosure to parents only for those activities. For instance, teens were asked whether they had ever gone to a party where teens were drinking alcohol; only teens responding affirmatively rated their voluntary disclosure to parents about this issue. Overall, the level of involvement in problem behaviors was low in this sample, although it increased with age. Similar to the findings just discussed, we found that controlling for age, sex, demographic background, behavioral control, and trust in the parent–adolescent relationship, adolescents' greater voluntary disclosure about personal and multifaceted issues was not significantly associated with problem behavior but it was significantly associated with lower levels of depressed mood. Underscoring the importance of focusing on the domain of the activities that adolescents voluntarily disclose to parents, we also found, employing the same controls, that adolescents who disclosed more about prudential activities (but not about personal and peer issues) reported lower levels of problem behavior (Smetana *et al.*, 2007a). Like our previous study, the study was cross-sectional, leaving causality to be determined in future research.

More generally, the findings from the analyses discussed in this chapter suggest that we need to focus less on parental surveillance, control, and adolescent compliance and more on the factors that facilitate adolescents' and parents' positive, trusting relationships. Furthermore, the findings suggest that adolescents construct domain-differentiated notions of appropriate disclosure that guide their willingness to talk to parents and that disclosure thus entails reciprocal, transactive processes between parents and adolescents. Thus, parents must balance their need to remain informed about their adolescents' behavior and whereabouts with a sensitivity to adolescents' developing autonomy, desires for greater personal freedom, and hence their need for parents not to intrude too deeply into their personal domains. Others have argued that "precision parenting" requires an appropriate and delicate balance between sufficient control to keep adolescents safe and not too much control, which will stifle adolescents' developing autonomy (Mason *et al.*, 1996). Likewise, precision parenting is needed to create an emotional climate that encourages adolescents' voluntary disclosure and permits parents to seek information when needed, without seeming coercive or controlling. Furthermore, our research suggests the need to take a developmental perspective on what constitutes healthy and unhealthy disclosure, parental solicitation of information, and adolescents' strategies for disclosure (Darling *et al.*, 2004; Marshall, Tilton-Weaver, & Bosdet, 2005) for different kinds of issues.

REFERENCES

Achenbach, T. M. (1991). *Manual for the Youth Self-Report and 1991 Profile*. Unpublished manual, University of Vermont.

Armsden, G. C. & Greenberg, M. T. (1987). The Inventory of Parent and Peer Attachment: Individual differences and their relationship to psychological well being in adolescence. *Journal of Youth and Adolescence, 16*, 427–454.

Barber, B. K., Olsen, J. E., & Shagle, S. C. (1994). Associations between parental psychological and behavioral control and youth internalized and externalized behaviors. *Child Development, 65*, 1120–1136.

Barnes, G. M. & Farrell, M. P. (1992). Parental support and control as predictors of adolescent drinking, delinquency, and related problem behaviors. *Journal of Marriage and the Family, 54*, 763–776.

Berndt, T. J. & Hanna, N. A. (1995). Intimacy and self-disclosure in friendships. In K. Rotenberg (ed.), *Disclosure Processes in Children and Adolescents* (pp. 57–77). Cambridge: Cambridge University Press.

Buhrmester, D. & Prager, K. (1995). Patterns and functions of self-disclosure during childhood and adolescence. In K. Rotenberg (ed.), *Disclosure Processes in Children and Adolescents* (pp. 10–56). Cambridge: Cambridge University Press.

Bumpus, M. F., Crouter, A. C., & McHale, S. M. (2001). Parental autonomy granting during adolescence: Exploring gender differences in context. *Developmental Psychology, 37*, 164–173.

Crouter, A. C., Bumpus, M. F., Davis, K. D., & McHale, S. M. (2005). How do parents learn about adolescents' experiences? Implications for parental knowledge and adolescent risky behavior. *Child Development, 76*, 869–882.

Crouter, A. C. & Head, M. R. (2002). Parental monitoring and knowledge of children. In M. Bornstein (ed.), *Handbook of Parenting, Vol. 3: Becoming and Being a Parent* (2nd edn, pp. 461–483). Mahwah, NJ. Erlbaum.

Crouter, A. C., Helms-Erikson, H., Updegraff, K., & McHale, S. M. (1999). Conditions underlying parents' knowledge about children's daily lives in middle childhood: Between- and within-family comparisons. *Child Development, 70*, 246–259.

Crouter, A. C. & McHale, S. M. (1993). Temporal rhythms in family life: Seasonal variation in the relation between parental work and family processes. *Developmental Psychology, 29*, 198–205.

Crouter, A. C., McHale, S. M. & Bartko, W. T. (1993). Gender as an organizing feature in parent-child relationships. *Journal of Social Issues, 49*, 161–174.

Csikszentmihalyi, M. & Larson, R. (1984). *Being Adolescent*. New York: Basic Books.

Daddis, C. (in press a). Influence of close friends on the boundaries of adolescent personal authority. *Journal of Research on Adolescence*.

Daddis, C. (in press b). Similarity between early and middle adolescent close friends' beliefs about personal jurisdiction. *Social Development*.

Darling, N., Cumsille, P., Hames, K., & Caldwell, L. L. (2004). *Adolescents as Active Agents in the Monitoring Process; Disclosure Strategies and Motivations*. Unpublished paper, Pennsylvania State University, College Park, PA.

Darling, N. & Steinberg, L. (1993). Parenting style as context: An integrative model. *Psychological Bull*etin, *113*, 486–496.

Finkenauer, C., Engels, R. C. M. E., & Meeus, W. (2002). Keeping secrets from parents: Advantages and disadvantages of secrecy in adolescence. *Journal of Youth and Adolescence, 2*, 123–136.

Finkenauer, C., Frijns, T., Engels, RCME, & Kerkhof, P. (2005). Perceiving concealment in relationships between parents and adolescents: Links with parental behavior. *Personal Relationships, 12*, 387–406.

Goodnow, J. J. (1988). Parents' ideas, actions, and feelings: Models and methods from developmental and social psychology. *Child Development, 59*, 286–320.

Grusec, J. E. & Goodnow, J. J. (1994). The impact of parental discipline methods on the child's internalization of values: A reconceptualization of current points of view. *Developmental Psychology, 30*, 4–19.

Hasebe, Y., Nucci, L., & Nucci, M. S. (2004). Parental control of the personal domain and adolescent symptoms of psychopathology: A cross-national study in the US and Japan. *Child Development, 75*, 815–828.

Helwig, C. C. & Turiel, E. (2003). Children's social and moral reasoning. In P. K. Smith & C. H. Hart (eds), *Blackwell Handbook of Childhood Social Development* (pp. 475–490). Oxford: Blackwell.

Jessor, R. & Jessor, S. L. (1977). *Problem Behavior and Psychosocial Development: A longitudinal Study of Youth*. New York: Academic Press.

Kerr, M. & Stattin, H. (2000). What parents know, how they know it, and several forms of adolescent adjustment: Further support for a reinterpretation of monitoring. *Developmental Psychology, 36*, 366–380.

Kerr, M., Stattin, H., & Trost, K. (1999). To know you is to trust you: parents' trust is rooted in child disclosure of information. *Journal of Adolescence, 22*, 737–752.

Killen, M., McGlothlin, H., & Kim, J. (2002). Heterogeneity in social cognition and culture. In H. Keller, Y, Poortinga, & A. Schoelmerich (eds), *Between Biology and Culture: Perspectives on Ontogenetic Development* (pp. 159–190). Cambridge: Cambridge University Press.

Kuczynski, L. (2003). Beyond bidirectionality: bilateral conceptual frameworks for understanding dynamics in parent-child relations (pp. 1–24). In L. Kuczynski (ed.), *Handbook of Dynamics in Parent-Child Relations*. Thousand Oaks CA: Sage.

Kuczynski, L. & Navara, G. S. (2006). Sources of innovation and change in internalization and socialization. In M. Killen & J. G. Smetana (eds), *Handbook of Moral Development* (pp. 299–327). Mahwah, NJ: Erlbaum.

Larson, R., Richards, M., Moneta, G. *et al.* (1996). Changes in adolescents' daily interactions with their families from ages 10–18: Disengagement and transformation. *Developmental Psychology, 32*, 744–754.

Lins-Dyer, T. (2003). *Mexican Adolescents' Perceptions of Parental Control and Academic Achievement: A Social Domain Approach*. Unpublished doctoral dissertation, College of Education, University of Illinois at Chicago, 2003.

Lins-Dyer, T. & Nucci, L. (2004). *The Impact of Social Class and Social Cognitive Domain on Northeastern Brazilian Mothers' and Daughters' Conceptions of Parental Control*. Unpublished manuscript, College of Education, University of Illinois at Chicago, 2004.

Loeber, R. & Stouthamer-Loeber, M. (1986). Family factors as correlates and predictors of juvenile conduct problems and delinquency. In M. Tonry & N. Morris (eds), *Crime and Justice: An Annual Review of Research, Vol. 7* (pp. 29–149). Chicago: University of Chicago Press.

Loeber, R. & Stouthamer-Loeber, M. (1998). Development of juvenile aggression and violence: Some common misconceptions and controversies. *American Psychologist, 53*, 242–259.

Marshall, S. K., Tilton-Weaver, L. C., & Bosdet, L. (2005). Information management: Considering adolescents' regulation of parental knowledge. *Journal of Adolescence*, 28, 633–647.

Mason, C. A., Cauce, A. N., Gonzales, N., & Hiraga, Y. (1996). Neither too sweet nor too sour: problem peers, maternal control, and problem behavior in African American adolescents. *Child Development, 67*, 2115–2130.

Noller, P. & Callan, V. J. (1990). Adolescents' perceptions of the nature of their communication with parents. *Journal of Youth and Adolescence, 19*, 349–362.

Nucci, L. P. (1996). Morality and personal freedom. In E. S. Reed, E. Turiel, & T. Brown (eds), *Values and Knowledge* (pp. 41–60). Mahwah, NJ: Erlbaum.

Nucci, L. P. (2001). *Education in the Moral Domain*. Cambridge: Cambridge University Press.

Nucci, L., Camino, C., & Milnitsky-Sapiro, C. (1996). Social class effects on Northeastern Brazilian children's conceptions of areas of personal choice and social regulation. *Child Development, 67*, 1223–1242.

Nucci, L P., Guerra, N., & Lee, J. (1991). Adolescent judgments of the personal, prudential, and normative aspects of drug usage. *Developmental Psychology, 27*, 841–848.

Nucci, L., Hasebe, Y., & Lins-Dyer, M. T. (2005). Adolescent psychological well-being and parental control of the personal. In J. G. Smetana (ed.), *New Directions for Child and Adolescent Development; Changing Boundaries of Parental Authority During Adolescence, No. 108* (pp. 17–30). San Francisco, CA: Jossey-Bass.

Perkins, S. A. & Turiel. E. (2007). To lie or not to lie: To whom and under what circumstances. *Child Development, 78*, 609–621.

Prinz, R. J., Foster, S. L., Kent, R. N., & O'Leary, K. D. (1979). Multivariate assessment of conflict in distressed and nondistressed mother-adolescent dyads. *Journal of Applied Behavior Analysis, 12*, 691–700.

Reis, H. T. & Shaver, P. (1988). Intimacy as an interpersonal process. In S. Duck (ed.), *Handbook of Research in Personal Relationships* (pp. 367–289). London: Wiley.

Robin, A. L. & Foster, S. I. (1989). *Negotiating Parent-Adolescent Conflict: A Behavioral Family Systems Approach*. New York: Guilford.

Searight, H. R., Thomas, S. L., Manley, C. M., & Ketterson, T. U. (1995). Self-disclosure in adolescents: A family systems perspective. In K. Rotenberg (ed.), *Disclosure Processes in Children and Adolescents* (pp. 204–225). Cambridge: Cambridge University Press.

Smetana, J. G. (1988). Adolescents' and parents' conceptions of parental authority. *Child Development, 59*, 321–335.

Smetana, J. G. (1989). Adolescents' and parents' reasoning about actual family conflict. *Child Development, 60*, 1052–1067.

Smetana, J. G. (1995). Morality in context: Abstractions, ambiguities, and applications. In R. Vasta (ed.), *Annals of Child Development, Vol. 10* (pp. 83–130). London: Jessica Kingsley.

Smetana, J. (1996). Adolescent-parent conflict: Implications for adaptive and maladaptive development. In D. Cicchetti & S. L. Toth (eds), *Rochester Symposium on Developmental Psychopathology, Vol. VII: Adolescence: Opportunities and Challenges* (pp. 1–46). Rochester, NY: University of Rochester Press.

Smetana, J. G. (2000). Middle-class African American adolescents' and parents' conceptions of parental authority and parenting practices: a longitudinal investigation. *Child Development, 71*, 1672–1686.

Smetana, J. G. (2002). Culture, autonomy, and personal jurisdiction in adolescent-parent relationships. In H. W. Reese and R. Kail (eds), *Advances in Child Development and Behavior, Vol. 29* (pp. 51–87). New York: Academic Press.

Smetana, J. G. (2006). Social domain theory: Consistencies and variations in children's moral and social judgments. In M. Killen & J. G. Smetana (eds), *Handbook of Moral Development* (pp. 119–153). Mahwah, NJ: Erlbaum.

Smetana, J. G. & Asquith, P. (1994). Adolescents' and parents' conceptions of parental authority and adolescent autonomy. *Child Development, 65*, 1147–1162.

Smetana, J. G., Campione-Barr, N., & Daddis, C. (2004). Developmental and longitudinal antecedents of family decision-making: Defining health behavioral autonomy for African American adolescents. *Child Development, 75*, 1418–1434.

Smetana, J. G. & Chuang, S. (2001). Middle-class African American parents' conceptions of parenting in the transition to adolescence. *Journal of Research on Adolescence, 11*, 177–198.

Smetana, J. G., Crean, H., & Campione-Barr, N. (2005). Adolescents' and parents' conceptions of parental authority. In J. G. Smetana (ed.), *New Directions for Child and Adolescent Development; Changing Boundaries of Parental Authority During Adolescence, No. 108* (pp. 31–46). San Francisco: Jossey-Bass.

Smetana, J. G. & Daddis, C. (2002). Domain-specific antecedents of psychological control and parental monitoring: The role of parenting beliefs and practices. *Child Development, 73*, 563–580.

Smetana, J. G. & Gaines, C. (1999). Adolescent-parent conflict in middle-class African American families. *Child Development, 70*, 1447–1463.

Smetana, J. G., Metzger, A., Gettman, D. C., & Campione-Barr, N. (2006). Disclosure and secrecy in adolescent-parent relationships. *Child Development, 77*, 201–217.

Smetana, J. G., Villalobos, M., Campione-Barr, N. *et al.* (2007a). *Domains of Disclosure, Parenting, and Adjustment during Adolescence*. Unpublished manuscript, University of Rochester.

Smetana, J. G., Villalobos, M., Tasopoulos, M. *et al.* (2007b). *Early and Middle Adolescents' Disclosure in Different Domains*. Unpublished manuscript, University of Rochester.

Stattin, H. & Kerr, M. (2000). Parental monitoring: A reinterpretation. *Child Development, 71*, 1072–1085.

Sullivan, H. S. (1953). *The Interpersonal Theory of Psychiatry*. New York: Norton.

Tilton-Weaver, L. C. & Galambos, N. L. (2003). Adolescents' characteristics and parents' beliefs as predictors of parents' peer management behaviors. *Journal of Research on Adolescence, 13*, 269–300.

Turiel, E. (1983). *The Development of Social Knowledge: Morality and Convention*. Cambridge: Cambridge University Press.

Turiel, E. (1998). Moral development. In N. Eisenberg (ed.), *Handbook of Child Psychology, Volume 3: Social, Emotional, and Personality Development* (William Damon, series editor) (5th edn, pp. 863–932). New York: Wiley.

Turiel, E. (2002). *The Culture of Morality: Social Development, Context, and Conflict*. Cambridge: Cambridge University Press.

Turiel, E. (2006). Moral development. In N. Eisenberg (ed.), *Handbook of Child Psychology, Volume 3: Social, Emotional, and Personality Development* (William Damon, series editor) (6th edn, pp. 789–857). New York: Wiley.

Waizenhofer, R. N., Buchanan, C. M., & Jackson-Newsom, J. (2004). Mothers' and fathers' knowledge of adolescents' daily activities: Its sources and its links with adolescent adjustment. *Journal of Marriage and the Family, 18*, 348–360.

Youniss, J. & Smollar, J. (1985). *Adolescents' Relations with Mothers, Fathers, and Friends*. Chicago: University of Chicago Press.

Part 2

The Roles of Adolescent Agency and Parenting Efforts in Relationships and Adjustment

CHAPTER 4

Parents React to Adolescent Problem Behaviors by Worrying More and Monitoring Less

Margaret Kerr, Håkan Stattin and Vilmante Pakalniskiene
Center for Developmental Research, Örebro University, Sweden

INTRODUCTION

As children mature into adolescents, they spend more time away from home and get into situations where they might be drawn into risky behavior such as delinquency. What can parents do to prevent this? We will argue that the majority of studies in the literature on parenting adolescents cannot answer this question, and we will not answer it in this study, either. Our study and many previous studies cannot show what parents can or might best do, but they show what parents do in the normal course of events. These, in our minds, are two very different phenomena, and they require different methods to study.

How could one discover what parents *can* do to prevent problems? There are two possible designs. One is an experimental study in which parenting behavior is manipulated, and parents are randomly assigned to conditions. Other things being equal, if adolescent behavior changes more in one condition than in another, then whatever parents in that condition did is an answer to the question. There might be other answers that have not been tested, but

The longitudinal study used in this research was financed by the Swedish Research Council. Work on this chapter was supported by The Bank of Sweden Tercentenary Foundation and the Swedish Council for Working Life and Social Research.

What Can Parents Do? New Insights into the Role of Parents in Adolescent Problem Behavior
Edited by Margaret Kerr, Håkan Stattin and Rutger C. M. E. Engels.

those results would give one. To answer the question with a nonexperimental design is trickier, but let us consider what that would entail. First, parents and adolescents would have to be followed over time. Second, one would need to show persistence in good youth behavior or a change in youth behavior from bad to good that is explained better by parents' behavior than by anything else. For persistent good youth behavior, one might want to show that the youth was at risk for bad behavior—had risk-prone personality characteristics or a delinquent peer group, for example—but did not fall into bad behavior. Then, one would need to rule out other potential protective factors and show that parents' behavior is the most reasonable explanation. For a change in youth behavior from bad to good, one would need to show that parents changed their behavior in some theoretically meaningful way prior to the change in the youth's behavior. Otherwise, it would be just as reasonable to assume that parents caused the *bad* youth behavior as the good. Then, one would have to rule out alternative explanations, leaving the change in parents' behavior as the most reasonable explanation. Although these strategies are possible, most non-experimental studies of parenting do not use them. Thus, they do not show what parents can do.

Our purpose is to examine what parents typically do in the face of problems such as adolescent delinquency and the defiance and secrecy at home that accompany it. We argue that this knowledge of what *does* happen does not set the limits for what *can* happen, but it is important for understanding undesirable adolescent development, the role of parenting, and what parenting behaviors might be targeted in studies that try to discover what *can* happen if parents' behaviors are changed for the better.

Although the vast majority of studies in the literature on parenting adolescents have focused on trying to show how parenting shapes youths' behaviors, there is growing awareness that parents also change their behavior in response to youth characteristics and behaviors. This is especially so in the parenting literature more broadly. Bell and Lytton have been two major figures in this move. More than three decades ago, Bell (1968) reviewed a number of experimental findings in which parents' and other adults' behaviors had changed in response to certain children's behaviors, and he argued that, because of these findings, parent–child correlations should not be interpreted as only parent-to-child effects. More recently, Lytton (1990) made a similar argument about experimental and observational studies, showing that parents change their behavior in response to conduct disordered behaviors such as aggression and noncompliance. Both these researchers have followed up with more recent reviews (Bell & Chapman, 1986; Lytton, 2000). In all, numerous experimental and longitudinal studies in the most visible developmental journals have shown that parents and other adults react to children's characteristics and adjust their behavior accordingly (e.g., Anderson, Lytton, & Romney, 1986; Buss, 1981; Dix *et al.*, 1986; Huh *et al.*, 2006; Mulhern & Passman, 1981; Passman & Blackwelder, 1981) or have shown good evidence for bidirectional effects (e.g., Chen, Liu, & Li, 2000; Hastings & Rubin, 1999; Kochanska, 1998; Mink & Nihira, 1986; Stice & Barrera, 1995). Behavioral genetic studies, too, argue for reciprocal effects (e.g., Ge *et al.*, 1996; Reiss *et al.*, 2000). Thus, the evidence is growing that a valid understanding of parenting will have to include reciprocal relationships—how parents react to children as well as how they shape them.

Concerning parenting and adolescent problem behavior, a number of studies have begun to look at parenting as both action and reaction to the youth. Not all are revealing about what parents do in reaction to adolescent problems, however. For instance, in one study, girls' unhealthy eating predicted poorer parent–child relationships over time (Archibald *et al.*, 2002) and in another there were reciprocal relations between parent–child relationships and internalizing and externalizing problems (Buist *et al.*, 2003). To the extent that these relationship measures can be considered measures of parenting (because the child is involved in the relationship, too), one can say that there is some evidence that parents responded to adolescent problems by doing things that resulted in the child reporting less positive relationships. But what they did is unknown. In another line of research, a number of studies have shown that youth problem behavior and parental knowledge (usually called monitoring) are reciprocally or mutually related (Fite *et al.*, 2006; Jang & Smith, 1997; Kandel & Wu, 1995; Laird *et al.*, 2003). It is not clear, however, whether the knowledge measure represents any action on the part of parents. Indeed, there is evidence that it does not primarily represent parental action (Kerr & Stattin, 2000; Stattin & Kerr, 2000). Consequently, one can neither say that this shows a parental reaction to youth behavior *nor* that it shows a youth reaction to parental behavior, and one cannot say what parents did. Thus, even though they appear to be studies of reciprocal relations, these studies lack information about what parents do in the face of adolescent problems.

Other studies have been more informative, however, and the results begin to paint a consistent picture. In one of the first such studies (Stice & Barrera, 1995), the authors used longitudinal data to examine perceived parental support and control in relation to adolescent drug use and externalizing problems. The effects were reciprocal for drug use, but for externalizing problems it appeared that parents reacted to these problems by relinquishing control and withdrawing support. There were no reciprocal effects. Another study tested an idea that was consistent with these results—that parents would react to a youth's deviant peers by disengaging and giving the youth more autonomy (Dishion, Nelson, & Bullock, 2004). The findings were that deviant peer processes were associated with reductions in family management over time. However, because the question was about how parents might react to youths' peer associations rather than to their own behavior, the results might underestimate parents' reactions to adolescents' own problem behaviors. Nonetheless, both these studies suggest that parents respond to adolescent problem behaviors by withdrawing emotionally and behaviorally. These studies, however, reveal little about the processes.

In our work, we have also examined how parents react to youth delinquency and whether that has an effect on later delinquency (Kerr & Stattin, 2003). Whereas the studies mentioned above used at-risk samples, however, we used a community sample, and we tested a larger model of the processes involved. For one thing, we included youth behaviors that correlate with delinquency and which parents might experience at home, behaviors such as defiance, nondisclosure, lying, and manipulation. Our thinking was that parents might react more to these behaviors than to the delinquency itself. We also included two kinds of parents' reactions to delinquency: (1) emotionally-tied, or "gut level" reactions such as worry, distrust, and lessened emotional support and (2) monitoring efforts such as setting and enforcing family rules that require the youth to give information about his or her free time activities (control) and asking for information from the youth, the youths' friends, and the friends' parents (solicitation). Our findings showed that parents tended to respond to the youth's negative behavior at home more than to the delinquency itself. The same was true when we substituted a measure of having deviant peers for the delinquency measure. On the gut level, parents reacted with worry, distrust, and lessened support and encouragement. Behaviorally, they reacted by slackening their monitoring efforts. According to these findings, then, parents of delinquents should appear more and more neglectful as time goes by, because they control less over time and give less emotional support.

Although that study was revealing about the processes going on in families that might otherwise have been labeled neglectful, it also raises several questions, which we will try to answer in this study. One question is whether this is a phenomenon of middle adolescence, after parents have tried other strategies and become exasperated, or whether it would show up in younger youths. In our previous study, we started with 14 year olds and followed them to 16 years, but the question remains whether parents would react the same to delinquency in younger offspring. To examine this, in this study, we start with youths aged 10 to 14 and follow them over two years. Second, it is counterintuitive that in our community sample, delinquency would be linked to a slackening of parental monitoring efforts rather than an escalation. In families with multiple problems, one might expect to see this kind of parental disengagement or premature autonomy process because disengaging might be a way for parents to cope with high levels of emotional stress. In a community sample, however, one would expect the opposite—that the majority of parents would step up their monitoring efforts if they started having trouble with their adolescent. The question is why this parental disengagement response appears as a general parenting phenomenon in an ordinary community. In our previous study, we offered several explanations and tried to test them indirectly by predicting different patterns of correlations among some of the measures used in the study. In this study, we have included measures of the constructs that seemed to provide the best explanations, and we use them to test the explanations directly.

In this study, then, we address several questions. The first is whether our earlier model of parents' responses to problem behavior will appear in a more age-heterogeneous population. The second is how parents and youths respond to each other over time. To answer this, we test a cross-lagged model using data from two time points. We also include gender in a multiple-groups analysis. Finally, we try with additional analyses to explain the mechanisms behind the links in the model.

METHOD

Participants

We used data from a longitudinal study of the development of criminality in adolescence that began in 2001. It was designed to build upon the most recent advances in the largely separate literatures on family, peers, and individual characteristics—assessing these factors simultaneously and testing an integrative theory about their combined effects on movements into and out of criminality in adolescence. Each year of the study we targeted nine cohorts (grades 4–12, or roughly ages 10 to 18). One new cohort came into the study each year (those entering the fourth grade) and one cohort left the study (those who graduated from high school the year before). Every second year parents received a questionnaire in the mail, and they participated by filling it out and returning it. Only parents of fourth through tenth graders were asked to participate, however, because many youths in eleventh and twelfth grades have reached the legal age of independence in Sweden (18), are living on their own, or both. In the analyses reported here, we use mainly parents' reports from Times 1 and 3 for youths who were in grades four through eight at Time 1 (ages 10 through 14), so that youths and their parents both participated at two time points.

At Time 1, we collected data from 1 641 youths (roughly 330 students in each grade, or 93 % of those registered in school). Two years later, we collected about the same information from 1 471 of these youths (90 % of the original subjects). The participants took part in the study unless their parents returned a form stating that they did not want their child to participate (1 % of the parents returned this form). Neither parents nor children were paid for their participation. At Time 1, 1 225 parents (75 %) responded. We did not ask parents to fill out separate questionnaires for all of their children if they had more than two. In that case, we randomly selected two and asked them about those. At Time 3, 77 % of the original 1 225 parents responded.

Measures

Delinquency

Youth-reported delinquency was measured with 21 questions about shoplifting; being caught by the police; vandalizing public or private property;

taking money from home; creating graffiti; breaking into a building; stealing from someone's pocket or bag; buying or selling stolen goods; stealing a bike; being in a physical fight in public; carrying a weapon; stealing a car; stealing a moped or motorcycle; using marijuana or hashish; and using other drugs. The alpha reliabilities were .92 and .93 at Times 1 and 3, respectively.

Negative behavior in the family

We formed a measure of the youths' negative behavior in the family as the mean of three scales: defiance, disclosure (reversed), and off-task behavior. *Defiance* was a three-item scale. Parents responded on 4-point Likert scales from "does not apply at all" to "applies exactly." The options were: "Often does things although we say several times that it is not allowed," "You often need to tell him/her several times when he/she has done something wrong to get him/her to stop," and "Usually it is sufficient to rebuke him/her one time to stop him/her from doing something that he/she is not allowed to do" (reversed). The scale had an alpha reliability of 0.82 at Time 1 and 0.83 at Time 3. *Disclosure* comprised five items. Parents reported on their child's disclosure of information about daily activities with items such as: "Does the child hide a lot from you about what he/she does during nights and weekends?" "Does the child talk at home about how he or she is doing in the different subjects at school?" and "Does the child keep a lot of secrets from you about what he or she is doing during his or her free time?" The alpha reliability was 0.81 at Time 1 and 0.78 at Time 3. *Off-task behavior* was an eight-item scale taken from a revised Strategy-Attribution Questionnaire (Nurmi, Salmela-Aro, & Ruotsalainen, 1994). Parents responded on a four-point scale from 1 (totally disagree) to 4 (totally agree). Some examples are: "It is too easy for him/her to think of other things, day dream or become lost in thought when he/she should concentrate on more important tasks," "He/she often finds other things to do when solving a difficult problem" and " If a hard task comes up, he/she quickly chooses to do something else." The alpha reliability at both times was 0.90. The mean intercorrelation among these three scales was 0.46, $p < 0.001$ (range $= 0.44$ to 0.49).

Parents' "gut-level" reactions

We used this label for emotionally tied reactions such as worries and distrust. Thus, gut-level reactions are the mean of two scales. *Worries* was a six-item scale. Parents responded to questions such as "Are you worried that the child will not make it in school?" "Are you worried that the child will end up in bad company?" and "Do you worry about what the child is doing together with friends on evenings and weekends?" The alpha reliability was 0.88 at both times. *Trust* (reversed) was a six-item scale. Parents responded to questions such as "Do you trust that your child does not enter into bad company?"

and "Do you trust that the child does not do anything dumb in his or her free time?" The alpha reliability for this scale was 0.80 at Time 1 and 0.81 at Time 3. The correlation between the two scales was 0.44 ($p < 0.001$).

Monitoring efforts

This measure was composed of the items from two scales—control and solicitation—which we developed previously to measure parents' active monitoring efforts (Kerr & Stattin, 2000). The scales tapped parents' efforts to keep track of the youth's whereabouts and associations by requiring the youth to do things such as check with parents before making plans to be out with friends (control) and by talking to the youth, the youth's friends, and the friends' parents in order to stay informed (solicitation). Five-point response scales were used. Five items that assessed *solicitation* were: "This month, have you been in contact with and talked to the parents of your child's friends?" "How often do you talk to the child's friends when they come over to your house (ask what they do, how they think and feel about different things)?" "During the past month, how often have you started a conversation with your child about his or her free time?" "How often do you ask the child to sit down and tell what has happened during an ordinary day in school?" and "Do you usually ask the child to tell about what happens in his or her free time (who he or she meets in town, leisure activities, etc.)?" Five items that tapped *control* were: "Does the child need to have your permission to stay out late on a weekday evening?" "Does the child need to ask you before he/she can decide with his/her friends what they will do on a Saturday evening?" "If the child has been out very late one night, do you require that he/she explains what he/she did and whom he/she was with?" "Do you always require that the child tells you where he/she has been at night, who he/she was with, and what they did together?" and "Before the child goes out on a Saturday night, do you require him/her to tell where he/she is going and with whom?" The alpha reliability for the 10-item monitoring efforts measure was –0.76 at Time 1 and 0.79 at Time 3.

Additional measures

Some additional measures were used to test follow-up questions. For ease of comprehension, their descriptions are integrated into the results section and presented just prior to the results where they are used.

Analyses

To examine associations between youths' behavior, such as delinquency and negative behavior at home, and parents' behavior, such as distrust, worry, and monitoring efforts, we performed structural path analyses with Mplus 4.0 (Muthén & Muthén, 2006). We also used multiple group analyses to examine the possible moderating effects of youths' gender and personality traits. For all analyses, we used full information maximum likelihood (FIML) because of missing data. The full information maximum likelihood techniques are thought to provide less biased estimates than listwise or pairwise deletion (Schafer & Graham, 2002), and are appropriate even when data are not missing at random or missing completely at random (Little & Rubin, 2002). The proportion of missing values may be calculated with a covariance "coverage" matrix. This provides an estimate of available observations for each pair of variables. The minimum recommended coverage is 0.10 (Muthén & Muthén, 2006). In this study, the coverage ranged from 0.71 to 0.94.

All structural models were evaluated using three goodness-of-fit indices: CFI (comparative fit index); RMSEA (root mean square error of approximation); and TLI (Tucker-Lewis index), also known as the Bentler-Bonett nonformed fit index. Comparative fit index and TLI values greater than 0.90 represent an adequate fit to the data (Bentler & Bonett, 1980); values greater than 0.95 suggest a good model fit (Hu & Bentler, 1998). Root mean square error of approximation values less than 0.08 represent reasonable errors of approximation; values less than 0.05 indicate a close model fit with the data (Browne & Cudeck, 1993).

RESULTS

Interrelations Among Variables

In Table 4.1, we present intercorrelations among the variables used in the main analyses. Above the diagonal are intercorrelations at Time 1 and below the diagonal are intercorrelations at Time 3.

Table 4.1 Intercorrelations among measures at time 1 (above the diagonal) and time 3 (below the diagonal)

		Parent-reported		
	Youth-reported delinquency	**Youth negative behavior**	**Parents' gut-level reactions**	**Parents' monitoring efforts**
Delinquency (YR)	–	0.23***	0.28***	−0.14***
Youth negative behavior (PR)	0.32***	–	0.56***	−0.34***
Parents' gut-level reactions (PR)	0.27***	0.46***	–	0.13***
Parents' monitoring efforts (PR)	−0.05	−0.27***	0.04	–

***$p < 0.001$; YR youth-reported; PR parent-reported

Parents' Reactions to Youth Delinquency

We ask, first, whether parents' reactions to delinquency and negative behavior at home in this sample of 10- to 14-year-olds are similar to what we found earlier in families of 14-year-olds. Here, we use parents' reports of all variables except delinquency, which is youth-reported, and we make assumptions about directionality in this model based on previous longitudinal findings (i.e., Kerr & Stattin, 2003). We started with a saturated model that contained as many parameter estimates as there were available degrees of freedom, and then removed paths that did not significantly contribute to the fit of overall model. The fit indices reported are for the model with nonsignificant paths removed. The results, shown in Figure 4.1, are remarkably similar to those found earlier for 14-year-olds. They show positive links between youth problem behaviors and parents' gut-level reactions (worry and distrust), with the link between negative behaviors at home and gut-level reactions being particularly strong. Thus, parents' worry and distrust are more tied to the problem behaviors they experience at home than to the youth's delinquency. As shown in Figure 4.1, gut-level reactions are weakly related to monitoring efforts, but the stronger associations with monitoring efforts are the negative links between them and youths' negative behaviors at home. The more defiance, secrecy, and off-task behavior youths show at home, the less parents tend to keep track of their comings and goings. In this model, monitoring efforts are not related to changes in delinquency over the next two years, but gut-level reactions predict increases in delinquency. In sum, we find strong concurrent associations

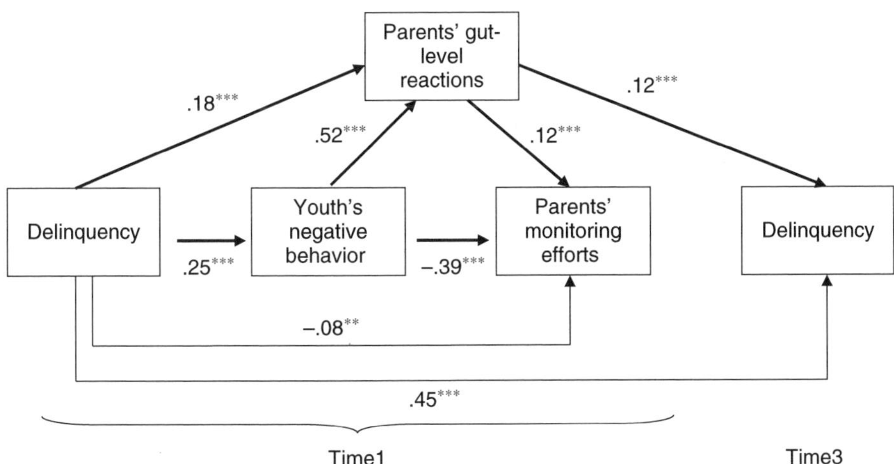

$\chi^2 = 4.480$, df = 2, $p = .105$, CFI = .998, TLI = .988, RMSEA = .027

Figure 4.1 A model of parents' reactions to youth delinquency and behaviors at home that correlate with delinquency

between youths' negative behavior at home and parents' gut-level reactions, which in turn, predict an increase over time in delinquency. The results also show that the more delinquent youths are and the more problematic they are at home, the fewer attempts parents make to track their movements away from home, but that is not related to a change in delinquency.

Reciprocal Effects Over Time

Apart from the inclusion of Time-3 delinquency in the model above, the data are cross-sectional. The directions assumed in the model were based on cross-lagged associations found in the earlier study (Kerr & Stattin, 2003) with one age cohort. To infer directions of effects in this more age-heterogeneous sample, we examined cross-lagged paths between all variables used in the previous model, controlling for stabilities over time and correlations between the variables within time. The model tested is shown in Figure 4.2. Again, we started with a saturated model and then removed paths that did not significantly contribute to the fit of overall model. The fit indices reported are for the model with nonsignificant paths removed.

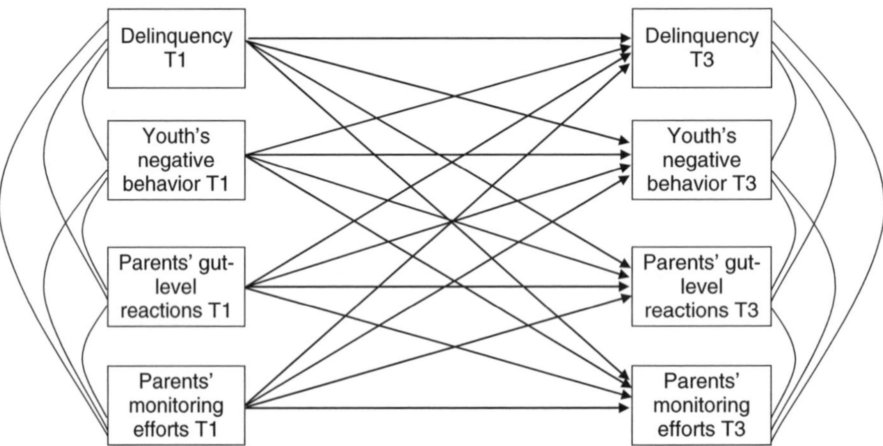

Figure 4.2 Model used to estimate change longitudinally

Children's and parents' behaviors were moderately stable over time (standardized path coefficients from 0.42 to of 0.52), and many of the cross-paths in the model were significant. The model fit was very good, $\chi^2 = 3.911$, d.f. = 3, $p = 0.270$, CFI = 0.999, TLI = 0.996, RMSEA = 0.013. For ease of interpretation, all significant cross-paths between youth behavior and parenting are presented in Figure 4.3. On the left side of the figure are the cross-paths predicting changes in parenting from youth behaviors. On the right side are paths predicting changes in youth behavior from parenting. The results in the left side of the figure suggest that parents react on the gut level (i.e., with distrust and worry) to negative (i.e., secretive, defiant, off-task) behavior at home. At the same time, in response to both negative behavior at home and the youth's delinquency, they make fewer efforts to track what the youth is doing away from home. That is, they relax the rules that would restrict the youth's movements and provide them with information, and they talk less to the youth and others to get information about the youth's whereabouts and associations away from home. All in all, then, it seems that when parents are faced with adolescent problem behaviors they react in ways that are unlikely to make the situation better. Thus, similar to what was suggested by the cross-sectional results, these longitudinal results show that the more problem behavior youths engage in, the more parents worry and distrust, and the less they monitor.

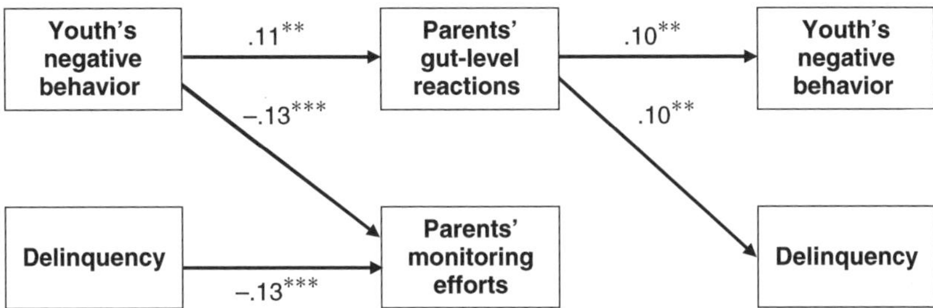

Figure 4.3 Significant cross paths between youth behaviors and parenting from longitudinal change model shown in Figure 4.2

Depicted in the right side of Figure 4.3 are the significant cross-paths from parenting to changes in youth behavior. Here, the only significant findings are for gut-level reactions. They predict increased negative behavior at home and delinquency over the following two years. Monitoring efforts are not significantly related to changes in problem behaviors. According to these results, then, it seems that in the normal course of events, a youth's problem behaviors do affect how parents act toward the youth, both in terms of emotional reactions and monitoring efforts, but it is only the emotional reactions that seem to have an effect on the youth.

Gender Differences in Changes Over Time

To determine whether these results generalize to boys and girls, we tested this change model for boys and girls with a multigroup analysis. Again, we started with saturated models and then removed paths that were nonsignificant for both groups. Paths that were nonsignificant for only one group were left in the model. Equal constraints in multiple group analyses were compared using χ^2 difference tests. The fit of the final model was very good, $\chi^2 = 3.382$, d.f. = 4, $p = 0.496$, CFI = 1.000, TLI = 1.000, RMSEA = 0.001. The cross-paths between youth behavior and parenting that were significant for either boys or girls appear in Figure 4.4. Although the similarities are striking, there are a couple of significant differences that emerged between boys and girls. First, one difference that is not shown in the figure that delinquency was more stable over time for boys than for girls (0.45 and 0.35, both $ps < 0.001$ for boys and girls, respectively). Second, as shown in the figure, a link from monitoring efforts to delinquency, which did not appear in the analyses combining boys and girls, now emerges and differs significantly between boys and girls. Monitoring efforts predict increases in boys' delinquency over the following two years, whereas they show a tendency ($p < 0.10$) to predict decreases in girls' delinquency. And parents' gut level reactions seem to affect boys' later delinquency significantly more than girls. Apparently, parents' gut-level reactions are part of an amplification of delinquency for boys and not girls, whereas low monitoring efforts might be part of an amplification of delinquency for girls but they are not for boys. In fact, for boys they seem to work in the opposite way, and for that we have no ready explanation.

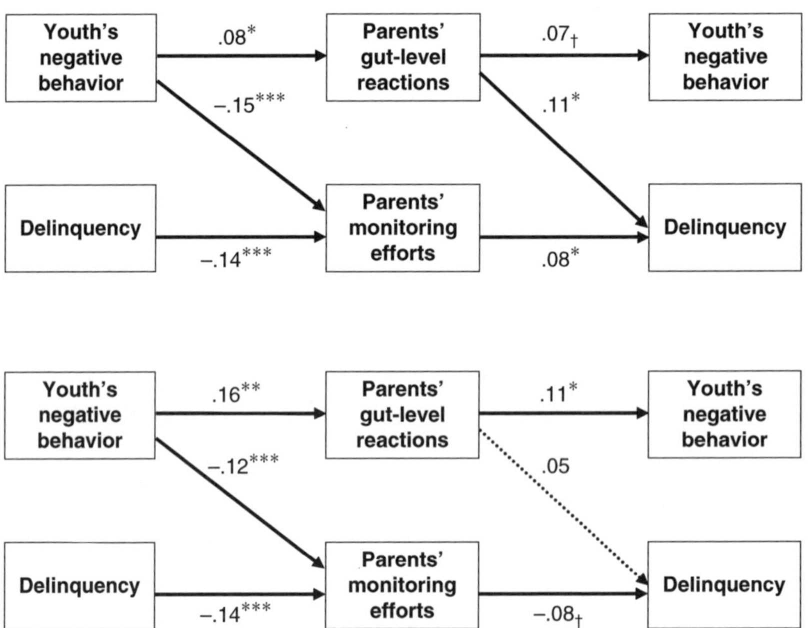

Figure 4.4 Significant cross paths between youth behaviors and parenting from multi-group analysis of longitudinal change—results for boys are in the upper panel and results for girls are in the lower panel

To summarize so far, youths' delinquency and negative behaviors seem to affect parents in different ways. Some seem reasonable but others are counter-intuitive. It is reasonable, for instance, to think that when a youth is defiant and secretive at home and has engaged in illegal acts, most parents would begin to worry and distrust the youth. These reactions are easy to understand. However, it is difficult to understand why most parents in an ordinary community sample would not try to take the situation in hand and monitor the youth's movements in order to limit the opportunities for further delinquency. They seem to do the opposite, and that is counterintuitive. Our goal is to understand why.

Why Do Parents Slacken Monitoring in the Face of Adolescent Problem Behavior?

We turn now to explaining why parents would slacken their monitoring efforts rather than increasing them when faced with adolescent problem behaviors such as being secretive about their whereabouts and activities, defying parents' requests and rules, and not concentrating on tasks such as school work. We propose and test three explanations.

Explanation one: parents believe the child needs autonomy

One explanation is that parents take their cues about the appropriate parenting actions from their children. They might interpret the youth's negative behavior at home as a signal that the youth has reached an age where he or she needs to be more autonomous, and they might not question this. Perhaps they then react by asking fewer questions about the youth's free time and slackening the rules that require the youth to give information in order to give the youth the autonomy that he or she seems to need. If so, then the youth's negative behavior at home should correspond to parents' attitudes about free time such that if youths are highly defiant and secretive parents should take this as a cue that their child is ready for them to back off, and they should believe that youths their child's age should be given much freedom and autonomy to decide what they do in their free time. To examine this, we looked at correlations between negative behavior and parents' attitudes about free time.

Parents' attitudes about youth free-time was a single-item measure that tapped parents' strict or lenient attitudes about whether youths should decide on their own free time activities. Parents were asked "What is your general attitude toward leisure time activities for someone your son's or daughter's age (leisure time activities means going out with friends, going to friends' houses or to town during evenings)?" They were asked to indicate which of four response options best fit their attitude: (1) At this age, parents must decide the child's leisure time activities. You should be able to demand to be told where children are going before they go out and that afterward, they tell you what they have done, where they have been and whom they have met (2) Parents should decide more than the child about children's leisure habits during this age. You should keep yourself informed on what is going on by asking on a regular basis. (3) Generally, you should let children do as they like. It is only when it is really needed that you should interfere. You should listen to what they tell you. (4) With children this age, you should absolutely let them do what they think is best. You should not interfere with what they do during leisure time; the children have to be able to do things without parents' insight.

These results appear in Table 4.2. We break them down by age because parents' attitudes about free time differ depending on the youth's age.

Table 4.2 Pearson correlations relating parents' attitudes about whether youths should govern their own free time with youth behavior and parents' monitoring efforts

	Correlations between parents' attitudes about youth free time and	
Approximate age (yrs)	**Negative behavior at home**	**Parents' monitoring efforts**
10	0.07	−0.17**
11	0.11	−0.26***
12	−0.04	−0.29***
13	−0.05	−0.27***
14	0.05	−0.19**

**$p < 0.01$; ***$p < 0.001$

In the first column of the table are the correlations between youths' negative behavior and parents' attitudes about free time. If the explanation is correct that parents are taking their cues from the youth's behavior about the amount of freedom that is appropriate for a youth their child's age, then these correlations should be positive and substantial. On the contrary, however, at every age the correlation between negative behavior and parents' attitudes about free time was nonsignificant and near zero. As shown in the other column of the table, parents' attitudes were linked to their actual monitoring behaviors, which suggests that their monitoring behaviors were consistent with their attitudes about how much autonomy youths should have in making decisions about their free time (the more freedom they think youths should have, the less they monitor). Thus, there is no evidence that parents take cues from the youth's negative behavior at home as a guide to what a normal level of independence should be for an adolescent of that age, so this explanation why parents reduce their monitoring in response to negative behavior at home is not supported by the data.

Explanation two: parents are intimidated

Another explanation why parents might slacken their monitoring efforts in response to a youth's secretive, defiant behavior is that they might be intimidated by the youth and reluctant to ask questions or try to enforce rules because these behaviors incite arguments. To the extent that this is so, controlling for intimidation should reduce the strength of the relation between youth negative behavior and parents' monitoring efforts. To examine this, we used parents' reports of how intimidated they were by their youth.

Intimidation was a five-item measure. The questions to parents were "Do you avoid taking up certain issues with your child due to bad experiences, e.g. how the child reacted earlier?" "Has it happened that you hesitated to set limits for the child since you know that the child will overreact?" "How often have you felt that it is better to avoid conflicts than to try to bring up certain things with the child?" "Has it happened the last month that you did not stick to certain rules for your child, since it would only leads to conflicts?" and "Do you feel like parenting sometimes is like walking on egg shells, since your child seems to react negatively to a majority of things you do?" Response scales ranged from (1) "no," to (5) "very often," or from (1) "has not happened" to (5) "happens all of the time." The alpha reliabilities were 0.80 and 0.82 at Times 1 and 3, respectively.

We predicted monitoring efforts from youth negative behavior in a multiple regression analysis in which we entered intimidation as a control. Parents' general attitudes about the youths' free time were entered as an additional control. The results appear in Table 4.3. Although intimidation is a significant predictor, the link between the youth's negative behavior at home and monitoring efforts remains substantial and significant. Thus, although intimidation seems to be one reason why parents reduce their monitoring efforts when faced with secretive, defiant, irresponsible youth behavior, it is in no way a complete explanation.

Table 4.3 Beta slopes from stepwise multiple regression models predicting parents' monitoring efforts

	Monitoring efforts beta
Step 1	
Negative behavior at home	-0.28^{***}
Step 2	
Parents' attitudes about youth free time	-0.24^{***}
Intimidation	-0.12^{***}
Negative behavior at home	-0.22^{***}

$^{***}p < 0.001$

Explanation three: parents respond to the youth

For a third explanation, we turn our focus to the other end of the distribution. We have been talking about secretive, defiant youth behavior and why parents react to that by reducing their monitoring efforts. At the same time, however, the results could be seen as suggesting that parents react to compliant, open youth behavior by maintaining or increasing their monitoring efforts. In other words, the relation between negative behaviors and monitoring could be explained, in part, by general social responses to the youth. For most of us, as we go about our everyday lives, when people show that they have no interest in talking to us, we tend to leave them alone, and when they are warm, open, and communicative, we tend to open up to them. Perhaps parents are doing a similar thing with their children. Perhaps when children are warm and open, parents respond by asking them a lot about their daily activities and generally keeping up with their friends and away-from-home activities. Conversely, perhaps if children are cold and closed, parents respond by leaving them alone much of the time. To test this idea, we performed a cluster analysis on two youth characteristics: warmth versus coldness and openness versus closedness.

We designed the measure of *youth warmth* to parallel what we ask youths about their parents' expressions of emotional warmth. We used four items. Parents were asked whether the child: "often says or does something nice without an obvious reason," "does small things to show tenderness (e.g., hugs, smiles)," "says that he or she is proud of us," and "shows that he or she likes us without a reason, almost regardless of what we do." Answers were given on a four-point scale ranging from (1) "does not apply at" all to (4) "applies exactly." The alpha reliability for the scale was 0.77 at Time 1 and 0.80 at Time 3.

With regard to *youth closedness*. The degree to which the youth seemed closed to parents' influence was measured with five items. Parents rated the following statements on a four-point scale ranging from (1) "does not apply at all," to (4) "applies exactly": "Our child keeps his/her feelings to him/herself when he/she is worried or upset." "Our child prefers to comfort him/herself." "Our child doesn't seem to think about keeping track of where he/she can reach us." Our child does not show who he/she really is." "Our child keeps his/her feelings to him/herself after we have been apart for a week or more." The alpha reliability for the scale was 0.78 at Time 1.

The results of the cluster analysis appear in Table 4.4. They show four clusters, which explain 64% of the total error sums of squares. The first three columns give the characteristics of the clusters. The largest, an "average" cluster, comprises youths who are near average on both variables. There is a "warm-open" cluster, consisting of youths who are high on warmth and open rather than closed, and a "closed" cluster, consisting of youths who are about average on warmth but highly closed. The smallest is a "cold-closed" cluster, comprising youths who are exceptionally low on warmth and exceptionally closed.

The last two columns in the table show mean monitoring efforts for these clusters both concurrently and two years later. As shown in the last two columns, parents' monitoring efforts seem to follow these youths' characteristics closely. Concurrently, monitoring efforts are highest for the warm-open

Table 4.4 Clusters of youths with different combinations of characteristics and their parents' monitoring over time

	Youth characteristics				
	Warm	**Closed**	*n*	**Monitoring efforts T1**[1]	**Change in monitoring T1 to T2**[2]
Warm-open	1.35	−0.97	192	0.44	0.17
Average	−0.05	−0.41	604	0.11	0.05
Closed	−0.11	1.13	248	−0.28	−0.15
Cold-closed	−1.70	1.29	118	−0.51	−0.10

[1] $F(3,1158) = 35.03$, $p < 0.001$
[2] $F(3,897) = 3.22$, $p = 0.02$

youths and lowest for the cold-closed youths. Then, over time, parents of the warm-open youths increase their monitoring relative to the rest of the sample and parents of the closed and cold-closed youths decrease their monitoring. Thus, it appears that parents' monitoring efforts are very much influenced by the youths' social signals. If youths are warm and open, parents seem to feel free to keep track of what they are doing. If they give signals that they do not want parents' involvement, parents seem to be reluctant to try to be involved.

DISCUSSION

What can parents do when they face parenting challenges such as having a child who defies socialization attempts or who begins to engage in delinquency? To get ideas about what parents *can* or might best do it is helpful to know what they typically do in these situations and how that seems to work out over time. In this study, we have shown that parents have predictable responses to delinquency and the secretive, defiant behavior at home that correlates with delinquency. Their strongest reactions seem to be to the behavior at home; the more secretive and defiant youths are, the more parents worry and distrust them and the less they monitor them. This slackening of monitoring seems to be primarily a normal, social response, in which parents respond to the youths' signals about how much involvement they want from parents. If youths are warm and open, parents stay involved by asking questions and keeping track of the youths' activities; if youths are cold and closed, parents back off.

We should keep in mind that there is a larger context that we have not tapped here. We did not include the contextual conditions that surround the family, the parents' marital relations, and parent, sibling, and peer characteristics that could have direct impacts on the way parents and youths act and react to each other. Nonetheless, our findings are revealing about processes inside the family, and this is one of few studies that provides this kind of information.

How do these findings fit with previous knowledge about parenting and adolescent problem behavior? Although there are few studies that have looked at parents' reactions to youth problems, there is some evidence in the literature that parents disengage emotionally or behaviorally in response to delinquency or deviant peers or both (e.g., Dishion, Nelson, & Bullock, 2004; Kerr & Stattin, 2003; Meeus, Branje, & Overbeek, 2004). What distinguishes our previous study (Kerr & Stattin, 2003) and this one from other studies in the literature is that we have tried to understand the mechanisms underlying these reactions. Do parents react to the delinquency itself or to the delinquent youth's behavior at home? Do their gut-level reactions lead them to slacken their monitoring efforts? What are the other possible explanations for their disengagement? In so doing, we have revealed that negative emotional reactions such as trust and worry seem to play a role in the amplification of delinquency. In contrast, we find no robust connections to delinquency for parents' monitoring efforts.

How can one explain the discrepancy between our finding that monitoring efforts play only a minor role in the amplification of problem behavior and the very large accumulated literature in which the strong conclusion is that monitoring is a critical factor? We believe that the main reason for the discrepancy is that there is little comparability between this study and the past literature. One reason for this is that the measures that are most commonly used in the literature do not measure parents' monitoring efforts. They measure parents' knowledge, but knowledge measures largely seem to tap the youth's willingness to give parents information (Kerr & Stattin, 2000; Stattin & Kerr, 2000). Obviously, a measure that represents the youth's willingness to provide information should have clear associations with problem behavior. It would be highly unlikely, for instance, for a delinquent youth to freely tell his or her parents a lot about what he or she is doing away from home (during the time when the delinquent acts are taking place). Knowing that most of parents' knowledge comes from the youth, it is difficult to conclude anything about parents' monitoring efforts from studies in which monitoring was operationalized as knowledge. A second reason this study is not comparable to most of the monitoring literature is that the bulk of those studies were either cross-sectional or considered only one direction of effects, with parents as the causal agents (e.g., Fletcher, Steinberg, & Williams-Wheeler, 2004). Thus, few studies have looked at how parents' monitoring changes in response to adolescent problem behaviors. At least one recent study has looked at this, but the measure of monitoring was parents' knowledge (Laird *et al.*, 2003), which again reveals little about parents' monitoring efforts. Thus, for these reasons, our results concerning monitoring efforts are not comparable to the past literature. Our findings do, however, suggest that a new literature on parental monitoring is needed—one that uses construct valid measures of parents' monitoring efforts and one that considers parents' reactions as well as their actions.

What is the mechanism linking parents' gut-level reactions with delinquency? Although we cannot bring any direct evidence to bear, we can offer a couple of speculations. One draws upon Hirschi's (1969) theory about the role of emotional attachment to parents in inhibiting delinquent behavior. The idea was that if youths are strongly attached to their parents they will not want to do anything such as engaging in delinquent behavior that would hurt or embarrass their parents. Hirschi suggested that when strongly attached youths face opportunities to commit delinquent acts, they actually think about their parents, and this psychological presence of their parents inhibits their behavior. One could imagine that if parents express their distrust, the youth might feel that there is little to lose in terms of disappointing parents and that might undermine the attachment mechanism, if it exists. Another possible explanation is a mechanism that we have called "context choice" (see Kerr *et al.*, 2003). In this line of reasoning, youths generalize feelings that arise from their interactions with parents to other situations that are structured and controlled by adults. If they feel valued and respected in their interactions with parents they will gravitate toward other adult-led structured settings because they elicit the same good feelings. If they feel unvalued, or perhaps distrusted, by parents at home, particularly if parents communicate their distrust in ways that make youths feel disrespected, they will gravitate toward situations that do not have the same negative emotions associated with them. These should be situations where adults are not present and do not influence youths' behaviors—situations that have been shown to put youths at risk for negative socialization by peers (e.g., Stattin *et al.*, 2005). In one recent test of the context choice idea, youths who reported negative feelings at home or who experienced negative parental treatment were less likely to join structured activities and were more likely to drop out of them and begin loitering on the streets (Persson, Kerr, & Stattin, 2007). Thus, there are at least two plausible theoretical explanations for the role that parents' gut-level reactions play in the escalation of delinquency. These await further testing.

What does this study say about attempts to manipulate parents' behaviors in order to prevent future problems or alleviate current problems? We started this chapter by saying that this is a study about what parents do in face of youth problems. It is not a study about what parents *can* do. We have examined what happens in families in a normal, community-wide sample, and we have used a longitudinal, correlational design. That is different from studies implementing and testing parenting interventions. At the same time, longitudinal studies are the first logical step to take when attempting to understand the complexities behind how parents and youths shape each others' behavior over time. Studies that use experimental manipulations have to be informed by longitudinal studies such as this. The findings reported here suggest some possible clues to prevention and intervention.

First, these findings suggest that asking parents to monitor more, per se, might not be the best preventive strategy. We do find marginally significant effects of monitoring efforts for girls, but not for boys. Patterson & Fisher

(2002) drew this same conclusion about monitoring as a limited single strategy for prevention. Second, our results suggest that prevention and intervention efforts must consider how parents react emotionally to the child and what they do with those emotions. Our findings suggest that parents' gut-level reactions to the child's negative behavior at home might escalate the risk for future delinquency. Third, our results suggest that whatever prevention and intervention efforts are used, they should aim to counterbalance the negative emotional effects that youth problem behaviors can have on parents.

In a broader sense, perhaps this whole area of enquiry has a lesson to teach. It is easy to let our research questions be guided by deeply rooted assumptions. This is perhaps never more true than in the parenting area, where large literatures such as the parenting styles literature have accumulated making bold, causal statements based on cross-sectional findings and longitudinal analyses that tested only one direction of effects—parent to child. Someone said that every time we as researchers test a hypothesis, we should also formulate and test the conceptual opposite hypothesis. We do not remember whom to credit with these wise words but we hope that we can remember to put them into practice in our own work.

REFERENCES

Anderson, K. E., Lytton, H., & Romney, D. M. (1986). Mothers' interactions with normal and conduct-disordered boys: Who affects whom? *Developmental Psychology, 22,* 604–609.

Archibald, A. B., Linver, M. R., Graber, J. A., & Brooks-Gunn, J. (2002). Parent-adolescent relationships and girls' unhealthy eating: Testing reciprocal effects. *Journal of Research on Adolescence, 12,* 451–462.

Bell, R. (1968). A reinterpretation of the direction of effects in studies of socialization. *Psychological Review, 75,* 81–95.

Bell, R. Q. & Chapman, M. (1986). Child effects in studies using experimental or brief longitudinal approaches to socialization. *Developmental Psychology, 22,* 595–603.

Bentler, P. M. & Bonett, D. G. (1980). Significance tests and goodness of fit in the analysis of covariance structures. *Psychological Bulletin, 88,* 588–606.

Browne, M. W. & Cudeck, R. (1993). Alternative ways of assessing model fit. In K. A. Bollen, & J. S. Long (eds), *Testing Structural Equation Models* (pp. 136–162). London: Sage.

Buist, K. L., Dekovic, M., Meeus, W., & van Aken, M. A. G. (2003). The reciprocal relationship between early adolescent attachment and internalizing and externalizing problem behaviour. *Journal of Adolescence, 27,* 251–266.

Buss, D. M. (1981). Predicting parent-child interactions from children's activity level. *Developmental Psychology, 17,* 59–65.

Chen, X., Liu, M., & Li, D. (2000). Parental warmth, control, and indulgence and their relations to adjustment in Chinese children: A longitudinal study. *Journal of Family Psychology, 14,* 401–419.

Dishion, T. J., Nelson, S. E., & Bullock, B. M. (2004). Premature adolescent autonomy: Parent disengagement and deviant peer process in the amplification of problem behaviour. *Journal of Adolescence, 27,* 515–530.

Dix, T., Ruble, D. N., Grusec, J. E., & Nixon, S. (1986). Social cognition in parents: Inferential and affective reactions to children of three age levels. *Child Development*, *57*, 879–894.

Fite, P. J., Colder, C. R., Lochman, J. E., & Wells, K. C. (2006). The mutual influence of parenting and boys' externalizing behavior problems. *Applied Developmental Psychology*, *27*, 151–164.

Fletcher, A. C., Steinberg, L., & Williams-Wheeler, M. (2004). Parental influences on adolescent problem behavior: Revisiting Stattin and Kerr. *Child Development*, *75*, 781–796.

Ge, X., Conger, R. D., Cadoret, R. J. *et al.* (1996). The developmental interface between nature and nurture: a mutual influence model of child antisocial behavior and parent behaviors. *Developmental Psychology*, *32*, 574–589.

Hastings, P. D. & Rubin, K. H. (1999). Predicting mothers' beliefs about preschool-aged children's social behavior: Evidence for maternal attitudes moderating child effects. *Child Development*, *70*, 722–741.

Hirschi, T. (1969). *Causes of Delinquency*. Berkeley: University of California Press.

Hu, L. & Bentler, P. M. (1998). Fit indices in covariance structure modeling: Sensitivity to underparameterized model misspecification. *Psychological Bulletin*, *3*, 424–453.

Huh, D., Tristan, J., Wade, E., & Stice, E. (2006). Does problem behavior elicit poor parenting? A prospective study of adolescent girls. *Journal of Adolescent Research*, *21*, 185–204.

Jang, S. J. & Smith, C. A. (1997). A test of reciprocal causal relationships among parental supervision, affective ties, and delinquency. *Journal of Research in Crime and Delinquency*, *34*, 307–336.

Kandel, D. B. & Wu, P. (1995). Disentangling mother-child effects in the development of antisocial behavior. In J. McCord (ed.), *Coercion and Punishment in Long term Perspectives* (pp. 106–123). New York: Cambridge University Press.

Kerr, M. & Stattin, H. (2000). What parents know, how they know it, and several forms of adolescent adjustment: Further evidence for a reinterpretation of monitoring. *Developmental Psychology*, *36*, 366–380.

Kerr, M. & Stattin, H. (2003). Parenting of adolescents: Action or reaction? In A. C. Crouter & A. Booth (eds) *Children's Influence on Family Dynamics: The Neglected Side of Family Relationships* (pp. 121–151). Mahwah, NJ: Lawrence Erlbaum.

Kerr, M., Stattin, H., Biesecker, G., & Ferrer-Wreder, L. (2003). Relationships with parents and peers in adolescence. In R. M. Lerner, M. A. Easterbrooks, & J. Mistry (eds) *Handbook of Psychology (Volume 6: Developmental Psychology)* (pp. 395–422). Hoboken, NJ: John Wiley & Sons.

Kochanska, G. (1998). Mother-child relationship, child fearfulness, and emerging attachment: A short-term longitudinal study. *Developmental Psychology*, *34*, 480–490.

Laird, R. D., Pettit, G. S., Bates, J. E., & Dodge, K. A. (2003). Parents' monitoring-relevant knowledge and adolescents' delinquent behavior: Evidence of correlated developmental changes in receprocal influences. *Child Development*, *74*, 752–768.

Little, R. J. A. and Rubin, D. B. (2002). *Statistical Analysis with Missing Data* (2nd edn). New York: John Wiley.

Lytton, H. (1990). Child and parent effects in boys' conduct disorder: A reinterpretation. *Developmental Psychology*, *26*, 683–697.

Lytton, H. (2000). Toward a model of family-environmental and child-biological influences on development. *Developmental Review*, *20*, 150–179.

Meeus, W., Branje, S., & Overbeek, G. J. (2004). Parents and partners in crime: a six-year longitudinal study on changes in supportive relationships and delinquency in adolescence and young adulthood. *Journal of Child Psychology and Psychiatry*, *45*, 1288–1298.

Mink, I. T. & Nihira, K. (1986). Family life-styles and child behaviors: A study of direction of effects. *Developmental Psychology*, *22*, 610–616.

Mulhern, R. K. Jr. & Passman, R. H. (1981). Parental discipline as affected by the sex of the parent, the sex of the child, and the child's apparent responsiveness to discipline. *Developmental Psychology, 17*, 604–613.

Muthén, L. K. & Muthén, B. O. (2006). Mplus users guide. Los Angeles, CA: Muthén & Muthén.

Nurmi, J.-E., Salmela-Aro, K., & Ruotsalainen, H. (1994). Cognitive and attributional strategies among unemployed young adults: A case of the failure-trap strategy. *European Journal of Personality, 8*, 135–148.

Passman, R. H. & Blackwelder, D. E. (1981). Rewarding and punishing by mothers: the influence of progressive changes in the quality of their sons' apparent behavior *Developmental Psychology, 17*, 614–619.

Patterson, G. R. & Fisher, P. A. (2002). Recent developments in our understanding of parenting: Bidirectional effects, causal models, and the search for parsimony. In M. H. Bornstein (ed.), *Handbook of Parenting: Vol. 5: Practical Issues in Parenting* (2nd edn, pp. 59–88). Mahwah, NJ: Lawrence Erlbaum Associates.

Persson, A., Kerr, M., & Stattin, H. (2007). Staying in or moving away from structured activities: explanations involving parents and peers. *Developmental Psychology, 43*, 197–207.

Reiss, D., Neiderhiser, J. M., Hetherington, E. M., & Plomin, R. (2000). *The Relationship Code: Deciphering Genetic and Social Influences on Adolescent Development*. Cambridge, MA: Harvard University Press.

Schafer, J. L. & Graham, J. W. (2002). Missing data: Our view of the state of the art. *Psychological Methods, 7*, 147–177.

Stattin, H. & Kerr, M. (2000). Parental monitoring: A reinterpretation. *Child Development, 71*, 1070–1083.

Stattin, H., Kerr, M., Mahoney, J. *et al.* (2005). Explaining why a leisure context is bad for some girls and not for others. In J. L. Mahoney, R. W. Larson, & J. S. Eccles (eds), *Organized Activities as Contexts of Development: Extracurricular Activities, After-school and Community Programs* (pp. 211–244). Mahwah, NJ: Erlbaum.

Stice, E. & Barrera, M. Jr. (1995). A longitudinal examination of the reciprocal relations between perceived parenting and adolescents' substance use and externalizing behaviors. *Developmental Psychology, 31*, 322–334.

CHAPTER 5

Vicissitudes of Parenting Adolescents: Daily Variations in Parental Monitoring and the Early Emergence of Drug Use

Thomas J. Dishion and Bernadette Marie Bullock
University of Oregon Child and Family Center, USA
Jeff Kiesner
Dipartimento di Psicologia DPSS, Università di Padova, Italy

INTRODUCTION

During the past century a considerable amount of research attention was paid to the role of parenting practices in general, and parental supervision in particular, in the development of problem behavior in adolescence (e.g., Hawkins & Catalano, 1992; Loeber & Dishion, 1983; McCord, 1979; Wilson, 1980). It was not until family therapy techniques were increasingly used

We gratefully acknowledge Cheryl Mikkola's editorial support for this study. In addition, this research was supported by the following grants: DA07031 and DA018374, both from the National Institutes of Health.

What Can Parents Do? New Insights into the Role of Parents in Adolescent Problem Behavior
Edited by Margaret Kerr, Håkan Stattin and Rutger C. M. E. Engels.

that questions of measurement and change of parenting behaviors became of interest (Haley, 1971; Minuchin, 1974). In the early 1980s Patterson coined the term *parent monitoring* after having worked with families struggling to manage their child's problem behavior, and as a potential target of measurement to guide future prevention and treatment efforts (Patterson, 1982; Patterson & Stouthamer-Loeber, 1984). Since then a great deal of empirical research has documented the empirical covariation between parental monitoring practices, child problem behavior, and health outcomes (Chilcoat & Anthony, 1996; Chilcoat, Dishion, & Anthony, 1995; Dishion & McMahon, 1998; Duncan *et al.*, 1998; Pettit *et al.*, 1999; Steinberg, Fletcher, & Darling, 1994). Although the construct of parental monitoring has promise for socialization theories and for prevention science, the measurement and conceptual underpinnings of parental monitoring are currently an issue of debate and empirical investigation.

PAST RESEARCH

In early research on parental monitoring, Patterson & Stouthamer-Loeber (1984) tested the roles of parental monitoring, parental discipline, problem solving, and reinforcement in the extent of youth delinquency and number of police contacts. The multiple indicator construct of parental monitoring was found to explain 2.5 times more variance in number of police contacts and involvement in delinquent lifestyle than did any of the other family management practices. Moreover, only the monitoring construct could differentiate between chronic and moderate police-recorded offenders.

Following this early work, a mechanism was proposed to explain how poor monitoring could lead to increased delinquency. Specifically, it was suggested that inadequate parental monitoring was especially problematic when the child or adolescent associated with delinquent peers (Dishion & Loeber, 1985; Snyder, Dishion, & Patterson, 1986). Using longitudinal data, Dishion *et al.* (1991) showed that poor parental monitoring at child age 10 significantly predicted deviant peer affiliation at age 12, after controlling for antisocial behavior, peer social preference, academic skills, and parental discipline (all of which also significantly predicted age 12 deviant peer affiliation). This pattern of results has been replicated across four US ethnic samples that include American Indians, Latinos, African Americans, and European Americans (Barrera *et al.*, 2001).

It would seem logical that parental monitoring and supervision would be most important in neighborhoods with high rates of criminal activity. Wilson (1980) found that parental supervision had a protective effect in the highest risk neighborhoods in London. In a more recent study examining social contextual factors (e.g., concentrated poverty) in relation to parenting behaviors, delinquent peer affiliation, and youth outcomes, Chung & Steinberg (2006) also found that neighborhood characteristics had direct effects on parenting behaviors and incidence of peer deviance, and that parenting had only an indirect effect on youth criminal offending, passing through peer deviance. Although the data presented were cross-sectional, this study provides further support for the hypothesis that parental monitoring serves a protective function against negative peer influence, and that these effects are likely to be most relevant in high-risk neighborhoods.

Of course, some adolescents are more difficult to supervise than are others. Stoolmiller (1990) defined *wandering* as a critical transition into adolescent deviance. This adolescent behavior involves avoiding adult supervision by not returning home on time and by maintaining secrecy about activities. Thus, reciprocal effects between parenting and adolescent problem behaviors are assumed to converge in determining long-term outcomes. For example, Laird and colleagues found that youth antisocial behavior predicted a deterioration in parent–child relationships, which in turn resulted in less parental monitoring of the child's whereabouts (Laird *et al.*, 2005), and that youth delinquency and parental knowledge showed reciprocal cross-lag effects over four annual assessments (Laird *et al.*, 2003). Similar findings were suggested in research by Stoolmiller (1990), in that antisocial youth tended to pull themselves out of the purview of supervising adults and actually became more difficult to monitor as they became more deviant.

It would also seem true that youth involved in problem behavior would be less willing to share and discuss their daily activities with parents, given a concern for avoiding parental scrutiny. The reality of such "child effects" is consistent with the inclusion of the youth's unsolicited disclosure measure by Kerr & Stattin (2000) as a key indicator of the reciprocal parent–child monitoring process. It was hypothesized and confirmed that adolescents' voluntary communication was as relevant to problem behavior as parents' knowledge of the youths' activities and whereabouts, efforts to solicit information, or control adolescent behavior.

This issue of child effects in the monitoring process in general and in communication in particular is reminiscent of the earlier work by Stoolmiller (1990) about adolescent wandering. As youth become more engaged in a deviant peer group, they actively pull away from adult efforts to track, monitor, and influence their behavior. The most succinct longitudinal test of this hypothesis is the study by Patterson (1993) that showed discipline and monitoring to be most predictive of the average level (intercept) of adolescent problem behavior, and wandering and associating with deviant peers predicted growth in problem behavior in adolescence.

Clearly, developmental researchers are converging on a pattern of findings that acknowledges the importance of both child effects and parenting behaviors in a process that could be referred to as *monitoring*. The interpretative challenge, however, is the divergent intensities of measurement, analytic strategies used, and samples of adolescents. We have developed a strategy that we refer to as *model building* that provides a framework for considering a complex set of issues related to questions such as the role of parenting in the etiology of problem behavior (Dishion & Patterson, 1999; Patterson, Reid, & Dishion, 1992). The goal of this pragmatic and quantitative approach is to account for variations in adolescent problem behavior.

The first step is to define and test the validity of a nomological network of constructs such as parenting by using multiple measurement methods (e.g., Campbell & Fiske, 1959; Cronbach & Meehl, 1955). The second step is to establish the predictive validity of constructs that are shown to be reliable and valid. The third step is to intervene on the causal variables to determine if changes in problem behavior ensue.

Without establishing the empirical foundation of the nomological network, it is difficult to know whether or not a set of findings is "misspecified." In a technical sense, a misspecified model is one in which a key construct is missing. Occlusion of important theoretical constructs in a multivariate model leads to overestimation of the effects of the construct included in the model. For example, examining the role of parental monitoring without considering the role of deviant peer involvement might lead to an oversimplified model and an overestimation of the effects of parental monitoring. Indeed, we found that the effect of parental monitoring (multiagent–multimethod measure) on youth early drug use dropped to zero after entering in the effect of deviant peer involvement. As one might suspect, the correlation between deviant peers and parental monitoring was 0.75 ($p < 0.0001$).

With regard to measurement, Dishion, Burraston, & Li (2002) examined the domain of family management (monitoring, limit setting, relationship quality, positive reinforcement, and problem solving) using a mulitagent–multimethod approach to confirmatory factor analysis. The approach to the analysis is summarized in Figure 5.1. Each construct was measured by parent report, youth report, and direct observation. Surprisingly, after estimating both method and trait factors, the model fitted the data well. Of considerable interest, however, was that the measurement method accounted for approximately 50 % of the variation in the indicators of parenting, much more than that accounted for by the parenting traits of interest themselves. This humbling empirical exercise revealed that much of what we get when we measure parenting is method variance, a conclusion reached by other researchers of parenting practices who have relied more exclusively on direct observations of parenting practices (Reid, 1978).

The second methodological hurdle in the analysis of bidirectional effects in the socialization process is analysis of longitudinal effects, which is not a trivial problem. At a minimum, it is important to control for a child's behavior at Time 1 when using a specific indicator of parenting behavior to account for a child's behavior at Time 2. Most developmental research is aware of this problem, and this minimal criterion is often met. However, much of the research on parental monitoring, oddly, is correlational and does not include longitudinal data. This problem is complicated in two ways: First, adolescence is a time of change, and one can expect some behaviors to increase and others to decrease. For problem behaviors such as substance use, an increase during

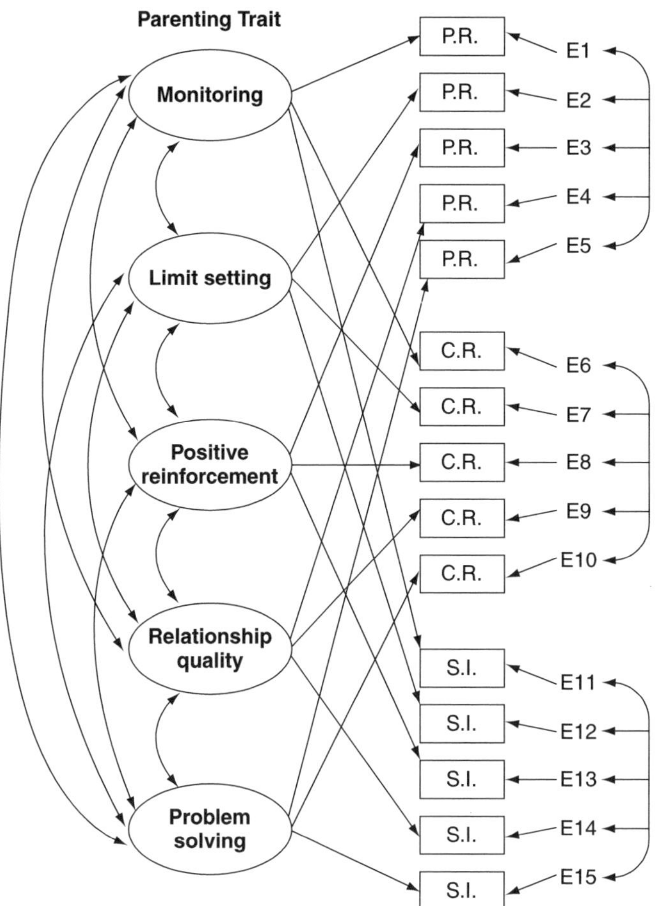

Figure 5.1 A multimethod–multitrait approach to the analysis of the validity of parenting constructs

Source: From Dishion, T. J. & Medici Skaggs, N. (2000). An ecological analysis of monthly "bursts" in early adolescent substance use. *Applied Developmental Science*, 4, 89–97.

adolescence is often observed, which provides a poor prognosis for long-term adjustment (Robins & Przybeck, 1985). Other behaviors, such as aggression and violence, are found to decrease through adolescence (e.g., Dishion *et al.*, 1997). It is important to account for the slope of change when considering the contribution of a parenting practice to adolescent adjustment. One would expect, for example, parental monitoring to account for changes in behaviors such as drug use from early to middle adolescence, and not merely change as measured in two points of time.

For example, Dishion, Nelson, & Bullock (2004) analyzed the longitudinal data of the Oregon Youth Study to define a process called *premature autonomy*.

From age 9 to 18, early-starting antisocial boys and successful boys were compared. It was found that in early adolescence, the parents of the early-starting boys disengaged from family management and monitoring, compared with those of successful boys, and that the negative effects of affiliating with deviant peers was most pronounced for boys whose parents decreased their family management practices. This study emphasizes the importance of considering how parent and peer effects interact and the importance of considering slopes of change as outcomes and predictors, rather than considering single time points.

There are major advantages of a model-building approach to understanding the relations between parental monitoring practices and adolescent problem behavior. First, model building affords the ability to evaluate the nomological network of constructs using multiple measurement strategies (Campbell & Fiske, 1959; Cronbach & Meehl, 1955; Dwyer, 1983). Several statistical innovations to structural equation modeling are particularly relevant to the study of longitudinal change in adolescence, all of which are based in latent growth curve modeling.

With innovations in the analysis of longitudinal change by use of latent growth curve modeling comes an improved ability to understand the role of parenting in predicting problem behavior. As discussed earlier, analyses can be conducted that differentiate factors that account for overall levels of problem behavior from those that predict change, as measured by (linear, quadratic, cubic) slope scores. Above we discussed two sets of findings that suggest it is the adolescents' time with peers without adult guidance that predicts growth in problem behaviors such as drug use (Dishion, Nelson, & Bullock, 2004; Patterson, 1993).

Finally, much of the work on parental monitoring has not emphasized a tight link between the actual measures and the construct being measured (Kerr & Stattin, 2000). Indeed, many of the actual behaviors assumed to be key to parental monitoring (such as tracking, etc.) are often not measured. Instead, scales are used that measure the potential effects of monitoring, such as "knowledge." Although some progress has been made in the measurement of parental monitoring by differentiating behaviors such as communication from solicitation by parents and the like, more work is needed if we wish to truly specify the day-to-day "vicissitudes" of parenting adolescents and, more important, produce knowledge that might actually be helpful to parents and clinicians so they can improve their practices when needed.

One strategy developed years ago is to move away from psychological scales, often designed to measure personality traits, and to assess more-specific behaviors within a specific time frame, for example, on a given day. The measurement of states and behaviors was an important contribution from behavior therapy, falling under the rubric *behavior assessment*. In our research we selected specific daily behaviors that we saw as tightly linked to a parent's ability to monitor an adolescent, considering the detailed discussions of the conceptual and methodological issues developed in the literature (e.g., Dishion & McMahon, 1999; Kerr & Stattin, 2000). Specifically, we examined daily reports of supervision of time spent with peers, communication about activities, affection, and shared family meals.

THE PRESENT STUDY

In this chapter we take a different approach to the analysis of parenting practices used when adolescents are exhibiting problem behavior. First, we examined parenting as it occurs on a daily basis, which reduces the need for informants such as parents and youth to recall and infer behaviors that unfold over longer time periods. Specifically, we used a telephone interviewing technique referred to in previous research as the Parent Daily Report (PDR) (Chamberlain & Reid, 1991). For this study, we collected reports of behavior from both the parent and the youth. Example questions include, "In the past 24 hours, how many hours were you with friends, unsupervised by adults?" or to the parent, "In the past 24 hours, how many hours was your child with friends, unsupervised by adults?" We asked youths several questions such as these at ages 12, 13, 14, and 15 years. A sample of adolescents at high risk and their parents were telephoned at least five times at each wave of data collection (at baseline, 3 months postintervention, and 1, 2, and 3 years after baseline). We used these data to create construct scores that summarized the parents' and adolescents' daily behavior.

Second, to examine the change in these behaviors over time we used time-sensitive analytic techniques generally referred to as *latent growth curve modeling* (Curran, 1993; Muthén & Muthén, 2004; Stoolmiller, 1995). Specifically, we tested hypotheses regarding the specific effects of daily monitoring (hours unsupervised), communication (talking about the day's activities), communality (eating meals together), and affection (hugs, kisses, and expressions of affection) as related to the adolescents' level of drug use.

METHOD

Sample and Design

The original 224 participants in this longitudinal study included 111 boys and 113 girls. Family participation was elicited through several sources, including newspaper advertisements, community flyers, school counselors, and other community professionals. A telephone interview was conducted with potential participants. Parents were asked to report on 10 areas of early adolescent risk for poor adjustment; those who reported the current presence of at least four of these risk factors were accepted as participants (Dishion & Andrews, 1995). Dishion *et al.* (1996) provide the details of these intervention outcomes and recruitment procedures. Recruiting the first sample of youth involved using newspaper ads to solicit families who had concerns about their teenagers. The second phase of recruitment was entirely through public middle schools, with letters sent to parents by way of school principals. In terms of the recruitment source, differences among the families were negligible (Dishion *et al.*, 1996) with respect to family demographics and young adolescents' adjustment, as indicated on both teacher and parent versions of the Child Behavior Checklist (CBCL; Achenbach, 1991).

At the beginning of this study, the 224 participants ranged in age from 10 to 14 years and were predominantly (90 %) European American (see Table 5.1 for full demographics). Baseline and termination assessments were completed on all families. Dishion & Andrews (1995) reported the short-term outcome of the intervention program and found effects for the Parent and Teen Focus interventions: Reductions in negative parent–child interactions, in reports of family conflict, and in teacher ratings of antisocial behavior. Parent reports of their children's aggressive behavior showed reductions across all intervention conditions, as did child and parent telephone interviews.

Table 5.1 Family demographics of study participants*

Average age (years)	12.2
Percentage single-parent households	42.9
Percentage two-parent stepfamilies	36.2
Percentage intact, two-parent families	21.0
Percentage receiving financial assistance	48.2
Percentage annual income of less than $20 000	60.0
High school graduate	
Percentage mothers	80.0
Percentage fathers	74.0
Percentage both parents, college graduate	17.0

Note * N = 224.

Telephone Interviews

Telephone interviews that asked specific questions about experiences in the previous 24 hours were administered to one parent and the target child. Parents and youth were interviewed on an average of five occasions at baseline, at three months after the intervention, and one, two, and three years after baseline. The telephone interviewing protocol is described in previous research (Chamberlain & Reid, 1987). The telephone interviews are highly structured, minimize incidental conversation, and take approximately 10–15 minutes to complete. The majority of the questions require a yes/no response or estimation of hours. The interviews with both the parent and youth are confidential in that efforts are made to ensure the privacy of each respondent.

Because this was a sample at high risk that included families who were undergoing multiple stressors, scheduling and ensuring cooperation with the monthly telephone interviews was challenging. Difficulties we encountered included families moving out of town, lack of phone access, youth who changed residences (e.g., those in divorced families), children who ran away from home or who were institutionalized, and youngsters and families who refused to continue participation.

Families were included in the current analyses if both the parents and child(ren) completed at least two telephone interviews within two weeks of one another at each wave of data collection. For the current study, 223 out of 224 families completed telephone interviews at baseline, 187 at termination, 147 at one-year follow-up, 152 at two-year follow-up, and 118 at three-year follow-up. Six constructs (four parenting constructs and two dependent variables) were formed from the daily reports of both the youth and parent.

- *Substance use*. This score consisted of the average number of "yes" responses concerning youth use of tobacco, alcohol, marijuana, or other substances in the past 24 hours. Responses of the parents and their youth were combined to develop a multiagent dependent variable.
- *Arrests*. The juvenile court records were searched for each child in the study to determine the number of police contacts up to the three-year follow-up. Police contacts were defined as any arrest for misbehavior (not parental neglect), regardless of the court adjudication. The measure of police contacts is a measure of the youth's problem behavior as detected or perceived by the police.
- *Friends' drug use*. The parents and their children were asked if, during the past 24 hours, the youngster had associated with friends who smoked tobacco, drank alcohol, or used marijuana.
- *Unsupervised time*. Parents and youth both were asked, "In the past day, how many hours did you spend with friends, unsupervised by adults?" This item assesses the extent to which the parent makes active efforts to structure the time and track the activities of the young adolescent, especially activities with peers. The correlation between parent and youth reports of the average number of hours reported unsupervised was the following for each of the follow-up probes: 0.50 at baseline, 0.46 at termination, 0.63 at the one-year follow-up, 0.79 at the two-year follow-up, and 0.80 at the three-year follow-up.
- *Communication*. Parents and youth both were asked, "In the past day, did you talk about the day's activities?" The average number of "yes" responses was averaged over the total number of interviews for each phase. The correlation between the youth and parent report was the following for each of the follow-up probes: 0.20 at baseline, 0.21 at termination, 0.30 at the one-year follow-up, 0.29 at the two-year follow-up, and 0.43 at the three-year follow-up.
- *Affection*. Parents and youth both were asked, "In the past day, did the parent hug or kiss the child?" The number of "yes" responses was averaged over the total number of interviews for each phase to render a score

reflecting the average level of physical affection shown that day. The correlation between the youth and parent report was the following for each of the follow-up probes: 0.41 at baseline, 0.46 at termination, 0.53 at the one-year follow-up, 0.47 at the two-year follow-up, and 0.60 at the 3-year follow-up.
- *Family meals.* Parents and youth both were asked, "In the past day, did you have a meal together?" The average number of "yes" responses was averaged over the total number of interviews for each phase to render a score reflecting the average level of family meals for that phase. The correlation between the youth and parent report was the following for each of the follow-up probes: 0.42 at baseline, 0.41 at termination, 0.62 at the one-year follow-up, 0.62 at the two-year follow-up, and 0.39 at the three-year follow-up.

Data Analysis

There were two phases to the data analyses. The first phase established the nomological network of the four parenting constructs with respect to the convergent validity of youth and parent report, as well as the covariation among the constructs when a confirmatory factor analysis is used. The second phase involved the analysis of predictive validity. First, we simply examined the level of covariation between the parenting constructs and the following indices of youth adjustment as measured for each observation phase: arrests, drug use, and friend drug use. For the constructs showing the highest levels of predictive validity, we examined the covariation between change in the parenting dynamics and changes in adolescent drug use. The Mplus program (Muthén & Muthén, 2004) for structural equation modeling was used for these analyses, and data imputation was used to address issues of missing data.

RESULTS

Convergent Validity

The first step in the analyses was to examine the convergent validity of the four parenting constructs. In general, youth and parent reports showed modest to high levels of convergent validity for each construct. The lowest levels of convergent validity were found for the communication construct; however, the correlation between youth and parent reports was statistically reliable. The highest level of convergent validity was observed for the youth and parent report of unsupervised hours with friends, which reached 0.80 at the three-year follow-up.

The number of youth hours unsupervised increased from early to middle adolescence, and the average number of times families had meals together decreased. The analyses of communication and affection were more complicated. Contrary to expectation, the average number of days youth talked with parents about their daily activities increased modestly from early to middle adolescence. Interestingly, the probability of displays of physical affection decreased sharply from baseline to termination (0.80 to 0.60), but remained stable thereafter.

Confirmatory factor analysis at baseline was conducted to examine the covariation among the four parenting constructs. The results of this structural equation model are shown in Figure 5.2. The *a priori* model was not a particularly outstanding fit to the data; however, there were no post hoc fitting adjustments to the overall model (e.g., measurement error covariation and the like). The key point of the model was to determine the viability of the measurement model. By and large, both youth and parent report converged for all of the constructs. Communication was most highly correlated with affection (0.78, $p < 0.001$), and affection and family meals were highly correlated (0.73, $p < 0.001$). Surprisingly, the unsupervised construct was uncorrelated with communication and family meals, suggesting that a fair number of parents

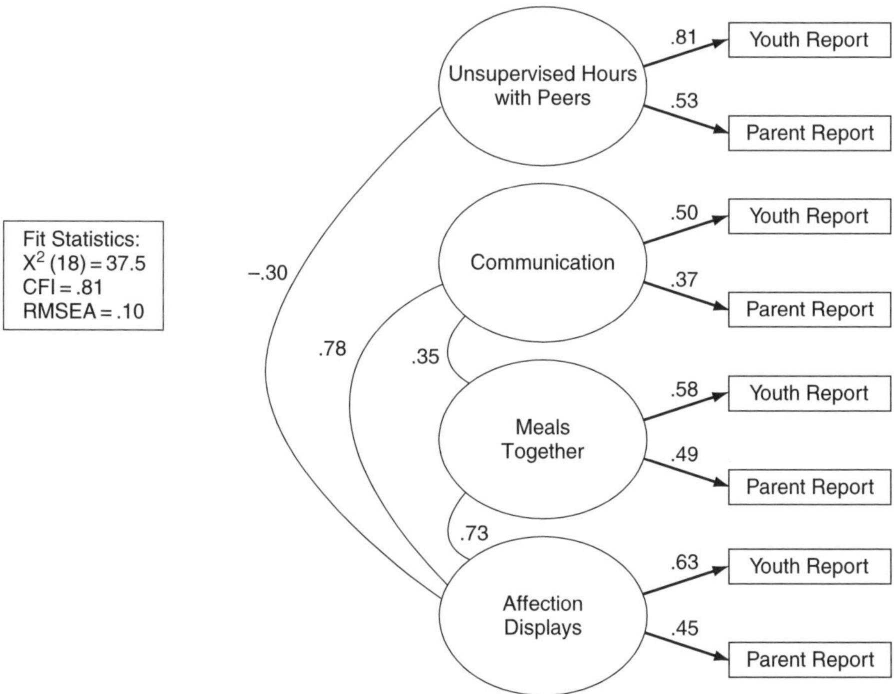

Figure 5.2 A confirmatory factor analysis of youth and parent report of daily parenting practices

discussed daily activities with their adolescents and the families had meals together, but nonetheless, allowed ample amounts of unsupervised free time with friends. Unsupervised was modestly correlated with lower levels of affection (−0.33, $p < 0.001$), suggesting a tendency toward supervision and emotional withdrawal.

Predictive Validity

Tables 5.2 and 5.3 provide the bivariate correlations between each of the four measures of parenting and adolescent drug use and police contacts, respectively. The correlations in Table 5.2 are concurrent and reflect the correlation between each parenting practice and drug use at each specific time. The correlations in Table 5.3 represent the correlation between each parenting construct and youth arrests through the follow-up period. Perusal of the correlations reveals that correlations between adolescent drug use and unsupervised time are quite high at all age points, ranging from 0.28 in early adolescence ($p < 0.05$) to 0.56 ($p < 0.001$) in middle adolescence. It is interesting to note that in addition, modest correlations were observed between family meals and adolescent drug use, ranging from −0.13 to −0.38 ($p < 0.05$) and reflecting a tendency for youth to use drugs when there was a low probability of conjoint

Table 5.2 Correlation between composite measures of daily parenting and adolescent drug use

Drug Use	**Unsupervised**	**Communication**	**Affection**	**Family meals**
Baseline (222)	0.28*	0.06	−0.13*	−0.13*
Termination (194)	0.32*	−0.11	−0.13	−0.23*
1-year FU(167)	0.31*	−0.04	−0.14	−0.38*
2-year FU (152)	0.56*	0.06	−0.26*	−0.22*
3-year FU (143)	0.53*	−0.14	−0.11	−0.06

Note FU = follow-up; * = $p < 0.05$

Table 5.3 Correlation between composite measures of daily parenting and youth arrests

Arrests (0,1,2)	**Unsupervised**	**Communication**	**Affection**	**Family meals**
Baseline (222)	0.20*	−0.11	−0.156*	−0.06
Termination (194)	0.25*	0.01	−0.09	−0.09
1-year FU (167)	0.32*	−0.05	−0.22*	−0.10
2-year FU (152)	0.15*	0.02	−0.11	0.07
3-year FU (143)	0.22*	0.04	−0.21*	−0.06

Note. FU = follow-up; * = $p < 0.05$

family meals. Affection and communication were virtually uncorrelated with adolescent drug use.

Similar findings were observed when we examined parenting with respect to youth arrests. Unsupervised time was by far the highest correlate of arrests among the four parenting constructs, compared with communication, affection, and family meals. However, there was some evidence linking the lack of affection displays to arrests in early and middle adolescence.

The next set of analyses involves the prediction of change in drug use. The first step in this analysis was to test a model for growth in substance use. Because substance use is typically covert and hidden from parents, we relied exclusively on youth report of substance use for this model. As can be seen in Figure 5.3, the overall latent growth curve model fit the data reasonably well. The intercept and the slope parameters were statistically reliable ($p < 0.05$), indicating significant variability in growth in self-reported substance use. The model fit was reliable ($p > 0.05$), with CFI = 0.99 and RMSEA = 0.08. Thus, there is reason to model the covariation between changes in parenting and adolescent self-reported drug use. A similar model was run and fit the data describing friend drug use (CFI = 0.99, RMSEA = 0.02), which was a construct defined by both parent and youth report.

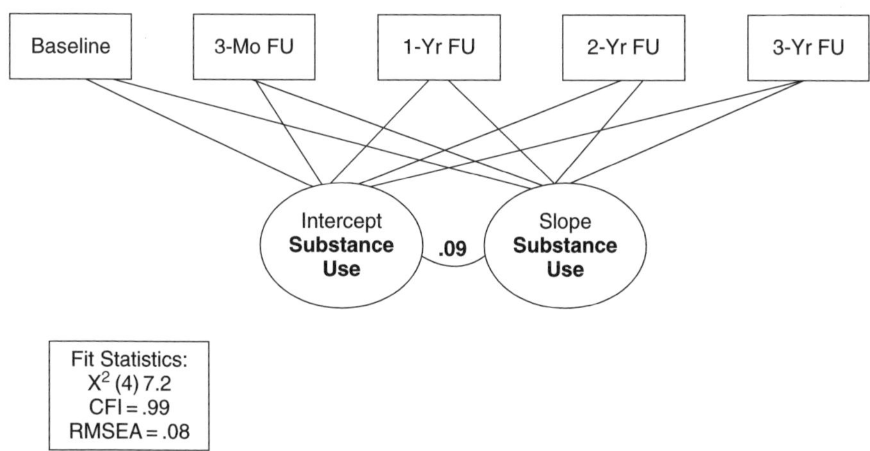

Figure 5.3 A latent growth model of drug use from early to middle adolescence

Because of the strong covariation between unsupervised hours and adolescent drug use, we tested a causal model showing that both the intercept and growth in unsupervised hours covaried with intercept and growth in adolescent drug use. This model is shown in Figure 5.4. This model showed a reasonable fit to the data (CFI = 0.96, RMSEA = 0.07). The intercept (average overall level) of the youths' hours spent unsupervised with friends was prognostic of the average overall level of drug use ($\beta = 0.42$, $p < 0.05$). In addition, the average overall growth in the youths' unsupervised time with peers predicted growth in adolescent drug use ($\beta = 0.63$, $p < 0.05$). These data suggest that the success or nonsuccess of parents' efforts to structure and track the activities of their adolescents (i.e., monitor) were prognostic of the emergence and growth of drug use in adolescence.

The most conservative test of the hypothesis that changes in parenting are associated with changes in adolescent drug use involves the testing of the parenting effect against that of peer exposure. Figure 5.5 examines the effect of degradation in parental monitoring and growth in drug use, controlling for friend drug use. As can be seen in Figure 5.5, increases in unsupervised time were highly prognostic of increased drug use, controlling for growth in friend drug use ($\beta = 0.8$, $p < 0.01$). However, increases in unsupervised time were also associated with increases in exposure to friends who use substances, as one might expect ($\beta = 0.62$, $p < 0.05$).

The same test was computed for arrests by age 15–16. Again, unsupervised time increased the probability of arrests, controlling for growth in friend drug use ($\beta = 0.2$, $p < 0.05$). However, the effect was much less strong and, paradoxically, having drug-using friends had a negative effect on the probability of arrests, which was the opposite of the expected finding (see Figure 5.6).

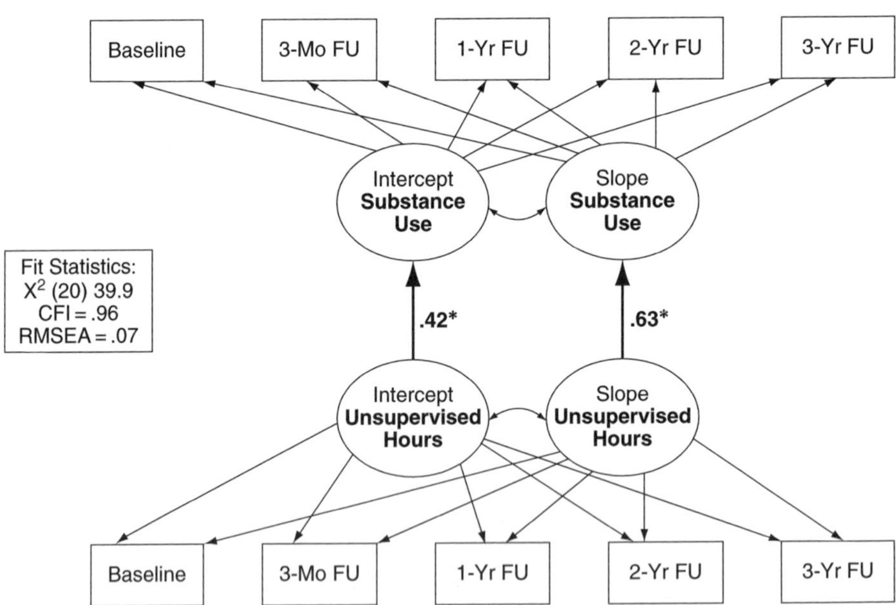

Figure 5.4 The predictive validity of unsupervised time to growth in adolescent drug use

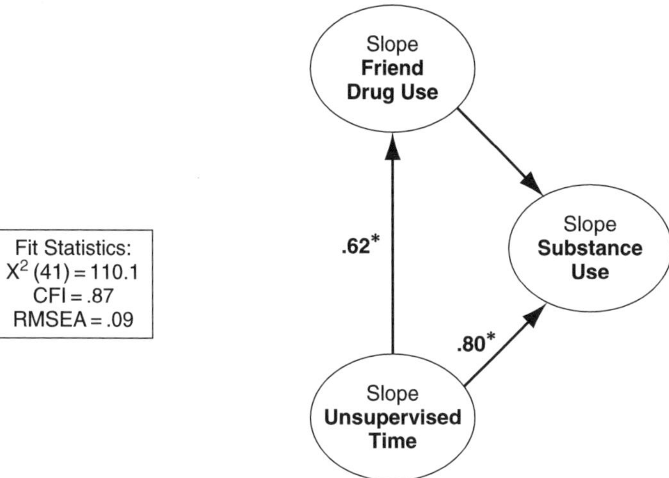

Figure 5.5 Multivariate prediction of growth in adolescent drug use: direct and indirect effects

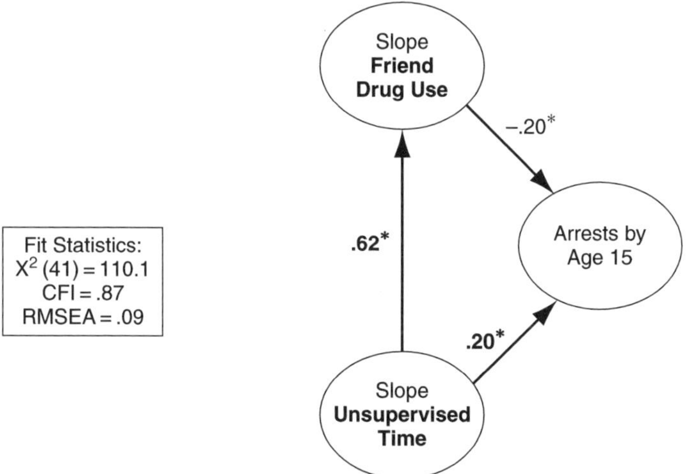

Figure 5.6 Multivariate prediction of police arrests: direct and indirect effects

DISCUSSION

These data support the proposition that the family management constructs used in previous research (see Dishion & McMahon, 1998) can be mapped onto daily parenting practices with adolescents at high risk. The map is imperfect, and certainly could be improved with further development of the brief daily report interviewing technique. For example, the communication construct was based on a measure of the adolescent and parent discussions of activities on a daily basis. It is unclear how much of these discussions involved the communication of information related to parents' monitoring of their adolescents' behaviors. However, it has been our clinical experience that many parents have a sibling-like relationship with their child, and open discussions of the adolescent's problem behavior do not lead to parental efforts to change. The inclusion of lax and strict parents into one group may obfuscate the covariation between communication and growth in drug use.

Family meals and affection are vulnerable to similar measurement questions regarding their utility as a measure of monitoring. Nevertheless, the fact that information about parental lack of supervision of youth activities, of shared meals, and of displays of affection converged with concurrent and longitudinal drug use and the number of arrests suggests that the infrequency of these family dynamics may lead to growth in adolescent antisocial behavior, more so than does purely adolescent communication itself. These results are consistent with a large body of research that points to parental monitoring and supervision of youth behaviors as a key mechanism in preventing or attenuating the growth of antisocial behaviors and drug use (Dishion & McMahon, 1998).

Particularly noteworthy is that the number of hours an adolescent spends with friends per day was easily measurable, and both youth and parents were able to report reliably on adolescents' unsupervised hours. Further, an increase in adolescents' unsupervised hours was predictive of growth in substance use and arrests. These findings are consistent with prior research that noted that a lack of parental involvement with their youths or the disengagement from active family management strategies is related to premature adolescent autonomy, migration into deviant peer groups, and the escalation of antisocial behaviors (Dishion, Nelson, & Bullock, 2004). In the present study, however, this phenomenon was captured using a brief measure of parent and youth daily reports of their behaviors.

When considering these findings in relation to the development of a nomological network of parenting constructs (Cronbach & Meehl, 1955; Patterson & Bank, 1986), this study accomplished several goals. First, data are consistent with the empirical literature linking parent involvement or lack thereof with poor child and adolescent adjustment. Second, our analyses are complex in that a number of theoretically related yet nonoverlapping constructs were considered jointly within a structural equation modeling framework using multiple indicators. Third, these analyses also permitted the evaluation of longitudinal patterns within the data. A clear relation between decreasing parental monitoring vis-à-vis increased unsupervised time with peers and growth in adolescent drug use was detected even after controlling for friends' drug use. These findings support a large literature in which deteriorating parental monitoring and tracking of the behaviors of adolescents are prognostic of increases in deviant peer affiliation, antisocial behavior, and substance use (Dishion & Patterson, 2006).

It is important to remind ourselves that these data do not prove the direction of effect. One could argue that it is the youth's drug use and association with drug-using friends that cause the increase in unsupervised time. Certainly there are grounds to draw that conclusion because some youth then become increasingly difficult to supervise. The random assignment intervention studies are useful in this regard in that there is ample evidence that interventions that target parenting practices in general, and monitoring and involvement in particular, reduce or eliminate growth in adolescent drug use (Liddle *et al.*, 2002). Moreover, randomized interventions reveal that reductions in drug use were mediated completely by improvements in direct observations of parental monitoring (Dishion, Nelson, & Kavanagh, 2003).

Thus the effects are bidirectional from an intervention standpoint—parenting practices are malleable, and parents are often amenable to change. In our analysis of the long-term effectiveness of our family interventions (see Dishion & Stormshak, 2007) from age 11 to 19, we found significant reductions in marijuana dependence and number of arrests. It is important to note that it was families most at risk who engaged in our Family Check-Up, defined by single-parent status, the youth's involvement with deviant peers, and teachers' ratings of school maladaptation.

Both a limitation and a strength of the current study was that the youth and families were involved in a series of pilot interventions leading to the development and refinement of our current ecological approach to family intervention and treatment (EcoFIT) described in detail by Dishion and Stormshak (2007). As with the findings described earlier, we found that random assignment to a parent intervention predicted reduced growth in unsupervised hours that was statistically reliable ($p < 0.05$). At the same time, however, some of the youth were also randomly assigned to interventions that aggregate adolescents (half of whom also received parenting support). Unfortunately, these analyses confirm those of earlier work showing an iatrogenic effect on the telephone interview data, with increasing drug use ($p < 0.05$). Indeed, the placement of youth in groups of deviant peers overwhelmed the effects of improved parental monitoring.

The relation between unsupervised time, affiliation with antisocial peers, number of arrests, and drug use was less clear. It is unclear why having drug-using peers was inversely related to the number of adolescent arrests in this sample at ages 15 and 16. It is likely that the base rates in the number of arrests compared with those of drug use were attenuated in this midadolescence sample, thus reducing the ability to detect effects. Further, arrests reflect an objective number of antisocial behaviors that have been recorded by the authorities and not the number of deviant acts actually committed by the adolescent. As such, it is quite possible that the relation between lower levels of parental monitoring and supervision when taken in the context of adolescent antisocial behavior would have yielded stronger effects after controlling for friends' drug use (Barrera *et al.*, 2001). This speaks more to a measurement issue rather than to a phenomenon in which poor monitoring is associated with higher levels of adolescent problem behavior.

These data add to the body of evidence that shows that family management practices, including parental monitoring and supervision, are central to child and adolescent socialization and growth in deviant peer affiliation, delinquency, and substance use (Dishion & Patterson, 2006). Longitudinal studies also clearly suggest that parent–child relationships, parenting effectiveness, and youth behavioral outcomes are moving targets. As such, our understanding of reciprocal effects within the dynamics of the parent–child relationship and their impact on parenting and youth development (Crouter *et al.*, 1990; Laird *et al.*, 2003) benefits from explorations that can be achieved only by a multiagent–multimethod measurement strategy to eliminate monomethod biases, and ideally, frequent assessment points to improve our understanding of this relational fluidity as opposed to relying on cross-sectional data or annual data collection.

Our study is limited in some respects. First, as previously mentioned, our measure of communication differs from the disclosure measure used by Kerr & Stattin (2000) and may be tapping into a different process. The advantage of our measurement strategy is that it is not biased with respect to reporting the type of communications between a parent and adolescent. It may be presumptuous, however, to link daily discussions of activities with meaningful disclosure. Second, these analyses were conducted on a sample of youth at high risk and must be evaluated and compared with those of typically developing adolescents. The issue may be a higher prevalence of dysfunctional parenting, such as the sibling parenting described earlier in this chapter. Last, missing data were more prevalent at later assessment waves. As such, these findings should be interpreted with some caution.

This work also suggests some exciting avenues for future investigation. The use of telephone reports emerged as a valid and reliable method for studying the dynamic interplay between parenting strategies and adolescent problem behavior. In addition, measurement of seemingly mundane daily activities such as sharing meals, showing affection, and youth communication of daily events contributed to our understanding of parent–youth dynamics and parent involvement in adolescent social and emotional development over time, and provides a promising direction for additional research. Further, the telephone report methodology is advantageous in that it is cost effective and can be collected at shorter intervals, in contrast to annual family assessments.

Analyses point to a direct link between the amount of time in which youths engage in unsupervised time with their peers and growth in drug use and problem behaviors, as well as the dynamic quality of these relationships over time. Last and most important, these findings suggest that parents' monitoring and supervision of their adolescents' activities is central to successful development, and that youth communication is embedded in the context of parent–child involvement and is not merely a static indicator of whether youths report the extent to which they inform their parents about what they are doing. As most parents and developmental and prevention scientists will concur, youth communication can become more obsequious with age. Therefore, interventions aimed at increasing parent–youth communication, problem-solving skills, and supervision and decreasing parental disengagement may serve to help families negotiate the vicissitudes of parenting adolescents.

REFERENCES

Achenbach, T. M. (1991). *Manual for the Child Behavior Checklist/4–18 and 1991 Profile*. Burlington, VT: University of Vermont, Department of Psychiatry.

Barrera, M., Jr., Biglan, A., Ary, D., & Li, F. (2001). Replication of a problem behavior model with American Indian, Hispanic, and Caucasian youth. *Journal of Early Adolescence, 21*, 133–157.

Campbell, D. T. & Fiske, D. W. (1959). Convergent and discriminant validation by the multitrait and multimethod matrix. *Psychological Bulletin, 56*, 81–105.

Chamberlain, P. & Reid, J. B. (1987). Parent observation and report of child symptoms. *Behavioral Assessment, 9*, 97–109.

Chamberlain, P. & Reid, J. B. (1991). Using a specialized foster care community treatment model for children and adolescents leaving the state mental hospital. *Journal of Community Psychology, 19*(3), 266–276.

Chilcoat, H. D. & Anthony, J. C. (1996). Impact of parent monitoring on initiation of drug use through late childhood. *Journal of the American Academy of Child and Adolescent Psychiatry, 35*, 91–100.

Chilcoat, H. D., Dishion, T. J., & Anthony, J. C. (1995). Parent monitoring and the incidence of drug sampling in urban elementary school children. *American Journal of Epidemiology, 141*, 25–31.

Chung, H. L. & Steinberg, L. (2006). Relations between neighborhood factors, parenting behaviors, peer deviance, and delinquency among serious juvenile offenders. *Developmental Psychology, 42*, 319–331.

Cronbach, L. J. & Meehl, P. E. (1955). Construct validity in psychological tests. *Psychological Bulletin, 52*, 281–302.

Crouter, A. C., MacDermid, S. M., McHale, S. M., & Perry-Jenkins, M. (1990). Parental monitoring and perceptions of children's school performance and conduct in dual- and single-earner families. *Developmental Psychology, 26*, 649–657.

Curran, P. J. (1993). *A Comparison of Latent Growth Curve and Auto-Regressive Longitudinal Analyses: Modeling Adolescent Substance Use*. Paper presented at the meeting of the Society for Research in Human Development, New Orleans.

Dishion, T. J. & Andrews, D. (1995). Preventing escalations in problem behaviors with high-risk young adolescents: Immediate and 1-year outcomes. *Journal of Consulting and Clinical Psychology, 63*, 538–548.

Dishion, T. J., Andrews, D. W., Kavanagh, K., & Soberman, L. H. (1996). Preventive interventions for high-risk youth: The Adolescent Transitions Program. In B. McMahon & R. D. Peters (eds), *Conduct Disorders, Substance Abuse and Delinquency: Prevention and Early Intervention Approaches* (pp. 184–214). Newbury Park, CA: Sage.

Dishion, T. J., Burraston, B., & Li, F. (2002). A multimethod and multitrait analysis of family management practices: Convergent and predictive validity. In W. J. Bukowski & Z. Amsel (eds), *Handbook for Drug Abuse Prevention Theory, Science, and Practice* (pp. 587–607). New York: Plenum.

Dishion, T. J., Eddy, J. M., Haas, E. *et al.* (1997). Friendships and violent behavior during adolescence. *Social Development, 6*, 207–223.

Dishion, T. J. & Loeber, R. (1985). Adolescent marijuana and alcohol use: The role of parents and peers revisited. *American Journal of Drug and Alcohol Abuse, 11*, 11–25.

Dishion, T. J. & McMahon, R. J. (1998). Parental monitoring and the prevention of child and adolescent problem behavior: A conceptual and empirical formulation. *Clinical Child and Family Psychology Review, 1*, 61–75.

Dishion, T. J. & McMahon, R. J. (1999). Parental monitoring and the prevention of problem behavior: A conceptual and empirical reformulation. Research meeting on drug abuse prevention through family interventions. In R. S. Ashery (ed.), *NIDA Research Monograph, 177*.Washington, DC: Government Printing Office.

Dishion, T. J., Nelson, S. N. & Bullock, B. M. (2004). Premature adolescent autonomy: parent disengagement and deviant peer process in the amplification of problem behavior. In J. Kiesner & M. Kerr (eds), Peer and family processes in the development of antisocial and aggressive behavior. *Journal on Adolescence* (special issue), *27*, 515–530.

Dishion, T. J., Nelson, S. E., & Kavanagh, K. (2003). The Family Check-Up for high-risk adolescents: preventing early onset substance use by parent monitoring. In J. E. Lochman & R. Salekin (eds), Behavior oriented interventions for children with aggressive behavior and/or conduct problems. *Behavior Therapy* (special issue) *34*, 553–571.

Dishion, T. J. & Patterson, G. R. (1999). Model-building in developmental psychopathology: A pragmatic approach to understanding and intervention. *Journal of Clinical Child Psychology, 28*(4), 502–512.

Dishion, T. J. & Patterson, G. R. (2006). The development and ecology of antisocial behavior in children and adolescents. In D. Cicchetti & D. J. Cohen (eds), *Developmental Psychopathology. Vol. 3: Risk, Disorder, and Adaptation* (pp. 503–541). New York: Wiley.

Dishion, T. J., Patterson, G. R., Stoolmiller, M., & Skinner, M. S. (1991). Family, school, and behavioral antecedents to early adolescent involvement with antisocial peers. *Developmental Psychology, 27*, 172–180.

Dishion, T. J. & Stormshak, E. (2007). *Intervening in Children's Lives: An Ecological, Family-Centered Approach to Mental Health Care*. Washington, DC: APA Books.

Duncan, S. C., Duncan, T. E., Biglan, A., & Ary, D. (1998). Contributions of the social context to the development of adolescent substance use: A multivariate latent growth modeling approach. *Drug and Alcohol Dependence, 50*, 57–71.

Dwyer, J. H. (1983). *Statistical Models for the Social and Behavioral Sciences*. New York: Oxford University Press.

Haley, J. (Ed.). (1971). *Changing Families*. New York: Grune & Stratton.

Hawkins, D. J. & Catalano, R. F., Jr. (1992). *Communities that Care: Action for Drug Abuse Prevention*. San Francisco, CA: Jossey-Bass.

Kerr, M. & Stattin, H. (2000). What parents know, how they know it, and several forms of adolescent adjustment: Further support for a reinterpretation of monitoring. *Developmental Psychology, 36*, 366–380.

Laird, R. D., Pettit, G. S., Bates, J. E., & Dodge, K. A. (2003). Parents' monitoring-relevant knowledge and adolescents' delinquent behavior: Evidence of correlated developmental changes and reciprocal influences. *Child Development, 74*, 752–768.

Laird, R. D., Pettit, G. S., Dodge, K. A., & Bates, J. E. (2005). Peer relationship antecedents of delinquent behavior in late adolescence: Is there evidence of demographic group differences in developmental processes? *Development & Psychopathology, 17*(1), 127–144.

Liddle, H. A., Santisteban, R. F., Levant, R. F., & Bray, J. H. (eds) (2002). *Family Psychology*. Washington, DC: American Psychological Association.

Loeber, R. & Dishion, T. (1983). Early predictors of male delinquency: A review. *Psychological Bulletin, 94*(1), 68–99.

McCord, J. (1979). Some child-rearing antecedents of criminal behavior in adult men. *Journal of Personality and Social Psychology, 9*, 1477–1486.

Minuchin, S. (1974). *Families and Family Therapy*. Oxford: Harvard University Press.

Muthén, L. K. & Muthén, B. O. (2004). *Mplus User's Guide* (3rd edn). Los Angeles, CA: Muthén & Muthén.

Patterson, G. R. (1982). *A Social Learning Approach: III. Coercive Family Process*. Eugene, OR: Castalia.

Patterson, G. R. (1993). Orderly change in a stable world: The antisocial trait as a chimera. *Journal of Consulting and Clinical Psychology, 61*, 911–919.

Patterson, G. R. & Bank, L. (1986). Bootstrapping your way in the nomological thicket. *Behavioral Assessment, 8*, 49–73.

Patterson, G. R. & Stouthamer-Loeber, M. (1984). The correlation of family management practices and delinquency. *Child Development, 55*, 1299–1307.

Patterson, G. R., Reid, J. B., & Dishion, T. J. (1992). *Antisocial Boys*. Eugene, OR: Castalia.

Pettit, G. S., Bates, J. E., Dodge, K. A., & Meece, D. W. (1999). The impact of after-school peer contact on early adolescent externalizing problems is moderated by parental monitoring, perceived neighborhood safety, and prior adjustment. *Child Development, 70*, 768–778.

Reid, J. B. (1978). The development of specialized observation systems: A social learning approach to family intervention: Vol II. *Observation in Home Settings*, pp. 43–49. Eugene, OR: Castalia.

Robins, L. N. & Przybeck, T. R. (1985). Age of onset of drug use as a factor in drug and other disorders. *National Institute of Drug Abuse: Research Monograph Series, 56*, 178–193.

Snyder, J., Dishion, T. J., & Patterson, G. R. (1986). Determinants and consequences of associating with deviant peers during preadolescence and adolescence. *Journal of Early Adolescence, 6*, 29–43.

Steinberg, L., Fletcher, A., & Darling, N. (1994). Parental monitoring and peer influences on adolescent substance use. *Pediatrics, 93*, 1060–1063.

Stoolmiller, M. S. (1990). *Parent Supervision, Child Unsupervised Wandering, and Child Antisocial Behavior: A Latent Growth Curve Analysis*. Eugene, OR: University of Oregon.

Stoolmiller, M. S. (1995). Using latent growth curve models to study developmental process. In J. M. Gottman (ed.), *The Analysis of Change* (pp. 105–138). Mahwah, NJ: Erlbaum.

Wilson, H. (1980). Parental supervision: A neglected aspect of delinquency. *British Journal of Criminology, 20*, 203–235.

CHAPTER 6

Reciprocal Development of Parent–adolescent Support and Adolescent Problem Behaviors

Susan J. T. Branje, William W. Hale III and Wim H. J. Meeus
Utrecht University, Netherlands

INTRODUCTION

Human development takes place in the context of relationships with others. These relationships are thought to influence individuals' behavior and developmental course (Reis, Collins, & Berscheid, 2000). Parent–child relationships are among the most important and central of human relationships, especially during the period of childhood and adolescence. Parents are an important source of support, although the relative impact of parental support may change over the life course. Perceived parental support concerns the perception of parents as available for support when needed. In the current chapter we will examine how parental support is related to adolescent adjustment over time.

ASSOCIATIONS BETWEEN PARENTAL SUPPORT AND ADOLESCENT ADJUSTMENT

Social support from parents is thought to be a major protective factor for adolescents (Wills & Resko, 2004). Adolescents who perceive higher levels of support generally have less problems and higher wellbeing than adolescents with lower levels of parental support. Lower levels of parental support tend to be concurrently related with higher levels of a variety of adjustment problems, including delinquent activities (Windle, 1992), violent behavior (Zimmerman, Steinman, & Rowe, 1998), antisocial behavior (Barnes & Farrell,

What Can Parents Do? New Insights into the Role of Parents in Adolescent Problem Behavior
Edited by Margaret Kerr, Håkan Stattin and Rutger C. M. E. Engels.

1992; Deković, Janssens, & Van As, 2003; Vazsonyi, 2004), aggression (Lopez *et al.*, 2006), alcohol and substance use (Maton & Zimmerman, 1992; Windle, 1992), depressive symptoms (McCarty *et al.*, 2006; Mounts, 2004; Windle, 1992), loneliness (Mounts, 2004) and lower levels of self-esteem (Parker & Benson, 2005).

In our own work we have also documented concurrent associations between parental support and adolescent adjustment. In particular, Helsen, Vollebergh & Meeus (2000) examined associations between parental support and emotional problems over the course of adolescence. They used data from the first wave of the six-year three-wave Dutch longitudinal project "Utrecht Study of Adolescent Development (USAD) 1991–1997" (Meeus & 't Hart, 1993), consisting of 2589 Dutch adolescents (1193 boys) in four age categories: early adolescence (between 12 and 14, $n = 549$), middle adolescence (between 15 and 17, $n = 798$), late adolescence (between 18 and 20, $n = 645$), and post adolescence (between 21 and 24, $n = 597$). The perceived level of parental support was measured by the role-relation method (Fisher, 1982; Meeus, 1989). The question asked was "when you are having problems in relations with someone else, or when you are feeling lonely, who helps you? Please note that this question refers to problems in relations with others, for example when you are quarrelling, when someone does not like you or when you are feeling lonely." The adolescents were asked to indicate on a 10-point scale the degree of support they received from father, mother, and friends when such problems arise. Parental support consisted of average scores of support from fathers and mothers. Emotional problems were measured by a composite of self-report measures: scales for psychological stress and depression, the feeling of general wellbeing and happiness, general physical health and complaints in bodily functioning, and the tendency to have suicidal thoughts. An exploratory factor analysis revealed a single-factor solution with loadings of 0.60 and higher, which explained 54.1% of the variance. Each adolescent was assigned a factor score, derived by using the short regression method, for the construct Emotional Problems.

Results of this study revealed a significant moderate correlation of parental support with emotional problems ($r = 0.25$). Multiple regression analyses of emotional problems on the support of parents and friends, age, and sex revealed that parental support interacted with all the other variables. Parental support was found to be stronger related to emotional problems for girls ($\beta = -0.32$) than for boys ($\beta = -0.16$). The effect of parental support also decreased during adolescence: parental support was stronger related to emotional problems for younger adolescents than for older adolescents. Adolescents of all ages who perceived low levels of support reported a high level of emotional problems. In particular younger adolescents with high levels of parental support reported lower levels of emotional problems. The interaction effect between parental support and the support of friends indicated that parental support is negatively related with emotional problems for all adolescents, but this effect is stronger among adolescents who perceive strong support from friends compared with those who perceive little support from friends. Among adolescents with higher parental support, peer support was associated with lower levels of depression, whereas among adolescents with lower parental support, peer support was associated with higher levels of depression. The latter finding might indicate a tendency to "turn to friends" in times of distress when parents are not available.

A study of the extent to which siblings affect each other's development and psychosocial adjustment during adolescence (Branje *et al.*, 2004) also included effects of parental support. The participants in this study were 285 Dutch middle-class two-parent families with at least two siblings between 11 and 15 years of age (older child M age = 14 years, younger child M age = 12 years), who participated in the Nijmegen Family and Personality Project (Haselager & Van Aken, 1999), a three-wave longitudinal study with one-year intervals between subsequent waves. Perceived parental support was measured with the Relational Support Inventory (RSI) (Scholte, Van Lieshout, & Van Aken, 2001). This inventory involves 24 questions representing four dimensions of perceived support measured by six items each along a five-point Likert-scale ranging from *very untrue of this person* (1) through *sometimes untrue, sometimes true of this person* (3) to *very true of this person* (5). The first support dimension, perceived Quality of Information, assesses the quality of information and withholding of information. A sample item is: "This person explains or shows how I can make or do something." The second support dimension is perceived Respect for Autonomy and assesses respect for autonomy and limit setting. For example, "This person lets me solve problems as much as possible on my own but also provides help when I ask for it." The third support dimension is perceived Emotional Support and assesses warmth as opposed to hostility. A sample item is: "In this person's view, I can't do anything right: he/she is always criticizing me." The fourth support dimension is perceived Convergence of Goals and assesses the perceived level of convergence as opposed to divergence of goals. For example: "This person and I have many conflicts with regard to my school achievement, future, or career opportunities" (reverse scoring). Adolescents judged the support they perceived from each other and from their father, mother, and best friend. The RSI total scores were averaged across all 24 items. Cronbach's alphas ranged between 0.80 and 0.87. To assess internalizing and externalizing behavior in a non-clinical setting, the Nijmegen Problem Behavior List (NPBL) (Scholte, Vermulste & De Bruyen, 2001) was used. Items are formulated to represent problem behavior. The NPBL contains 16 items on a five-point scale and is validated as both a self-report measure and as an other-report measure. Internalizing and externalizing problem behavior of adolescents was assessed by self-ratings of the adolescents and by ratings of fathers and mothers. Ratings of fathers and mothers were averaged. Internalizing behavior is measured with nine items measuring withdrawn and anxious/depressed behavior (e.g., "I withdraw from others, I feel sad, unhappy"). Cronbach's alpha varies from 0.81 to 0.88 for the different versions. Externalizing behavior is measured with seven items measuring aggressive and delinquent behavior (e.g., "I readily threaten others with violence," "I cheat others"). Cronbach's alpha varies between 0.77 and 0.89.

Perceived parental support was found to correlate significantly with both self-reported and parent-reported internalizing and externalizing behavior, except for younger siblings' parent-reported internalizing behavior (see Table 6.1).

Table 6.1 Correlations between parental support and internalizing and externalizing problem behavior

	Perceived paternal support	**Perceived maternal support**
Internalizing behavior		
Younger sibling, self-report	−0.29**	−0.29**
Younger sibling, parent-report	−0.08	−0.06
Older sibling, self-report	−0.36**	−0.31**
Older sibling, parent-report	−0.20**	−0.17**
Externalizing behavior		
Younger sibling, self-report	−0.40**	−0.41**
Younger sibling, parent-report	−0.24**	−0.21**
Older sibling, self-report	−0.51**	−0.52**
Older sibling, parent-report	−0.34**	−0.30**

**$p < 0.01$

A series of multiple regression analyses in which internalizing and externalizing behavior were regressed on several background variables, support from father, mother, best friend, and sibling, and sibling problem behavior, revealed that father support was still significantly related to older adolescents' self-reported ($\beta = -0.31$) and parent-reported ($\beta = -0.34$) externalizing behavior and older adolescents' self-reported internalizing behavior ($\beta = -0.33$), with older adolescents who perceived more support from father revealing less problems. Longitudinal effects of parental support on externalizing or internalizing behavior were also examined, thereby controlling for stability of problem behavior. Results showed that paternal and maternal support did not predict changes in adolescent problem behavior one year later.

In sum, many studies have provided evidence for concurrent associations between parental support and adolescent internalizing and externalizing problem behavior. Although most of these studies assumed that higher levels of parental support lead to better psychosocial adjustment, the opposite direction of effects is equally possible, with adolescent problem behavior leading to changes in parental support. Other possibilities are that parental support and adolescent problem behavior reciprocally affect each other, or that third variables cause their relation. Longitudinal studies that focused on the direction of effects between parental support and adolescent problem behavior while controlling for stability and initial associations between problem behavior and support are sparse, however. In the remainder of this chapter we will discuss different theoretical perspectives regarding the underlying processes of the associations between parental support and adolescent problem behavior, as well as longitudinal evidence for these perspectives.

THEORETICAL FRAMEWORKS FOR THE LINKS BETWEEN PARENTAL SUPPORT AND ADOLESCENTS' ADJUSTMENT

Several theoretical perspectives offer explanations for the links between parental support and adolescent adjustment problems. Most of these perspectives focus on effects of parental support on adolescent problem behaviors. These socialization theories have been summarized by Hartup (1978) under the label of social mold model. According to these theories, parental socialization efforts literally mold a child's behavior, and a lack of parental support leads to adolescent problem behavior. Other perspectives emphasize effects of adolescent problem behavior on parental support or bidirectional effects between parental support and adolescent problem behavior.

Effects of Parental Support on Adolescent Problem Behavior

Stress-buffering Model

According to the stress-buffering model (Cohen & Wills, 1985; Windle, 1992), parental support can protect against adolescent problem behavior by neutralizing the adverse effects of a risk factor such as stressful life events. Similarly, a vulnerability-buffering model suggests that parental support might reduce the effects of a personal characteristic such as negative affect on problem behavior (Cohen & Wills, 1985). In contrast to a direct effects model, the stress-buffering model suggests that parental support is only protective under conditions of stress and moderates the negative consequences of high levels of stress. The perception of being accepted and valued is thought to boost self-esteem, confidence, and efficacy (Pierce *et al.*, 2000) and makes it easier to cope effectively with stressful life events. Feeling supported and loved by one or both parents is thought to ameliorate the effects of stress on depression (Wills & Cleary, 1996). Similarly, supportive relationships with parents are thought to be related to adaptive coping that promotes prosocial behavior, whereas unsupportive relationships with parents are thought to be related to patterns of maladaptive coping that might lead to externalizing behavior problems (Wills & Resko, 2004).

There is not much empirical evidence for the stress-buffering hypothesis. Cross-sectional studies offer mixed support and there are only a few studies that have addressed the stress-buffering hypothesis using longitudinal designs.

Burton, Stice & Seeley (2004) did not find any support for parental support buffering the effects of negative life events on depression in a longitudinal study among adolescent girls aged 11 to 15 years. DuBois *et al.* (1992) tested the stress-buffering hypothesis in a sample including 61% African-American and 39% White adolescents. They found no moderating effect for parental support on the relations of major life events and daily hassles with psychological adjustment and academic performance over a two-year period. Windle (1992) examined the stress-buffering effects of parent and friend support on alcohol consumption, alcohol problems, delinquent activity, and depressive symptoms among White, predominantly middle-class, adolescent males and females. He found no support for the buffering hypothesis of parental support among both males and females. Also, longitudinally, no support for the stress-buffering hypothesis was found for alcohol and marijuana use (Zimmerman *et al.*, 2000). Similarly, no support was found for the vulnerability-buffering model regarding the onset of substance abuse (Measelle, Stice, & Springer, 2006). The increased risk of substance abuse onset due to negative emotionality or depressive symptoms did not decrease as a function of higher levels of perceived parental support.

Some support for the stress-buffering hypothesis was found in a study by Ge *et al.* (1994), who used latent growth curve models in a four-year longitudinal study to examine the moderating effect of maternal support on the link between depression and stressful life events. Their findings showed that the level of depressive symptoms is related to the level of life events for both boys and girls and that maternal support buffers these effects of stress on depressive symptoms of adolescents. However, only for girls with less supportive mothers, change in depressive symptoms is significantly related to change in stressful events.

In sum, longitudinal studies provide only limited support for the stress-buffering hypothesis. Perhaps stressful life events have an immediate effect on adolescents but have only minimal lasting consequences (Zimmerman *et al.*, 2000), which might explain why the buffering role that parental support has been found to play in cross-sectional studies is often not found in longitudinal designs.

Three other models regarding relations between parental support and adolescent problem behavior can be distinguished, that is, a direct effects model, a child-effects model, and a reciprocal effects model. These models will be discussed below. As studies that examined these models often addressed two or more of these models at the same time, we will present empirical evidence for each of the models after describing the three models.

Direct effects model

A direct effects model assumes that parental support has a generalized positive effect on adolescents. Deficits in parental support might have a main effect on adolescent problem behavior and directly increase the risk for problem behaviors (Baumrind, 1991; Windle, 1992). Hirschi's Social Control Theory (Hirschi, 1969) is an example of a perspective in the social mold tradition that assumes direct effects of parental support on externalizing behavior: Adolescents who have stronger ties to parents would have higher self-control and restrain from delinquent behavior. Deficits in parental support might lead to a weaker bond and identification with parents and subsequently to more delinquent behavior. Adolescents who experience deficits in parental support are thought to identify with their parents to a lesser extent, which in turn interferes with the internalization of parental norms and leads to deviant behavior or substance abuse. Internalizing problems can also be affected by direct effects of parental support. The perception of being accepted and valued boosts self-esteem and self-efficacy, which protects against depressive feelings (Windle, 1992).

Effects of Adolescent Problem Behavior on Parental Support Child Effects Model

The direction of effects between parental support and adolescent problem behavior could also go from child to parent. Child characteristics are thought to be important in shaping parenting (Belsky, 1984; Patterson, 1982). Bell (1968) was among the first to emphasize *child effects* in socialization processes, and proposed a child-effects model, which suggests that children and adolescents basically mold parents' behaviors in an attempt to adjust to their children's behaviors (Bell & Chapman, 1986). This perspective suggests that parents react to the actions of their children (Kerr & Stattin, 2003). According to this perspective, adolescent behavior would elicit more or less parental support.

In respect to depression, Coyne (e.g., Coyne, Burchill, & Stiles, 1991) has proposed depression as a gradual escalation of depressed persons initially eliciting supportive behaviors from significant others (such as parents or partners) by means of their display of depressive behaviors (e.g., Hale, 2001). The depressed person specifically looks for support from others to offset their negative cognitive beliefs that others are rejecting them (e.g., Beck *et al.*, 1979).

These interpersonal interactions between the depressed person and the other are believe to induce a negative mood in the other person. Hence, over time, this initial supportive interaction becomes increasingly rejecting and a process of support erosion emerges in which people are likely to stop supporting depressed individuals as a consequence of their negative self-statements, complaints, apathy, reassurance seeking, and social inadequacy (Coyne, 1976). This rejection confirms depressed individuals' negative beliefs that they were being rejected by others all along (e.g., Hollon & Beck, 1994). This interpersonal theory of depression has received support in both (young-)adult (e.g., Segrin & Dillard, 1992) and adolescent studies (e.g., Joiner, 1999). Additionally, a recent longitudinal study by Hale *et al.* (in press) of young adolescents and perceived parental rejection also lends credence to this theory.

For externalizing behavior, similar patterns have been described. Adolescents' behavior could elicit aversive reactions and a decrease in support of parents (Patterson, 1982). Also, parents might emotionally reject their adolescent with externalizing problem behavior (Baumrind & Moselle, 1985) and become less supportive. Parents might also become increasingly tolerant to the behavior of their child, however (Bell & Chapman, 1986), and remain supportive. Moreover, parents might try to get their adolescent with externalizing problem behavior back on a nondeviant track by increasing their level of support, although at the present time we are not aware of any empirical evidence of this.

Reciprocal Effects Between Parental Support and Adolescent Problem Behavior

Different theories emphasize bidirectionality of effects, in which relationship partners influence each other and contribute to individual developmental outcomes (Bell, 1968; Bell & Chapman, 1986; Lollis & Kuczynski, 1997; Sameroff, 1983). In recent decades, the transactional character of relations between individual characteristics and family relationships has been emphasized: family members develop in a continuous process of transactions, in which individual characteristics and relationship characteristics influence each other reciprocally (Lollis & Kuczynski, 1997; Maccoby, 1984; Sameroff, 1983). Thus, it is likely that parental support and adolescent problem behavior mutually affect each other, with adolescent problem behavior eliciting changes in support and parental support influencing adolescent behavior.

Although many studies have investigated associations between adolescent behavior and parental support, most of these studies used concurrent or cross-lagged correlations that do not permit conclusions about the underlying processes (Neyer & Asendorpf, 2001). To examine transactions between parental support and adolescent behavior, longitudinal causal models are needed, such as path analyses with cross-lagged effects or growth-curve models, which control for concurrent relations at time 1, stability, and correlated change of adolescent behavior and parental support when estimating the reciprocal effects between these variables. Only this type of analysis can disentangle the extent to which differences in parental support predict changes in adolescent problem behavior over time and vice versa. It should be noted, however, that this analysis does not provide conclusive evidence for causal direction of effects because alternative explanations, such as third variables, may still play a role.

Evidence for Direct Effects, Child Effects, and Reciprocal Effects

Longitudinal studies examining direct or reciprocal effects between parental support and problem behavior while controlling for initial associations and stability of problem behavior are relatively sparse. Most of these studies only tested direct effects of parental support instead of reciprocal effects between support and problem behavior. In a study among adolescent girls aged 11 to 15 years, no effects of parental support on changes in depression were found (Burton, Stice, & Seeley, 2004). Also, deficits in parental support predicted future increases in alcohol use among adolescents aged 12–17 (Stice, Barrera Jr., & Chassin, 1998). Similarly, in a five-year longitudinal study of adolescent girls using hazard models, deficits in parental support were found to predict future substance abuse onset (Measelle, Stice, & Springer, 2006). Moreover, using a pretest-posttest design, Yang & Yeh (2006) found that enacted parental support predicted changes in anxiety among Taiwanese adolescents who went through the final school examinations but this effect was moderated by intimacy with parents. Anxiety was reduced when adolescents perceived high relationship intimacy with parents, and increased when there was low relationship intimacy.

Gender differences in the effects of parental support have also been found. For example, among middle adolescents, higher parental support was found to predict decreases in alcohol problems, delinquent activity and depressive symptoms for girls but not for boys (Windle, 1992). Meadows, Brown, & Elder (2006) investigated gender differences in the associations among stressful life events, parental support, and depression during late adolescence and emerging adulthood. Their results showed that both maternal and paternal support reduce depressive symptoms during late adolescence but not during emerging adulthood. Maternal support and depressive symptoms were more strongly related for females than for males, but no gender difference was found for support from fathers. Also, whereas maternal support seemed to be more effective for females than paternal support, for males no differences between the relation of support from mothers and fathers with depressive symptoms was found.

Some studies examining reciprocal effects between parental support and adolescent problem behavior found further evidence for direct effects of parental support. For instance, in a sample of male African-American adolescents, Zimmerman *et al.* (2000) found that parental support predicted a decrease in anxiety and depression six months later, but not in alcohol and marijuana use or for delinquency. However, anxiety and depression did not predict parental support over time, indicating that adolescents' problems do not elicit increased levels of parental support longitudinally. Additionally, Sheeber *et al.* (1997) found that family support at time 1 significantly predicted depression one year later for 14 to 20 year olds: adolescents who received less family support had more depressive symptoms one year later. Time 1 depression did not significantly predict time 2 family support. Furthermore,

Stice, Ragan, & Randall (2004) tested bidirectional effects between perceived parental support and depression using longitudinal data from adolescent girls. Deficits in parental support predicted future increases in depressive symptoms as well as onset of major depression. In contrast, initial depressive symptoms and major depression did not predict future decreases in parental support. These results are consistent with the direct effect model of parental support. Rather than depression leading to support erosion, these findings suggest that low parental support has a direct effect on depressive symptoms over time.

In a community sample, regression analyses revealed that parental support was not independently related to adolescents' depression two years later when controlling for time 1 depression (Young *et al.*, 2005). Also, time 1 depression did not predict changes in parental support over time. However, the authors did find that the interaction between parental support and peer support significantly predicted depression, which was interpreted as parental support moderating the relationship between peer support and depression. Anticipated peer support was found to lead to less depression among adolescents with high parental support, and to higher levels of depression for adolescents with low parental support. Nevertheless, these results could also be interpreted as peer support moderating the effect of parental support. If this is the case then this would indicate that when relationships with peers are supportive, higher parental support leads to less depression, but when relationships with peers are nonsupportive, higher parental support leads to more depression. Among adolescents with low anticipated peer support, higher parent support did not buffer for depressive symptoms. Thus, these data suggest a direct effects model of parental support, whereby the direction of the effect is moderated by supportiveness of peers.

Thus, evidence for the direct effect model of parental support to adolescent problems is mixed. Results are much more consistent regarding effects of parental support on internalizing problems than regarding effects of parental support on externalizing problems. Furthermore, effects of internalizing problems on parental support were mostly found to be non-significant. Although many of the studies did not test reciprocal effects and can therefore not rule out possible effects of problem behavior on support, the studies that tested reciprocal effects mostly did not find effects of problem behavior on support. Only one study found evidence for support erosion in relation to depression (Slavin & Rainer, 1990). Depressive symptoms were found to predict a decrease in perceived family support for girls but not boys during late adolescence.

Some evidence for support erosion in response to externalizing behavior has been reported in studies examining reciprocal effects, however. Using the same dataset as Measelle, Stice, & Springer (2006), Huh *et al.* (2006) tested the hypothesis that perceived parenting would show reciprocal relations with adolescents' problem behavior. They found that higher externalizing behavior and substance abuse predicted future decreases in perceived parental support. Low parental support did not predict increases in externalizing or substance abuse symptoms. These results suggest that for girls during middle adolescence, externalizing problem behavior is a more consistent predictor of parental support than parental support is of externalizing problem behavior.

Only one study was found that reported full reciprocal effects between parental support and adolescent externalizing problems. Stice & Barrera (1995) used covariance structural modeling to examine prospective reciprocal relations between perceived parenting and adolescents' substance use and externalizing symptoms among a community sample of adolescents and their parents, within which half of the adolescents were at risk for problem behavior because of parental alcoholism. Full reciprocal relations between adolescent self-reported substance use and levels of parental support were found: higher substance use predicted less support over time and higher support predicted less substance use over time. Also, adolescent self-reported externalizing behaviors prospectively predicted parental support, with higher levels of externalizing leading to less parental support. Parental support was not prospectively related to externalizing behavior, however. These findings support the reciprocal effects model for substance use and the support erosion model for externalizing behavior.

In sum, empirical evidence so far suggests a direct effects model of parental support on internalizing behavior, a child effects model of externalizing behavior on parental support characterized by support erosion, and a reciprocal effects model for substance use. As many studies did not use a full reciprocal model to test for effects between parental support and problem behavior, further research is needed to confirm these findings. At the Adolescent Development Research Centre we have also examined bidirectional effects between parental support and various types of problem behavior, covering an age period from early adolescence until early adulthood. In the remaining part of this chapter we will describe the results of several of these studies.

LONGITUDINAL ASSOCIATIONS BETWEEN PARENTAL SUPPORT AND INTERNALIZING AND EXTERNALIZING BEHAVIOR DURING ADOLESCENCE

Using data from the second and third wave of the CONAMORE (CONflict And Management Of RElationships, Meeus *et al.*, 2004) longitudinal study, Hale III *et al.* (2005) examined longitudinal bidirectional effects between parental support and internalizing behavior during adolescence. In this study, conflict with parents was also included, so findings for conflict will also be presented. For the current chapter we repeated these analyses for externalizing behavior. We hypothesized that parental support would predict lower levels of internalizing problems and that externalizing behavior would predict less parental support over time. As some studies found that stronger effects of parental support for females than for males, we also explored gender differences in the associations between parental support and problem behavior. Of the 1 313 adolescents who longitudinally participated in the CONAMORE study, 1 185 (578 boys, 607 girls) had complete data on all the measures used in the current study. Of these 1 185 adolescents, 841 were early adolescents (13–14 years in wave 2) and 344 were middle adolescents (17–18 years in wave 2). 86% of the adolescents were of Dutch origin; the other 14% came from other ethnic minorities.

Perceived support from mother and father and conflict with mother and father were measured using the short version of the Network of Relationship Inventory (Furman & Buhrmester, 1992). The participants indicated on a five-point Likert scale (ranging from 1 = *a little or not at all*, 5 = *more is not possible*) the amount of support they received from their parents and the frequency of conflict in the relationship with their parents, for the relationships with their mother and father separately. Examples of items are: "Does your mother/father like or approve of the things you do?" (support), and "Do you and your mother/father get on each other's nerves?" (conflict). Internal consistencies were high with alphas ranging from .87 to .92.

Internalizing problems consisted of a measure for depression and anxiety. *Depression* was measured with the Children's Depression Inventory (CDI) (Kovacs, 1985), a symptom-based measure consisting of 27 items rated on a three-point Likert scale ranging from *not true* to *very true*. Sample items are: "I worry all the time about all kind of things", "I feel tired all the time", and "I don't have any friends." Cronbach's alpha for this measure in the current sample was 0.92. *Anxiety* was measured with the SCARED (Screen for Child Anxiety Related Emotional Disorders) (Birmaher *et al.*, 1997), a reliable and valid DSM-IV-related self-report questionnaire (Birmaher *et al.*, 1999; Hale III *et al.*, 2005). The SCARED includes subscales for panic disorder (e.g., "When I am scared I have difficulties with breathing"), separation anxiety (e.g., "I worry that something bad will happen to my parents"), social anxiety (e.g., "I feel nervous around people I don't know well"), school anxiety (e.g., "I worry about going to school"), and generalized anxiety (e.g., "I worry if I am going to be fine"). Items were rated on a three-point scale: 0 (almost never), 1 (sometimes), 2 (often), and were averaged to compute a total anxiety score. Cronbach's alpha for this scale was 0.93.

Externalizing problems contained a scale for aggression and delinquency. *Aggression* was measured by the Direct and Indirect Aggression Scales (DIAS) (Björkqvist, Lagerspetz, & Osterman, 1992). We used the 17 items from the subscales for direct aggression (e.g., "I kick or strike the other one" or "I call the other one names") and indirect aggression (e.g., "I spread vicious rumors as revenge" or "I tell others not to associate with that person"), which have good reliability (Björkqvist, Lagerspetz, & Osterman, 1992). Adolescents indicated on a four-point Likert scale ranging from *never* to *very often* the extent to which they show certain behaviors when they are angry at someone in the classroom. A total aggression score was computed by averaging direct and indirect aggression scores ($\alpha = 0.89$). *Delinquency* was measured by a 16- item minor delinquency questionnaire (Baerveldt, van Rossem, & Vermande, 2003). Adolescents were asked to rate on a four-point scale ranging from *never* to *four times or more* how often they had shown certain forms of delinquent behavior (e.g., "stolen a bike", "deliberately broken something on street") during the last 12 months. This measure has good internal consistency and is sufficiently one-dimensional (Baerveldt, van Rossem, & Vermande, 2003). Cronbach's alpha in the current sample was 0.90.

Latent path analyses were conducted using Structural Equation Modeling (AMOS), in which paternal and maternal support were indicators of a latent parental support factor, conflicts with father and mother were indicators of a latent conflict with parents factor, anxiety and depression were indicators of a latent internalizing problems factor, and aggression and delinquency were indicators of a latent externalizing problems factor. Bidirectional effects over time were estimated between support, conflict, and problem behavior, thereby controlling for time 1 correlations, stability, and correlated change of support, conflict, and problem behavior (see Figure 6.1). Fit indices are displayed in Table 6.2 and results are displayed in Table 6.3.

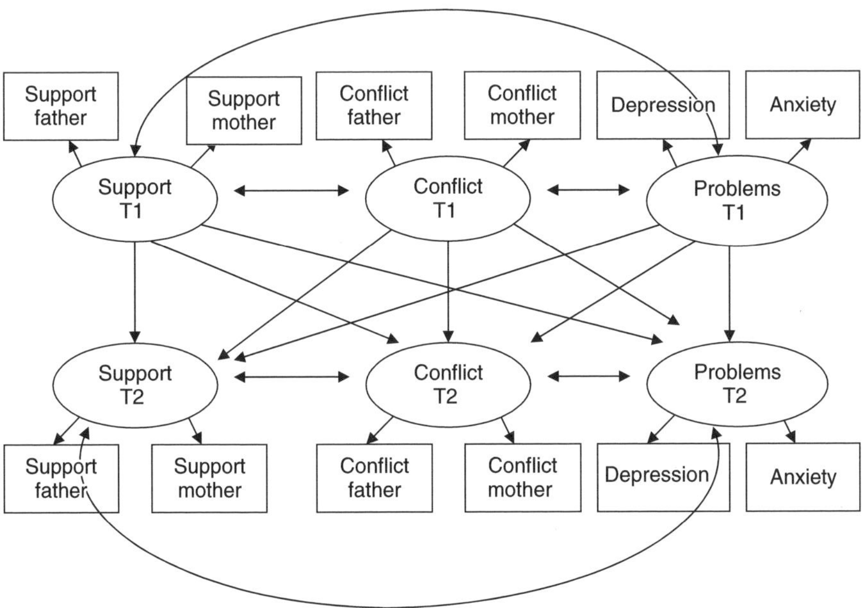

Figure 6.1 Estimated model of parental support, conflict with parents and problem behavior

Table 6.2 Model fit summary for path analyses

Model	χ^2	*df*	NNFI	CFI	RMSEA
Externalizing	213.12**	36	0.91	0.95	0.08
Internalizing	175.48**	36	0.94	0.97	0.07
Internalizing multigroup:					
1. invariant	751.15**	220	0.90	0.92	0.05
2. different paths	693.57**	193	0.89	0.92	0.05
3. diff paths boys v. girls	**721.18****	**211**	**0.90**	**0.92**	**0.05**
4. diff paths young v. old	741.75**	211	0.90	0.92	0.05

** $p < 0.01$

Table 6.3 Correlations and effects among parental support, parental conflict, and problem behavior

	Externalizing	Internalizing		
	Total sample	Total sample	Girls	Boys
Time 1 correlations				
Support – conflict	−0.53**	−0.52**	−0.58**	−0.58**
Conflict – problem behavior	0.62**	0.48**	0.54**	0.54**
Support – problem behavior	−0.29**	−0.24**	−0.33**	−0.33**
Time 2 correlations				
Support – conflict	−0.35**	−0.33**	−0.47**	−0.47**
Conflict – problem behavior	0.44**	0.32**	0.32**	0.32**
Support – problem behavior	−0.28**	−0.20**	−0.30**	−0.30**
Regression Weights (β)				
Support t1 – support t2	0.67**	0.67**	0.69**	0.69**
Conflict t1 – conflict t2	0.76**	0.70**	0.73**	0.81**
Problem behavior t1 – problem behavior t2	0.75**	0.71**	0.84**	0.61**
Support t1 – conflict t2	0.02	0.02	0.01	0.16*
Conflict t1 – support t2	−0.06	−0.05	−0.06	0.09
Support t1 – problem behavior t2	−0.10	0.02	−0.00	−0.00
Conflict t1 – problem behavior t2	−0.06	−0.01	−0.12	0.11
Problem behavior t1 – conflict t2	−0.02	0.11*	0.05	0.08
Problem behavior t1 – support t2	−0.05	−0.10*	−0.05	−0.14*

* $p < 0.05$; ** $p < 0.01$

Parental support was found to be negatively associated with internalizing and externalizing behavior at time 1 and time 2. Higher levels of parental support were related to lower levels of externalizing and internalizing problems ($r = -0.29$ and -0.24, respectively), and a greater decrease in parental support was related to a greater increase in externalizing and internalizing problem behavior ($r = -0.28$ and -0.20, respectively). In contrast to our hypothesis, no cross-lagged effects between parental support and externalizing problem behavior were found. For internalizing behavior, we found an effect on parental support and conflict with parents, but again this effect disconfirmed our hypothesis: adolescents who had higher internalizing problems at time 1 perceived less support and more conflict with parents at time 2 ($\beta = -0.10$ and 0.11, respectively). We examined sex and age differences in this effect using multigroup models. Chi-square difference tests revealed that a model with sex differences and no age differences between early and middle adolescents in cross-lagged paths provided the best fit to the data. Estimates for this model showed that the detrimental effect of internalizing problems for parental support were significantly stronger for boys than for girls (see Figure 6.2).

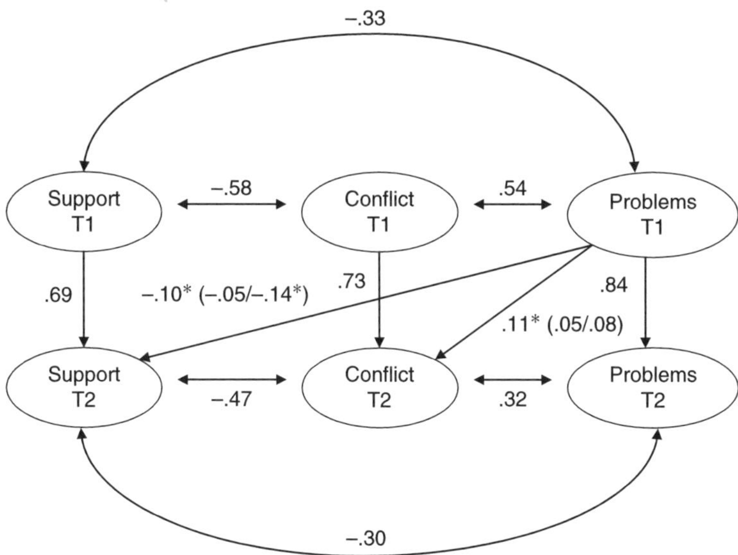

Figure 6.2 Associations between parental support, conflict with parents, and internalizing problem behavior over time

LONGITUDINAL ASSOCIATIONS BETWEEN PARENTAL SUPPORT AND INTERNALIZING AND EXTERNALIZING BEHAVIOR DURING ADOLESCENCE AND YOUNG ADULTHOOD

In two studies, we examined the bidirectional associations of parental support with internalizing behavior (i.e., emotional problems) and externalizing behavior (i.e., delinquency) in the context of adolescents' and young adults' romantic relationships. Both studies used data from the Utrecht Study of Adolescent Development (USAD) 1991–1997 (Meeus & 't Hart, 1993; see the study of Helsen, Vollebergh, & Meeus, 2000, described earlier). The development of intimacy and commitment to romantic partners is one of the important tasks for adolescents and young adults (Erikson, 1968), although relations with parents and friends remain important for support and intimacy (Seiffge-Krenke, 1997; Shulman & Scharf, 2000). As romantic partners become more important both with age and with extended experience with romantic partners (Shulman & Scharf, 2000), they will eventually replace the parent as the most important attachment figure (Hazan & Shaver, 1987). Thus, it might be that parental support is no longer related to emotional problems when adolescents and adults have a romantic partner. This effect might be stronger for young adults who have more mature romantic relationships.

Similarly, it has been found that once young adults have a romantic partner, their parents no longer have any influence on their delinquency and the quality of the relationship with the romantic partner is predictive of delinquency (see for an overview Meeus, Branje, & Overbeek, 2004). Studies that only considered the association between the relationship with parents and delinquency did report an association between the quality of the relationship with parents and delinquency. However, these studies only focused on adolescence and not on young adulthood (i.e., after 20 years of age). The difference between these studies might be due to a moderation effect of having a romantic partner on the association between the relationship with parents and delinquency, but could also reflect that the influence of parents diminishes as the adolescent grows older regardless of partnership status.

We investigated how involvement with romantic partners moderates the effect of parental support on delinquency and emotional problems. We expected that parental support is predictive of the degree of delinquency and emotional problems when adolescents have no romantic partners but not predictive if they do have such a partner. We also expected that for adolescents with romantic involvement, parental support is stronger related to less delinquency and emotional problems than for young adults because romantic partners are thought to become more important and effects of parental support might diminish with age.

As the effects of romantic partner might be especially strong when there is extended experience with romantic partners, we distinguished three *partnership status* groups: (1) Six year partner group: respondents who have had a romantic partner at time 1 and time 2 six years later, and consequently had experience with one or more partners for a period that spanned, although not necessarily continuously, a period of six years, (2) T2 partner group: respondents who moved from having no partner at time 1 to having a partner at time 2, (3) Never partner group: respondents who never had a partner. Respondents who did not fall into one of these patterns were excluded from the study. In order to examine whether the diminished influence of the parents could be attributed to the existence of a romantic partner or to age alone, we distinguished adolescents (aged 12–18 in wave 1) and young adults (aged 21 in wave 1).

LONGITUDINAL EFFECTS BETWEEN PARENTAL SUPPORT AND DELINQUENCY

The first study examines how romantic involvement moderates the effect of parental support on delinquency. Meeus, Branje & Overbeek (2004) used the same three partner groups of the USAD study to examine longitudinal associations between parental support and delinquency. *Parental support* was the average of paternal and maternal support. *Partner support* was assessed by means of a list of three questionnaire items. Respondents indicated on a 10-point scale (range 10–100) the degree of social support they received in the domain of personal relationships, leisure time and school/work from their romantic partner. Cronbach's alphas for partner support were 0.82, 0.75, and 0.74 at wave 1, wave 2 and wave 3 respectively. *Delinquency* was assessed in an oral interview as the number of delinquent acts the respondents reported over the past 12 months. The delinquency measure consists of 21 items pertaining to three types of delinquent behavior: violent crime (e.g., "Have you ever wounded anybody with a knife or other weapon?"), vandalism (e.g., "Have you ever covered walls, buses, or entryways with graffiti?"), and crime against property (e.g., "Have you ever bought something which you knew was stolen?"). Subjects indicated whether they had behaved in one of these ways during the past 12 months on a two-point scale (0 = no, to 1 = yes). The scores on the 21 items were summed with ranges between 0–10 in wave 1, 0–9 in wave 2, and 0–6 in wave 3; mean scores were 0.81, 0.70 and 0.48 respectively. In the structural equation models standardized scores were used. Results are displayed in Figures 6.3a–6.3c.

Multigroup path analyses (with six groups: three partner groups by two age groups) revealed that parental support was related to a reduction in the level of delinquency over time for adolescents and young adults who have never had a partner and for adolescents who only have a partner at time 2 six years later. For these adolescents and young adults, higher levels of parental support were associated with lower levels of delinquency six years later. For adolescents and young adults who consistently had a romantic partner across the waves and for young adults who moved into a relationship with an romantic partner, parental support was not related to a reduction of delinquency over time. Furthermore, delinquency was found to lead to reduced parental support for adolescents and young adults who had a romantic relationship at time 2 only, but not for any of the other groups of adolescents. These findings show that delinquency can be an obstacle for maintaining good relationships with parents.

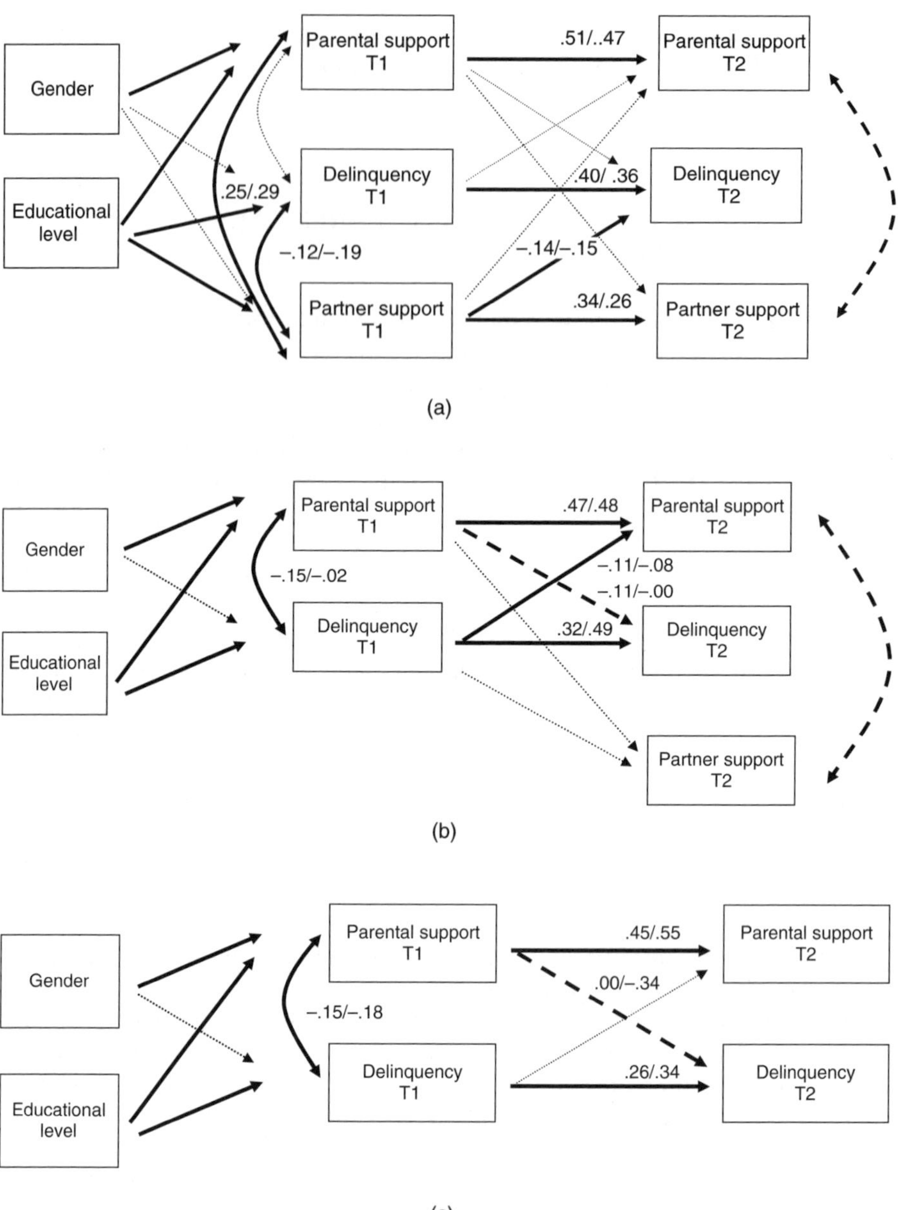

Figure 6.3 Models of relations between parental support and delinquency for the systematic romantic partner groups (a), the best friend to romantic partner groups (b), and no romantic partner groups (c). Statistics of the relevant significant parameters of both age groups within the relationship status groups are printed. The first statistic is that of the youngest group, the second that of the oldest. Only significant estimates are shown. Broken lines indicate correlations or paths that were significant in only one group

In sum, these findings offer evidence for the moderating role of the relationship with a romantic partner on the effects of parental support on delinquency. In adolescents and young adults who have a romantic partner, parental support is not important in reducing delinquency and partners seem to have taken this role from parents. For adolescents and young adults who have never had a partner, as well as for adolescents who do not have a partner yet, parental support is important in reducing delinquency. Confirming our expectations regarding age, adolescents who are on their way to finding a romantic partner are still influenced by parental support, whereas young adults who are forming relationships with romantic partners are not affected in this stage of their lives by parental support.

LONGITUDINAL EFFECTS BETWEEN PARENTAL SUPPORT AND EMOTIONAL PROBLEMS

The second study describes how involvement with romantic partners moderates the effect of parental support on emotional adjustment. Meeus *et al.* (in press) examined longitudinal associations of parental support with emotional problems as part of a study on longitudinal relations of parental support and emotional adjustment with commitment to romantic partners and best friends. The longitudinal sample consisted of 1,302 participants, of whom 550 were males. The respondents were evenly distributed over four age categories: 321 early adolescents (25%), 341 middle adolescents (26%), 261 late adolescents (20%), and 379 young adults (29%). For this study, the three youngest age groups were combined to create one adolescent group.

Parental support was computed as the average of support of father and mother (see also Helsen, Vollebergh, & Meeus, 2000). Cronbach's alphas for parental support were 0.87, 0.88, and 0.87 at wave 1, wave 2, and wave 3 respectively. *Emotional adjustment* was assessed as a composite of scales for psychological stress and depression, general well being and happiness, and the consideration of suicide (see also Helsen, Vollebergh, & Meeus). *Relational commitment to best friend and romantic partner* was assessed with the relational commitment scale of the Utrecht-Groningen Identity Development Scale (U-GIDS) (Meeus, 1996). Adolescents who had a romantic partner rated this partner, other adolescent rated a best friend. The six-item scale includes items tapping commitment to stay in the relationship and involvement in the relationship. Examples of the items are: "My best friend/romantic partner allows me to face the future with optimism' (intent to persist in the relationship"), and "I'm sure my best friend/romantic partner was the best choice for me" (psychological attachment to the relationship). A five-point Likert type scale was used with response categories ranging from 1 = "completely untrue" to 5 = "completely true." Cronbach's alphas of the scale for relational commitment were 0.88, 0.89, and 0.89 at wave 1, wave 2, and wave 3 respectively.

Table 6.4 Standardized maximum likelihood estimates between parental support, relational commitment and emotional problems

Parameter	Age group by relationship status group					
	12–20			21–23		
	T1 + 3 partner n = 157	**T3 partner n = 262**	**No partner n = 305**	**T1 + 3 partner n = 234**	**T3 partner n = 38**	**No partner n = 45**
T1 correlations						
Relational commitment T1 – Emotional problems	0.04_b	-0.05_b	0.06_b	-0.27^{***}_a	-0.04_b	0.07_b
T1Parental support T1 – Emotional problems	-0.24^{***}	-0.30^{***}	-0.36^{***}	-0.18^{***}	-0.29^{***}	-0.32^{***}
T1Parental support T1 – Relational commitment T1	0.03_b	0.03_b	0.03_b	0.27^{***}_a	0.03_b	0.03_b
Stability paths						
Relational commitment T1 – T3	0.22^{***}_b	0.23^{***}_b	0.21^{***}_b	0.37^{***}_a	0.27^{***}_b	0.24^{***}_b
Parental support T1 – T3	0.51^{***}	0.43^{***}	0.39^{***}	0.56^{***}	0.77^{***}	0.71^{***}
Emotional problems T1 – T3	0.38^{***}	0.34^{***}	0.28^{***}	0.27^{***}	0.41^{***}	0.30^{***}
T3 associations						
Relational commitment T3 – Emotional problems T3	-0.04_b	-0.16^{***}_a	-0.06_b	-0.15^{***}_a	-0.23^{***}_a	0.09_b
Parental support T3 – Emotional problems T3	-0.03	-0.26^{***}	-0.17^{**}	-0.18^{**}	-0.16	0.09
Parental support T3 – Relational commitment T3	0.05	0.16^{**}	0.05	0.03	0.02	0.16

Notes Estimates sharing a common subscript across columns are not significantly different from each other
$^{*}p < 0.05$. $^{**}p < 0.01$ $^{***}p < 0.00$

We performed multigroup path analyses using AMOS to estimate links over time between parental support, partner/best friend commitment and emotional problems for the six groups of adolescents and young adults with and without a romantic partner (three partner status groups by two age groups). Results of this study are displayed in Table 6.4.

Results showed that parental support was related to less emotional disturbance at time 1 for all groups, and that this relation is stronger for adolescents without a romantic partner than for adolescents with a romantic partner. At time 2, there was correlated change between parental support and emotional problems: a decline in parental support was related to an increase in emotional problems for young adults with a romantic partner at both time points, for adolescents without a partner, and for adolescents with a partner at time 2 only (that are late adolescents or young adults by this time). Against our expectation, there were no crosslagged effects from parental support to emotional problems or from emotional problems to parental support for any of the groups. These findings suggest that parental support is more strongly related to emotional problems for adolescents than for young adults, however when young adults are systematically involved in romantic relationships, parental support is related to emotional problems as well. Thus, disconfirming our hypothesis, romantic partners only partially take over the role of parents in young adulthood. An explanation for this findings might be that relationships with parents become more egalitarian when adolescents are older and parents are more likely to be accepted as supportive when dealing with romantic relationships in young adulthood than in adolescence.

DISCUSSION

The aim of this chapter was to compare longitudinal evidence for associations between parental support and adolescent problem behavior to theoretical perspectives that offer explanations for these associations. Theoretical perspectives focusing on direct effects of parent, direct effects of child, and reciprocal effects were compared. Longitudinal results confirm the importance of assessing bidirectional effects and generally suggested that parental direct effects are found predominantly for internalizing problems, whereas child direct effects or bidirectional effect are more likely to occur for externalizing problems. The review of empirical findings confirms that parents play a pronounced role in adolescent adjustment, particularly in internalizing problems (Baumrind, 1991). Adolescents rely on parents to provide several types of support (Furman & Buhrmester, 1992), and they might be deeply effected by a lack of parental support because of the permanent nature of the parent–child relationship (Collins & Laursen, 1992).

For both depression and anxiety, most support was found for direct effects of parental support. These effects were more often found for adolescents than for young adults and when gender differences were found, effects tended to be stronger for girls. Youth who experience deficits in parental provision of support seem to be more likely to feel depressed. Although these results suggest that parental support promotes ways of coping in adolescents that enables them to deal more effectively with problems or daily hassles and may help them to regulate their emotional states (Eisenberg & Fabes, 1992; Wills & Cleary, 1996), not much support was found for stress-buffering effects of parental support, although the possibility remains that parental support compensates for other (unidentified) vulnerability factors. Also, only limited evidence was found for erosion of parental support as a consequence of effects in reaction to adolescent depressive and anxiety symptoms. Perhaps internalizing problems are more likely to promote erosion of support in relationships with peers that are more voluntary than in relationships with parents (Stice, Ragan, & Randall, 2004). Surprisingly, the results of our own studies are not in agreement with these general findings. In one study we did not find effects over time between parental support and emotional problems, in the other study we found evidence for support erosion, in particular for boys with internalizing problems. One reason for this unexpected finding is that, until now, hardly any studies have examined reciprocal effects between support and internalizing behavior for girls and boys separately. This finding might reflect that parents accept internalizing behavior less from boys than from girls and reduce their support to boys but not to girls in response to internalizing behavior.

For externalizing behavior, longitudinal results most consistently revealed evidence for adverse effects of adolescent problem behavior on parental support, indicating that parents tend to detach emotionally from their externalizing adolescent and reduce their support to the adolescent as a consequence of the externalizing behavior. Although there was less support for the assertion that deficits in parental support unilaterally foster adolescent problem behaviors, reciprocal effects were also found, in particular for substance use. These effects suggest cycles of influence in which youths prone to externalizing behavior repulse their parents because of their problem behavior (Patterson *et al.*, 1998) and the adolescents subsequently use illicit substances or display acting-out behavior as a means of coping with this perceived deficit in parental support. Again, our own results were not in agreement with these conclusions. One study did not reveal effects over time between externalizing behavior and parental support; the other study showed that parental support was related to delinquency but only for adolescents who had a romantic partner in late adolescence only (time 2 of the study) and for young adults who did not have a romantic partner during the study. Further research is needed to see if reciprocal effects between parental support and externalizing behavior will be found when controlling for initial relationships, stability, and correlated change.

The findings discussed in this chapter demonstrate that longitudinal relations of parental support with internalizing and externalizing problems are not the same under all conditions. The precise pattern of effects between parental support and adjustment problems for adolescents might depend on a number of factors, including adolescents' individual characteristics (e.g., ethnicity, sex, age) and types of problem behaviors (e.g., depression, anxiety). Also, social support may be provided by peers, teachers, mentors, and other persons in the network of youngsters, and effects of parental support can have a differential impact in the context of other relations, such as siblings (Branje *et al.*, 2004), romantic partners (Meeus *et al.*, 2004, in press), and friends (Young *et al.*, 2005).

The extent to which parental support and child problem behavior affect each other might depend on the developmental period under study. During childhood, parental effects might be larger than during adolescence, whereas during adolescence child effects might be larger than during childhood. Additionally, when both problem behavior and parental support are stable over time it is likely that reciprocal influences between problems and support have been established during childhood and remain stable over time. Therefore, few reciprocal effects will be observed. Effects might further decrease during late adolescence, when adolescents move out of their parents' home, either to continue their education or begin their own families, and peer support may become more important than parental support (Furman & Buhrmester, 1992; Helsen, Volleburgh, & Meeus, 2000; Wilkinson, 2004). The vanishing effect of support from parents as adolescents age into adulthood (Meadows, Brown, & Elder, 2006; Meeus, Branje, & Overbeek, 2004) might reflect the changing role of parents during the transition to adulthood when adolescents begin to establish independent lives (Helsen, Vollebergh & Meeus, 2000; Furman & Buhrmester, 1992).

The findings presented in this chapter seem consistent with the assertion that parents continue to affect adolescent development (Collins *et al.*, 2000). Nevertheless, third variables may be involved that are not included in the study and influence the relations between problem behavior and perceived support. An example of such a third variable is genetic resemblance between family members. Because parents and children are genetically related, the relations between parental support and adolescent adjustment problems might in part be explained by genetic similarity between parents and children (Caspi, 2000). Genetic factors that influence parents' ability to provide support to their children might be the same as the genetic factors accounting for child problem behavior (Harris, 1998; Jaffee *et al.*, 2004).

Moreover, most studies have assessed adolescents' *perceived* parental support and thus effects between parental support and adolescent problem behavior might exist in the eye of the beholder: adolescents with higher levels of problems might perceive their environment differently than adolescents with lower levels of problems. The correlations between reports of parents and adolescents on parental support are not very high and mean levels substantially differ. Perceiver effects play a relatively strong role in adolescents' perceptions of support from fathers and mothers (Branje, Van Aken, & Van Lieshout, 2002), indicating that the meanings that adolescents make of their experiences with parents are important to understand. Because similar experiences may mean different things to different adolescents, the same experiences may lead to different outcomes for different adolescents. These large perceiver effects might also explain why generally not many differences between effects of paternal support and maternal support are found. Future research should address whether the results for adolescent reported parental support generalize to more "objective" measures of parental support.

To conclude, results suggest that parental effects are found predominantly for internalizing problems, whereas child effects and bidirectional effect are found predominantly for externalizing problems. Future longitudinal research should examine the processes mediating the effects between parental support and problem behavior. Does a lack of parental support lead to ineffective ways of coping (Wills & Cleary, 1996)? Does lack of parental support interfere with socialization processes and internalization of parental norms (Baumrind, 1991)? Does a lack of parental support lead to externalizing behavior through a process of affiliation with deviant peers (Patterson, 1982; Dishion, Nelson, & Bullock, 2004)? Or does adolescent problem behavior lead to parent emotional rejection (Baumrind & Moselle, 1985)? Knowledge of the underlying mechanisms would greatly increase our understanding of the associations between adolescent problem behavior and parental support.

REFERENCES

Baerveldt, C., Rossem van, R., & Vermande, M. (2003). Pupils' delinquency and their social networks: a test of some network assumptions of the ability and inability models of delinquency. *Netherlands Journal of Social Sciences*, *39*, 107–125.

Barnes, G. M. & Farrell, M. P. (1992). Parental support and control as predictors of adolescent drinking, delinquency, and related problem behaviors. *Journal of Marriage and the Family*, *54*, 763–776.

Baumrind, D. (1991). Parenting styles and adolescent development. In J. Brooks-Gunn, R. Lerner & A. C. Petersen (eds), The Encyclopedia of Adolescence (pp. 746–758). New York: Garland.

Baumrind, D. & Moselle, K. A. (1985). A developmental perspective on adolescent drug abuse. *Advances in Alcohol and Substance Abuse*, *4*, 41–67.

Beck, A. T., Rush, A. J., Shaw, B. F., & Emery, G. (1979). *Cognitive Therapy of Depression*. New York: Guilford Press.

Bell, R. (1968). A reinterpretation of the direction of effects in studies of socialization. *Psychological Review*, *75*, 81–95.

Bell, R. Q. & Chapman, M. (1986). Child effects in studies using experimental or brief longitudinal approaches to socialization. *Developmental Psychology*, *22*, 595–603.

Belsky, J. (1984). The determinants of parenting: A process model. *Child Development*, *55*, 83–97.

Birmaher, B., Khetarpal, S., Brent, D. *et al.* (1997). The Screen for Child Anxiety Related Emotional Disorders (SCARED): Scale construction and psychometric characteristics. *Journal of the American Academy of Child and Adolescent Psychiatry*, *36*, 545–553.

Birmaher, B., Brent, D. A., Chiappetta, L. *et al.* (1999), Psychometric properties of the Screen for Child Anxiety Related Emotional Disorders (SCARED): A replication study. *Journal of the American Academy of Child and Adolescent Psychiatry, 38,* 1230–1236.

Bjorkqvist, K., Lagerspetz, K. M. J., & Osterman, K. (1992). *The Direct and Indirect Aggression Scales.* Vasa, Finland: Abo Akademi University, Department of Social Sciences.

Branje, S. J. T., Van Aken, M. A. G., & Van Lieshout, C. F. M. (2002). Relational support in families with adolescents. *Journal of Family Psychology, 16,* 351–362.

Branje, S. J. T., Van Lieshout, C. F. M., Van Aken, M. A. G ., & Haselager, G. J. T. (2004). Perceived support in sibling relationships and adolescent adjustment. *Journal of Child Psychology and Psychiatry, 45,* 1385–1396.

Burton, E., Stice, E. & Seeley, J. R. (2004). A prospective test of the stress-buffering model of depression in adolescent girls: No support once again. *Journal of Consulting and Clinical Psychology, 72,* 689–697.

Caspi, A. (2000). The child is father of the man: personality continuities from childhood to adulthood. *Journal of Personality and Social Psychology, 78,* 158–172.

Cohen, S. & Wills, T. A. (1985). Stress, social support, and the buffering hypothesis. *Psychological Bulletin, 98,* 310–357.

Collins, W. A. & Laursen, B. (1992). Conflict and relationships during adolescence. In C. U. Shantz & W. W. Hartup (eds), *Conflict in Child and Adolescent Development* (pp. 216–241). New York: Cambridge University Press.

Collins, W., Maccoby, E. E., Steinberg, L. *et al.* (2000). Contemporary research on parenting: the case for nature and nurture. *American Psychologist, 55,* 218–232.

Coyne, J. C. (1976). Depression and the response of others. *Journal of Abnormal Psychology, 85,* 186–193.

Coyne, J. C., Burchill, S. A. L. & Stiles, W. B. (1991). An interactional perspective on depression. In C. R. Snyder & D. O. Forsyth (eds), *Handbook of Social and Clinical Psychology* (pp. 327–349). New York: Pergamon.

Deković, M., Janssens, J. M. A. M & Van As, N. M. C. (2003). Family predictors of antisocial behavior in adolescence. *Family Process, 42,* 223–235.

Dishion, T. J., Nelson, S. E., & Bullock, B. M. (2004). Premature adolescent autonomy: Family management and deviant peer process in the amplification of problem behavior. *Journal of Adolescence, 27,* 515–530.

DuBois, D. L., Felner, R. D., Brand, S. *et al.* (1992). A prospective study of life stress, social support, and adaptation in early adolescence. *Child Development, 63,* 542–557.

Eisenberg, N. & Fabes, R. A. (1992). Emotion, regulation, and the development of social competence. In S. C. Margaret (ed.), *Emotion and Social Behavior. Review of Personality and Social Psychology: Vol. 14* (pp. 119–150). Newbury Park, CA: Sage.

Erikson, E. (1968). *Identity, Youth and Crisis.* New York: Norton.

Fisher, C. S. (1982). *To Dwell Among Friends. Personal Networks in Town and City.* Chicago University Press, Chicago.

Furman, W. & Buhrmester, D. (1992). Age and sex differences in perceptions of networks of personal relationships. *Child Development, 63,* 103–115.

Ge, X., Lorenz, F. O., Conger, R. D. *et al.* (1994) Trajectories of stressful life events and depressive symptoms during adolescence. *Developmental Psychology, 30,* 467–483.

Hale III, W. W. (2001). Behavioral social support between remitted depressed patients with partners and strangers. *Journal of Affective Disorders, 64,* 285–289.

Hale III, W. W., Branje, S. J. T., Raaijmakers, Q. A. W., & Meeus, W. H. J. (2005). *Why Me? Adolescent Problems and Parental Support and Conflict*. Symposium paper presented at the Twelfth European Conference on Developmental Psychology, Tenerife, Spain, August 24–27, 2005.

Hale III, W. W., Raaijmakers, Q., Muris, P., & Meeus, W. (2005). Psychometric properties of the Screen for Child Anxiety Related Emotional Disorders (SCARED) in the general adolescent population. *Journal of the American Academy of Child and Adolescent Psychiatry*, *44*, 283–290.

Hale III, W. W., Van der Valk, I., Akse, J., & Meeus, W. (in press). The interplay of early adolescent depressed mood, aggressive behavior and perceived parental rejection: A four year longitudinal community study.

Harris, J. R. (1998). *The Nurture Assumption: Why Children Turn Out the Way They Do*. New York: Free Press.

Hartup, W. W. (1978). Perspectives on child and family interaction: Past, present, and future. In R. M. Lerner & G. B. Spanier (eds), *Child Influences on Marital and Family Interaction: A Life-Span Perspective* (pp. 23–46). San Francisco: Academic Press.

Haselager, G. J. T. & Van Aken, M. A. G. (1999). *Codebook of the Research Project Family and Personality: Vol. 1. First Measurement Wave*. Nijmegen, The Netherlands: University of Nijmegen, Faculty of Social Science.

Hazan, C. & Shaver, P. (1987). Romantic love conceptualized as an attachment process. *Journal of Personality and Social Psychology*, *52*, 511–524.

Helsen, M., Vollebergh, W., & Meeus, W. (2000). Social support from parents and friends and emotional problems in adolescence. *Journal of Youth and Adolescence*, *29*, 319–335.

Hirschi, T. (1969). *Causes of Delinquency*. Berkeley, CA: University of California Press.

Hollon, S. D. & Beck, A. T. (1994) Cognitive and cognitive-behavioral therapies. In A. E. Bergin & S. L. Garfield (eds), *Handbook of Psychotherapy and Behavior Change* (4th edn, pp. 428–466). Chichester: John Wiley & Sons.

Huh, D., Tristan, J., Wade, E., & Stice, E. (2006). Does problem behavior elicit poor parenting? A prospective study of adolescent girls. *Journal of Adolescent Research*, *21*, 185–204.

Jaffee, S. R., Polo-Tomas, M., Taylor, A. *et al.* (2004). The limits of child effects: Evidence for genetically mediated child effects on corporal punishment but not on physical maltreatment. *Developmental Psychology*, *40*, 1047–1058.

Joiner, T. E. (1999). A test of interpersonal theory of depression in youth psychiatric inpatients. *Journal of Abnormal Child Psychology*, *27*, 77–85.

Kerr, M. & Stattin, H. (2003). Parenting of adolescents: Action or reaction? In A. C. Crouter & A. Booth (eds), *Children's Influence on Family Dynamics: The Neglected Side of Family Relationships* (pp. 121–152). Mahwah, NJ: Erlbaum.

Kovacs, M. (1985). The children's depression inventory. *Psychopharmacology Bulletin*, *21*, 995–998.

Lollis, S. & Kuczynski, L. (1997). Beyond one hand clapping: Seeing bidirectionality in parent–child relations. *Journal of Social and Personal Relationships*, *14*, 441–461.

Lopez, E. E., Olaizola, J. H., Ferrer, B. M & Ochoa, G. M. (2006). Aggressive and nonaggressive rejected students: An analysis of their differences. *Psychology in the Schools*, *43*, 387–400.

Maccoby, E. E. (1984). Socialization and developmental change. *Child Development*, *55*, 317–328.

Maton, A. & Zimmerman, K. I. (1992). Life-style and substance use among male African-American urban adolescents: A cluster analytic approach. *American Journal of Community Psychology*, *20*, 121–138.

McCarty, C. A., Van der Stoep, A., Kuo, E. S., & McCauley, E. (2006). Depressive symptoms among delinquent youth: testing models of association with stress and support. *Journal of Psychopathology and Behavioral Assessment*, 28, 85–93.

Meadows, S. O., Brown, J. S., & Elder, G. H. (2006). Depressive symptoms, stress and support: Gendered trajectories from adolescence to young adulthood. *Journal of Youth and Adolescence, 35,* 89–99.

Measelle, J. R., Stice, E., & Springer, D. W. (2006) A prospective test of the negative affect model of substance abuse: Moderating effects of social support. *Psychology of Addictive Behaviors, 20,* 225–233.

Meeus, W. (1989). Parental and peer support in adolescence. In Hurrelmann, K. & Engel, U. (eds), *The Social World of Adolescents* (pp. 167–185). New York: De Gruyter.

Meeus, W. (1996). Studies on identity development in adolescence: an overview of research and some new data. *Journal of Youth and Adolescence, 25,* 569–598.

Meeus, W., Akse, J., Branje, S. J. T. *et al.* (2004). *Codeboek van het onderzoeksproject CONflicts and MAnagement of Relationships (CONAMORE). Eerste meetronde: 2001.* [Codebook of the research project CONflicts and MAnagement of Relationships (CONAMORE) First wave: 2001.] Unpublished manuscript, Utrecht University, The Netherlands.

Meeus, W., Branje, S. J. T., & Overbeek, G. J. (2004). Parents and partners in crime: a six year longitudinal study on changes in supportive relationships and delinquency in adolescence and young adulthood. *Journal of Child Psychology and Psychiatry and Allied Disciplines, 45,* 1288–1298.

Meeus, W. H. J., Branje, S. J. T., Van der Valk, I., & De Wied, M. (2007). Relationships with intimate partner, best friend, and parents in adolescence and early adulthood: A study of the saliency of the intimate partnership. *International Journal of Behavioral Development, 31,* 569–580.

Meeus, W. & 't Hart, H. (1993). *Jongeren in Nederland* [Young people in the Netherlands]. Amersfoort: Academische Uitgeverij.

Mounts, N. S. (2004). Contributions of parenting and campus climate to freshmen adjustment in a multiethnic sample. *Journal of Adolescent Research, 19,* 468–491.

Neyer, F. J. & Asendorpf, J. B. (2001). Personality-relationship transaction in young adulthood. *Journal of Personality and Social Psychology, 81,* 1190–1204.

Parker, J. S. & Benson, M. J. (2005). Parent-adolescent relations and adolescent functioning: Self-esteem, substance abuse, and delinquency. *Family Therapy, 32,* 131–142.

Patterson, G. R. (1982). *A Social Learning Approach: III. Coercive Family Process*. Eugene, OR: Castalia.

Patterson, G. R., Forgatch, M. S., Yoerger, K. L., & Stoolmiller, M. (1998). Variables that initiate and maintain an early-onset trajectory for juvenile offending. *Development and Psychopathology, 10,* 531–547.

Pierce, R., Frone, M., Russell, M. *et al.* (2000). A longitudinal model of social contact, social support, depression, and alcohol use. *Health Psychology, 91,* 28–38.

Reis, H. T., Collins, W. A., & Berscheid, E. (2000). The relationship context of human behavior and development. *Psychological Bulletin, 126,* 844–872.

Sameroff, A. J. (1983). Developmental systems: Contexts and evolution. In W. Kessen (ed.), *Handbook of Child Psychology: Vol. 1. History, Theory, and Methods* (4th edn, pp. 237–294). New York: Wiley.

Scholte, R. H. J., Van Lieshout, C. F. M., & Van Aken, M. A. G. (2001). Perceived relational support in adolescence: Dimensions, configurations, and adolescent adjustment. *Journal of Research in Adolescence, 11,* 71–94.

Scholte, R. H. J., Vermulst, A. A., & De Bruyn, E. E. J. (2001). Instrument Development and Validation. Poster presented at the 6th European Association of Psychological Assessment. Aachen, Germany, September 2–5.

Segrin, C. & Dillard, J. P. (1992). The interactional theory of depression: A meta-analysis of the research literature. *Journal of Social and Clinical Psychology, 11*, 43–70.

Seiffge-Krenke, I. (1997). Wie verändern sich die familiären Beziehungen im Jugendalter? Diskrepanz in der Einschätzung von Jugendlichen und ihren Eltern. *Zeitschrift für Entwicklungspsychologie und Pädagogische Psychologie, 29*, 133–150.

Sheeber, L., Hops, H., Alpert, A. *et al.* (1997). Family support and conflict: Prospective relations to adolescent depression. *Journal of Abnormal Child Psychology, 25*, 333–344.

Shulman, S. & Scharf, M. (2000). Adolescent romantic behaviors and perceptions: Age- and gender-related differences, and links with family and peer relationships. *Journal of Research on Adolescence, 10*, 99–118.

Slavin, L. A. & Rainer, K. (1990). Gender differences in emotional support and depressive symptoms among adolescents: A prospective analysis. *American Journal of Community Psychology, 18*, 407–421.

Stice, E. & Barrera, M. (1995). A longitudinal examination of the reciprocal relations between perceived parenting and adolescents' substance use and externalizing behaviors. *Developmental Psychology, 31*, 322–334.

Stice, E., Barrera, M., & Chassin, L. (1998). Prospective differential prediction of adolescent alcohol use and problem use: Examining mechanisms of effect. *Journal of Abnormal Psychology, 107*, 616–628.

Stice, E., Ragan, J., & Randall, P. (2004). Prospective relations between social support and depression: Differential direction of effects for parent and peer support? *Journal of Abnormal Psychology, 113*, 155–159.

Vazsonyi, A. T. (2004). Parent–adolescent relations and problem behaviors: Hungary, the Netherlands, Switzerland, and the United States. *Marriage and Family Review, 35*, 161–187.

Wilkinson, R. B. (2004). The role of parental and peer attachment in the psychological health and self-esteem of adolescents. *Journal of Youth and Adolescence, 33*, 479–493.

Wills, T. A. & Cleary, S. D. (1996). How are social support effects mediated? A test with parental support and adolescent substance use. *Journal of Personality and Social Psychology, 71*, 937–952.

Wills, T. A. & Resko, J. A. (2004). Social support and behavior toward others: some paradoxes and some directions. In A. G. Miller (ed.) *The Social Psychology of Good and Evil* (pp. 416–443). New York: Guilford.

Windle, M. (1992). Temperament and social support in adolescence: Interrelations with depressive symptoms and delinquent behaviors. *Journal of Youth and Adolescence, 21*, 1–21.

Yang, Y. & Yeh, K. (2006). Differentiating the effects of enacted parental support on adolescent adjustment in Taiwan: Moderating role of relationship intimacy. *Asian Journal of Social Psychology, 9*, 161–166.

Young, J. F., Berenson, K., Cohen, P., & Garcia, J. (2005). The role of parent and peer support in predicting adolescent depression: A longitudinal community study. *Journal of Research on Adolescence, 15*, 407–423.

Zimmerman, M. A., Steinman, K. J & Rowe, K. J. (1998). Violence among urban African American adolescents: The protective effects of parental support. In X. B. Arriaga & S. Oskamp (eds), *Addressing Community Problems: Psychological Research and Interventions* (pp. 78–103). Thousand Oaks: Sage Publications.

Zimmerman, M. A., Ramirez-Valles, J., Zapert, K. M., & Maton, K. I. (2000). A longitudinal study of stress-buffering effects for urban African-American male adolescent problem behaviors and mental health. *Journal of Community Psychology, 28*, 17–33.

CHAPTER 7

Linkages between Parenting and Peer Relationships: A Model for Parental Management of Adolescents' Peer Relationships

Nina S. Mounts
Northern Illinois University, USA

INTRODUCTION

Drawing on Bronfenbrenner's (1979) ecological theory, researchers have devoted much effort to examining the linkages between parent–child and peer relationships. Recently, there has been recognition in the literature that there are several facets to parental influences on children's peer relationships (Darling & Steinberg, 1993; Mize, Russell, & Pettit, 1998; Parke & O'Neil, 1999). Researchers suggest a distinction between indirect parental influences and direct parental influences on peer relationships. Indirect influences act outside of the domain of peer relationships (Ladd & LeSieur, 1995) and can include the way in which parenting style (Fuligni & Eccles, 1993; Mounts & Steinberg, 1995) affects peer relationships. In contrast, direct parental influences have

---

This material is based upon work supported by the National Science Foundation under Grant No. 0131664. Any opinions, findings, and conclusions or recommendations expressed in this material are those of the author and do not necessarily reflect the views of the National Science Foundation.

What Can Parents Do? New Insights into the Role of Parents in Adolescent Problem Behavior
Edited by Margaret Kerr, Håkan Stattin and Rutger C. M. E. Engels.

specific goals and content such that when parents use these practices their focus is on affecting the peer relationships of children.

Despite the progress in understanding linkages between parental management of peers and the peer relationships of young children, the research examining parental management of peer relationships during adolescence is limited. In this chapter, research on parental management of peers during adolescence will be reviewed, a model of peer management will be proposed, and some issues for future consideration will be introduced.

CONCEPTUALIZING MANAGEMENT OF PEER RELATIONSHIPS

The study of management of adolescents' peer relationships is relatively new, so the conceptual models available for describing it are relatively undeveloped. However, the literature on management of younger children's peer relationships provides some useful models for conceptualizing parental management of adolescents' peer relationships. In particular, Ladd & LeSieur (1995) and Ladd & Pettit (2002) suggested that the management of peer relationships of younger children might be described using a four-category model. These categories are a useful starting point in conceptualizing parental management of adolescents' peer relationships as well. In this chapter, I will review investigations that examine these four categories. Because this is a relatively new literature, in most cases, not all four aspects of the model are included in the investigations on peer management.

Parents as Designers of Adolescents' Environments

The first way in which parents manage peer relationships is that parents act as *designers* of the environment for adolescents by choosing particular neighborhoods, after school programs, extracurricular activities, and schools (Ladd & LeSieur, 1995; Ladd & Pettit, 2002). One way parents could design the environment of adolescents is by choosing particular types of neighborhoods. In their study of children's lives outside of school, Medrich *et al.* (1982) suggested that neighborhood configuration affected the extent to which young adolescents had contact with their peers. Neighborhoods with sidewalks, parks and schoolyards in close proximity and with many children offered more possibility for peer interaction than neighborhoods without sidewalks, few children, and busy streets.

The extent to which parents can act as designers of their children's environments by selecting neighborhoods is at least partially dependent upon socioeconomic status. Parents who are more affluent have the means to select and live in neighborhoods that support their values. On the other hand, parents living in poverty might be unable to move to better neighborhoods, despite their desire to provide their children with a better living situation (Furstenberg *et al.*, 1999). Furstenberg and colleagues suggest that in these cases parents might rely on other techniques to manage the peer relationships of their children. Likewise, one might expect parents to rely on similar strategies if they are unable to move to better school districts.

Another way in which parents could design the environment of adolescents is through their decisions about out-of-school care (Ladd & LeSieur, 1995; Ladd & Pettit, 2002). Steinberg (1986) suggested that adolescents in self-care after school reported higher levels of susceptibility to peer influence than adolescents who were in adult care or were in self-care in their homes. Similarly, Galambos & Maggs (1991) in their longitudinal investigation of sixth graders, found that adolescents who were in self-care out of their own homes after school and during the summer reported higher levels of peer involvement than adolescents in adult care or in self care at home. In addition, boys in self-care out of their homes reported having more deviant peers than boys who reported adult care or self-care in their own homes. Girls in self-care out of their homes reported higher levels of problem behavior than those in adult care or self-care in their own home. Taken together, these results suggest that parents do function as designers of the environments of young adolescents' through their selection of after-school arrangements and that these arrangements have consequences for peer relationships.

A final way in which parents could function as designers of the environments of adolescents is by encouraging adolescents to participate in community or extracurricular activities (Ladd & LeSieur, 1995; Ladd & Pettit, 2002). In one study, Fletcher, Elder & Mekos (2000) reported that parental reinforcement of adolescents' involvement in community activities was related to their ninth-grade involvement in activities as well as their tenth-grade involvement in activities for adolescents whose parents did not model community involvement through their own activities. For adolescents whose parents modeled community involvement through their own activities, parental reinforcement of adolescents' involvement in community activities was related to ninth-grade involvement in activities, but not tenth-grade involvement in activities. In another investigation, parents reported that involving their children in religious organizations was a means to provide them with peer groups that would have a positive influence on their development (Furstenberg *et al.*, 1999).

One question that emerges from the research on parents as designers of adolescents' environments is whether parents are making decisions about neighborhoods, after school care, or community activities as a means of managing peer relationships. Few of the investigations described above explicitly speak to the issue of whether these environmental design choices are active or passive (Ladd & Pettit, 2002). It could be that parents are considering peer relationships as they think about the neighborhoods they will live in, the kind of care their children will receive after school, and the types of activities they encourage their children to be in. On the other hand, it could be that parents do not generally consider the effects of these decisions on adolescents' peer relationships.

In one investigation, my research team explicitly asked primary caregivers whether they encouraged their young adolescents to participate in extracurricular activities so that they would meet other children. A total of 78 seventh graders (mean age = 12.6 years) and their primary caregivers from ethnically diverse backgrounds participated in the investigation. During a home visit the primary caregivers were asked "what kinds of activities have you encouraged your child to join so that he/she will meet other kids?"

Responses to the open-ended question were transcribed verbatim from the audiotapes. Content coding was conducted to assess for specific issues in the interviews. The codes for the content coding were generated by first having coders examine the transcripts and record all possible responses to a question. Subsequently, the list was consolidated to create unique codes and operational definitions were written. Finally, the data were coded using the coding list. Inter-rater reliability was assessed using Cohen's kappa.

The initial coding of this question produced 47 different activities that the parents encouraged their children to join so that they would meet other adolescents. Each interview protocol was coded by two coders and Cohen's kappa was calculated for each of the 47 codes. Kappas ranged from 0.49 to 1.00. Eighty-three percent of the kappas were 1.00, 8% of the kappas were between 0.90 and 0.99, 2% were in the 0.80 to 0.89 range, 4% were in the 0.70 to 0.79 range, 2% were in the 0.60 to 0.69 range, and the remaining 1% were below 0.60. In order to make the 47 activities more interpretable, three coders then collapsed the 47 activities into six categories: youth organizations (e.g., 4-H, girl/boy scouts, park district activities, YMCA/YWCA classes), arts (e.g., art classes, band, choir/chorus, dance classes, drama classes), sports (e.g., baseball, football, cheerleading, swimming, soccer), religious activities, school based clubs (e.g., book, debate, pep, yearbook), and summer activities (e.g., summer camps, summer school). Approximately 54% of the caregivers reported that they encouraged activities so that their children would meet other children. Figure 7.1 presents the percentages of specific activities encouraged by the caregivers for boys and girls.

Chi-square analyses suggested child gender differences in the types of activities encouraged by caregivers. Significant gender differences were found for encouragement of participation in youth organizations, χ^2 (1, $N = 78$) = 4.75, $p < 0.05$), encouragement of participation in arts, χ^2 (1, $N = 78$) = 8.16, $p < 0.01$), encouragement of religious activities, χ^2 (1, $N = 78$) = 8.56, $p < 0.01$), and encouragement of summer activities χ^2 (1, $N = 78$) = 4.92, $p < 0.05$). Caregivers were more likely to encourage participation in youth organization, religious activities, and summer activities for boys than for girls. In contrast, caregivers were more likely to encourage participation in art programs for girls than for boys. There were no gender differences in caregiver encouragement of participation in sports activities χ^2 (1, $N = 78$) = 0.07, $p = ns$). It could be that

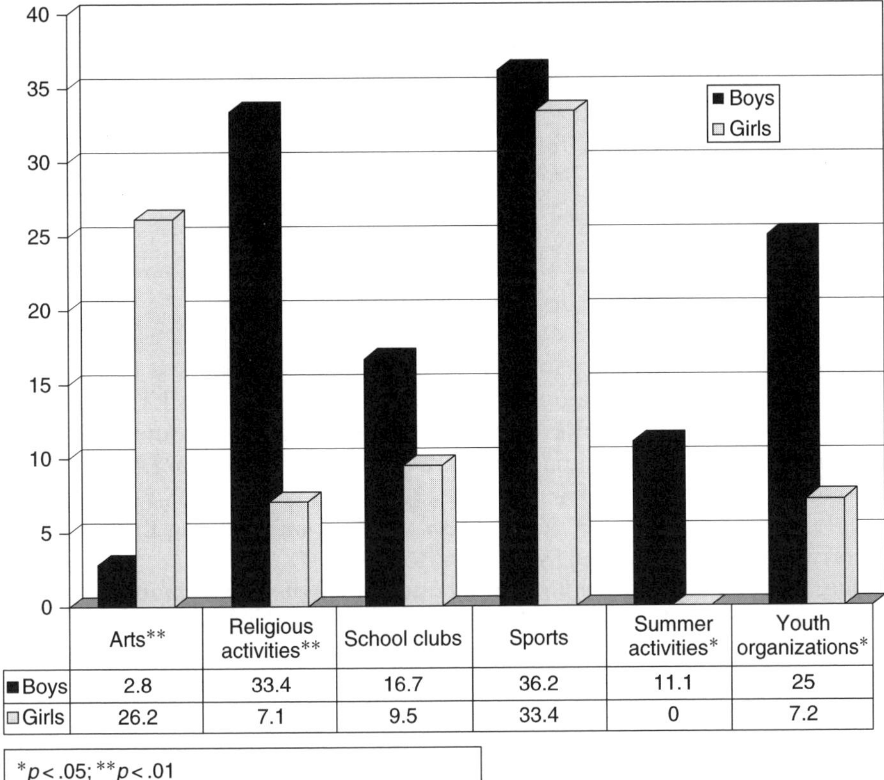

	Arts**	Religious activities**	School clubs	Sports	Summer activities*	Youth organizations*
■ Boys	2.8	33.4	16.7	36.2	11.1	25
□ Girls	26.2	7.1	9.5	33.4	0	7.2

Figure 7.1 Activities encouraged by caregivers so that adolescents will meet other adolescents

caregivers are more concerned with adolescent boys' involvement in misbehavior in the presence of their friends. Because of this, they encourage them to meet friends in contexts that are more structured or which might have a positive effect on adolescents' development. In contrast, caregivers might be less concerned with the misbehavior of girls and tend to encourage involvement in gender stereotypical activities. Future research on parental goals should explore this issue more fully. We did not explicitly ask whether the parents encouraged their children to participate in activities so that they would avoid affiliating with deviant peers, so it is not clear whether this was the goal in facilitating involvement in extracurricular activities.

Results of these analyses suggest that slightly over half of the caregivers reported that they encouraged their young adolescents' participation in extracurricular activities so that they would meet other adolescents. In addition, there were gender differences in the types of activities that parents encouraged. This provides some preliminary evidence that parents are acting as designers of extracurricular activities so that adolescents will meet other children. Further research is needed that examines whether peer relationships are a consideration in selection of neighborhoods, schools, or after school programs. Furthermore, as mentioned above, more information is needed whether parents are focusing on their children cultivating friendships in general or whether there are peers with specific characteristics (e.g., low problem behavior) which they are hoping to find in these settings.

Parents as Mediators of Adolescents' Peer Relationships

The second way in which parents manage peer relationships is that parents act as *mediators* of peer relationships (Ladd & LeSieur, 1995; Ladd & Pettit, 2002). As mediators, parents help their adolescents arrange meetings with peers and also help them manage their interactions with their peers. Following Ladd and colleagues (Ladd & LeSieur, 1995; Ladd & Pettit, 2002), this might include helping adolescents build a peer network and helping them arrange opportunities to get together with friends.

One study that examined potential mediators of peer relationships was conducted by Vernberg *et al.* (1993). Four groups of friendship facilitation strategies were identified that were useful in helping early adolescents form friendships after a move to a new school. Parents reported that they met with other parents, facilitated proximity to peers, talked with their adolescents about peer relationships, and encouraged interactions with other adolescents as strategies for helping their young adolescent make new friends after a family relocation. Adolescents whose parents reported the highest frequency of friendship facilitation strategies had greater success in making friends. This study provides some evidence that parents of adolescents do function as mediators in peer relationships.

Parents as Supervisors of Peer Relationships

The third way in which parents manage peer relationships is that parents act as *supervisors* of adolescents' peer relationships (Ladd & LeSieur, 1995; Ladd & Pettit, 2002). As supervisors, parents might help adolescents avoid undesirable friends by directing their children's action and provide rules or guidelines for peer interactions (Parke *et al.*, 2003). In contrast to *mediating*, in which parents facilitate peer interactions, the focus of *supervising* is much more directive. In the case of adolescents, supervision that occurs in regard to peer relationships could take the form of monitoring, although other types of direct supervision have also been found. Through monitoring, parents have knowledge of the child's activities with peers. There is a considerable body of research that examines parental monitoring during adolescence (Bogenschneider *et al.*, 1998; Jacobson & Crockett, 2000; Stattin & Kerr, 2000; Steinberg *et al.*, 1994). There is strong support in the literature for the relation between parental monitoring and involvement with deviant peers during adolescence (Brown *et al.*, 1993; Loeber & Stouthamer-Loeber, 1998). However, recently, there has been considerable debate regarding the nature of parental monitoring. In particular, Stattin & Kerr (2000) suggested that much of what prior researchers label as parental monitoring has really been parental knowledge. That is, parents have knowledge of the child's whereabouts although this knowledge often comes from sources other than the parent seeking information from the child. In fact, they suggest that the largest determinant of parental knowledge is the child offering information to the parent. In examining parents' roles as supervisors of adolescents' peer relationships, the primary interest is in parental solicitation of information as opposed to adolescent's free disclosure of information. Earlier investigations, which examined monitoring, do not make the distinction between child disclosure and parental solicitation, making it more difficult to draw firm conclusions regarding the extent to which parents are using this aspect of peer management.

Several other aspects of supervising have also been examined. Youniss, DeSantis, & Henderson (1992) examined supervising in regard to peers with problem behaviors. Parents were asked to write out the strategy they would be most likely to use in handling a hypothetical situation in which their child was involved in several types of peer interactions (e.g., their child is hanging around with adolescents who are troublemakers). Results suggested that parents would exert a moderate amount of control in a situation where the friends were known to be troublemakers and less control in situations where the parents did not know the friends. This research, using hypothetical situations, is consistent with results reported by Furstenberg *et al.* (1999). In their study, 64 % of the parents reported that they told their adolescents not to hang around with certain adolescents.

Continuing this theme of parental prohibitions of peer contacts, Mounts (2000) examined the relation between prohibiting and characteristics of ninth-graders' friends using a short-term longitudinal study. Parental prohibiting at Time 1 was associated with peer selection at Time 1 but not at Time 3. That is, when parents engaged in prohibiting, adolescents were likely to have friends who were engaged in antisocial behavior. Because the significant effect was present at Time 1, but not at Time 3, this suggests that parents might have been prohibiting in response to their child's selection of a particular friend rather than the prohibiting functioning to have an effect on peer influence processes.

In two short-term longitudinal studies of ninth graders, Mounts (2001) examined parental prohibiting of peer relationships. Because prohibiting of peer relationships might be considered by adolescents to be more intrusive than other types of peer management, a curvilinear relation was expected for the prohibiting variable. Adolescents who reported moderate levels of parental prohibiting of peer relationships at time 1 reported lower levels of time 1 drug use and time 1 delinquent behavior. Moreover, moderate levels of prohibiting of peer relationships at time 1 were associated with having friends with lower levels of time 1 drug use and time 1 delinquent behavior. Significant curvilinear relations between time 1 prohibiting and time 3 (nine months later) grade point average and time 3 educational expectations were found such that moderate levels of prohibiting at time 1 were associated with higher grade point averages and higher educational expectations at time 3.

Parents might also supervise peer relationships by providing rules regarding peer relationships. Although not specifically focused on examining the rules that parents have in regard to peer relationships, several investigations provide some information about this issue. Furstenberg *et al.* (1999) reported that parents in impoverished neighborhoods enforced a variety of rules regarding peer relationships as a strategy to prevent their children from being adversely affected by peers. For example, parents had rules about where the adolescents could socialize or rules constraining the amount of contact adolescents could have with peers who might have a negative influence. In a longitudinal investigation by Way & Greene (2005), girls reported more stringent rules regarding socializing with friends than did boys. Simpkins & Parke (2002) examined the relation between mothers' play rules about peer relationships and sixth graders' play with peers. To be specific, rules about behavior with peers were a fairly global measure. They included prohibitions about aggressive behavior with peers, rules about playing with children engaging in undesirable behavior, rules encouraging prosocial behavior with peers, and rules about managing conflicts with peers. Results suggested that peer-rated aggressive girls had more rules about play with peers than nonaggressive girls. In addition, boys who were rated by peers as having higher levels of shyness had more rules about peer play than boys who were not rated as shy by peers and boys who engaged in less prosocial behavior had more peer play rules than boys who engage in more prosocial behavior. The cross-sectional nature of the investigation made it impossible to examine whether the children's behaviors were the result of restrictive maternal rules about peer relationships or whether the restrictive maternal rules about peer relationships were emerging in response to the children's behaviors.

Parents as Consultants Regarding Peer Relationships

The fourth way in which parents management peer relationships is that parents act as *consultants* in peer relationships. Ladd and colleagues (Ladd & LeSieur, 1995; Ladd & Pettit, 2002) suggested that, in their role as consultants, parents are usually engaged in consulting when the child is not in the peer context. That is, parents might help adolescents think about solving problems with peers or give advice about various aspects of peer relationships. Parke *et al.* (2003) suggest that consulting is more likely to occur as parents move beyond the direct involvement in peer relationships that is seen in early childhood.

In addition, Ladd and colleagues (Ladd & LeSieur, 1995; Ladd & Pettit, 2002) suggested that consulting could occur in response to specific incidences involving peers or it could occur as parents see a need for preparing their children for the possibility of having certain types of experiences with peers.

In the investigation by Vernberg *et al.* (1993), parents reported talking with their children about friendships as a means to assist them in meeting new friends after a move to a new school. Higher levels of talking to adolescents about friendships were related to higher levels of intimacy in young adolescents' friendships. The items for the scale used in this investigation tended to focus on preparing the child for particular types of peer relationships as opposed to focusing on specific incidences involving peers.

As a type of consulting, Mounts (2000) examined guiding, in which the parent helped the adolescent think about friendships and the way in which potential friendships might affect them. Guiding appeared to have an effect on the selection of friends. Adolescents whose parents used higher levels of guiding selected friends who had lower levels of antisocial behavior and higher levels of academic achievement.

In further investigation, Mounts (2004) created another measure of parental consulting in regard to peer relationships. In contrast to the measure of guiding used by Mounts (2000), the majority of the items on the consulting measure focused on parents helping their children solve problems in regard to specific incidences with their friends as opposed to parents talking about potential friendship issues. Mounts (2004) reported that higher levels of consulting were related to higher levels of positive friendship quality. Not included in the Mounts (2004) investigation, however, was an assessment of the relation between this measure of consulting and adolescents' or their friends' antisocial behaviors.

At this time, the research is mixed as to whether advice given to adolescents in regard to peer relationships would be related to poor social relationships or whether it would be related to more positive social relationships (Parke *et al.*, 2003). It could be that parents provide advice to adolescents when they believe their child is lacking in social skills. Alternatively, it could be that too much advice from the parent might interfere with the development of appropriate social skills. Another alternative might be that the provision of advice contributes positively to the development of social skills in adolescents. Longitudinal investigations are needed to ascertain the nature of this association.

In sum, there is accumulating evidence that there are several aspects to parental management of peers during the period of adolescence. More research is needed to understand fully the nature of these four aspects of management. In particular, more studies are needed which examine all four aspects of management simultaneously in order to understand the way in which the various aspects might work together to support the development of healthy peer relationships.

CONCEPTUAL FRAMEWORK FOR PARENTAL MANAGEMENT OF ADOLESCENTS' PEERS

It appears that Ladd & LeSieur's (1995) model of parental management of young children's peer relationships might be useful for conceptualizing parental management of adolescents' peer relationships. Using Ladd and colleagues (Ladd & LeSieur, 1995; Ladd & Pettit, 2002) as a starting point, in this section of the chapter I will suggest a conceptual framework for parental management of adolescents' peer relationships. Figure 7.2 presents a conceptual framework of the relation between some hypothesized predictors of parental management of peers, parental management of peers, and outcomes associated with the management of peer relationships.

Some aspects of the model have been the focus of research investigations; other aspects of the model are strictly theoretical. Many of the relations between the various aspects of the model are believed to be bidirectional, although empirical support for bidirectionality is limited. In particular, there are limited investigations that examine the relation between adolescent behavior and subsequent parental management of peer relationships.

Although Ladd & LeSieur's (1995) model does not explicitly address the ways in which the four aspects of management are related to one another, there is some suggestion in the literature that in cases where parents cannot exercise control over the design of the environment in which children are spending their time, they are likely to use other types of peer management (Furstenberg *et al.*, 1999). O'Neil, Parke, & McDowell (2001) also found support for parental regulation of peer relationships as a mediator between neighborhoods and child competence in a sample of younger children. Thus, in drawing the theoretical model, I have separated parents as *designers* into a separate component of the model and have indicated that design of the environment predicts other aspects of management of peers. That is, when parents can exercise a relatively high degree of control over the environment in terms of the friends that their children can select parents might feel less inclined to engage in mediating, supervising, and consulting about peer relationships. In contrast, when parents have little control over the environment, they might rely more heavily on other types of management such as mediating, supervising or consulting.

Predictors of Parental Management of Peers

Missing from the growing literature on parental management of adolescents' peer relationships is a consideration of the reasons why parents manage peer relationships during this developmental period. In this section we will consider several factors that could be predictors of parental management of peers.

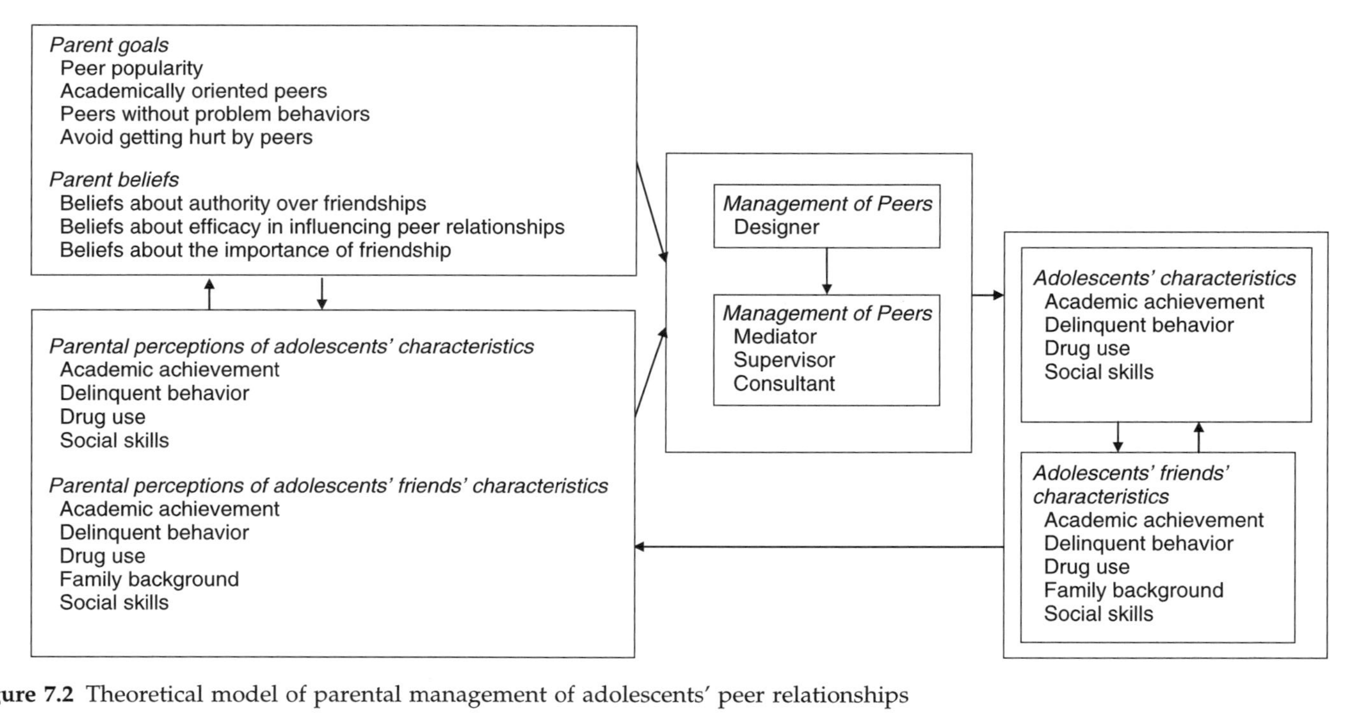

Figure 7.2 Theoretical model of parental management of adolescents' peer relationships

Parental goals

One factor that might contribute to parental management of peers is the goals that parents have in regard to peer relationships. In considering parental management of peers to be a direct influence on peer relationships, there is an assumption that the management is occurring with the goal of affecting peer relationships. Yet, there is little research that explores whether this is in fact the case. Parents might have several goals in managing peer relationships. This might include goals for having positive peer relationships such as having friendships with adolescents who are doing well in school. Other goals might include avoiding contact with peers whom parents believe to be negative influences, such as avoiding interactions with adolescents who are involved in drug use or delinquent activity. Still other goals might be related to issues of peer popularity. As described in an earlier section of this chapter, our analyses suggested that parents were encouraging seventh graders to participate in extracurricular activities because they had the goal of their child meeting other children. Several other analyses were conducted on those data, collected on an ethnically diverse sample, to further examine parental goals in regard to peer relationships.

During the interview portion of the home visit, caregivers were asked to indicate whether they had any of several goals in mind when becoming involved in their adolescents' peer relationships. The goals were: they wanted their child to be popular, they were concerned about their child being hurt by other children, they wanted their child to have better peer relationships, they wanted their child to have more friends, they intervened because their child misbehaved, and they intervened because their child's friend misbehaved.

Figure 7.3 presents the percentages of caregivers reporting these goals in regard to peer relationships. More than 40 % of the caregivers reported being involved in adolescents' peer relationships because they were concerned about their child being hurt by other children, they wanted their child to have better peer relationships, their child's misbehavior, and their child's friend's misbehavior.

Although there were few gender differences in caregivers' goals in involving themselves with peer relationships, there were significant gender differences for caregivers' involvement because of children's misbehavior. Caregivers were significantly more likely to become involved in peer relationships because of the misbehavior of their sons than of their daughters, $\chi^2 (1, N=78)=3.83$, $p<0.05$).

Using the theoretical model as a guide, these goals should be related to caregiver's management of peer relationships. In a second set of analyses, I examined whether caregivers' goals were related to caregivers' reports of mediating and consulting in regard to peer relationships. Six 2 (child gender) by 2 (goal present versus goal absent) MANOVAs were conducted to assess

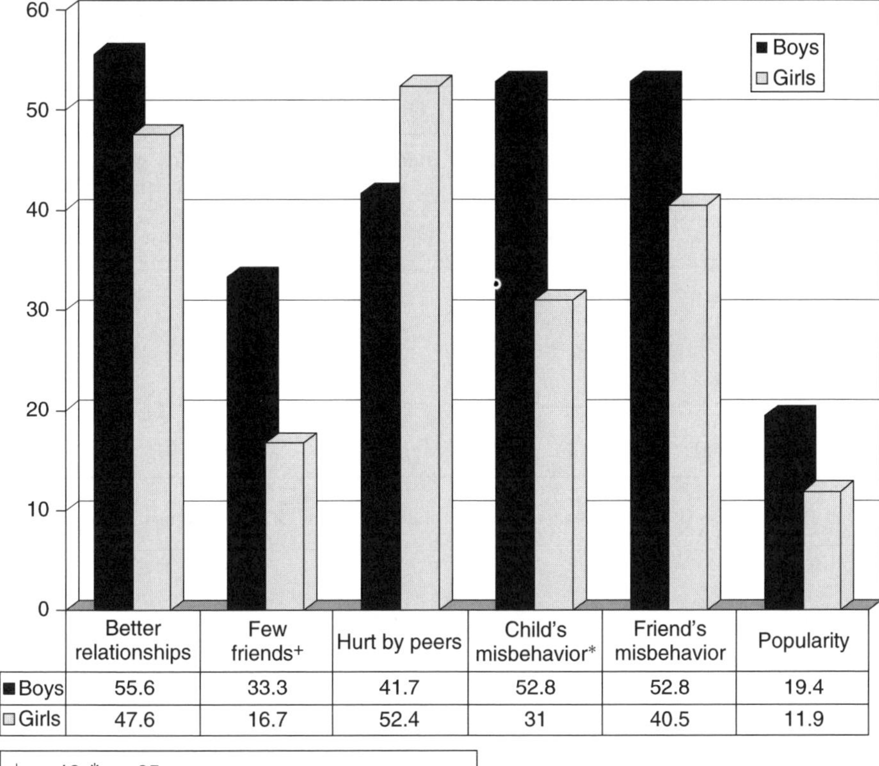

	Better relationships	Few friends+	Hurt by peers	Child's misbehavior*	Friend's misbehavior	Popularity
■ Boys	55.6	33.3	41.7	52.8	52.8	19.4
□ Girls	47.6	16.7	52.4	31	40.5	11.9

$^{+}p < .10$; $^{*}p < .05$

Figure 7.3 Reasons for becoming involved in peer relationships

whether there were differences in caregivers' reports of management based on the six goals that were described above. Table 7.1 presents the results of the MANOVAs.

As can be seen from the table, significant differences emerged in caregivers' reports of mediating and consulting when they reported having goals of their child being popular with other kids, their child had few friends, and their child's friends misbehaved. These results give partial support to the notion that parental goals are related to their management behaviors.

Taken together, these results suggest that parents do have specific goals in mind in regard to the peer relationships of their adolescents and that these goals are related to management of peer relationships. More detailed investigations are needed in the future to explicitly detail the way in which particular goals that parents have are related to specific management behaviors. In addition, more research is needed to examine the range of goals that parents have in regard to peer relationships.

Table 7.1 Hierarchical regression analyses of adolescents' and maternal perceptions of mediating in peer relationships on perceptions of parental authority over peer relationships

	Outcome variables					
	Maternal reports of mediating (n = 119)			**Adolescent reports of mediating (n = 117)**		
Predictor variables	**B**	**Beta**	**R^2 Change**	**B**	**Beta**	**R^2 Change**
Block 1						
Gender	–0.07	–0.11		–0.09	–0.13	
Parental education	–0.02	–0.07	0.02	–0.02	–0.08	0.02
Block 2						
Health	0.06	0.07		0.17	0.21*	
Personal	0.22	0.35***		0.20	0.29**	
Social-conventional	0.19	0.32***	0.35***	–0.20	–0.31**	0.09**

* $p < 0.05$; ** $p < 0.01$; *** $p < 0.001$

Note B indicates unstandardized regression coefficients and Beta indicates standardized regression coefficients

Parental beliefs

A second factor that might predict parental management of peers is parents' beliefs. There are several types of beliefs that might be related to parental management of peers. Parental beliefs regarding authority over peer relationships, parental beliefs regarding their efficacy in influencing adolescents' peer relationships, and parental beliefs regarding the importance of friends all might be related to the extent to which parents manage peer relationships and the types of management strategies that parents select.

The first type of parental belief that might be related to management of peers is parental beliefs regarding their authority over adolescents' peer relationships. Smetana & Asquith (1994) examined parent beliefs regarding their authority about a number of issues related to adolescents including peer relationships. They suggested that although adolescents believe that friendship is an issue of personal choice, parents view friendships as something that they maintain jurisdiction, or authority, over. Parents believe that because issues of friendship often include psychological concerns as well as conventional concerns that they should maintain control over adolescents' friendships. These results are relevant for beginning to explore the reasons why parents are involved in the peer relationships of adolescents.

The work of Smetana & Asquith (1994) might lead us to hypothesize that parents who believe they have higher levels of authority over peer relationships should use higher levels of management than those who believe that adolescents should have authority over their own peer relationships. One interesting question is whether variations in parental beliefs about authority over friendships has implications for the amount of peer management that parents engage in as well as the types of peer management that they use.

In a pilot investigation, our research team examined the relation between beliefs that parents of adolescents have regarding their authority over peer relationships and three aspects of parental management of peer relationships. The sample was an ethnically diverse sample of 121 seventh and eight graders and their primary caregivers. Beliefs about parental authority over peer relationships were assessed using items adapted and modeled after Tisak & Tisak (1990). Eighteen items were developed that assessed the degree to which parents believed they had a right to make rules regarding various types of friendship situations. An example item is, "Do you have a right to make rules about your child's friendships when his/her friends use drugs?" Caregivers used a three-point scale in which 0 = "no," 1 = "maybe," and 2 = "yes."

Parallel analysis was used in conjunction with factor analysis for determining the factor structure of this scale (Longman *et al.*, 1989). The *Social-conventional situations* scale assessed situations where social conventional rules apply such as language use or behavior in a school. An example item for this eight-item scale is, "Do you have a right to make rules regarding friendships because your child's friends use bad language?" Cronbach's alpha on this scale was 0.89. A second three-item factor was labeled *Health situations* and assessed situations in which the child's friend was engaging in behaviors with adverse health consequences. An example item is, "Do you have a right to make rules regarding friendships because your child's friends smoke marijuana?" Cronbach's alpha on this scale was 0.78. The remaining seven items loaded on a factor named *Personal situations,* which assessed situations in which the friend was engaging in behaviors which did not seem to have any significant consequence. An example item is "Do you have a right to make rules regarding your child's friendships because you don't like the way your child's friend dresses?" Cronbach's alpha for this scale was 0.81. A high score on these scales indicated that the caregiver believed that parents did have the right to make rules about adolescents' friendships based on this issue.

Parental management of peer relationships was assessed using the Parental Management of Peers Inventory (PMPI) (Mounts, 2002, 2004). Adolescents used a four-point Likert-type scale such that responses ranged from a score of 1 = *Strongly disagree* to 4 = *Strongly agree.* Following Mounts (2004) three subscales were used to describe parental management of adolescents' peer relationships. A 10-item measure of *Consulting* was used and was intended to assess some of the more proactive aspects of parental management of peer relationships in which parents help adolescents engage in problem solving in regard to peer relationships. A sample item for this scale is "When I am having a problem with a friend, I can ask my caregiver for help in solving it." Cronbach's alpha for *Consulting* for adolescents participating in the current investigation was 0.85. Cronbach's alpha for *Consulting* for the caregivers was 0.73. *Mediating* is an 18-item scale intended to assess the extent to which parents are involved in the peer relationships of their adolescents. A sample item for this scale is "My caregiver tells me that who I have for friends will affect my future." Cronbach's alpha for *Mediating* for the adolescents was 0.76 for the current investigation. Cronbach's alpha for *Mediating* for the caregivers was 0.79. *Autonomy-granting with peers* is a four-item scale, which assesses the extent to which parents allow adolescents control over their peer relationships. A sample item for this scale is "My parents tell me that who I have as friends is my personal choice." Cronbach's alpha for *Autonomy-granting* for adolescents in the current investigation was 0.58 and the alpha for the caregivers was 0.44. The mean scores of these scales were used in the analyses.

Hierarchical regression analyses were conducted to ascertain whether parental beliefs about authority over peer relationships were related to parental management of peer relationships. Parental education and child gender were entered in the first block of the analyses. The three subscales of the beliefs about parental authority over peers scale were then entered into the second block of the regression analyses. Adolescent and caregiver reports of parental mediating, consulting, and autonomy-granting in regard to peer relationships were used as dependent variables in the analyses. Results regarding mediating as the dependent variable are presented in Table 7.2.

Caregivers who reported believing that they had higher levels of authority over personal issues related to friendship also reported higher levels of mediating in peer relationships. Similarly, higher levels of authority over personal issues related to friendship were related to adolescents reporting higher levels of parental mediating in peer relationships. Adolescents whose caregivers reported higher levels of authority over health issues related to

Table 7.2 Hierarchical regression analyses of adolescents' and maternal perceptions of consulting in peer relationships on perceptions of parental authority over peer relationships

	Outcome variables					
	Maternal reports of consulting (n = 119)			**Adolescent reports of consulting (n = 117)**		
Predictor variables	**B**	**Beta**	**R^2 Change**	**B**	**Beta**	**R^2 Change**
Block 1						
Gender	0.06	0.08		0.04	0.03	
Parental education	−0.01	−0.03	0.01	−0.03	−0.07	0.01
Block 2						
Health	0.11	0.14		0.20	0.14	
Personal	−0.02	−0.02		−0.26	−0.22*	
Social-conventional	−0.14	−0.22	0.05	−0.10	−0.09	0.08**

* $p < 0.05$; ** $p < 0.05$; ** $p < 0.001$

Note B indicates unstandardized regression coefficients and Beta indicates standardized regression coefficients

peers also reported higher levels of mediating. Caregivers who believed that they had higher levels of authority over social-conventional issues also reported higher levels of mediating. In contrast, adolescents whose caregivers believed that they had a higher level of authority over social-conventional issues reported lower levels of mediating on the part of their caregivers. This is likely due to differences in parents' versus adolescents' perceptions of mediating. The correlation between mothers' and adolescents' reports of mediating was 0.11, suggesting that there were differences in the perceptions of mediating. Because the adolescents are becoming increasingly autonomous during this developmental period, they may be less likely to notice or report parental attempts at management.

The results were more limited for parental consulting about peer relationships (see Table 7.3). None of the caregiver reports of authority over peer relationships subscales was a significant predictor of caregiver reports of consulting. Higher caregiver reports of authority over personal friendship issues were related to lower adolescent reports of consulting regarding peer relationships. Because of the nature of the issues assessed in the personal domain seemed like they should be under the authority of the adolescent, it could be that when caregivers interfere with these issues, adolescents regard them as behaving in ways less like a consultant.

Table 7.3 Hierarchical regression analyses of adolescents' and maternal perceptions of autonomy-granting in peer relationships on perceptions of parental authority over peer relationships

	Outcome variables					
	Maternal reports of autonomy-granting (n = 119)			Adolescent reports of autonomy-granting (n = 117)		
Predictor variables	**B**	**Beta**	**R^2 Change**	**B**	**Beta**	**R^2 Change**
Block 1						
Gender	0.11	0.10		0.25	0.18	
Parental education	0.02	0.04	0.01	0.03	0.07	0.04
Block 2						
Health	−0.22	−0.17		−0.17	−0.10	
Personal	−0.18	−0.17		−0.16	−0.12	
Social-conventional	−0.26	−0.25*	0.19***	0.06	0.05	0.02

* $p < 0.05$; ** $p < 0.01$; *** $p < 0.001$

Note B indicates unstandardized regression coefficients and Beta indicates standardized regression coefficients

The results for the parental autonomy-granting in regard to peer relationships were also more limited (see Table 7.4). Caregivers who reported higher levels of authority over social-conventional peer relationships issue reported lower levels of autonomy-granting in regard to peer relationships. None of the

Table 7.4 Results of MANOVA examining gender and goal (presence versus absence) differences in caregiver's reports of mediating and consulting in regard to peer relationships

Goal	Present	Absent	F
Popular with other kids			3.22*
Consulting	3.45(.09)	3.33(.04)	1.49
Mediating	3.04(.11)	2.73(.05)	6.19*
Hurt by other kids			0.89
Consulting	3.36(.05)	3.31(.05)	0.43
Mediating	2.84(.07)	2.72(.06)	1.73
Better relationships			0.73
Consulting	3.33(.05)	3.36(.05)	0.12
Mediating	2.82(.06)	2.73(.07)	0.99
Few friends			4.75*
Consulting	3.33(07)	3.36(04)	0.15
Mediating	3.01(.09)	2.72(.05)	7.83**
Child's misbehavior			2.33
Consulting	3.28(.06)	3.39(.05)	2.56
Mediating	2.82(.07)	2.74(.06)	0.71
Friend's misbehavior			2.49+
Consulting	3.35(.05)	3.35(.05)	0.01
Mediating	2.88(.07)	2.69(.06)	4.53*

$^{+}p < 0.10$; * $p < 0.05$; ** $p < 0.01$

caregiver reports of authority over peer relationships subscales was a significant predictor of adolescent reports of autonomy-granting in regard to peer relationships.

The results of this pilot investigation suggest that caregiver beliefs regarding authority over peer relationships were related to both caregiver reports as well as adolescents' reports of peer management. The low reliability for the autonomy-granting variable limit the interpretation of the results associated with that variable. The results for the mediating and consulting variables seem to suggest that beliefs about authority over peer relationships are likely to influence mediating of peer relationships in particular. Given that mediating is more focused on regulating peer relationships than is consulting it seems reasonable that stronger relations would be found between mediating and beliefs about authority. On the other hand, because consulting is more focused on advice or problem-solving about peers, beliefs about parental authority over peers might not play as strong a role in determining consulting.

A second type of parental belief that might be related to parental management of peers is parental beliefs about efficacy. Parents' beliefs about efficacy in influencing adolescents' peer relationships might also determine the level and nature of peer management. In their review of self-efficacy and parenting quality, Coleman & Karraker (1997) suggest that the encouragement of children's recreation and social development could be considered one of several domains of parenting which would be included in a Bandurian self-efficacy model. A positive relation between parental beliefs about self-efficacy and a number of positive parental competencies has been found (see Coleman & Karraker, 1997 for review). Few investigations of parental self-efficacy, however, explore the relation of self-efficacy to parenting and management of peer relationships. In one study, Shumow & Lomax (2002) found that maternal beliefs about efficacy, in particular how efficacious they felt in regard to helping their adolescents avoid problems with peers, were positively related to mothers' as well as adolescents' reports of monitoring. These results are suggestive of a relation between parental beliefs about efficacy over peers and management of peer relationships.

In another investigation, Tilton-Weaver & Galambos (2003) examined the relation between parental efficacy beliefs in regard to influencing adolescents' peer relationships and management of peers. Paternal efficacy beliefs were positively related to three aspects of management of peers including communicating preferences about peers, communicating disapproval about peers, and information seeking about peers. Maternal efficacy beliefs were not related to any aspect of peer management.

A third type of belief that might play a role in determining management of peers is parental beliefs about the importance of friends. Using qualitative and quantitative methods, Way & Greene (2005) suggested variations across ethnic groups, adolescent gender group, and socioeconomic status group in parental attitudes about friends. In particular, Asian American and African-American adolescents reported that their parents saw less value in friendships than did Latino adolescents. In addition, adolescents reported changes in parental attitudes about friends over time with parents becoming more positive about friends as children progressed beyond middle adolescence. Although not addressed by Way and Greene, it is likely that the attitudes that parents have regarding the importance of friends is related to management strategies. For instance, parents who do not think that friends are important might engage in more prohibiting of peer relationships and less consulting when their children are having problems with peer relationships.

Taken together, the few studies that do exist regarding parental beliefs and management of peer relationships suggest that there is evidence to support this relation. Future investigations might examine these different types of beliefs more systematically and their relation to peer management using longitudinal designs.

Child characteristics

A third factor that might predict parental management of peer is parents' perceptions of child characteristics. Several researchers have suggested that parenting practices are likely to be affected by parents' perceptions of their children's characteristics (Kerr & Stattin, 2003; Profilet & Ladd, 1994;

Tilton-Weaver & Galambos, 2003). Indeed, Kerr & Stattin (2003) suggest that many of the parenting effects that are reported in the literature are likely to be child effects. There are likely to be numerous instances of parents responding to children's behavior in regard to peers and children responding to parents' attempts to manage peer relationships. In one investigation, Tilton-Weaver & Galambos (2003) reported that adolescents' problems behaviors were positively related to mothers' reports of communicating disapproval about peers and seeking information about peers six months later. In addition, adolescents' problem behaviors were related to higher levels of communicating disapproval about peers for fathers six months later.

Adolescents' friends' characteristics

A fourth factor hypothesized to predict parental management of adolescents' peers is the characteristics of adolescents' friends. Parents might become aware that certain friends with whom their child is interacting are engaging in behaviors or have characteristics that they view as undesirable. As a result, parents might modify their management practices in response to a particular friend. Mounts (2000) reported that parental prohibiting at Time 1 was associated with peer characteristics at Time 1 but not at Time 3. This result suggests that parents might have been prohibiting in response to their child's selection of a particular friend. Similarly, Tilton-Weaver & Galambos (2003) found that adolescents' reports of having deviant friends was positively related to mothers' reports of communicating preferences about peers and communicating disapproval about peers six months later. In addition, adolescents' reports of having deviant friends was negatively related to fathers' support of friendships six months later. Mothers' and fathers' reports of concerns about friends were positively related to communicating disapproval about friends. Taken together, these studies suggest that child friendship selections are, in part, responsible for parental management of peers.

Considering adolescents' characteristics and the characteristics of adolescents' friends suggests a need for more investigations which can examine issues of bidirectionality. There is a need for more longitudinal investigations that examine the bidirectional relation between child behavior (or friends' behaviors) and parent management of peers during adolescence. In addition, methodologies that allow a more fine-grained analysis of the processes leading up to parental management of peers are also needed to more fully understand the links between adolescent behaviors and parental management of peers. A final point to be made in regard to adolescents' characteristics and adolescents' friends' characteristics is that there is likely to be a bidirectional relation between parents goals and beliefs and their perceptions of adolescents' characteristics and adolescents' friends' characteristics (see Figure 7.1). That is, parents might modify their goals and beliefs depending on the characteristics of their children. For instance, parents initially might want their children to be popular with other children. However, if a child has many problems developing friendships with other children parents might modify their goal to be that the child has some good friendships. In depth longitudinal investigations would allow for a consideration of the interplay between goals, beliefs, and perceptions of adolescents and the subsequent effect on parental management of peers.

Outcomes of Parental Management of Peers

Finally, there are two ways in which parents might have an impact on adolescents' adjustment through the use of peer management. First, management might affect adolescent social skills and adjustment directly. Second, parental management of peers might affect the types of friends that a child selects, and this, in turn, through processes of peer influence, affects adolescent adjustment. As outlined in earlier sections of this paper, much of the existing research on the parental management of peer relationships has focused on these two issues.

Additional Issues

In addition to research directions that arise from the proposed model, there are several other issues related to parental management of adolescents' peers which warrant further attention.

Parental management of peers across cultural or ethnic contexts

Much of the literature on parental management of adolescents' peer relations is based on samples of White, middle-class adolescents. A limited amount of research has been conducted that examines the ways in which parenting practices directed toward peer relationships might occur within different cultural or ethnic contexts. There are two issues that are relevant in considering ethnicity and parental management of peer relationships. The first issue of interest regarding culture and ethnicity is to examine the management of peers for adolescents from differing cultural or ethnic groups. Examining whether the theoretical model outlined above functions similarly across cultural and ethnic contexts is an important step in developing this literature. For instance, parents from differing cultural or ethnic groups might have different goals or beliefs in regard to adolescents' peer relationships, they might have different ways of managing peer relationships, or their management strategies might have different effects on their adolescents.

As described above, Way & Greene (2005) suggested that there were ethnic differences in the beliefs that parents had regarding the importance of peer relationships. In another investigation, Mounts (2004) reported mean differences in management across African-American, Latino, and White ethnic groups as well as differences in the correlations between management and several outcome variables across the three groups. That is, mean differences were found in consulting such that African-American and Latino adolescents reported lower levels of consulting than did White adolescents. In addition, higher levels of consulting were related to lower levels of delinquent activity for the White adolescents but not for the African-American or the Latino adolescents. This would suggest that the lower levels of consulting that exist in these minority groups might not necessarily be something of concern. Future investigations should consider not only mean similarities and differences in management of peer relationships across ethnic groups, but also similarities and differences in the relations between peer management and outcome variables across ethnic groups. Mounts (2004) suggests that there could be ethnic differences in means and ethnic differences in patterns of correlations. Alternatively, there could be ethnic differences in means but a similar pattern of correlations across ethnic groups. There could also be similar means, but ethnic differences in the pattern of correlations. Or, there could be similarities across groups in both means as well as correlations.

A second issue of interest regarding culture and ethnicity is to examine the extent to which ethnicity or culture is a focus when parents manage adolescents' peer relationships. This might be considered to be one aspect of ethnic socialization. There are a few research investigations that suggest that concerns with the ethnicity of peers do play a role in parental management of peers. Brown, Hamm, & Meyerson (1996) suggested that African-American and Latino parents actively encouraged their children to establish same-race friendships and cautioned their children about the dangers of cross-race romantic relationships. A similar pattern of findings was reported by Peshkin (1991) who reported that parents seemed unconcerned about issues of ethnicity as far as friendships were concerned and voiced objections only when their children were romantically involved with an adolescent from another ethnic group. In another study, Hamm (2001) suggested that White parents do not feel particularly motivated (and in some cases reluctant) to encourage their children to have friendships across ethnic groups. In contrast, African-American parents voiced greater concerns with managing the peer relationships around issues of ethnicity.

This small number of studies suggests that parents manage peer relationships with an eye toward cross-ethnic relationships. Further investigation of this issue might include the way in which ethnic identity is important in parents' consideration of management, ethnicity, and culture. In addition, in order to minimize responses that mask parent's true views regarding cross-ethnic relationships, future investigations might use assessments of parental management of peers around issues of ethnicity where issues of race are implicit as opposed to explicit. That is, parents might recognize that certain responses to questions regarding cross-ethnic relationships might be regarded as racist. They, therefore, might not provide responses regarding cross-ethnic relationships that are completely honest. By assessing, management of cross-ethnic peer relationships using measures that do not ask about cross-ethnic relationships explicitly, researchers might better assess the extent to which parents do manage cross-ethnic relationships.

Parents' versus adolescents' reports of management

Much of the existing literature on management is based on either parents' or adolescents' reports of management of peer relationships. More research is needed to explore differences in parents' and adolescents' reports of management. The issue of discrepancy in report of family members during adolescence is important for theoretical reasons. The development of autonomy, especially autonomy from parents, is an issue that becomes increasingly important during adolescence (Steinberg, 1990). Growth in adolescent autonomy might affect the extent to which adolescents believe that parental involvement in their peer relationships is appropriate, making parental involvement in adolescent peer relationships more challenging than the parental management of the peer relationships of younger children. Indeed, Smetana & Asquith's (1994) work suggests that adolescents believe that friendship selection is a personal choice over which their parents should have little authority. Parents, on the other hand, often believe that they have legitimate authority over friendships because the effects of adolescents' friendships may carry over into other domains of the adolescents' life, such as moral domains. Because of a growing need for autonomy during the early adolescent period, Carlson, Cooper, & Spradling (1991) suggest that issues such as friendship decisions might be an area where discrepancies between parents and adolescents might be related to more positive outcomes for adolescents.

In one investigation of differences in maternal and adolescent perceptions of management of peers, Mounts (2007) found significant differences in maternal and adolescent reports of management of peer relationships. The correlations among the adolescent and maternal reports of mediating were not significant and the correlation between adolescent and maternal reports of consulting was modest in size. Similarly, there were significant reporter mean differences in mediating peer relationships and consulting in peer relationships, with mothers reporting significantly higher levels of mediating peer relationships and consulting in regard to peer relationships than adolescents. In addition, discrepancies between mothers' and adolescents' reports of management were related to adolescents' adjustment.

More research is needed that examines the nature of the differences between adolescents' and their parents' reports of management, the way in which these discrepancies are related to autonomy development, and their subsequent effect on adjustment. Investigations that ask adolescents and their parents to report separately on specific instances of management of peers—for instance, peer management that occurred on a particular day—might allow researchers to understand better the nature of the discrepancies between parents' and adolescents' reports of management.

Age differences

One of the limitations with the existing literature on parental management of adolescents' peer relationships is that there has been no examination of age differences in management. The extent to which management varies across adolescents of different ages is not known. Age differences have not been addressed with cross-sectional investigations nor have age changes been addressed using longitudinal investigation. Although there have been a few short-term longitudinal investigations that examined parental management of peer relationships, no examination of age related changes were conducted using those data sets. Changes in management that occur as adolescents age are particularly important because of the push toward autonomy that occurs during the adolescent years. One would expect, that as adolescents' age, and as they become more autonomous from parents, parental management of peers diminishes. In particular, one would expect that management in which parents are exerting high levels of control over peer relationships would probably be most noticeably absent as adolescents age and become more autonomous. On the other hand, some types of management, such as consulting, might persist even into the college years as late adolescents make the transition into college and must live with peers who are considerably different from themselves.

Parental management of dating relationships

Missing from most of this literature on parental management of peers is a consideration of the ways in which parents manage dating relationships. Given the growing importance of dating during the period of early adolescence, it is important to consider the ways in which parents might be involved in dating. Although there is evidence that parenting style, parent–child attachment, or modeling might play a role in the development of romantic relationships (Gray & Steinberg, 1999), there is little research that examines particular parenting practices associated with managing dating relationships. Indeed, because exploration of romantic relationships is beginning during the early adolescence period, parents might find it necessary to be increasingly involved in managing dating relationships during this time period. Gray & Steinberg (1999) suggest that parents might have a number of concerns with dating including concerns about pregnancy or less time with family. These concerns might be precursors of parental management of dating relationships.

CONCLUSION

To summarize, there is a growing literature that examines parental management of adolescents' peer relationships. Despite the growth in the literature, there are few models available for guiding future research in the field. Ladd and colleagues' (Ladd & LeSieur's, 1995; Ladd & Pettit, 2002) model for management of young children's peer relationships appears to have some utility for organizing the literature on parental management of adolescents' peer relationships. The proposed model considers potential predictors of peer management as well as outcomes of peer management. In addition, ethnicity, age differences in peer management, and parents' versus adolescents' differences in reports of management are important considerations for future investigations.

REFERENCES

Bogenschneider, K., Wu, M., Raffaelli, M., & Tsay, J. (1998). Parent influences on adolescent peer orientation and substance use: the interface of parenting practices and values. *Child Development, 69*, 1672–1688.

Bronfenbrenner, U. (1979). *The Ecology of Human Development: Experiments by Nature and Design*. Cambridge, MA: Harvard University Press.

Brown, B. B., Hamm, J. V., & Meyerson, P. (1996). Encouragement, empowerment, detachment: Ethnic differences in approaches to parental involvement with peer relationships. In B. B. Brown (Chair), *Buzz Off or Butt In? Parental Involvement in Adolescent Peer Relations*. Symposium conducted at the biennial meeting of the Society for Research on Adolescence, Boston.

Brown, B. B., Mounts, N. S., Lamborn, S. D., & Steinberg, L. (1993). Parenting practices and peer group affiliation in adolescence. *Child Development, 64*, 467–482.

Carlson, C., Cooper, C., & Spradling, V. (1991). Developmental implications of shared versus distinct perceptions of the family in early adolescence. *New Directions for Child Development, 51*, 13–32.

Coleman, P. K. & Karraker, K. H. (1997). Self-efficacy and parenting quality: findings and future applications. *Developmental Review, 18*, 47–85.

Darling, N. & Steinberg, L. (1993). Parenting style as context: an integrative model. *Psychological Bulletin, 113*, 487–496.

Fletcher, A. C., Elder, G. H., & Mekos, D. (2000). Parental influences on adolescent involvement in community activities. *Journal of Research on Adolescence, 10*, 29–48.

Fuligni, A. J. & Eccles, J. S. (1993). Perceived parent-child relationships and early adolescents' orientation towards peers. *Developmental Psychology, 29*, 622–632.

Furstenberg, F. F., Cook, T. D., Eccles, J., Elder, G. H., & Sameroff, A. (1999). *Managing to Make It: Urban Families and Adolescent Success*. Chicago: University of Chicago Press.

Galambos, N. L. & Maggs, J. (1991). Out-of-school care of young adolescents and self-reported behavior. *Developmental Psychology, 27*, 644–655.

Gray, M. R. & Steinberg, L. (1999). Adolescent romance and the parent-child relationship: A contextual perspective. In W. Furman, B. B. Brown, & C. Feiring (eds), *The Development of Romantic Relationships in Adolescence* (pp. 235–265). New York, NY: Cambridge University Press.

Hamm, J. V. (2001) Barriers and bridges to positive cross-ethnic relations: African-American and White parent socialization beliefs. *Youth and Society, 33*, 62–98.

Jacobson, K. & Crockett, L. J. (2000). Parental monitoring and adolescent adjustment: an ecological perspective. *Journal of Research on Adolescence, 10*, 65–97.

Kerr, M. & Stattin, H. (2003). Parenting adolescents: action or reaction? In A. C. Crouter & A. Booth (eds), *Children's Influence on Family Dynamics* (pp. 121–151). Mahwah, NJ: Erlbaum.

Ladd, G. W. & LeSieur, K. D. (1995). Parents and children's peer relationships. In M. Bornstein (ed.), *Handbook of Parenting, Volume 4: Applied and Practical Parenting* (pp. 377–409). Hillsdale, NJ: Erlbaum.

Ladd, G. W. & Pettit, G. S. (2002). Parenting and the development of children's peer relationships. In M. Bornstein (ed.), *Handbook of Parenting, Volume 5: Practical Issues in Parenting* (pp. 269–309). Mahwah, NJ: Erlbaum.

Loeber, R. & Stouthamer-Loeber, M. (1998). Development of juvenile aggression and violence: Some common misconceptions and controversies. *American Psychologist, 53*, 242–259.

Longman, R. S., Cota, A. A., Holden, R. R., & Fekken, G. C. (1989). A regression equation for the parallel analysis criterion in principal components analysis: Mean and 95th percentile eigenvalues. *Multivariate Behavioral Research, 24*, 59–69.

Medrich, E., Roizen, J., Rubin, V., & Buckley, S. (1982). *The Serious Business of Growing Up: A Study of Children's Lives Outside of School*. Berkeley, CA: University of California Press.

Mize, J., Russell, A., & Pettit, G. S. (1998). Further explorations of family-peer connections: the role of parenting practices and parenting style in children' development of social competence. In P. T. Slee & K. Rigsby (eds), *Children's Peer Relations* (pp. 31–44). New York: Routledge.

Mounts, N. (2000). Parental management of adolescent peer relationships: what are its effects on friend selection? In K. A. Kerns, J. M. Contreras, & A. M. Neal-Barnett (eds), *Family and Peers: Linking Two Social Worlds* (pp. 167–193). Westport, CT: Greenwood/Praeger.

Mounts, N. (2001). Young adolescents' perceptions of parental management of peer relationships. *Journal of Early Adolescence, 21*, 92–122.

Mounts, N. (2002). Parental management of adolescent peer relationships in context: the role of parenting style. *Journal of Family Psychology, 16*, 58–69.

Mounts, N. (2007). Adolescents' and their mothers' perceptions of parental management of peer relationships. *Journal of Research on Adolescence, 17*, 169–178.

Mounts, N. S. (2004). Adolescents' perceptions of parental management of peer relationships in an ethnically diverse sample. *Journal of Adolescent Research, 19*, 446–467.

Mounts, N. & Steinberg, L. (1995). An ecological analysis of peer influence on adolescent grade-point-average and drug use. *Developmental Psychology, 31*, 915–922.

O'Neil, R., Parke, R. D., & McDowell, D. J. (2001). Objective and subjective features of children's neighborhoods: relations to parental regulatory strategies and children's social competence. *Applied Developmental Psychology, 22*, 135–155.

Parke, R. D., Killian, C. M., Dennis, J. *et al.* (2003). Managing the external environment: the parent and child as active agents in the system. In L. Kuczynski (ed.), *Handbooks of Dynamics in Parent-child Relations* (pp. 247–270). Thousand Oaks, CA: Sage.

Parke, R. D. & O'Neil, R. (1999). Social relationships across contexts: family-peer linkages. In W. A. Collins & B. Laursen (eds), *Relationships as Developmental Contexts: The Minnesota Symposium on Child Psychology, Vol. 30* (pp. 211–239). Mahwah, NJ: Lawrence Erlbaum.

Peshkin, A. (1991). *The Color of Strangers, the Color of Friends*. Chicago: University of Chicago Press.

Profilet, S. M. & Ladd, G. (1994). Do mothers' perceptions and concerns about preschoolers' competence predict their peer-management practices? *Social Development, 2*, 205–221.

Shumow, L. & Lomax, R. (2002). Parental efficacy: predictor of parenting behavior and adolescent outcomes. *Parenting: Science and Practice*, *2*, 127–150.

Simpkins, S. D. & Parke, R. D. (2002). Maternal monitoring and rules as correlates of children's social adjustment. *Merrill-Palmer Quarterly*, *48*, 360–377.

Smetana, J. G. & Asquith, P. (1994). Adolescents' and parents' conceptions of parental authority and personal autonomy. *Child Development*, *65*, 1147–1162.

Stattin, H. & Kerr, M. (2000). Parental monitoring: a reinterpretation. *Child Development*, *71*, 1072–1085.

Steinberg, L. (1986). Latchkey children and susceptibility to peer pressure: an ecological analysis. *Developmental Psychology*, *22*, 433–439.

Steinberg, L. (1990). Autonomy, conflict, and harmony in the family relationship. In S. S. Feldman & G. R. Elliott (eds), *At the Threshold: The Developing Adolescent* (pp. 255–276). Cambridge, MA: Harvard University Press.

Steinberg, L., Lamborn, S., Darling, N. *et al.* (1994). Over-time changes in adjustment and competence among adolescents from authoritative, authoritarian, indulgent, and neglectful families. *Child Development*, *65*, 754–770.

Tilton-Weaver, L. C. & Galambos, N. (2003). Adolescents' characteristics and parents' beliefs as predictors of parents' peer management behaviors. *Journal of Research on Adolescence*, *13*, 269–300.

Tisak, M. & Tisak, J. (1990). Children's conceptions of parental authority, friendship, and sibling relations. *Merrill-Palmer Quarterly*, *36*, 347–367.

Vernberg, E., Beery, S., Ewell, K., & Abwender, D. (1993). Parents' use of friendship facilitation strategies and the formation of friendships in early adolescence: a prospective study. *Journal of Family Psychology*, *3*, 356–369.

Way, N. & Greene, M. (2005). Exploring adolescents' perceptions of parental attitudes and rules about friendships. Brown, B. (Chair), *Parental Involvement in Child and Adolescent Peer Relationships: Ethnic and Cultural Variations*. Symposium paper presented at the biennial meeting of the Society for Research in Child Development, Atlanta.

Youniss, J., DeSantis, J., & Henderson, S. (1992). Parents' approaches to adolescents in alcohol, friendship, and school situations. In I. Sigel, A. V. McGillicuddy-Delisi, & J. J. Goodnow (eds), *Parental Belief Systems: The Psychological Consequences for Children* (pp. 199–216). Hillsdale, NJ: Lawrence Erlbaum.

CHAPTER 8

From Coercion to Positive Parenting: Putting Divorced Mothers in Charge of Change

Marion S. Forgatch, Zintars G. Beldavs, Gerald R. Patterson and David S. DeGarmo
Oregon Social Learning Center, USA

INTRODUCTION

Once, not long ago, the traditional family consisting of children living together with their biological parents and siblings was the norm. Today, with 50 % of marriages facing separation or divorce, only half of the families in the USA are so-called traditional. Parents are likely to repartner and repartnered couples are even more likely to separate (Brody, Neubaum, & Forehand, 1988; Bumpass & Sweet, 1989; Bumpass, Sweet, & Martin, 1990). These transitions place families at risk for parenting problems and other adversities including mental and physical illness; substance abuse; antisocial behavior; couple conflict; decreased social support; financial problems; downward economic mobility; and the instability that comes with changing residences, neighborhoods, and schools (Amato, 1993; Hetherington & Stanley-Hagan, 1999; Simons *et al.*, 1993; Zill, Morrison, & Coiro, 1993). Parenting problems increase the likelihood of a myriad of difficulties for children including internalizing, externalizing, academic difficulty, deviant peer association, delinquency, and

Support for this project was provided by Grant Nos. RO1 DA 16097 from the Prevention Research Branch, NIDA, U.S. PHS; and RO1 MH 38318 from the Child and Adolescent Treatment and Preventive Intervention Research Branch, DSIR, NIMH, U.S. PHS. Special thanks to Kelly Bryson for her editorial expertise. Correspondence concerning this chapter should be addressed to Marion S. Forgatch, Oregon Social Learning Center, 10 Shelton McMurphey Boulevard, Eugene, Oregon 97401; 541.485.2711; 541.485.7087 (fax); marionf@oslc.org.

What Can Parents Do? New Insights into the Role of Parents in Adolescent Problem Behavior
Edited by Margaret Kerr, Håkan Stattin and Rutger C. M. E. Engels.

children's adjustment problems. These challenges, in turn, increase the risk of coercion and decrease the likelihood of positive parenting, which can result in a negative spiral proving increasingly difficult to overcome (Amato, 1987; Anderson *et al.*, 1999; Hetherington, 1999; Zill, Morrison & Coiro, 1993). This chapter describes an important intervention for divorced families that can reverse these negative effects and help families achieve multilateral success by reducing coercive parenting and increasing positive parenting, thereby preventing growth in rates of delinquency for boys.

Parenting through Change (Forgatch, 1994) is the intervention that grew out of the Oregon Divorce Study (ODS), a set of two studies spanning 20 years of research on the sequelae of separation and divorce. Study 1 used a passive longitudinal design to develop assessment tools and test models of adjustment for mothers and their school-aged children. The sample of 197 mothers and sons and 40 sibling sisters was assessed within the first 18 months of separation and three times over the subsequent four years. Study 2 focused on a new sample of 238 mothers and sons with 40 sibling sisters to extend and test the models from Study 1. In Study 2, families were randomly assigned to intervention or no-intervention control groups and assessed before intervention and nine times over the next nine years. The aims of Study 2 were:

- to develop and test the intervention
- to conduct an experimental test of the theory underlying the intervention by altering parenting practices and thereby preventing boys' antisocial behavior problems and delinquency; and
- to evaluate the manner in which intervention effects on parenting and child outcomes would impact maternal adjustment.

In this chapter, we focus on a single outcome for the boys and two sets of parenting variables. The youth outcome is delinquency measured through assessments taken over nine years from teacher reports for the children involved in the study. The parenting variables are the two types of family management practices specified in our model and repeatedly found to predict antisocial and delinquent behavior: coercive parenting and positive parenting. Coercive parenting is based on specific microsocial processes associated with antisocial behavior, namely negative reciprocity, escalation, and negative reinforcement. Positive parenting comprises a set of five parenting skills associated with amelioration of antisocial behavior and promotion of prosocial adjustment. These five positive parenting practices are skill encouragement, limit setting, monitoring, problem solving, and positive involvement. All parenting variables were assessed via direct observation of parent–child interactions. In this chapter, we describe the two sets of parenting variables and how they unfold in relationship to delinquent outcomes for the boys. Our analyses of the findings suggest that mothers can significantly help their children adjust to changes following marital separation if they reduce coercive parenting and increase positive parenting, as shown in Figure 8.1.

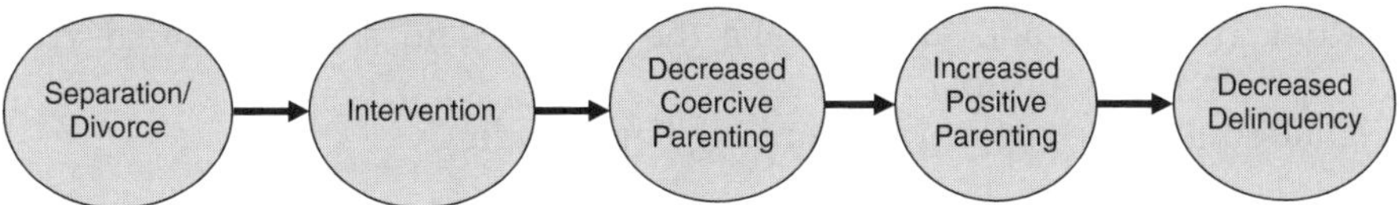

Figure 8.1 How intervention can affect divorce sequelae

WHAT IS COERCION?

Programmatic applied and basic research on families with antisocial children led to a carefully articulated theory about the role coercion plays in the development of delinquency (Patterson, 1982). Significant effects found in passive longitudinal and intervention studies demonstrate that the frequency and duration of coercive bouts is greater in families with antisocial children compared to those that are better adjusted (Patterson, 1982; Patterson, Reid, & Dishion, 1992; Reid, Patterson, & Snyder, 2002). Along with the importance of coercion, analyses of progressions from mild to serious behavior problems indicate that noncompliance is the keystone for progressions in both overt and covert kinds of deviant behavior (Chamberlain & Patterson, 1995; Patterson, Reid & Dishion, 1992; Shaw, Keenan, & Vondra, 1994). These findings helped to create the theory for the Oregon model of Parent Management Training (PMTO) in which one of the first steps is the introduction of strategies to decrease coercion and noncompliance in children while bolstering prosocial and compliant behaviors.

Children who live in families with high rates of coercion are likely to overlearn patterns of coercive behavior themselves and these overlearned patterns can generalize across social settings. In the intervention described in this chapter, our approach is to reduce and replace coercive tactics with positive parenting strategies. As we describe below, coercive interactions set negative reinforcement traps that ensnare everyone involved in a pattern of increasingly nonproductive interactions. One of the great battlegrounds for parents and children is the grocery store, where the tactic of choice is more often than not an exercise in coercion. Here is one example between a mother and her little girl:

Child: Mommy, I want those cookies.
Mom: Sorry, honey, but you can't have them now. We're having dinner soon.
Child: (raising her voice) But mommy, mommy, I want those cookies! NOW!
Mom: (Frowning and raising her voice) No! I said no, and I mean NO!
Child: (At full blast) I WANT COOKIES!! I WANT COOKIES!! I WANT COOKIES!! I WANT, I WANT, I WANT . . .

Mom: (Defeated and angry) Take the cookies and shove them in your mouth, and shut up!
Child: (takes the cookies and smiling begins eating).

What the child learns in this sequence is that when her mother refuses her requests, success can be attained through an escalation in her use of aversive behaviors. The steps are as follows: (1) request; (2) denial (a negative toward the child); (3) negative reciprocation with negative behaviors; (4) escalation; (5) win for child (gets cookies); and (6) termination of the child's negative behavior (escape from negative for mother). The child is positively reinforced with cookies for using aversive behavior and the mother is negatively reinforced with the termination of her child's embarrassing public behavior. Patterson (1982) refers to this double set of contingencies as "the reinforcement trap." Though on occasion we all become entrapped in coercive interchanges, when people rely on coercion as a standard means of accomplishing their aims, this pattern can become a way of life and negative outcomes are sure to follow.

POSITIVE PARENTING TO REPLACE COERCION

To reduce coercion and increase positive parenting, PMTO intervention calls for parents to be proactive in settings in which problems are likely to occur. Positive parenting takes careful planning and an integrated preventive approach. For example, here is a positive parenting method for application to the grocery store situation:

- *Step 1:* Parents specify appropriate grocery-store behaviors, e.g., stay with me, follow my directions, and accept no. These behaviors are clearly defined and role plays of positive and negative examples for specific behaviors are practiced.
- *Step 2:* Parents establish a plan to provide positive reinforcement for appropriate behaviors while in the grocery store. This can be done with tokens, points, or other simple strategies to encourage successful behavior. With each token, the parent comments positively on the behavior that earns the token ("Good job staying right with me. Here's a penny."). A goal is set for the number of tokens (in this case, pennies) necessary to get a reward upon leaving the grocery store. The goal should be easy for the child to achieve, and the reward should be one the parent is willing and able to provide and the child considers worth working for.
- *Step 3:* Before the next shopping trip, parents explain the grocery store game to the child during a pleasant time at home. Parents and children practice several examples of right- and wrong-way behaviors. The practice is designed to be fun and instructive.

- *Step 4:* On the way to the store, parents remind children of how the game is played. While in the store, parents actively attend to children's positive behaviors, encouraging success. Parents should consider the first few trips to the store as training sessions. For this reason, the first trips should be short.
- *Step 5:* Upon leaving the store, parents provide children with the earned reward. If the child was not successful, the parent is encouraging ("You earned almost enough pennies for your reward. Next time, I *know* you will make it. Shall we try again tomorrow?")
- *Step 6:* When children misbehave, parents stop the grocery store expedition and go home. Parents are not negative but matter of fact. ("Today's not a good day to play this game. We'll try again another time.") The next trial should be short. The ultimate goal is the child's successful behavior. Practice will produce the desired results.

THE BASIC PMTO INTERVENTION

The Oregon model of Parent Management Training, was first developed in the mid 1960's by Gerald R. Patterson and has been evolving since as a result of the work of Patterson's colleagues at the Oregon Social Learning Center.

The program has been applied in a series of efficacy trials with prevention and treatment samples by Patterson's colleagues at the Oregon Social Learning Center (OSLC) (Chamberlain & Reid, 1991; Forgatch & DeGarmo, 1999; Patterson, Chamberlain, & Reid, 1982; Reid *et al.*, 1999). One of the hallmarks of this program is the structured focus on youngsters with antisocial behavior and concurrent related problems, such as noncompliance, depression, school failure, deviant peer association, substance use, and delinquency. The intervention is hypothesized to operate by reducing coercion within the family and increasing positive parenting. This, in turn, is hypothesized to benefit child adjustment. The model goes on to specify that improvement in child adjustment will decrease parental stress and depression, which will lead to improved parenting. Thus, intervention shortly after marital separation can disrupt the previously described cycle of deviance. Hypothetically, reducing coercion and strengthening positive parenting will result in reductions in trajectories of delinquency.

The Oregon model of Parent Management Training, is based on the model of social interaction learning (SIL: Patterson, 1982; Patterson, Reid & Dishion, 1992; Reid, Patterson & Snyder, 2002). The overarching principle in the SIL model is that people learn patterns of behavior that are shaped within their social environments. Repeated reinforcement leads some patterns to become overlearned. The more consistent the social environment, the more likely the patterns are to become habitual and generalize across social settings such as from home to school (Ramsey, Patterson, & Walker, 1990). The agents that shape behavior differ according to social context. In the family context, parents or caregivers are presumed to be the most proximal socializing agents for their children, with siblings and other peers following closely. Of particular relevance within the SIL is the role that parents play in terms of their parenting practices as mediating mechanisms between family contexts and youth adjustment (Dishion, Patterson, & Kavanagh, 1992; Forgatch, Patterson, & Ray, 1996; Patterson, 2005). The social contexts in which families live are also assumed to affect youngsters' adjustment, but these effects are presumed to be mediated through socialization processes taking place with parents and peers.

The PMTO method has been applied effectively with mixed family structures (i.e., single mothers, two-parent biological, and stepfamilies) and interventions are delivered one family at a time or in group formats (Forgatch & DeGarmo, 1999; Forgatch, DeGarmo, & Beldavs, 2005; Patterson, Chamberlain, & Reid, 1982; Reid & Eddy, 2002). Preventive PMTO interventions have been tested in randomized studies for at-risk populations of the recently divorced, recently remarried, and those living in high-crime neighborhoods. Clinical programs have proven effective in randomized trials for elementary-school-aged children referred for antisocial behavior problems, children who steal, multiple offending delinquent adolescents, children who have been physically abused, and delinquent youth referred for out-of-home placement (Bank *et al.*, 1991; Chamberlain & Moore, 1998; Patterson, Chamberlain & Reid, 1982; Reid, Hinojoa-Rivera & Lorber, 1980; Reid & Kavanagh, 1985).

PARENTING THROUGH CHANGE: PMTO FOR SINGLE MOTHERS

The Parenting through Change program (Forgatch, 1994) was designed specifically for recently separated mothers, provided in group format to offer a supportive context in which mothers could learn new strategies and share their struggles and successes. Meetings took place at suppertime in an easy to reach location, with a choice of groups taking place two or three evenings a week. Transportation assistance was provided on a need basis. Childcare and meals were part of the fare for mothers and their children. To enhance attendance, two drawings were held each night with awards of $5 as incentives for attendance and completing homework assignments. To provide a clean test of the theoretical model in the present study, we intervened with the mothers, not the children. In this way, we were able to test the impact of the PMTO child-rearing strategies as mechanisms of child adjustment following divorce. In most PMTO programs, children are included in the intervention sessions.

The number of sessions for the intervention reflected a balance between providing sufficient information for mothers to help their children make a successful passage through the separation/divorce transition and few enough sessions to ensure attendance. The pilot group participated in 16 sessions; we pared this to 14 sessions by the time the study began. The PMTO theory and methods require the following content:

- *Introduction to change* as a process and learning to *identify and track strengths*
- attention to *parental directives*, effective and ineffective, and tracking children's *compliance*
- *skill encouragement*, which involves identifying a goal behavior, breaking it into appropriate sized steps, identifying incentives for small steps toward success, establishing a chart to track daily progress, and practicing how to talk about the procedures with children
- *limit setting* as a means of reducing deviant behavior, with short time outs backed up with short privilege removal for relatively small but critical problem behaviors, such as noncompliance
- *balancing encouragement and discipline* so that parents provide a goal ratio of five-to-one positive to negative contingencies to their children
- *monitoring* children's whereabouts, activities, behavior, peer associations, and development
- using *problem-solving* strategies in interpersonal situations to make plans, establish agreements, negotiate conflict, and otherwise prevent and manage stressors
- *positive involvement* in terms of showing genuine interest and attention to children's issues and concerns, and to providing the kinds of care and support that help children feel loved; and
- *holding the course* following group termination in the face of likely setbacks.

With nine sessions designated as necessary by theory, we were frugal in further supplementing the fundamental structure but did want to explore some additional areas in this study. The literature provided many suggestions with which to enrich the intervention. We chose the following arenas: children's academic achievement, effective communication, management of interpersonal conflict (especially with the ex-partner), and regulating emotions (for mothers and for children). The challenge, of course, was to integrate these issues in a sequence that would bolster maternal family management skills. Each of the additional components was framed within the context of the core PMTO structure.

The academic dimension model was divided into two sessions: school-related success at home and success at school. At home, mothers learned to break the goal of doing homework into small steps (e.g., establishing a consistent and relatively short time for daily academic training, using a specific place with good light and appropriate materials, creating a quiet environment for the whole family) and providing small incentives for carrying out these steps. For the at-school component, we helped mothers specify school goals that could be accomplished on a daily or weekly basis and techniques to monitor children's behavior while they were away from home. We encouraged the group of mothers to use problem-solving strategies such as identifying goal behaviors, brainstorming strategies to achieve goals, designing a plan, negotiating contingencies, and engaging teachers and children in the process.

Within the PMTO method, parents learn strategies to regulate their own emotional expression, to recognize and reduce negative emotional expression and increase positive expression with special application to each of the five parenting dimensions. Role plays help parents to understand situations and differing perspectives by allowing them to experience differences learned when playing their own role or that of their children. We role play the many varieties of negative emotion, including anger, contempt, fear, sadness, and combinations of these. Using a questioning process that guides parents to identify specific nonverbal dimensions relevant to affective expression, mothers explore the effects that hostile and friendly approaches to children can have. Instead of encouraging parents to "let it all out," we facilitate the use of neutral and positive expression as well as strategies for managing negative emotions. For children's emotional expression, mothers learn to differentiate their own feelings from those of their children and practice ways to engage their youngsters in activities that make it safe for the children to talk about their own feelings. Mothers learn to listen without negative reactions when their children talk about upsetting issues.

Many of the difficulties between children's divorced parents have to do with managing the small details of life, e.g., making arrangements concerning the children, planning activities, sharing holidays, and issues coordinating visitation. We taught families to manage conflict and other emotional situations in the context of interpersonal problem solving. Mothers learn to set specific goals that lead to agreements, to communicate directly with their ex, to communicate clearly and in a neutral manner, to paraphrase statements and advance the interaction, to write down the agreements, and to keep their children out of these interactions. Mothers practice replacing negative affect with neutral affect.

Early reports of findings resulting from Parenting through Change have been positive. At 1 year post-baseline, parenting practices had improved relative to the control group, and these improvements contributed to 1-year improvements in teacher reports of adaptive, prosocial, and externalizing behavior at school; maternal reports of child depression, anxiety, and externalizing; and child report of depression and peer relations. Although the intervention did not have direct effects on these child outcomes at Year 1, the indirect effects through parenting practices were significant (Forgatch & DeGarmo, 1999). By three years after baseline, the intervention demonstrated direct effects on several child outcomes, including observed noncompliance (Martinez & Forgatch, 2001), teacher ratings of externalizing and internalizing behavior (DeGarmo, Patterson, & Forgatch, 2004), and teacher ratings of delinquency (DeGarmo & Forgatch, 2005). In all of these models, the intervention effects on child outcomes were mediated by parenting practices as observed during parent–child interactions. In the delinquency study, child report of deviant peer association also mediated intervention effects on delinquency. Growth curve analysis of nine-year followup data provided evidence that teacher ratings of delinquency continued to show significant intervention benefits for boys in the experimental group and that this intervention effect was similar for police arrest data over the same nine-year interval. Improvements in parenting practices and diminished deviant peer association mediated the direct effects on both teacher ratings and arrest records (Forgatch *et al.*, submitted).

As mentioned earlier, Parenting through Change was successful in reducing noncompliance, and in line with the SIL model, benefits to parenting mediated the intervention's effect in reducing noncompliance over the course of three years (Martinez & Forgatch, 2001). Of particular relevance for this chapter, parenting practices were measured separately for coercive and positive parenting and changes in each evinced unique effects on changes in noncompliance as anticipated. It is interesting to note that changes in positive parenting contributed significantly more variance to change in noncompliance than did change in coercive parenting. This differential effect had not been anticipated and raised a set of chicken-or-egg questions that we address in the present report:

- What is the sequence of change in parenting resulting from intervention?
- How do coercive and positive parenting relate to each other and to long-term effects on child behavior?

In the following sections we describe the measures, results, and analyses used to examine our hypothesis that long-term delinquency for children is reduced by treatment of PMTO and that this reduction is mediated by immediate reduction in coercive parenting and mid-term increase of positive parenting. First the measures used are described, then the results and presented, and a discussion of these results and implications is presented in conclusion.

Measures

We conducted multiple-method assessments, which included structured interviews with mothers and children, observations of mother-child interactions in the laboratory, and questionnaires filled out by mothers, youngsters, and teachers. For Phase 1 of the ODS efficacy trial, we collected teacher data annually over a 36-month time span and parent and child data semi-annually over a 30-month time span. Phase 2 of the trial was initiated after a three-year hiatus, the sixth year following the baseline assessment. We collected teacher and family questionnaire data annually and observational data two times on alternate years.

- *Boys' age* was used to control for differences in development. Boy ages were calculated by subtracting the date of birth from the date of assessment.

- *Delinquency* was evaluated using the Delinquency T-score attained through administration of the Teacher Report Form (TRF) of the Child Behavior Checklist (CBCL) (Achenbach, 1991). The delinquency T-score is a nationally normed measure of teacher ratings of delinquent acts. The T-score consisted of nine items rated on a three-point scale from 0 (*not true*) to 2 (*very true or often true*). Sample items include: steals, physically attacks people, and destroys others property, lies, or cheats. Cronbach's alphas for sequential assessments were 0.76, 0.71, 0.75, and 0.72 for phase 1 and 0.76, 0.82, 0.80, and 0.83 in Phase 2.

Parenting Practices

We observed parenting behaviors in the laboratory during structured interaction tasks (SIT) lasting 45 minutes. The tasks included mother-son problem-solving discussions about current hot conflicts, a teaching task, an unstructured activity, a forbidden toy situation, and a refreshment break. We scored microsocial data using the Interpersonal Process Code (IPC) (Rusby, Estes, & Dishion, 1991) in real time data entry on computers. The IPC is a 13-code system used to code information on respondent, recipient, sequence, content, affect, context, and duration of behaviors. Behaviors are deemed aversive if negative in content (e.g., refusal or criticism) or affective tone (e.g., hostile or sad). Behaviors are identified as positive if they are either positive in content, such as positive interpersonal and endearment with neutral or positive affect, or neutral in content, such as talking with positive affect, including happy and caring. Coders also rated their overall impressions of interaction following coding of microsocial behaviors with a rating instrument (Forgatch, Knutson, & Mayne, 1992). At each wave, approximately 15% of the interactions were scored for interrater reliability. Two factor scores were measured: coercive parenting and positive parenting. Each factor demonstrated convergence (Forgatch & DeGarmo, 2002). Positive parenting included positive involvement, skill encouragement, and monitoring. Coercive parenting consisted of negative reinforcement, negative reciprocity, and aversive discipline.

Positive involvement was obtained from global coder ratings following each of the eight SIT tasks. Likert-scale items included: warm, empathetic, encouraging, affectionate, and treated child with respect. Cronbach alphas for sequential assessments were 0.97, 0.97, 0.97, 0.96, and 0.97. The intraclass correlation coefficients (ICCs) were 0.83, 0.90, 0.82, 0.79, and 0.93.

Skill encouragement for mothers was measured using the global coder ratings of ability to promote child skill development through contingent encouragement and scaffolding strategies observed during the 10-minute teaching task. The measure consists of 11 Likert-scale items, which include items such as "breaks task into manageable steps," "reinforces success," "prompts appropriate behavior," and "corrects appropriately." Cronbach's alphas were 0.69,

0.73, 0.81, 0.70 and 0.67 from baseline to 30 months. The ICCs of coder agreement were 0.73, 0.67, 0.66, 0.48, and 0.77, respectively.

Monitoring consisted of five items rated by coders and parent interviewers. Coders rated how skilled the mother was in supervising the child, keeping close track of the youngster's behavior, and obtaining information from the child. Interviewers rated how well the mother knew what the boy does on day-to-day basis and tracked antisocial behavior. Cronbach's alphas for the scale score were 0.72, 0.64, 0.71, 0.70, and 0.55.

Negative reinforcement was defined as the frequency of conflict bouts initiated by the mother and terminated by the child. Bouts consisted of an exchange in which the mother introduced an aversive behavior and the child responded in kind. The bout continued until a period of at least 12 seconds of interaction without an aversive behavior by either party. An example would be: the mother gave the child a command, the child shouted a refusal, the mother withdrew the command, and the interaction became neutral. In this sense, the child escaped the aversive situation provided by the mother by introducing his own aversive behavior, which resulted in the mother backing down and thereby negatively reinforcing the boy's use of aversive behavior. The ICCs were 0.78 and 0.47 for baseline and 12 months.

Negative reciprocity was measured with the Haberman binomial z score (Gottman & Roy, 1990), reflecting the conditional likelihood that the mother reciprocated the child's aversive behavior with an aversive behavior of her own. The ICCs were 0.65 and 0.54 for baseline and 12 months.

Aversive discipline was based on global ratings. The discipline score was the mean of 13 items, scaled from 1 to 5, indicating inconsistent, erratic, or otherwise ineffective discipline. Sample items rated whether the mother was overly strict and authoritarian, used nagging or nattering to get compliance, expressed anger/hostility while disciplining, seemed indecisive or unsure when disciplining, or used inappropriate discipline. Cronbach's alphas were 0.91 and 0.92 and ICCs were 0.70 and 0.78 for baseline and 12 months.

Results

Our analyses focused on testing the hypothesis that treatment with PMTO would significantly reduce growth in delinquency and that this treatment effect will be mediated by growth in positive parenting practices. Furthermore, we hypothesized that an early reduction in coercive processes resulting from the intervention would mediate the effect of treatment on positive parenting, which, in turn, would mediate a reduction in long-term growth of adolescent delinquency. These models use teacher rated reports of delinquency over the entire nine-year course of the intervention study (Phases 1 and 2), including seven full waves of data.

We used a structural equation-modeling framework to estimate latent variable growth models of the time series teacher-reported data. Growth curve models provide several advantages in conducting prevention analyses including more reliable estimates of change and intervention effects (Kraemer & Thiemann, 1989), more accurate representation of the time spacing of assessment (Biesanz *et al.*, 2004; DeGarmo & Forgatch, 2005), and the ability to partial out measurement error for the time series data while simultaneously conducting prevention tests of mediation and direct and indirect effects of the intervention (Cheong, MacKinnon, & Khoo, 2001; Duncan *et al.*, 1997).

In these analyses, growth curve factors were specified with a latent factor for initial level of delinquency over nine years and a latent factor for "rate of growth" using the continuous level teacher-reported data. These factors were specified using appropriate time weights or fixed chronometric factor loadings. For the nine-year average level latent factor, these weighted time loadings in the unstandardized model were fixed at 1 for each of the repeated measures indicators. For the linear growth-rate latent factor, time weights were fixed at 1, 3, 5, 7, 15, 17, and 19 representing the available data obtained from teachers from baseline to the nine-year follow-up. Boys' age is controlled as a time-varying covariate in each subsequent growth model. In all analyses we used intent-to-treat (ITT) group assignment, a conservative estimate of intervention effects that is in keeping with the maxim, once randomized always analyzed. Effect sizes can be underestimated using the ITT approach (Jo & Muthen, 1997) because data from all participants is included whether or not they attended intervention sessions.

Test of treatment impact on delinquency reduction

The model depicted in Figure 8.2 is used to test the hypothesis that treatment has a direct effect on reduction in nine-year growth of delinquency. This model demonstrates adequate fit to the data ($\chi^2_{(77)} = 112.049$, $p < 0.01$, CFI = 0.99, $\chi^2/df = 1.46$, RMSEA = 0.04). As predicted, this model indicates that intervention resulted in a significant direct reduction in growth of delinquency ($\beta = -0.22$, $p < 0.05$).

Mediation of treatment effect on delinquency by three-year growth in positive parenting

The model depicted in Figure 8.3 tests the hypothesis that positive parenting practices mediate the direct intervention effect on nine-year growth in delinquency. This model demonstrates acceptable fit to the data ($\chi^2_{(121)} = 195.48$, $p < 0.01$, CFI = 0.98, $\chi^2/df = 1.62$, RMSEA = 0.05). To demonstrate mediation, upon inclusion of the mediating variable, direct paths to and from this variable must be significant and the direct effect from the independent variable to the dependent variable must be rendered nonsignificant (Baron & Kenny, 1986). As is observed in Figure 8.3, the regression paths are significant from treatment to three-year growth in positive parenting ($\beta = 0.27$,

Notes: $\chi^2_{(77)} = 112.05$, $\boldsymbol{p} = .01$, **CFI** = .99, $\chi^2/df = 1.46$, **RMSEA** = .04, $^*\boldsymbol{p} < .05$.

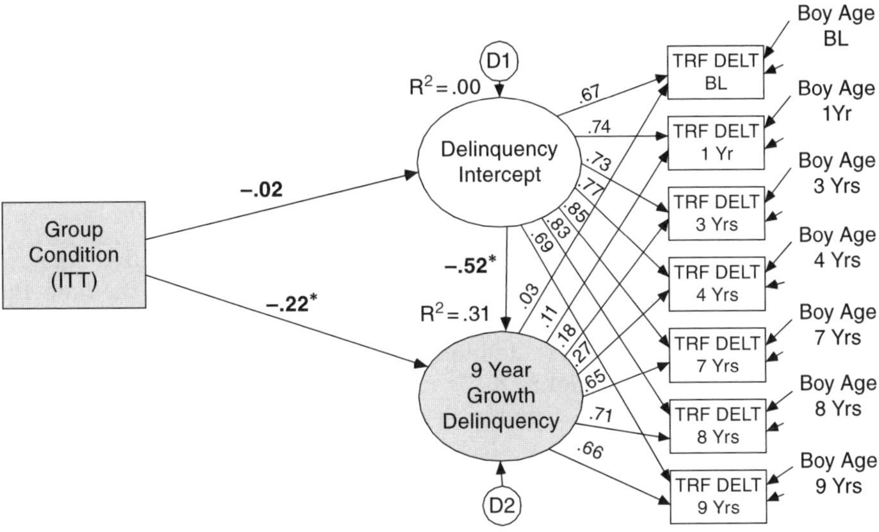

Figure 8.2 Latent variable growth model for test of intervention effect on 9-year teacher-rated delinquency data

Notes: $\chi^2_{(121)} = 195.48$, $p = < .01$, CFI = .98, $\chi^2/df = 1.62$, RMSEA = .05, $^*p < .05$.

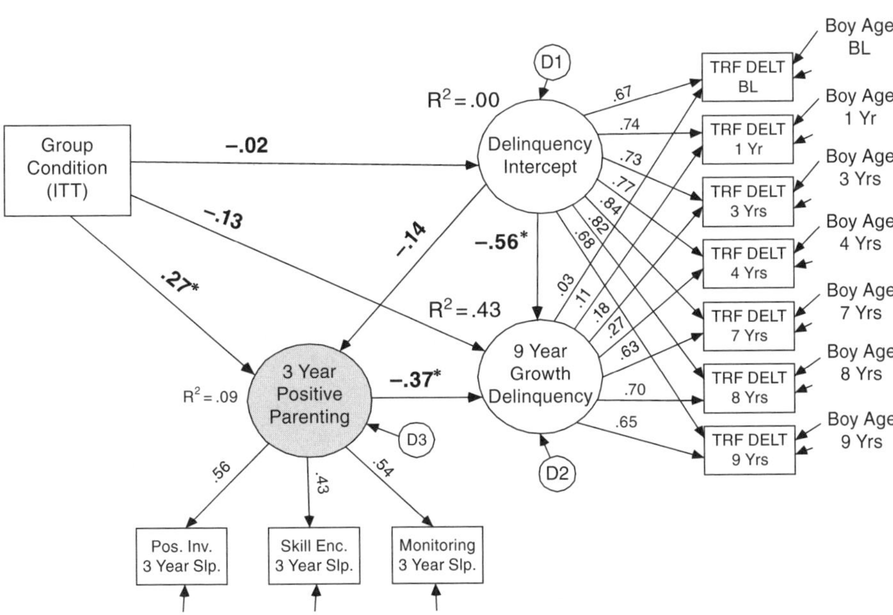

Figure 8.3 Latent variable growth model for test of intervention effects on 9-year teacher-rated delinquency data mediated by 3-year growth in parenting

$p < 0.05$) and from positive parenting to growth in delinquency ($\beta = -0.37$, $p < 0.05$). Inclusion of the positive parenting slope factor rendered the direct treatment effect on delinquency non significant, indicating that growth in positive parenting factors acts to mediate treatment effects on the reduction in delinquency.

Mediation of positive parenting by early change in coercive parenting

Next, we examine the full model which includes the hypothesis that changes in coercive parenting practices from baseline to Year 1 act to mediate the growth in positive parenting from baseline to three years, which significantly decreases growth of adolescent delinquency.

The model depicted in Figure 8.4 is used to examine this hypothesis. This model also demonstrates acceptable fit to the data ($\chi^2_{(135)} = 218.10$, $p < 0.01$, CFI $= 0.98$, $\chi^2/df = 1.62$, RMSEA $= 0.05$). As can be seen in this model, the direct effect on delinquency remains nonsignificant and the direct effect on positive parenting has been rendered nonsignificant. Concurrently, there is a significant path from treatment to one-year change in coercive parenting ($\beta = -0.23$, $p < 0.01$), change in coercive parenting to three-year positive parenting ($\beta = -0.28$, $p < 0.01$), and positive parenting to delinquency ($\beta = -0.41$, $p < 0.01$).

Notes: $\chi^2_{(135)} = 218.10$, $p = < .01$, $CFI = .98$, $\chi^2/df = 1.62$, RMSEA $= .05$, $^*p < .05$. $^{**}p < .01$.

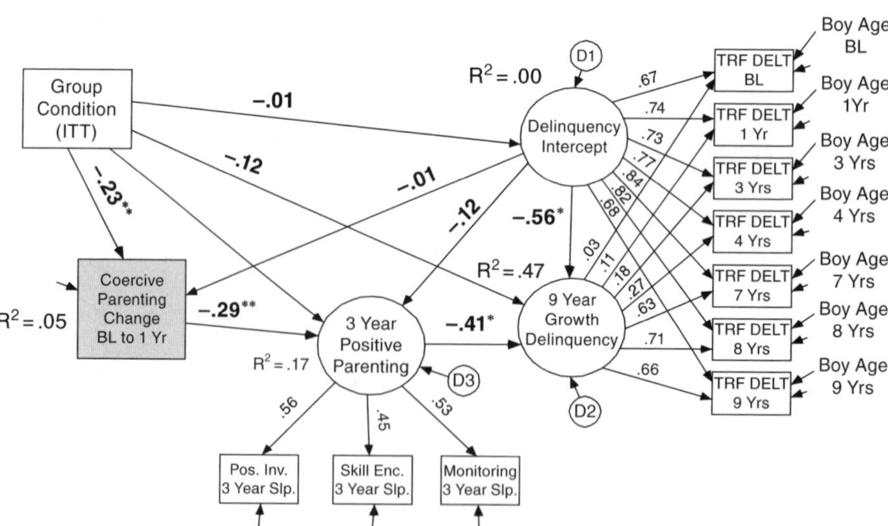

Figure 8.4 Latent variable growth model for test of intervention effects on 9-year teacher-rated delinquency data mediated by 1-year change in coercive parenting and 3-year growth in positive parenting

Discussion

Taken together, these models support the hypotheses set forth in the introduction. Our analyses used an intent-to-treat, randomized, experimental design with multiple-agent and method assessments and classical mediational analyses. We first demonstrated a direct treatment effect with nine-year reductions in teacher-reported delinquency for boys. Secondly, we demonstrated the delinquency reduction to be mediated by three-year growth in positive parenting as observed in parent child interactions. Finally, we demonstrated that the mediating effect of positive parenting was further mediated by one-year reduction in observed coercive parenting practices. The overall implications of these analyses support our hypothesis of a fully mediated pathway from intervention to reduction in delinquency whereby coercive parenting over one year is decreased, positive parenting over three years increased, and ultimately growth in delinquency over nine years is decreased. These findings have important implications for intervention programs for families at risk child behavior problems because of their parents' marital separation. Separating mothers can prevent their sons' delinquency following divorce if (1) they can reduce their coercive tactics and (2) they can increase their positive parenting practices.

Following separation, a disproportionate number of youngsters are identified with adjustment problems, some temporary and some enduring. Several investigators have examined whether these problems existed before the separation or developed afterwards and whether the problems tend to be short lived or long lasting. Findings indicate that there are many trajectories for these children: some are well adjusted before the separation and remain so; others who were healthy struggle for a while but recover; on the other hand some previously well-functioning youngsters fall onto a negative path that continues well into their adult lives. Yet another set of children develop problems only after their parents separate. Those who have or develop difficulties experience differing topographies, durations and intensities for their adjustment problems (e.g., Amato & Fowler, 2002; Chase-Lansdale, 1995; Shaw, Winslow, & Flanagan, 1999). Although decades of work will be required to understand fully the mechanisms of divorce adjustment, theory-based prevention programs can help at-risk families so long as they are efficacious and do not introduce iatrogenic outcomes. Working directly with the custodial parents can have the added benefit of helping other children in the family. For example, in the small subsample of 40 sibling sisters in the study, mothers were found to reduce their coercive interactions, and the girls reported fewer internalizing problems (Forgatch & DeGarmo, 2002).

The Parenting through Change program empowered single mothers with a brief preventive intervention focused on effective parenting in the face of stressful life circumstances. Positive outcomes emerged for mothers and their children in the ensuing years. With improvement in parenting practices there were benefits to boys' adjustment that included reduced delinquent behavior as reported by teachers and in official police arrest records, reduced noncompliance observed between boys and their mothers, reduced internalizing behavior and deviant peer association as reported by the boys themselves, and increases in academic performance as measured through standardized test scores (Beldavs *et al.*, 2006; DeGarmo & Forgatch, 2004, 2005; DeGarmo, Patterson, & Forgatch, 2004; Forgatch & DeGarmo, 1999, 2002; Forgatch *et al.*, (submitted)). Benefits to the boys, specifically reductions in externalizing behavior, in turn led to reductions in self-reported maternal depression (DeGarmo, Patterson & Forgatch, 2004), and mothers whose depression improved responded with more effective parenting (Patterson, DeGarmo, & Forgatch, 2004). Another family benefit from the intervention involved significant increases in mothers' per capita annual income accompanied by reductions in financial stress (Forgatch & DeGarmo, in press). Thus, supporting mothers with parenting information during a stressful transition can produce long lasting and diverse positive outcomes in a manner that can spread throughout the family system.

The Parenting through Change program is currently being tested in adaptations for other populations and contextual stressors. In the present study, the sample was drawn from an ethnically restricted pool. The robustness of the findings from this program will be greatly enhanced with replication and application to multiple ethnicities. Two replication studies are under way that employ randomized designs using Parenting through Change with Latino families (Domenech-Rodriguez, 2003–2008; Wieling, 2003–2008). A replication is also being conducted within battered women's shelters (Gewirtz, 2005–2009). We await findings from these PMTO adaptations.

REFERENCES

Achenbach, T. M. (1991). *Manual for the Teacher's Report Form and 1991 Profile*. Burlington: University of Vermont.

Amato, P. R. (1987). Family processes in one-parent, stepparent and intact families: The child's point of view. *Journal of Marriage and Family, 49*, 327–337.

Amato, P. R. (1993). Children's adjustment to divorce: Theories, hypotheses, and empirical support. *Journal of Marriage and Family, 55*(February), 23–38.

Amato, P. R. & Fowler, F. (2002). Parenting practices, child adjustment, and family diversity. *Journal of Marriage and Family, 64*(3), 703–716.

Anderson, E. R., Greene, S. M., Hetherington, E. M., & Clingempeel, W. G. (1999). The dynamics of parental remarriage: Adolescent, parent, and sibling influence. In Hetherington, E. M. (ed.), *Coping with Divorce, Single Parenting, and Remarriage: A Risk and Resiliency Perspective* (pp. 295–319). Mahwah, NJ: Erlbaum.

Bank, L., Marlowe, J. H., Reid, J. B. *et al.* (1991). A comparative evaluation of parent-training interventions of families of chronic delinquents. *Journal of Abnormal Child Psychology, 19*(1), 15–33.

Baron, R. M. & Kenny, D. A. (1986). The moderator-mediator variable distinction in social psychological research: Conceptual, strategic, and statistical considerations. *Journal of Personality and Social Psychology, 51*, 1173–1182.

Beldavs, Z. G., Forgatch, M. S., Patterson, G. R., & DeGarmo, D. S. (2006). Reducing the detrimental effects of divorce: Enhancing the parental competence of single mothers. In Heinrichs, Haalweg & Döpfner (eds), *Strengthening Families: Evidence-Based Approaches to Support Child Mental Health* (pp. 143–185). Münster: Verlag für Psychotherapie.

Biesanz, J. C., Deeb-Sossa, N., Papadakis, A. A. *et al.* (2004). The role of coding time in estimating and interpreting growth curve models. *Psychological Methods, 9*(1), 30–52.

Brody, G. H., Neubaum, E., & Forehand, R. (1988). Serial marriage: A heuristic analysis of an emerging family form. *Psychological Bulletin, 103*(2), 211–222.

Bumpass, L. L. & Sweet, J. A. (1989). National estimates of cohabitation. *Demography, 26*(4), 615–625.

Bumpass, L. L., Sweet, J., & Martin, T. C. (1990). Changing patterns of remarriage. *Journal of Marriage and Family, 52*(August), 747–756.

Chamberlain, P. & Moore, K. J. (1998). A clinical model of parenting juvenile offenders: A comparison of group versus family care. *Clinical Child Psychology and Psychiatry, 3*, 375–386.

Chamberlain, P. & Patterson, G. R. (1995). Discipline and child compliance in parenting. In Bornstein (ed.), *Handbook of Parenting* (Vol. 4, pp. 205–225). Hillsdale, NJ: Erlbaum.

Chamberlain, P. & Reid, J. B. (1991). Using a specialized foster care community treatment model for children and adolescents leaving the state mental hospital. *Journal of Community Psychology, 19*, 266–276.

Chase-Lansdale, P. L. (1995). The long-term effects of parental divorce on the mental health of young adults: A developmental perspective. *Child Development, 66*, 1614–1634.

Cheong, J. W., MacKinnon, D., & Khoo, S. T. (2001). A latent growth modeling approach to mediation analysis. In Collins & Sayer (eds), *New Methods for the Analysis of Change: Decade of Behavior* (pp. 390–392). Washington DC: American Psychological Association.

DeGarmo, D. S. & Forgatch, M. S. (2004). Putting problem solving to the test: replicating experimental interventions for preventing youngsters' problem behaviors. In Conger, R. D., Lorenz, F. O. & Wickrama, K. A. S. (eds), *Continuity and Change in Family Relations* (pp. 267–290). Mahwah, NJ: Erlbaum.

DeGarmo, D. S. & Forgatch, M. S. (2005). Early development of delinquency within divorced families: Evaluating a randomized preventive intervention trial. *Developmental Science, 8*(3), 229–239.

DeGarmo, D. S., Patterson, G. R., & Forgatch, M. S. (2004). How do outcomes in a specified parent training intervention maintain or wane over time? *Prevention Science, 5*(2), 73–89.

Dishion, T. J., Patterson, G. R., & Kavanagh, K. A. (1992). An experimental test of the coercion model: linking measurement theory, and intervention. In McCord & Tremblay (eds), *The Interaction of Theory and Practice: Experimental Studies of Intervention* (pp. 253–282). New York: Guilford Press.

Domenech-Rodriguez, M. (2003–2008). *Parenting Intervention for Spanish-speaking Latinos*, Grant No. KOI MH 066297. Bethesda: MD. National Institute of Mental Health.

Duncan, T. E., Duncan, S. C., Alpert, A. *et al.* (1997). Latent variable modeling of longitudinal and multilevel substance use data. *Multivariate Behavioral Research, 32*(2), 275–318.

Forgatch, M. S. (1994). *Parenting Through Change: A Programmed Intervention Curriculum for Groups of Single Mothers*. Eugene: Oregon Social Learning Center.

Forgatch, M. S. & DeGarmo, D. S. (1999). Parenting through change: An effective prevention program for single mothers. *Journal of Consulting and Clinical Psychology, 67*, 711–724.

Forgatch, M. S. & DeGarmo, D. S. (2002). Extending and testing the social interaction learning model with divorce samples. In Reid, Patterson & Snyder (eds), *Antisocial Behavior in Children and Adolescents: A Developmental Analysis and Model for Intervention* (pp. 235–256). Washington, DC: American Psychological Association.

Forgatch, M. S. & DeGarmo, D. S. (submitted). Accelerating recovery from poverty: Prevention effects for recently separated mothers. *Journal of Early and Intensive Behavioral Intervention.*

Forgatch, M. S., DeGarmo, D. S., & Beldavs, Z. (2005). An efficacious theory-based intervention for stepfamilies. *Behavior Therapy, 36*(4), 357–365.

Forgatch, M. S., Knutson, N. M., & Mayne, T. (1992). *Coder Impressions of ODS Lab Tasks.* Eugene, OR: Oregon Social Learning Center.

Forgatch, M. S., Patterson, G. R., DeGarmo, D. S., & Beldavs, Z. G. (manuscript submitted for publication). An experimental test of the Oregon Delinquency Model.

Forgatch, M. S., Patterson, G. R., & Ray, J. A. (1996). Divorce and boys' adjustment problems: Two paths with a single model. In Hetherington, E. M. (eds), *Stress, Coping, and Resiliency in Children and Families* (pp. 67–105). Mahwah, NJ: Erlbaum.

Gewirtz, A. (2005–2009). *Integration of Evidence-based Treatment into Community Systems of Care for Traumatized Children*, Grant No. SM 56177. Minnesota Child Response Center, Minneapolis-St. Paul, MN: Substance Abuse and Mental Health Services Administration.

Gottman, J. M. & Roy, A. K. (1990). *Sequential Analysis: A Guide for Behavioral Researchers.* Cambridge: Cambridge University Press.

Hetherington, E. M. (ed.). (1999). *Coping with Divorce, Single Parenting, and Remarriage: A Risk and Resiliency Perspective.* Mahwah, NJ: Erlbaum.

Hetherington, E. M. & Stanley-Hagan, M. (1999). The adjustment of children with divorced parents: a risk and resiliency perspective. *Journal of Child Psychology and Psychiatry, 40*(1), 129–140.

Jo, B. & Muthen, B. (1997). *Finite Mixture Modeling of Non-compliance in Intervention Studies: Multivariate Models with Mediators* (unpublished manuscript). Los Angeles: University of California.

Kraemer, H. C. & Thiemann, S. (1989). A strategy to use soft data effectively in randomized controlled clinical trials. *Journal of Consulting and Clinical Psychology, 57*(1), 148–154.

Martinez, C. R., Jr. & Forgatch, M. S. (2001). Preventing problems with boys' noncompliance: effects of a parent training intervention for divorcing mothers. *Journal of Consulting and Clinical Psychology, 69*, 416–428.

Patterson, G. R. (1982). *Coercive Family Process.* Eugene, OR: Castalia.

Patterson, G. R. (2005). The next generation of PMTO models. *Behavior Therapist, 28*(2), 25–32.

Patterson, G. R., Chamberlain, P., & Reid, J. B. (1982). A comparative evaluation of a parent-training program. *Behavior Therapy, 13*, 638–650.

Patterson, G. R., DeGarmo, D. S., & Forgatch, M. S. (2004). Systematic changes in families following prevention trials. *Journal of Abnormal Child Psychology, 32*(6), 621–633.

Patterson, G. R., Reid, J. B., & Dishion, T. J. (1992). *Antisocial Boys* (Vol. 4). Eugene, OR: Castalia.

Ramsey, E., Patterson, G. R., & Walker, H. M. (1990). Generalization of the antisocial trait from home to school settings. *Journal of Applied Developmental Psychology, 11*, 209–223.

Reid, J. B. & Eddy, J. M. (2002). Preventive efforts during the elementary school years: the linking the interests of families and teachers project. In Reid, J. B., Patterson, G. R. & Snyder, J. (eds), *Antisocial Behavior in Children and Adolescents: A Developmental Analysis and Model for Intervention* (pp. 219–233). Washington DC: American Psychological Association.

Reid, J. B., Eddy, J. M., Fetrow, R. A., & Stoolmiller, M. (1999). Description and immediate impacts of a preventive intervention for conduct problems. *American Journal of Community Psychology, 27*(4), 483–517.

Reid, J. B., Hinojoa-Rivera, G., & Lorber, R. (1980). *A Social Learning Approach to the Outpatient Treatment of Children Who Steal* (unpublished manuscript). Eugene, OR: Oregon Social Learning Center.

Reid, J. B. & Kavanagh, K. (1985). A social interactional approach to child abuse: risk, prevention, and treatment. In Chesney, M. A. & Rosenman, R. (eds), *Anger and Hostility in Behavioral and Cardiovascular Disorders* (pp. 241–257). New York: Hemisphere/McGraw-Hill.

Reid, J. B., Patterson, G. R., & Snyder, J. (eds). (2002). *Antisocial Behavior in Children and Adolescents: A Developmental Analysis and Model for Intervention*. Washington DC: American Psychological Association.

Rusby, J. C., Estes, A., & Dishion, T. (1991). *The Interpersonal Process Code (IPC)* (unpublished manuscript). Eugene, OR: Oregon Social Learning Center.

Shaw, D. S., Keenan, K., & Vondra, J. I. (1994). Developmental precursors of externalizing behavior: Ages 1 to 3. *Developmental Psychology, 30*, 355–364.

Shaw, D. S., Winslow, E. B., & Flanagan, C. (1999). A prospective study of the effects of marital status and family relations on young children's adjustment among African American and European American families. *Child Development, 70*, 742–755.

Simons, R. L., Beaman, J., Conger, R. D., & Chao, W. (1993). Stress, support, and antisocial behavior trait as determinants of emotional well-being and parenting practices among single mothers. *Journal of Marriage and Family, 55*, 385–398.

Wieling, E. A. (2003–2008). *Implementing the PTC Program with Latina Single Mothers;* Grant No. KOI MH 064506. Bethesda, MD: National Institute of Mental Health.

Zill, N., Morrison, D. R., & Coiro, M. J. (1993). Long-term effects of parental divorce on parent-child relationships, adjustment, and achievement in young adulthood. *Journal of Family Psychology, 7*(1), 91–103.

PART 3

LESSONS FROM PARENTING RESEARCH ON YOUNGER CHILDREN

CHAPTER 9

Stepping Up without Overstepping: Disentangling Parenting Dimensions and their Implications for Adolescent Adjustment

Wendy S. Grolnick, Krista L. Beiswenger, Carrie E. Price
Clark University, USA

INTRODUCTION

The period of adolescence has received an increasing amount of research attention in the past decade. New research has focused on both psychological and biological aspects of adolescents. The conclusions that have emerged from this research base have been important and have shaped policies that affect adolescents. However, the messages derived from this research have been somewhat conflicting, at least on the surface, in their implications for parenting.

One theme emerging from the literature is the increasing independence of adolescents and its importance for their development and adjustment. Theorists view adolescents as moving away from parents and toward peers, spending more time with friends and less with parents as they move through adolescence (Berndt, 1979; Meeus & Dekovic, 1995). Steinberg & Silverberg (1986), for example, suggested that adolescents need to develop "emotional

What Can Parents Do? New Insights into the Role of Parents in Adolescent Problem Behavior
Edited by Margaret Kerr, Håkan Stattin and Rutger C. M. E. Engels.

autonomy" or rely less on parents, to make their own decisions, and to have a say in issues that affect them. Eccles and her colleagues (Eccles *et al.*, 1991), in their developmental match hypothesis, suggested that adolescents prefer more input into decision making as they approach and move through adolescence. If it is true that adolescents function best when provided greater independence, the message to parents would be to allow their adolescents more say in decisions and greater space to be on their own, perhaps moving away from them, emotionally and physically.

On the other hand, there is increasing concern for adolescent problem behaviors expressed in the literature. In particular, research has documented a high level of risk-taking behavior (Centers for Disease Control, 2006; Leigh & Stall, 1993; Substance Abuse and Mental Health Service Administration, 2005). Adolescence is a period of experimentation, with increases in drug and alcohol use and risky sexual behaviors. Adolescents' increased engagement in risky behavior poses a serious danger to their health, safety, and future. Further, new biological studies suggest that the brain is not fully developed until the early to mid-twenties, with increasing "gyrification" occurring until that time (Armstong *et al.*, 1995). The immaturity of the brain has been cited as the reason for the low impulse control and responsibility adolescents often exhibit. Thus, from this perspective, adolescents are viewed as potentially displaying poor judgment and are therefore at risk of engaging in problem behavior, especially as their increasing mobility allows them greater access to risky substances and behaviors. The message here is that adolescence is a period in which parents need to be on heightened alert with regard to their adolescents and to monitor carefully and control their activities.

At first glance, the discrepancy between these messages is striking. Allowing for greater independence as a goal of parenting seems at odds with the importance of being highly involved and aware of what adolescents are doing and providing boundaries and limits. However we suggest that this is not the case—allowing for greater decision making and input is not at odds with high involvement and monitoring. We suggest that the confusion in these issues is, at least in part, a result of confusion in the literature over various terms. In particular, the terms "autonomy" and "independence" are often conflated. In addition, a large part of the problem stems from the multiple definitions and uses of the term "parental control" when it comes to adolescents. This term, often preceded by modifiers such as behavioral, psychological and firm, has been used in various ways by researchers. Such a situation makes for potentially misleading recommendations to parents and caregivers regarding how to best care for their adolescents.

We suggest that some of this confusion can be clarified by taking a theoretical stance in relation to the issue of parenting facilitative of adolescent adjustment—importantly linking such parenting to what adolescents need. Self-determination theory (SDT) (Deci & Ryan, 1985) provides just such a lens through which to view parenting. This view can then be integrated with what we know about the developmental period of adolescence.

SELF-DETERMINATION THEORY

From a self-determination theory framework individuals have three psychological needs: autonomy, competence, and relatedness (Deci & Ryan, 1985). Autonomy concerns the need to feel like an initiator of one's actions, or the locus of one's own behavior, rather than feeling coerced, either internally or externally, with the experience of behavior as initiated from outside oneself. Competence is the need to feel effective in one's interactions with the environment. Finally, relatedness is the need to feel connected with important others in the social surround. When these needs are satisfied, intrinsic motivation and self-regulation are facilitated and individuals' well-being is enhanced (Deci & Ryan, 1985).

While competence and relatedness are relatively straightforward, positing a need for autonomy has elicited much controversy. For example, critics point to cultures that value interdependence rather than an individual self and suggest that this is at odds with a universal need for autonomy. As suggested earlier, we believe that this disagreement can be rectified with a clarification of terms. First is the need to differentiate between "independence" and "autonomy." Hill & Holmbeck (1986) argued that two dominant conceptualizations of autonomy in the literature on adolescence are detachment from parents and freedom from social influence. Both of these definitions involve separation from others and thus, we would suggest, relate more to independence than autonomy. Independence is the opposite of dependence—dependence referring to relying on others and independence referring to not relying on others. Autonomy, as described earlier, connotes the experience of being behind one's actions and feeling agentic with respect to them, and is moot on the issue of reliance on others. Thus, from a self-determination perspective, where one stands on the issue of independence is orthogonal to that of autonomy. One can be choicefully or willingly reliant on others or, conversely, feel coerced into relying on others. On the other hand, one can be autonomously self-reliant or conversely feel forced into relying upon oneself because either one has no one on whom to rely or lacks trust in the availability and consistency of others (Ryan & Lynch, 1989). Consistent with this argument, emotional autonomy, which was measured as lack of reliance on parents and detachment from them, was associated with negative outcomes such as internal distress and lower grades (Beyers & Goossens, 1999; Ryan & Lynch, 1989). Conversely, autonomy, assessed as experiencing oneself as an initiator and as choiceful and volitional, has been associated with positive outcomes in a variety of domains (see Deci & Ryan, 2000 for a review) including academics (e.g., Fortier, Vallerand, & Guay, 1995; Grolnick, Ryan, & Deci, 1991; Vansteenkiste *et al.*, 2004), after-school activities (e.g., Beiswenger & Grolnick, 2006) work contexts (e.g., Baard, Deci, & Ryan, 2004; Soenens & Vansteenkiste, 2005), and friendships (Soenens & Vansteenkiste, 2005). Thus, positing a need for autonomy is not at odds with a value for interdependence. Autonomy is how choicefully one engages in activities or behaviors valued by a culture (Chirkov, Ryan, Kim, & Kaplan, 2003).

A corollary of the theory positing three needs is that environments, be they physical or social, that enhance adjustment and well-being are those that facilitate the satisfaction of these needs. Self-determination theory has specified three social-contextual dimensions that facilitate need satisfaction. First, the degree to which contexts support autonomy versus control behavior, is relevant to the need for autonomy. Autonomy supportive environments support individuals' initiations and encourage active problem solving. Thus, autonomy support is an active process in which parents and other caregivers engage. By contrast, environments that are controlling coerce and pressure people toward specified outcomes and solve problems for them. A second social–contextual dimension—structure—is one that facilitates competence. Structure concerns the degree to which the environment provides a systematic framework though which individuals can orient themselves, including rules, guidelines, and clear expectations. Such a framework allows the individual to anticipate the effects of his or her actions and thus facilitates a sense of control and efficacy (Grolnick & Ryan, 1989; Skinner, Johnson, & Snyder, 2005). Finally, positive involvement includes warmth and provision of resources such as time, attention, and support, which facilitate a sense of relatedness.

According to self-determination theory, these three dimensions are relatively orthogonal. Thus, parents can be high on autonomy support while promoting or not promoting structure. Further, they can be high on structure, providing rules, expectations, and guidelines, while doing so in an autonomy supportive or a controlling manner. Finally, parents can be highly involved and either facilitating or inhibiting of autonomy.

We suggest that positing three social-contextual dimensions that can be crossed can solve some of the apparent discrepancies in the literature. Referring to the two themes in the literature with which we began, there is nothing conflictual about suggesting that parents need to support their adolescents' autonomy by taking their perspectives, allowing them input into decisions, and encouraging them to solve their own problems and being both highly involved and knowledgeable about their lives and providing clear and consistent guidelines in the home. Thus, taking a self-determination perspective integrates theories that suggest that adolescents function best when they are allowed autonomy and those suggesting that adolescents function best when their parents are active in their lives and provide rules, guidelines, and consistent consequences for action. Further, it provides a justification for the importance of the three dimensions, highlighting the ways in which they facilitate the fulfillment of children's needs, and subsequently promote adolescents' well-being and adjustment.

DISENTANGLING DIMENSIONS IN PREVIOUS WORK—TOWARD A SYNTHESIS

Before reviewing evidence for the facilitative effects of these three dimensions during adolescence, we illustrate how this framework might clarify apparent discrepancies in previous research. We review a number of distinctions that have been made in the literature and then explain how many confound two or even three of these dimensions—leading to problematic conclusions.

Types of Control

One way in which key dimensions of parenting have been conceptualized is as types of control. For example, Schaefer (1965) empirically differentiated between psychological control, which included intrusiveness and was defined as "covert psychological methods of controlling the child's activities and behaviors that would not permit the child to develop as an individual apart from the parent," and firm control, which referred to the absence versus presence of permitting extreme independence (e.g., allowing children to go anywhere they like without asking and letting children go out as often as they please) and lax discipline (e.g., letting children get away without doing work they have been told to do and excusing children's bad conduct). One distinction frequently made in the current literature is between psychological control and behavioral control. Barber (1996, p. 3296) defined psychological control as parents' "attempts to intrude on the psychological and emotional development of the child" (e.g., thinking processes, self-expression, and attachment to the parent). Behavioral control, by contrast was defined as parents' attempts to manage or control children's behavior. It is often operationalized as parents' monitoring of children's behavior outside the home or parents' involvement in decision making in the home (versus children making decisions such as when to come home on their own). Sometimes the term control is used without a modifier —for example, Fletcher, Steinberg, & Williams-Wheeler (2004) used the term "parental control" to refer to the extent to which parents are involved in key decisions involving adolescents. Kerr & Stattin (2000) used the term "parental control" to refer to the degree to which parents require their adolescents to ask permission and let them know where they are going and what they are doing.

Thus, in the current literature, control can be positive if it refers to parent involvement and creating rules and clarity, or it can be negative if it intrudes upon the psychological life of the child. However, because these subtle distinctions are often not picked up by the parents who are the targets of our research, we suggest that reserving the term *control* for pressuring and dominating behavior on the part of parents might be most fruitful (Grolnick & Pomerantz,

2007). The term *structure* might be used to refer to the behaviors that are encompassed by terms like behavioral control and firm control, which refer to rules, expectations and guidelines. The use of this dimensionalization would encourage researchers to be clear that their structure terms do not include elements of control. This was apparently the case for Kerr & Stattin's (2000) measurement of parental control, which focused on requirements within the home. Here, parental control was positively related to adolescents' experience of feeling controlled. This may be why it did not relate positively to adjustment, as expected.

Other Terms

As researchers recognized that there were three dimensions of parenting, rather than the two that had emerged in the literature (warmth and control), a number of other dimensions were proposed. Baumrind (1971) used the term *firm enforcement* to refer to the parent's ability to enforce regulations when children were noncompliant. While it contained elements of structure, such as consistency of rule enforcement and provision of guidelines, it also included the use of force to ensure compliance, which would be seen as controlling. The term *demandingness* has also been used to refer to parental provision of clear expectations and defined responsibilities. Durbin, Darling, & Steinberg (1993) described demanding parents as providing clear guidelines and expectations for children's behavior but also as using external consequences to guide behavior such as rewarding compliance. Lamborn *et al.* (1991) used a strictness/supervision scale to measure demandingness. Rodrigo, Janssens, & Ceballos (1999) included limit setting and holding children responsible, as well as overprotection and punishment, which would be controlling, in their construct of demandingness. Finally, some researchers labeled their dimension demandingness/control, reflecting a purposeful combination of the two dimensions. Grigorenko & Sternberg (2000), for example, measured demandingness as the extent to which parents agree to statements, such as "children must conform to the rules and demands of authorities, parents always know what is best for their children, and strict discipline is good for children's character."

Our brief review of terms used in the parenting literature suggests the need for researchers to distinguish carefully dimensions of parenting. In the next section, we review what we know about parenting of adolescents, organizing our review along the three dimensions of autonomy supportive to controlling, involvement, and structure. Where appropriate, we translate terms used by other researchers and point out where confusion in terms has led to what seem like contradictory conclusions. In fact, when carefully examining the types of behaviors researchers are examining in their studies, rather than using their labeling of the constructs alone, the literature tells a rather consistent story about parenting that facilitates adjustment and well-being in adolescents.

Autonomy Support to Control

In our work, we have defined parental autonomy supportive behaviors as those that encourage and support children's initiatives and help children solve their own problems. By contrast, controlling behaviors involve using pressure to motivate children and solving problems for them (Grolnick & Ryan, 1989; Grolnick, 2003). Our first studies of parental autonomy supportive to controlling behavior were conducted with younger children. In one study (Grolnick & Ryan, 1989), we interviewed 64 mothers and 50 fathers of elementary-age children. The interviews focused on how parents motivated their children for school and home behaviors (e.g., doing homework, doing chores) and how they handled conflict around those behaviors. Interviews were rated for autonomy support to control, involvement, and structure. Autonomy support to control included three ratings: the degree to the parent valued autonomy in their child (versus valued compliance first and foremost), the degree to which the parent used autonomy supportive techniques such as limit setting and discussion (versus controlling techniques such as rewards and punishment) and the degree to which the parent involved the child in decisions and routines (versus imposed these). Parental autonomy support was associated with children's more autonomous regulation of their school and home activities, greater perceived competence, and higher grades and achievement test scores. As discussed, our first studies involved younger children and were also completed at one time point. Of course, it is likely that the findings represent a bidirectional process. Parents, through their support of their children's agency and initiative may facilitate their autonomy and competence. Alternatively, and consistent with SDT's depiction of the child as an active creator of his or her own socialization, children who are more self-regulating may evoke less control from their parents.

A more recent study examined older children and, in addition, added a longitudinal component (Grolnick *et al.*, 2000). Transitioning to junior high school is a time when young adolescents may be prone to developing adjustment difficulties in the classroom or peer context. We wondered whether parental support of autonomy, along with parent involvement, might buffer children from experiencing declines in adjustment. In this study, parent involvement and autonomy support were measured when the children were in sixth grade and then again in seventh grade. Children's motivational resources as well as grades and teacher ratings of adjustment were also measured at both times. Results indicated that children of parents higher in autonomy support at sixth grade showed lesser increases in acting-out and learning problems across the transition. Further, children of parents who increased their levels of autonomy support over the transition did not show the same declines in self-worth, control understanding, and reading grades as those whose parents became more controlling over the transition (Grolnick *et al.*, 2000).

Self-determination research by others has also illustrated the importance of autonomy support in adolescence. Soenens & Vansteenkiste (2005) have linked mothers' and fathers' autonomy-supportive parenting to positive outcomes for adolescents in many domains, including adolescents' perceived autonomy in academic, friendship, and job-search contexts. Adolescents' perceived autonomy in school and friendships was in turn associated with greater academic performance, perceived academic competence, and perceived social competence. In addition, fathers' autonomy-supportive parenting was linked with adolescents' perceived sense of autonomy about job-search behavior, which was in turn associated with greater exploration, commitment, and job-search intention. Soenens & Vansteenkiste's (2005) study also showed positive effects of teachers' autonomy support in these three areas.

Research on authoritative parenting also lends support to the importance of parents fostering a sense of autonomy in adolescence. Previous studies by Steinberg and colleagues (see Steinberg, 2001 for a review) have shown that adolescents benefit from authoritative parenting environments. In their work, authoritative parenting has been defined as parenting behaviors that are warm, firm, and accepting of children's needs for psychological autonomy (Steinberg, 2001). Steinberg and colleagues have also used Maccoby & Martin's (1983) reconceptualization of Baumrind's authoritative parenting framework by crossing two dimensions of parenting (acceptance/involvement and strictness/supervision) to yield four categories of parenting: authoritarian, authoritative, indulgent/permissive, and neglectful (Lamborn *et al.*, 1991).

In adolescence, authoritative parenting has been linked with positive outcomes in many domains, including higher levels of academic competence, school and work orientation, and lower levels of school misconduct, as compared to adolescents who characterize their caregivers as providing authoritarian, indulgent, or neglectful parenting (Lamborn *et al.*, 1991). Results from a longitudinal follow-up of this study one year later suggested that the differences in adjustment and competence between these groups were either maintained or increased over time (Steinberg *et al.*, 1994). In particular, the adjustment gap between adolescents of authoritative and neglectful homes widened, such that the academic competence of adolescents of authoritative parents increased and their school misconduct decreased. However, the authors also acknowledge the possibility that well-adjusted adolescents may evoke authoritativeness in their parents, which is consistent with a model of bidirectional or reciprocal parent–child influences.

Given that the construct of authoritative parenting has been conceptualized as multidimensional, Gray & Steinberg (1999) attempted to unpack this definition further by examining its subconstructs separately (acceptance-involvement; strictness-supervision or "behavioral control," and psychological autonomy-granting). From our self-determination theory framework, these subconstructs would be conceptualized as involvement, structure, and autonomy support, respectively. In their study of 14–18 year olds, Gray & Steinberg (1999) found that psychological autonomy-granting and involvement were positively associated with indices of adolescents' psychosocial development, such as work orientation (i.e., adolescents' pride in successful completion of tasks), self-reliance (i.e., adolescents' feelings of internal control and ability to make decisions without extreme reliance on others), and global self-esteem. In addition, psychological autonomy-granting and acceptance-involvement were negatively associated with adolescents' internal distress, which included both somatic and psychological symptoms. These authors also found that strictness-supervision or "behavioral control" (which we conceptualize as structure) was negatively associated with adolescents' behavioral problems. Finally, all three dimensions of authoritative parenting were positively associated with self-perceptions of academic competence. Thus all three component of authoritative parenting appear to have positive effects, although these findings also illustrate that it may be useful to conceptualize them separately, as self-determination theory suggests, for they may be somewhat differently related to different outcomes. Differentiating among the components of authoritative parenting is not only theoretically useful but may also help parents understand and develop their skills in each respective area, given that it is possible to be competent in one area and not the other (e.g., a parent may be involved or provide structure in a controlling or an autonomy supportive manner).

In their study of 10–16 year old adolescents, Steinberg, Elmen, & Mounts (1989) also explored the three components of authoritative parenting separately (acceptance, psychological autonomy, and behavioral control) in order to test the hypothesis that authoritative parenting facilitates, rather than simply accompanies, school success. They found that not only does authoritative parenting facilitate academic success but that each component of authoritativeness makes an independent contribution to achievement, thus suggesting the importance of all three components of authoritative parenting, which we view as involvement, autonomy support, and structure, respectively. Further, the positive effects of authoritative parenting on school achievement were partially mediated by a sense of autonomy and healthy work orientation (sense of competence). Thus adolescents who are provided with warmth, democratic, and firm parenting (which in SDT terms would be described as involvement, autonomy support, and structure) are more likely to develop a positive sense of self, and feelings of autonomy and competence in the academic and work context which in turn likely contribute to their success in school (Steinberg, Elmen, & Mounts, 1989).

Although not focused on autonomy support per se, a longitudinal study by Goldstein, Davis-Kean, & Eccles (2005) explored relations between adolescents' perceptions of their relationships with their parents and adolescent problem behaviors in the peer context. In this study, *parental intrusiveness* was measured with items such as "Your parents have too many rules for you" and "Your parent always tells you what to do and how to act," which from a self-determination theory perspective might be defined as controlling behavior, or providing structure in a controlling manner. These authors found that seventh-grade adolescents who perceived a high level of parental intrusiveness in their daily activities were more likely to associate with negative peers in eighth grade, engage in unsupervised social activities, and hold an extreme peer orientation (i.e., a tendency to go along with potentially problematic peer behavior in order to fit in with one's peer group), which in turn predicted later problem behavior. In addition, seventh-grade adolescents who experienced their parents as intrusive also tended to feel less positively about their relationship with their parents. However, the authors also acknowledge that adolescents who are already engaging in problem behaviors in seventh grade may, over time, perceive their parents as increasingly intrusive, which may predict increases in later problem behavior above and beyond previous problem behavior. Thus the bidirectionality of these results must be considered.

Goldstein, David-Kean, & Eccles (2005) examined "social autonomy," which they defined as the extent to which adolescents perceive they have "jurisdiction" over their daily activities (e.g., "In your family, how do you make most of the decisions about which friends you can spend time with?" and "In your family, how do you make decisions about how late you can stay out at night?"). Higher scores on these items indicate greater social autonomy. These authors found that adolescents who perceived themselves to have high levels of freedom over their daily activities in seventh grade (e.g., how late they can stay out at night, whether they can date), were more likely to engage in unsupervised socializing in eighth grade, which in turn predicted problem behavior in eleventh grade. The authors concluded that too much autonomy may lead to problematic peer behavior. However, autonomy as it was measured in this study should not be equated with autonomy support as conceptualized from a self-determination theory framework. Although Goldstein *et al.*'s study appears to measure autonomy in the form of adolescents feeling "free" about decision-making, endorsement of these items may most reflect a lack of parental involvement or structure in the family, given that permissive or neglectful parents may grant adolescents much latitude in decision-making by not providing structure or supervision. It is important for adolescents to experience a sense of choice and freedom about spending time with peers, but we suggest that autonomy support provided with parental involvement and structure (in particular, structure provided in an autonomy supportive manner) would predict more adaptive outcomes in terms of peer group affiliations and problem behavior.

Along these lines, previous work by Barber and colleagues (e.g., Barber, 1996; Barber, Olsen, & Shagle, 1994) makes a distinction between what they consider two different types of control, psychological control and behavioral control, which we would reframe as controlling parenting behavior and structure, respectively. In a review of the literature on adolescent problem behaviors, Barber (1992, p. 72) identified two negative family contexts—psychological overcontrol and behavioral undercontrol—that place adolescents at risk for internalizing and externalizing problems. Psychological overcontrol is defined as "an environment that intrudes on the psychological and emotional development of a child, either through the forced inclusion of others in the child's definition of self, or through manipulation of the child's emotions . . . parental interference in the psychological autonomy of the child," whereas behavioral undercontrol is characterized as "an environment that provides insufficient regulation of the child's behavior as in a lack of rules and restrictions, or a lack of knowledge or surveillance of the child's behavior." Barber's research has consistently shown psychological control to be more predictive of internalizing symptoms (e.g., depression), whereas behavioral control has been associated with adolescents' externalizing problems (e.g., delinquency—Barber, 1996; Barber, Olsen, & Shagle, 1994). These relations have also been demonstrated longitudinally (Barber, 1996), although bidirectionality of effects must also be considered. For example, the authors acknowledge that adolescents who are perceived as socially isolated and withdrawn may have parents who increase their attempts to elicit interaction with their child by using psychological control. On the other hand, parents of adolescents who are acting out more may feel that their children are beyond their control and become lax in their supervision.

In sum, a variety of studies conducted during adolescence show positive effects of autonomy support and negative effects of controlling styles. When parents support children's initiatives and make an effort to take their perspectives, adolescents are more likely to feel connected to their parents, develop a sense of competence about the tasks they undertake, and develop a sense of autonomy about their actions, which fosters their self-esteem and sense of self. On the other hand, when adolescents feel pressured or controlled by their caretakers, they may be less likely to show initiative in the future, which undermines their sense of competence and autonomy in the world, as well as complicating feelings of connectedness to their parent. Thus parents can best support their adolescents' development by remaining involved, connected, and providing guidance, but by doing so in a way that supports their adolescent's initiatives and sense of choice.

Involvement

Along with the provision of autonomy support and structure, parental involvement is a dimension of parenting that facilitates the fulfillment of children's needs, particularly, their need for relatedness. Parental involvement refers to the extent to which parents are interested in, knowledgeable about, and play an active role in their children's lives (Grolnick & Slowiaczek, 1994). Involvement can also be described as the provision of resources by the parent to the child. These resources can be tangible, such as books for school, or more emotional, such as warmth, availability, and time devoted to the child. Research has shown that when children feel as though their parents are interested in and aware of what happens in their lives on a day-to-day basis, their feelings of connection and relatedness are greatly enhanced (Cookston &

Finlay, 2006; Grolnick *et al.*, 2000; Grolnick & Slowiaczek, 1994; Hill & Taylor, 2004).

Parent involvement has been investigated by numerous researchers, often using terms such as warmth or acceptance, and has been related to a host of positive outcomes for children. Much of the research on parent involvement has been in the realm of school, examining relations with children's achievement and other academic outcomes. Although less research has focused on fathers than mothers, father involvement has been positively associated with adolescents' adjustment (Cookston & Finlay, 2006), intellectual development (Williams & Radin, 1993), social competence, internal locus of control, and their ability to empathize (Amato, 1994).

In a study of parent involvement in elementary-aged children, Grolnick & Ryan (1989) found that the children of highly involved parents (those who were rated as knowledgeable about their children's activities and preferences, high in time spent with children, and appeared to enjoy this time) did better and had fewer problems in school. It is important to note that highly involved parents were not necessarily in the home more; however, when they were home, they spent more time engaged in activities with their children as compared to less involved parents. In a subsequent study of 11–14 year olds, Grolnick & Slowiaczek (1994) found when parents were more involved intellectually (engaging in activities at home such as talking about current events with children and going to the library) and at school (going to school activities and events and volunteering in the classroom), children felt more competent in school and more in control of their school successes and failures. These motivational resources, in turn, predicted higher school performance.

Parental involvement in children's education has been repeatedly associated with improvements in school behavior, social competence, school performance, and school achievement across grade levels (Eamon, 2005; Grolnick & Ryan, 1989; Grolnick & Slowiaczek, 1994; Hill & Craft, 2003; Steinberg *et al.*, 1992). Hill & Taylor (2004) found that, for adolescents, discussions amongst parents, teachers, and school administrators, as well as conversations between parents and adolescents about school and future plans have the strongest relations with academic outcomes.

The positive effects of parental involvement in education have been examined and documented in families varying in ethnicity and SES. In a study of Latino high-school students and their immigrant parents, Ibanez *et al.* (2004) found that parent involvement was positively related to achievement motivation, school expectations, and the importance of schooling. Hill & Craft (2003) found that parent involvement was related to improved school performance for both African–American and European–American children. Interestingly, the authors identified different pathways by which parental involvement affects school performance. For African–Americans, parent academic involvement was associated with improved academic skills, which improved school performance, whereas for European–Americans, academic involvement was associated with improved social competence, which in turn, improved school performance.

In another study, Hill *et al.* (2004) found differences in the impact of parental involvement on children's achievement depending on parents' education levels. Among families with lower parental education levels, parent involvement increased adolescents' educational and career aspirations but was not effective in changing school behavior or achievement. In families with higher parental education levels academic involvement was related to school behavior problems, and in turn, achievement and aspirations. However, in a study of 10,000 socioeconomically and ethnically diverse high school students, Steinberg *et al.* (1991) found that the positive correlates of authoritative parents (of which involvement is a key component) transcend ethnicity, SES, and family structure.

In the aforementioned study of children transitioning to junior high school, Grolnick *et al.* (2000) found positive relations between personal and academic involvement and children's adjustment. Children whose mothers were involved with their children in intellectual activities at home in sixth grade did not show the same declines in feelings of competence in school and in reading grades as did children whose parents were less involved. In addition, children whose mothers were higher in personal involvement were less likely to drop in reading grades and less likely to show increased acting out and learning problems in the classroom. Findings from this study highlight the importance of parental involvement during the transition to junior high school. Mothers who increased or maintain their involvement had children whose feelings of self-worth did not reduce over the transition to junior high.

Given the emphasis on adolescent individuation and autonomy strivings, many parents wonder whether they should become less involved in their children's lives as they enter adolescence. The simple answer is no. The involvement literature is quite clear: when parents are involved, children do better in school. In addition, parental involvement during the teenage years has been positively related to adolescents' formation of a healthy identity and the avoidance of common pitfalls such as drug use, school misconduct, anxiety, and depression (Gray & Steinberg, 1999). In fact, Purdie, Carroll, & Roche (2004) found that parental involvement was the most important parenting behavior (beyond autonomy granting and strictness/supervision), with respect to adolescents' self-regulatory behaviors. Therefore, the important message for parents is that children do not need their parents to become less involved as they get older, but rather, parents should remain highly involved throughout their children's development.

Structure

Many researchers have recognized that a third dimension of parenting, in addition to involvement and support/control of autonomy, is crucial to adolescent development. However, this dimension has been more difficult to categorize and measure than the other two. We suggest that this is at least in part due to a lack of theory concerning its importance. From a self-determination theory perspective, the third dimension is one that facilitates the need for competence. To be competent, one needs to have information about how one's actions are related to outcomes, or a perception of control (Connell, 1985). Further, one needs to feel that one can enact the behaviors that will lead to desired outcomes or a sense of perceived competence. These motivational resources are most likely to be present when the social context specifies what behaviors are expected or valued, what the consequences of various behaviors are, and provides guidelines or information about how to achieve desired outcomes. We conceptualize such information as structure. Thus, structured homes include a framework or organization with clear and consistent guidelines, expectations, and rules for children as well as predictable consequences for children's actions and clear feedback. By contrast, an environment low in structure would be haphazard, unpredictable or chaotic. Such an environment would result in children not feeling in control of key outcomes and experiencing themselves as ineffective.

In our work on parenting with younger children discussed earlier (Grolnick & Ryan, 1989), we rated interviews of parents for two dimensions of structure; parents' provision of clear rules, expectations and guidelines for behavior and the stipulation of consequences for not meeting expectations and the degree to which rules and expectations were consistently applied or promoted. Children of parents high on these dimensions reported more knowledge about how successes and failures occur (control understanding) than children low on these dimensions. Using a similar conceptualization of structure, Skinner, Johnson, & Snyder (2005) showed that children's and parents' reports of parental structure were positively related to children's psychological functioning including their perceived control, engagement in school, and self-worth. Farkas & Grolnick (2006) studied young adolescents' perceptions of whether there were rules and expectations in the home. Adolescents in homes with more rules and expectations reported engaging in fewer antisocial behaviors, a decreased likelihood of following peer pressure, and perceptions of antisocial behavior as more wrong.

Structure is clearly related to dimensions of firm control, decision making and other variables examined during adolescence. For example, Barber's (1996) concept of behavioral control refers to attempts to control or manage children's behavior. However, previous operationalizations of this construct have not allowed for clear recommendations to parents. The most common way of measuring behavioral control for example, has been to ask parents how much their parents "really know" about their activities and whereabouts. Parents' knowledge assessed in this way has been related to key outcomes, such as depression, delinquency, drug use and behavior problems (e.g., Barber & Olsen, 1997; Fletcher, Darling, & Steinberg, 1994; Gray & Steinberg, 1999; Laird Pettit, & Bates, 2003). However, Kerr & Statin (2000) illustrated that it was child disclosure, rather than active parent strategies, which was most responsible for parental knowledge. Accordingly, such measures of behavioral control probably index parent–child relationship quality rather than parenting strategies.

Other work has addressed parts of the construct of structure with measures that more likely index parenting strategies. For example, with regard to rules, Patterson & Stouthamer-Lober (1984) asked children about rules in the home, including telling parents when they will be home and leaving a note when they go out. Though combined with other measures, including knowledge of boys' whereabouts, more rules were associated with lower levels of delinquency (Patterson & Stouthamer-Loeber, 1984). Barnes & Farrell (1992) found that adolescent reports of the number of rules in the home were inversely related to children's antisocial behavior. Another aspect of structure—whether there are consistent consequences for action or predictability—is captured in Forehand and Nousiainen's (1993) measure of *firm* versus *lax control*, which has been associated with child adjustment. Inconsistent discipline, which would involve inconsistent consequences for action and so unpredictability, has been connected to child depression and conduct problems in both low income Mexican-American and European-American samples (Hill, Bush, & Roosa, 2003; Patterson & Stouthamer-Loeber, 1984).

Recently, Farkas, & Grolnick (2006) developed a six-component conceptualization of structure. This conceptualization was a first attempt at distinguishing the ways in which parents set up a consistent framework for the development of competence and a way to organize some of the previous work on the structure dimension. The first—clear and consistent communication of expectations—includes clearly provided and consistently endorsed rules, guidelines and expectations. The second—opportunities to meet or exceed expectations—concerns parents' provision of opportunities for children to behave within guidelines, such as necessary materials or support (e.g., if the rule is to clean one's room before a specific time, there is time allotted for this to be completed and tools available to do so). Third, predictability is clearly conveyed and consistent consequences of and contingencies for actions. Fourth, informational feedback involves feedback from the environment on children meeting expectations. Fifth, provision of rationales for expectations involves caretakers explaining the reasons for rules and expectations so that these rules can be internalized or taken on by children. Finally, authority of caretakers involves caretakers taking a leadership role in the home and serving as ultimate authorities. This dimension would encompass parents involving themselves in decision making rather than allowing adolescents to make key decisions (e.g., curfew) on their own.

In a first study of these six components in young adolescents, we interviewed 75 mothers and their adolescents about six domains of importance to adolescents: homework, grades, curfew, bedtime, after-school activities and activities when unsupervised. For each domain, parents and children were asked about rules and expectations, how parents respond if rules are not followed, whether parents provide rationales for the rules and whether feedback is provided about children's behavior. From their responses, parents are rated on 16 subscales associated with the six dimensions. Results indicated that the dimensions were moderately correlated, supporting the notion that they were separable yet related. Second, they were correlated with key outcomes—in particular, clear and consistent guidelines were positively correlated with children's control understanding, while clear and consistent guidelines, predictability, and opportunity were each positively related to children's perceived competence. The results provide support for the new conceptualization and method. Further studies are planned, which will focus on parental structure as children make the transition to middle school. We are hypothesizing that parental structure will provide the stability and clarity that will help young adolescents manage the transition, which often involves major organizational changes. Further, we will include economically diverse European-American and Hispanic/Latino samples so that we can begin to address the ways in which culture and socioeconomic circumstances affect the way in which structure is provided as well as its concomitants.

Crossing Parenting Dimensions

As previously discussed, the three parenting dimensions (autonomy support, structure, and involvement) are relatively orthogonal—for example, one can be highly involved or provide structure in either an autonomy supportive or controlling way. Therefore, it is important to do work that examines the interaction of these dimensions. Our work, and that of others, has begun to do so. First, we have looked at whether some types of involvement are experienced in different ways from others. For example, in a diverse sample of early adolescents (Benjet, 1994; Grolnick, Gehl, & Manzo, 1997) we asked children about their parents' involvement and autonomy support. Findings suggest that children who saw their parents as autonomy supportive tended to be positive about their parents' involvement and wanted them to be involved, whereas children who saw their parents as controlling tended to be more negative about their parents' involvement. Studies also show that some types of involvement can have more or less beneficial effects. Steinberg *et al.* (1992) divided their sample of 14–18 year olds into four authoritativeness groups (authoritative, somewhat authoritative, somewhat nonauthoritative, and nonauthoritative). While parent involvement was positively associated with school performance for all groups, the weakest relations were found for the nonauthoritative group. This indicates that authoritarian parenting can partially undermine the beneficial effects of parental involvement. Weiss & Grolnick (1991) found that parents of seventh to eleventh graders who were rated as high on involvement and high in autonomy support had adolescents with the fewest internalizing and externalizing symptoms. However, the combination of high involvement and low autonomy support yielded a high level of symptoms. The results suggest that when parents are involved in a controlling way, the involvement can have a harmful effect on child outcomes.

According to our conceptualization, a combination of high involvement and high autonomy support is ideal for facilitating children's needs. Ryan, Stiller, & Lynch (1994) demonstrated the importance of the combination of parental involvement and autonomy support. Junior high and high-school students reported low relatedness when they described their parents as uninvolved and controlling. On the other hand, when autonomy support and involvement were present, adolescents reported high relatedness.

PREDICTORS OF PARENTING

As we begin to garner some consensus about the parenting styles and behaviors that facilitate adolescent adjustment and well-being, we need to turn our attention to factors that make it more likely or less likely that parents will display these attitudes and behaviors. Thus, our recent work has also begun to explore factors that facilitate parents' provision of autonomy support, involvement, and structure. A full review of this work is not possible due to space constraints but we present some of our findings around what we regard as a key factor—pressure that may challenge and complicate parents' efforts to support their adolescents. We consider three forms of pressure that may impact upon parenting: (1) *pressure from above* (environmental and situational pressures), (2) *pressure from below* (child characteristics), and (3) *pressure from within* (parent internal characteristics).

Pressure from Above

Pressures in the larger and immediate context may undermine parenting by taking the time, psychological energy, and physical resources that such parenting requires. Previous research has shown that stressful life events (Conger, Patterson, & Ge, 1995), lack of resources (Dodge, Petit, & Bates, 1994), and unemployment (McLoyd, 1989) have each been predictive of less supportive parenting.

In our previous work we examined possible environmental predictors of the parenting of adolescents. Grolnick *et al.* (1996) measured the number of stressful life events that parents of adolescents experienced in the past three months. They then interviewed parents and rated their parenting on autonomy support, involvement, and structure. Mothers who reported more stressful life events were rated as more controlling and as providing less involvement and structure. In a study focused on types of involvement in children's schooling, parents who described a difficult context, including high levels of stressful life events and low resources, were lower in several types of involvement than those who described less difficult circumstances (Grolnick *et al.*, 1997).

Our work has also begun to examine situational pressure, or more immediate aspects of the situation, such as evaluation and performance standards. In our laboratory studies (Grolnick *et al.*, 2002, 2007), we introduced situational pressure in the form of high-pressure/evaluation and low-pressure/no-evaluation conditions. We found that when mothers are given performance standards (told their child is expected to perform well) or subjected to the pressure of evaluation (told their child will be evaluated) they may be more likely to interact with their child in a controlling manner while their child is completing a laboratory task, although some of the effects of environmental pressure may depend upon characteristics of the parent, which will be discussed further below.

Taken together, these results illustrate the potentially harmful effects that environmental and situational pressure may have on parent–child interactions. Thus it is important to help parents become aware of how such pressure may impact upon the level of autonomy support, involvement, and structure they provide to their children.

Pressure from Below

Another form of pressure that parents may experience is that which arises from the unique needs of one's child. Children are born with different temperaments, personalities, social skills, and intellectual abilities. As adolescents grow older, they may be developing their competencies solidly in some areas, but could be struggling in others. In particular, parents of less competent adolescents may worry about how their child is doing and become involved in their adolescent's life in ways that, although well-meaning, could be detrimental to their child's development.

Our previous work has begun to examine this form of pressure in parent–adolescent relationships (Grolnick *et al.*, 1996). We found that mothers who perceived their adolescent as more "difficult" were more controlling than mothers who rated their adolescent as easier. Although parents may experience their use of control as consistent with their view that their difficult adolescent "needs" more control, controlling parenting undermines a child's sense of autonomy and competence, which may forestall rather than promote development.

Another child characteristic that may induce experiences of "pressure from below" on parents is child competence. In our laboratory study of third-grade children we found that mothers of children who had lower grades in reading and math in school were more controlling while their children completed a laboratory task (Grolnick *et al.*, 2002). Similarly, Pomerantz, & Eaton (2001) found that mothers of children who received lower grades in school were more likely to endorse and use control than were mothers of higher performing children. Perhaps when parents perceive their children as struggling, they attempt to overcompensate for their child's difficulties by exerting more control.

Pressure from Within

Pressures within parents may also affect how parents interact with their adolescents. Our recent work has examined the effects that parent characteristics such as making their self-worth contingent on their children's performance or outcomes (Contingent Self-worth—CSW) can have on levels of autonomy supportive versus controlling behavior.

Eaton & Pomerantz (2004) found that mothers with high CSW were perceived as more controlling by their college student children. Similarly, in our laboratory study (Grolnick *et al.*, 2007), we found that mothers with CSW in their child's social outcomes were more likely to be controlling while their child completed a social self-presentation task. We also examined interactions between CSW and situational pressure and found that mothers who believed their children would be evaluated and had high CSW were the most controlling.

Another form of internal pressure comes from parents' perceptions of threat for their children. Gurland & Grolnick (2005) found that mothers who perceived the "world out there" as threatening (competitive, unstable, scarce resources) were more likely to endorse controlling parenting attitudes and were more likely to interact with their fourth-grade children in a controlling manner while their children completed an achievement-oriented laboratory task.

In conclusion, there are many forms of pressure that may affect parents' ability to provide adequate autonomy support, involvement, and structure for their adolescent children. Pressure from above (environmental stress, threat, situational pressure), pressure from below (child temperament, competence), and pressure from within (parenting attitudes, contingent self-worth) can undermine parents' well-meaning attempts to support their children's development. Although our work has focused mostly on the effects of pressure in relation to autonomy support and controlling parenting behavior, the above factors likely also have implications for parental involvement and structure, important areas which may the focus of future research.

CHALLENGES AND FUTURE DIRECTIONS

We end our chapter with some thoughts regarding challenges of studying parenting of adolescents, as well as some ideas for future research directions. One important challenge that must be addressed in future research is the concept of bidirectionality. Given recognition of the active role of children in their socialization (Bell, 1968), studies have increasingly begun to see parent–child relations as a bidirectional process. For example, Stattin & Kerr (2006) examined parenting and child outcomes in a large sample of 10–18 year olds over four waves. Using cross-lagged analyses, their findings suggest that adolescent problem behavior largely drives parents' knowledge and monitoring efforts, with more problem behavior resulting in decreased efforts over time. Future studies should continue to investigate the cyclical relations between parenting and adolescent behavior.

The debate concerning the universality of the dimensions of parenting is one of the more lively ones in the parenting literature. This has been a particularly controversial issue regarding parental control. Are the effects of control moderated by setting or culture? Specifying what might be general and what specific to culture is clearly a challenge for researchers.

It seems that there are several issues included in this larger question. First, are the major constructs of parenting the same in different cultures? For example, Chao (2001) suggested that Asian parents organize their parenting around the concept of training, or Chiao Sun, which involves high levels of support and encouragement to succeed along with high standards. Such a concept cannot be linked to just one dimension of parenting. Promising techniques to determine whether parenting constructs are meaningful in various cultures such as means and covariance structure analyses (Little, 1997) can be used to address this question. Second, measurement issues can become highly problematic—for example, the same item or parenting technique can be experienced as controlling to one culture and autonomy supportive to another. Data from Rohner & Pettengill (1985) are a case in point, with Korean adolescents indicating positive correlations between parental control and warmth. This is in sharp contrast to the usual negative relations found in European–American samples. The authors suggest that the items that were meant to elicit feelings of control were actually perceived as actions demonstrating love and caring. This illustrates a challenge for researchers in this area: to understand how items or techniques are perceived to determine whether the literature across cultures is consistent or inconsistent.

One issue that has plagued this area is confusion over control and structure. A case in point is the dangerous neighborhood hypothesis. This hypothesis suggests that the effects of control are moderated by the level of dangerousness of the environment. In environments that are risky or dangerous, control might have positive effects but in safer or less challenging neighborhoods there are negative effects. In citing evidence for this hypothesis, researchers often evoke the findings of a study by Baldwin, Baldwin, & Cole (1990). These authors followed a group of children from the time their mothers were pregnant through adolescence. The families were divided into those that were high risk and those that were low risk on the basis of socioeconomic circumstances, parent education, minority status and absence of the father. They also divided the children into highly competent and less competent groups on the basis of their IQ and school achievement. Parents were interviewed extensively about their parenting, including rules and expectations in the home and how these rules and expectations were conveyed. Ratings were conducted on restrictiveness (how numerous and circumscribed the rules are), clarity of rules, and democracy (whether rules were imposed or whether adolescents had a say in the rules). Restrictiveness was associated with positive outcomes for children in the high-risk group but negatively with outcomes for children in the low risk group. However, democracy was positively associated with outcomes in both high- and low-risk groups.

The authors conclude that these results demonstrate that "restrictive authoritarian" family patterns were successful in high-risk situations, but when the results are differentiated by structure and control they suggest that the moderation was apparent for rules (the structure portion) where democracy (the facet most related to control) was not moderated. In fact, when examined closely, many of the studies finding moderation have looked at dimensions closer to structure than control (e.g., Coley & Hoffman, 1996; McCarthy, Lord & Eccles, 1993).

We hope that our dimensionalization of parenting will prove useful as researchers attempt to identify key parenting constructs in various cultures and settings, generate items that have equivalent meaning across cultures, and determine how context might moderate particular aspects of parenting. Our current work focuses on multimethod measurement of parenting dimensions including observation, in-depth interviews, and questionnaires with parents and children across a variety of contexts and domains. Such an approach will allow us to continue refining our understanding of how the parenting dimensions of autonomy support, involvement, and structure operate and interact to affect adolescents' development, adjustment, and well-being.

REFERENCES

Amato, P. R. (1994). Father-child relations, mother-child relations, and offspring psychological well-being in early adulthood. *Journal of Marriage and the Family, 56,* 1031–1042.

Armstong, E., Schleicher, A., Omran, H. *et al.* (1995). The ontogeny of human gyrification. *Cerebral Cortex, 1,* 56–63.

Baard, P., Deci, E. L., & Ryan, R. M. (2004). Intrinsic need satisfaction: A motivational basic of performance and well-being in two work settings. *Journal of Applied and Social Psychology, 34,* 2045–2068.

Baldwin, A. L., Baldwin, C., & Cole, R. E. (1990). Stress-resistant families and stress-resistant children. In J. Rolf, A. S. Masten, D. Cicchetti *et al.* (eds), *Risk and Protective Factors in the Development of Psychopathology* (pp. 257–280). New York: Cambridge University Press.

Barber, B. K. (1992). Family, personality, and adolescent problem behaviors. *Journal of Marriage and the Family, 54,* 69–79.

Barber, B. K. (1996). Parental psychological control: revisiting a neglected construct. *Child Development*, 67, 3296–3319.

Barber, B. K. & Olsen, J. E. (1997). Socialization in context: Connection, regulation, and autonomy in the family, school, neighborhood, and with peers. *Journal of Adolescent Research*, *12*, 287–315.

Barber, B. K., Olsen, J. E., & Shagle, S. C. (1994). Associations between parental psychological and behavioral control and youth internalized and externalized behaviors. *Child Development*, 65, 1120–1136.

Barnes, G. M. & Farrell, M. P. (1992). Parent support and control as predictors of adolescent drinking, delinquency, and related problem behaviors. *Journal of Marriage and the Family*, *54*, 763–776.

Baumrind, D. (1971). Current patterns of parental authority. *Developmental Psychology*, *4*, 1–103.

Beiswenger, K. L. & Grolnick, W. S. (2006). Autonomy in adolescents' after-school activities: Relations with peer relatedness, perceived competence, and well-being. Unpublished manuscript, Clark University.

Bell, R. Q. (1968). A reinterpretation of the direction of effects in studies of socialization. *Psychological Review*, *75*, 81–95.

Benjet, C. (1994). *The Impact of Parental Involvement on Children's Motivation and School Performance*. Unpublished master's thesis, Clark University, Worcester, MA.

Berndt, T. J. (1979). Developmental changes in conformity to peers and parents. *Developmental Psychology*, *15*, 606–616.

Beyers, W. & Goossens, L. (1999). Emotional autonomy, psychosocial adjustment, and parenting: Interactions, moderating and mediating effects. *Journal of Adolescence*, *22*, 753–769.

Centers for Disease Control (2006). Youth risk behavior surveillance—United States, 2005. *Morbidity and Mortality Weekly Report*, 55(SS-5), 1–108.

Chao, R. K. (2001). Extending research on the consequences of parenting style for Chinese American and European Americans. *Child Development*, *72*, 1832–1843.

Chirkov, V., Ryan, R. M., Kim, Y., & Kaplan, U. (2003). Differentiating autonomy from individualism and independence: A self-determination theory perspective on internalization of cultural orientations and well-being. *Journal of Personality and Social Psychology*, *84*, 97–109.

Coley, R. L. & Hoffman, L. W. (1996). Relations of parental supervision and monitoring to children's functioning in various contexts: Moderating effects of families and neighborhoods. *Journal of Applied Developmental Psychology*, *17*, 51–68.

Conger, R. D., Patterson, G. R., & Ge, X. (1995). It takes two to replicate: A mediational model for the impact of parents' stress on adolescent adjustment. *Child Development*, *66*, 80–97.

Connell, J. P. (1985). A new multidimensional measure of children's perceptions of control. *Child Development*, *56*, 1018–1051.

Cookston, J. T. & Finlay, A. K. (2006). Father involvement and adolescent adjustment: Longitudinal findings from add health. *Fathering*, *4*, 137–158.

Deci, E. L. & Ryan, R. M. (1985). *Intrinsic Motivation and Self-determination in Human Behavior*. New York: Plenum.

Deci, E. L. & Ryan, R. M. (2000). Self-determination theory and the facilitation of intrinsic motivation, social development, and well-being. *American Psychologist*, *55*, 68–78.

Dodge, K. A., Pettit, G. S., & Bates, J. E. (1994). Socialization mediators of the relations between socioeconomic status and child conduct problems. *Child Development* (special issue: children and poverty), *65*, 649–665.

Durbin, D. L., Darling, N., & Steinberg, L. (1993). Parenting style and peer group membership among European-American adolescents. *Journal of Research on Adolescence*, *3*, 87–100.

Eamon, M. K. (2005). Social-demographic, school, neighborhood, and parenting influence on the academic achievement of Latino young adolescents. *Journal of Youth and Adolescence, 34,* 163–174.

Eaton, M. M. & Pomerantz, E. M. (2004). *Parental Contingent Self-Worth Scale.* Unpublished manuscript, University of Illinois.

Eccles, J. S., Buchanan, C. M., Flanagan, C. *et al.* (1991). Control versus autonomy during early adolescence. *Journal of Social Issues, 47,* 53–68.

Farkas, M. S. & Grolnick, W. S. (2006). *Toward a New Model of Parental Structure.* Unpublished manuscript, Clark University.

Fletcher, A. C., Darling, N. & Steinberg, L. (1994). Parental supervision and peer influences on adolescent substance use. In J. McCord (ed.), *Coercion and Punishment in Long-term Perspectives* (pp. 259–288). New York: Cambridge University Press.

Fletcher, A. C., Steinberg, L., & Williams-Wheeler, M. (2004). Parental influences on adolescent problem behavior: Revisiting Stattin & Kerr. *Child Development, 75,* 781–796.

Forehand, R. & Nousiainen, S. (1993). Maternal and paternal parenting: Critical dimensions in adolescent functioning. *Journal of Family Psychology, 7,* 213–221.

Fortier, M. S., Vallerand, R. J., & Guay, F. (1995). Academic motivation and school performance: Toward a structural model. *Contemporary School Psychology, 20,* 257–274.

Goldstein, S. E., Davis-Kean, P. E., & Eccles, J. S. (2005). Parents, peers, and problem behavior: A longitudinal investigation of the impact of relationship perceptions and characteristics on the development of adolescent problem behavior. *Developmental Psychology, 41,* 401–413.

Gray, M. R. & Steinberg, L. (1999). Unpacking authoritative parenting: Reassessing a multidimensional construct. *Journal of Marriage and the Family, 61,* 574–587.

Grigorenko, E. & Sternberg, R. J. (2000). Elucidating the etiology and nature of beliefs about parenting styles. *Developmental Science, 3,* 93–112.

Grolnick, W. S. (2003). *The Psychology of Parental Control: How Well-meant Parenting Backfires.* Mahwah: Lawrence Erlbaum Associates.

Grolnick, W. S., Benjet, C., Kurowski, C. O., & Apostoleris, N. H. (1997). Predictors of parent involvement in children's schooling. *Journal of Educational Psychology, 89,* 538–548.

Grolnick, W. S., Gehl, K., & Manzo, C. (1997). *Longitudinal Effects of Parent Involvement and Autonomy Support on Children's Motivation and School Performance.* Washington, DC: Society for Research in Child Development.

Grolnick, W. S., Gurland, S. T., DeCourcey, W., & Jacob, K. (2002). Antecedents and consequences of mothers' autonomy support. *Developmental Psychology, 38,* 143–155.

Grolnick, W. S., Kurowski, C. O., Dunlap, K., & Hevey, C. (2000). Parental resources and the transition to junior high. *Journal of Research on Adolescence,* 10, 465–480.

Grolnick, W. S. & Pomerantz, E. (2007). *Issues and Challenges in the Study of Parental Control.* Unpublished manuscript, Clark University, Worcester, MA.

Grolnick, W. S., Price, C. E., Beiswenger, K. L., & Sauck, C. (2007). Evaluative pressure in mothers: Effects of situation, maternal and child characteristics on autonomy-supportive versus controlling behavior. *Developmental Psychology, 43,* 991–1002.

Grolnick, W. S., & Ryan, R. M. (1989). Parent styles associated with children's self-regulation and competence in school. *Journal of Educational Psychology, 81,* 143–154.

Grolnick, W. S. Ryan, R. M., & Deci, E. L. (1991). Inner resources for school achievement: Motivational mediators of children's perceptions of their parents. *Journal of Educational Psychology, 83,* 508–517.

Grolnick W. S. & Slowiaczek, M. (1994). Parents' involvement in children's schooling: A multidimensional conceptualization and motivational model. *Child Development,* 65, 237–252.

Grolnick, W. S., Weiss, L., McKenzie, L., & Wrightman, J. (1996). Contextual, cognitive, and adolescent factors associated with parenting in adolescence. *Journal of Youth and Adolescence, 25*, 33–54.

Gurland. S. T. & Grolnick, W. S. (2005). Perceived threat, controlled parenting, and children's achievement orientations. *Motivation and Emotion, 29*, 103–121.

Hill, N. E., Bush, K. R., & Roosa, M. W. (2003). Parenting and family socialization strategies and children's mental health: Low-income Mexican-American and European-American mother and children. *Child Development, 74*, 189–204.

Hill, N. E., Castellino, D. R, Lansford, J. E. *et al.* (2004). Parent academic involvement as related to school behavior, achievement, and aspirations: Demographic variations across adolescence. *Child Development, 75*, 1491–1509.

Hill, N. E. & Craft, S. A. (2003). Parent-school involvement and school performance mediated pathways among socioeconomically comparable African-American and Euro-American families. *Journal of Educational Psychology*, 95, 74–83.

Hill, J. P. & Holmbeck, G. N. (1986). Attachment and autonomy during adolescence *Annals of Child Development, 3*, 145–189.

Hill, N. E. & Taylor, L. C. (2004). Parental school involvement and children's academic achievement: Pragmatics and issues. *Current Directions in Psychological Science, 13*, 161–164.

Ibanez, G. E., Kuperminc, G. P., Jurkovic, G., & Perilla, J. (2004). Cultural attributes and adaptations linked to achievement motivation among Latino adolescents. *Journal of Youth and Adolescence, 33*, 559–568.

Kerr, M. & Stattin, H. (2000). What parents know, how they know it, and several forms of adolescent adjustment: Further support for a reinterpretation of monitoring. *Developmental Psychology, 36*, 366–380.

Laird, R. D., Pettit, G. S., & Bates, J. E. (2003) Parents' monitoring-relevant knowledge and adolescents' delinquent behavior: Evidence of correlated developmental changes and reciprocal influences . *Child Development 74*, 752–768.

Lamborn, S. D., Mounts, N. S., Steinberg, L., & Dornbusch, S. M. (1991). Patterns of competence and adjustment among adolescents from authoritative, authoritarian, indulgent, and neglectful families. *Child Development, 62*, 1049–1065.

Leigh B. & Stall, R. (1993). Substance use and risky sexual behavior for exposure to HIV: Issues in methodology, interpretation, and prevention. *American Psychologist, 48*, 1035–1043.

Little, T. D. (1997). Mean and covariance structure (MACS) analysis of cross-cultural data: Practical and theoretical issues. *Multivariate Behavioral Research, 32*, 53–76.

Maccoby, E. & Martin, J. (1983). Socialization in the context of the family: Parent-child interaction. In E. M. Hetherington (ed.), P. H. Mussen (series ed.), *Handbook of Child Psychology: Vol. 4. Socialization, Personality, and Social Development* (pp. 1–101). New York: Wiley.

McCarthy, K. A., Lord, S. E., & Eccles, J. S. (1993). Contextual factors related to family management strategies in high risk environments. Poster presented at the biennial meeting of the Society for Research in Child Development, New Orleans.

McLoyd, V. C. (1989). Socialization and development in a changing economy: The effects of paternal job and income loss on children. *American Psychologist, 44*, 293–302.

Meeus, W. & Dekovic, M. (1995). Identity development, parental and peer support in adolescence: Results from a national Dutch survey. *Adolescence, 30*, 931–944.

Patterson, G. R. & Stouthamer-Loeber, M. (1984). The correlation of family management practices and delinquency. *Child Development, 55*, 1299–1307.

Pomerantz, E. M. & Eaton, M. M. (2001). Maternal intrusive support in the academic context: Transactional socialization processes. *Developmental Psychology, 37,* 174–186.
Purdie, N., Carroll, A., & Roche, L. (2004). Parenting and adolescent self-regulation. *Journal of Adolescence, 27,* 663–676.
Rodrigo, M. R., Janssens, J., & Ceballos, E. (1999). Do children's perceptions and attributions mediate the effects of mothers' child-rearing actions? *Journal of Family Psychology, 13,* 508–522.
Rohner, R. P. & Pettengill, S. M. (1985). Perceived parental acceptance-rejection and parental control among Korean adolescents. *Child Development, 56,* 524–528.
Ryan, R. M. & Lynch, J. (1989). Emotional autonomy versus detachment: Revisiting the vicissitudes of adolescence and young adulthood. *Child Development, 60,* 340–356.
Ryan, R. M., Stiller, J., & Lynch, J. (1994). Representations of relationships to teachers, parents, and friends as predictors of academic motivation and self-esteem. *Journal of Early Adolescence,* 14, 226–249.
Schaefer, E. S. (1965). Children's reports of parental behavior: an inventory. *Child Development, 36,* 413–424.
Skinner, E., Johnson, S., & Snyder, T. (2005). Six dimensions of parenting: A motivational model. *Parenting: Science and Practice, 5,* 175–235.
Soenens, B. & Vansteenkiste, M. (2005). Antecedents and outcomes of self-determination in three life domains: The role of parents' and teachers' autonomy support. *Journal of Youth and Adolescence, 34,* 589–604.
Stattin, H. & Kerr, M. (2006). Parents' reactions to and effects on adolescent development. Paper presented at Autonomy Conference, Mitzpe Ramon, Israel.
Steinberg, L. (2001). We know some things: Parent–adolescent relationships in retrospect and prospect. *Journal of Research on Adolescence, 11,* 1–19.
Steinberg, L. & Silverberg, S. B. (1986). The vicissitudes of autonomy in early adolescence. *Child Development, 57,* 841–851.
Steinberg, L., Elmen, J. D., & Mounts, N. S. (1989). Authoritative parenting, psychosocial maturity, and academic success among adolescents. *Child Development,* 60, 1424–1436.
Steinberg, L., Lamborn, S. D., Dornbush, S. M., & Darling, N. (1992). Impact of parenting practices on adolescent achievement: Authoritative parenting, school involvement, and encouragement to succeed. *Child Development, 63,* 1266–1281.
Steinberg, L., Mounts, N., Lamborn, S., & Dornbush, S. (1991) Authoritative parenting and adolescent adjustment across various ecological niches. *Journal of Research on Adolescence, 1,* 19–36.
Steinberg, L., Lamborn, S. D., Darling, N. *et al.* (1994). Over-time changes in adjustment and competence among adolescents from authoritative, authoritarian, indulgent, and neglectful families. *Child Development, 65,* 754–770.
Substance Abuse and Mental Health Services Administration (2005). *Overview of Findings from the 2004 National Survey on Drug Use and Health.* Rockville, MD: Office of Applied Studies.
Vansteenkiste, M., Simons, J., Lens, W. *et al.* (2004). Motivating learning, performance, and persistence: The synergistic role of intrinsic goals and autonomy support. *Journal of Personality and Social Psychology, 87,* 246–260.
Weiss, L. A. & Grolnick, W. S. (1991). *The Roles of Parental Involvement and Support for Autonomy in Adolescent Symptomatology.* Paper presented at the biennial meeting of the Society for Research in Child Development, Seattle, WA, April.
Williams, E. & Radin, N. (1993). Paternal involvement, maternal employment, and adolescents' academic achievement: An 11-year follow-up. *American Journal of Orthopsychiatry, 63,* 306–312.

CHAPTER 10

What is the Nature of Effective Parenting? It Depends

Joan E. Grusec
University of Toronto, Canada

INTRODUCTION

Martin Hoffman, one of the major contributors to our understanding of the socialization process, characterizes effective discipline as "a blend of frequent inductions, occasional power assertion, and a lot of affection" (Hoffman, 2000). Discipline, of course, is not the only context in which children are socialized. In addition to reacting to undesirable behavior on the part of their children, parents also expose them to models of appropriate behavior, provide them with opportunities to engage in cultural practices and routines that characterize the social group, protect them from exposure to undesirable and inappropriate behavior, talk to them about acceptable and unacceptable actions, and so on. Nevertheless, in accord with Hoffman's statement, reasoning, modest levels of enforcement of rules and standards of behavior, and warmth and acceptance have been trademark features of most approaches to the understanding of effective parenting.

There are numerous examples of these trademark features figuring in analyses of parent–child and teacher-child relationships. For example, Baumrind (1967, 1971) in her seminal work on parenting styles points to authoritative parenting—firm control but in the context of sensitive responsiveness to the reasonable needs of the child—as a good predictor of self-esteem, social skills, prosocial behavior, and academic achievement. The contrast is with authoritarian parenting, which involves excessive and/or rigid control and lack of acceptance of the child and the child's needs and, in contrast to authoritative parenting, is associated with modest academic performance and social skills. Baumrind also identified a permissive parenting style that was a predictor of poor self-control and academic performance. Parke (1977)

What Can Parents Do? New Insights into the Role of Parents in Adolescent Problem Behavior
Edited by Margaret Kerr, Håkan Stattin and Rutger C. M. E. Engels.

reported that children who participated in an experimental setting involving a resistance-to-temptation task were more likely to develop self-control if they received punishment from a warm adult, accompanied by reasons for why resistance to temptation was important. Deci and his colleagues (e.g., Deci & Ryan, 1985; Grolnick, Deci, & Ryan, 1997) argue that the internalization of social standards (i.e., taking over societal values as one's own) is best accomplished when agents of socialization are supportive of the child's autonomy by employing gentle control and appropriate choice, when they provide structure by setting clear expectations, and when they are interpersonally involved by being warm and caring and showing interest in the child. They note that autonomy support promotes the child's perception that behavior is self-generated rather than externally imposed (an important criterion for successful socialization), structure makes clear what is expected of the child, and warmth makes the child willing to accept the structure.

The similarity of conclusions reached by various theoreticians and researchers concerning the nature of effective parenting suggests that there is some reasonable merit in Hoffman's depiction of good socialization practices. It has become clear in recent years, however, that the picture is somewhat more complicated than the simple formula of explanation, moderate power assertion, and parental warmth. In this chapter I will describe some of these complexities and offer a somewhat different definition of what constitutes effective parenting. I will focus on three kinds of complexity in particular. The first involves the fact that parents have different goals in socialization interactions with their children and that these parenting goals direct the way in which they act. The second complexity is that different behaviors require different kinds of parent actions. The third is that features of parenting such as warmth and control have a different impact on children depending on characteristics such as their temperament, mood, age, and sex. I will then suggest a more nuanced formula for the nature of effective parenting than the general one of explanation, minimal power assertion, and warmth.

PARENTING GOALS AND THEIR IMPACT ON PARENTING ACTIONS

Dix (1992) notes that goals, or hoped-for outcomes, play an organizational role as parents monitor the progress of interactions with their children, search for factors that are affecting their progress to the goal, and adjust their behavior accordingly. These cognitive activities are accompanied by emotions—positive ones when the goal is approached and negative ones when attainment of the goal appears to be blocked. Dix suggests that parenting goals can be divided into three categories: parent- or self-oriented goals, which include obedience and short-term compliance; child-centered or socialization goals, which involve teaching the child important lessons about values; and empathic goals, which are focused on satisfying the child's emotional needs. A main distinction between child-centered and empathic goals is that the former are oriented toward long-term outcomes or benefits for the child whereas the latter are geared toward pleasing the child in the short term.

There are no doubt other parenting goals. Safety of the child is an obvious one, given the central role of parents in protecting their children from harm. Another has to do with the maintenance of positive, harmonious, and mutually satisfying relationships among family members (Goodnow, 1992; Grusec & Goodnow, 1994), a goal that might be particularly likely to underlie the actions of parents in collectivist cultural contexts where family harmony and interdependence is valued. Indeed, Japanese and US mothers differ significantly in the way they handle their children's socialization. Rothbaum *et al.* (2000) summarize some of these differences. They note that US mothers are quite directly controlling whereas Japanese mothers avoid confrontations and often back down when their children fail to comply. Japanese mothers use indirect methods of control by removing something from the child or by becoming silent or apparently indifferent. A particularly favored practice is to appeal to the child's awareness of the consequences of his or her behaviour on others. These differences in strategies of interaction, then, may well be motivated by different emphases on the importance of relationship maintenance.

My colleagues and I have assessed some of these ideas empirically, both with respect to parenting in an Anglo-European, individualist, context and in a collectivist context. We were interested in the kinds of variations that individuals report in their goals when dealing with their children's misdeeds, as well as how these goals might determine the strategies they employed to achieve those goals.

Goals and Parent Reactions

In an initial study (Hastings & Grusec, 1998) parents were asked to describe recent situations in which their children had engaged in an undesirable action. They were asked to say what their goal was, or what they had hoped to achieve in the subsequent interaction, as well as how they had responded in order to achieve their goal. Parents reported both short- and long-term parent–centered, child-centered, and relationship-centered goals. They also reported safety goals, albeit infrequently. Their reactions covered a wide range of possibilities, including accepting the child's wishes, acknowledging the child's perspective, bribing, comforting, commanding, diverting attention, inducing guilt, humiliating, negotiating for partial compliance, physical force, physical punishment, praising, questioning to learn about the child's perspective, reasoning, other-oriented reasoning, threatening, verbally disapproving, verbally forcing, withdrawing love, and withdrawing privileges. These reactions were reduced to four categories depicted in Table 10.1—force, direction, reasoning, and cooperation—and assessed for their linkages to the goals the parents had reported. There was a clear relation between goals and reactions (see Table 10.1), with force used more for parent-centered goals than for child- or relationship-centered goals, reasoning more for child- than parent-centered goals, and cooperation more for relationship- than parent- or child-centered goals. The data certainly suggest the possibility, then, that goals direct actions.

Table 10.1 Means for the interaction of focus of parenting goal and parenting behavior (standard deviations in parentheses)

	Behavior			
	Dominate	**Direct**	**Reason**	**Cooperate**
Par-centered N=49	$_{1}0.36^{a}$(0.35)	$_{1}0.88^{b}$(0.26)	$_{1}0.43^{a}$(0.50)	$_{1}0.22^{a}$(0.31)
Child-centered N=32	$_{2}0.20^{a}$(0.29)	$_{1}0.89^{b}$(0.28)	$_{2}0.69^{b}$(0.47)	$_{1}0.27^{a}$(0.28)
Rel.-centered N=13	$_{2}0.13^{a}$(0.17)	$_{1}0.96^{b}$(0.14)	$_{12}0.62^{ab}$(0.51)	$_{2}0.50^{a}$(0.35)

Means in a column not preceded by a common subscripted NUMBER differ at least at $p < 0.06$.
Means in a row not followed by a common superscripted LETTER differ at least at $p < 0.06$.

We also considered determinants of goals that individuals adopt. We found that the setting in which the dyadic interaction occurred had an impact on the parent's goal. When the misbehavior took place in public—for example, when a child began to fight with a sibling when the family was in a store—parents reported a greater concern with parent-centered goals of obedience and immediate compliance than when the misbehavior occurred in private. Clearly the presence of an audience reduces at least an immediate interest in teaching general principles of prosocial behaviour or maintaining a harmonious and cooperative relationship. In another part of this same study, participants were presented with vignettes describing a variety of different kinds of misdeeds and asked to rate the probability of different goals being elicited by different misdeeds. The misdeeds included a child using derogatory terms to describe the losing team in a swimming race, wanting to watch television before tidying toys left in the hallway, getting upset when a parent tries to delay a promised game due to friends of the parent visiting unexpectedly, accusing a parent of preferring a younger sibling, and behaving badly in a grocery store. The impact of situation on goals was apparent in the fact that parent-centered goals received the highest ratings when the child was behaving badly in a public setting (the grocery store), child-centered goals the highest rating in the case of derogatory language, and relationship-centered goals in the case of sibling rivalry.

In summary, parents have different goals and they appear to adopt different strategies to achieve those goals. This finding would seem to indicate that asking what effective parenting entails must also include a consideration of what the parent is trying to achieve. Our data indicate that the same parent has different goals at different points in time, and that these goals are determined by variables such as anxiety about public embarrassment as well as the content of the child's misdeed. They may also be determined by a general philosophy of child rearing adopted by a parent, with some parents more focused on teaching general values, some on obtaining respect and obedience, and some on ensuring the child is happy and satisfied and the family unit a harmonious one. Indeed, these different goals seem to find a parallel with authoritative, authoritarian, and permissive parenting styles and Baumrind's research would suggest that, at least in the Anglo-European context, child-centered goals are optimal for children's outcomes. The point, however, is that even an authoritative parent has authoritarian or permissive goals at one point or another in time, and that analyses of socialization must take this fact into account.

Goals in Different Cultural Settings

In a second set of studies, my colleagues and I have considered this analysis of goals from the perspective of differences between members of individualist and collectivist cultural groups. We recognize that the individualist-collectivist distinction is a rough one at best (see Oyserman, Coon, & Kemmelmeier, 2002 and associated commentaries, e.g., Miller, 2002 for an excellent overview of the strengths and weaknesses of the distinction). Nevertheless, it has proved a useful one in our work in the sense that it helps to explain at least some of the variance in our data.

People who live in individualist cultures, on average, are alleged to emphasize competition, self-actualization, dominance, and open expression of emotion. In contrast, those who live in collectivist cultures, on average, are concerned with interrelatedness and connectedness with the group, social harmony, and the organization of behavior around relationships with others. Their values include an emphasis on cooperation, empathy, accommodating the needs of others, subtle expression of emotion, and, in some cases, deference to the authority of others. (As an aside, it should be noted that collectivists comprise the largest portion of the earth's population and that most of our understanding of the parenting process is, in fact, based on the characteristics of a smaller proportion of the world's inhabitants who live in countries where the predominant culture is Western and industrialized.)

In cultures that emphasize interdependence, authoritarian or strict parenting appears to be more the rule. For example, Indian parents utilize strict parenting strategies (Sinha, 1981), cultures with economic systems that require interdependence tend to emphasize obedience in children (Oyserman, Coon, & Kemmelmeier, 2002), Latina and Asian mothers score high on measures of authoritarianism (Chao, 1994; Oyserman, Coon, & Kemmelmeier, 2002), and Puerto Rican mothers are more restrictive when feeding infants and more likely to restrain infants during social play (Harwood, Miller, & Irrizary, 1995; Harwood *et al.*, 1999; Miller & Harwood, 2001). The question becomes why collectivism should be associated with authoritarianism, whether this association is linked to negative outcomes for children, and what authoritarianism might mean in different cultural contexts.

We have argued that the values of collectivist cultures—inhibition of one's own needs and deference to those of the group, as well as deference to authority in many cases—are best served by a parenting approach that emphasizes the goal of obedience, that is, to use terminology from Hastings & Grusec (1998), by an approach that is parent centered. (Noted above was the possibility that collectivists also endorse more relationship-oriented goals, although only parent-centered goals and their implications have been assessed in our research to date.) Thus, in order to achieve an outcome of obedience and deference to the group, highly controlling practices may be needed. In a cultural context that encourages autonomy and separation (albeit it while maintaining positive family relationships), however, negotiation and responsiveness to children's input may be more appropriate.

Are authoritarian practices harmful in a collectivist context? The data suggest they are not. As some examples, the link between authoritative parenting and academic achievement is stronger for European-American than for Asian- and African-American adolescents (Darling & Steinberg, 1993), authoritarian parenting has positive effects on adolescents' school performance among the Chinese in Hong Kong (Leung, Lau, & Lam, 1998), corporal punishment is associated with externalizing problems in European-American but not African-American children (Deater-Deckard *et al.*, 1996), supervision and consistency of discipline are negatively related to delinquency among European-Americans but unrelated among Mexican-Americans (Smith & Krohn, 1995), and authoritarianism is positively related to externalizing problems for European-Americans but unrelated for Mexican-Americans (Lindahl & Malik, 1999).

What does authoritarian parenting mean in different cultural contexts? Kağiçıbası (1996) argues that children in more interdependent cultures see strong parental control as normal, and therefore not necessarily as reflecting parental rejection in the same way it would in the individualist context where this parenting style is less frequently employed. And Trommsdorf (1985) suggests that Japanese adolescents feel rejected by parents who exert little control and allow considerable autonomy. Rudy & Grusec (2001, 2006) have pursued this line of thinking by looking at correlates of authoritarian parenting. They reasoned that authoritarian parenting may have quite a different meaning for individualists and collectivists by virtue of the context in which it is administered. If it is a normative style for collectivists then it need not be associated with hostile thoughts and feelings. On the other hand, if it is less normative for individualists, then it might be more likely an outcome of rejection, anger, and frustration and therefore associated with hostile thoughts and negative affect on the part of the parent. Indeed, there is substantial evidence that authoritarian parenting is associated with rejection and lack of warmth (Baumrind, 1967), attributions of children's misbehavior to intentionality on the child's part (Dix, Reinhold, & Zambarano, 1990), and mothers' perceptions that their children have more control over difficult situations than they themselves do (Bugental, Blue, & Cruzcosa, 1989).

Across two studies, Rudy & Grusec (2001, 2006) assessed maternal warmth, mothers' general feelings of negativity in interactions with their children, positive and negative views of the child's characteristics, and anger felt in specific situations in which the child had misbehaved. They also studied negative descriptions of the child and attributions for the child's misbehavior (whether the child knew he or she was acting badly or improperly, whether the child thought his or her behavior would upset the mother, how reasonable the mother believed it was to expect her child to know better, and how much blame the mother thought her child deserved). Participants consisted of mothers from Anglo-Canadian backgrounds and collectivist mothers from Egypt, Iran, Iraq, India, and Pakistan. Mothers were additionally assessed for collectivism (using the Bardis Nuclear and Bardis Extended Familism subscales—Rao & Rao, 1979), and Triandis's (1995) measure of vertical collectivism), as well as authoritarianism (specifically, the frequently used measure devised by Kochanska, Kuczynski, & Radke-Yarrow, 1989, which assesses authoritarian control, supervision of the child, and control by anxiety induction).

Results indicated that the only differences between the two groups of mothers were for collectivism and authoritarianism (see Table 10.2, which provides measures from Rudy & Grusec, 2006). The results from Rudy & Grusec (2001) were similar. The two groups did differ in collectivist values, and the collectivist group scored higher on authoritarianism than did the individualist group. Table 10.2 also provides the scores on the measures of affect and cognition where there was notably no difference between the two groups of mothers. Thus, although collectivists may be more controlling in their behavior they are no different from individualists in the way they think and feel about their children.

Table 10.2 Differences between collectivists and individualists on measures of collectivism, authoritarianism, and parenting affect and cognition

	Collectivist	Individualist
Collectivism $p < 0.01$	7.39	5.62
Authoritarianism $p < 0.01$	6.38	4.87
Warmth *ns*	9.08	9.07
Responsivity *ns*	9.11	9.38
Negative affect *ns*	3.26	2.95
Positive view of child *ns*	8.03	7.55
Negative view of child *ns*	4.24	4.35
Anger *ns*	4.26	4.64
Negative descriptors *ns*	1.64	1.91
Negative attributions *ns*	5.76	6.78

Table 10.3 shows the correlations between authoritarianism and parenting affect and cognitions (with some of the measures aggregated). An omnibus test indicates that, overall, these measures were significantly correlated for the individualists but not the collectivists ($p < 0.005$). The findings suggest, then, that authoritarian parenting has a more benign meaning for collectivists, being less associated with anger, hostility, and rejection, and (we speculate) more likely to be a reflection of the values that predominate in the collectivist context. That does not mean, of course, that some individualists never use authoritarian parenting for purposes of teaching their children rather than as a reflection of their irritation. But it would appear to be the case that the teaching aspect of authoritarianism is more predominant when goals are more collectivist in their orientation.

Table 10.3 Correlations between authoritarianism and parental cognitions and affect for collectivist and individualist groups

	Authoritarianism within cultural group	
Maternal and child variables	**Collectivist**	**Individualist**
Collectivism	0.47*	0.10
Maternal affect and cognition warmth	0.07	−0.31†
CRPR negative affect	0.18	0.30
General view of child – positive	−0.07	−0.32†
Neg. cognition-discipline situation	0.18	0.48*
Anger-discipline situation	0.07	0.15

*$p < 0.05$; †$p < 0.10$

In a recent study we have found more evidence for the proposition that authoritarian parenting is more benign in a collectivist context. In this study (Grusec, 2005), adults from a variety of ethnic backgrounds were asked if their parents had spanked them when they were young and, if so, why they believed their parents had done so. There was no difference between participants who scored high and those who scored low on a measure of collectivism in the amount of spanking they reported. Individuals low in collectivism, however, were more likely to report that the more their parents had spanked them the more they did so because they were angry and because they wanted to teach them to be obedient. There were no correlations between amount of spanking for high collectivists and the reasons they gave for the spanking. These results suggest, then, that spanking may be perceived somewhat more benignly by high collectivists. Interestingly, this perception was accompanied by differences between the two groups in different aspects of prosocial behavior: For low collectivists, the amount of spanking was negatively correlated with taking the perspective of others while, for high collectivists, the amount of spanking predicted *higher* levels of empathic concern. In other words, spanking that occurred in a context of anger was linked to negative outcomes, as one would expect. That which occurred in a more benign context, however, appeared to be linked to a positive outcome.

Conclusion

The studies reported here underline the fact that effective parenting appears to depend on the goal a parent wishes to achieve. These studies have pointed to links between goals and parenting strategies, although they do not speak directly to the question of whether particular strategies are better employed to achieve particular goals. The inference, however, is that this is indeed the case.

Specificity of Links between Child Behavior and Parenting Strategies

The second complexity that makes it difficult to pinpoint a specific feature of parenting as particularly effective is that different behaviors require different kinds of parent actions. Frequently, many aspects of positive parenting behavior are subsumed under one term, such as "sensitive and responsive parenting," or parenting that promotes a positive relationship within the dyad. The argument here is that what constitutes positive or effective parenting depends on the behavior that is being socialized. Different kinds of positive parenting are needed to promote or deal with different kinds of child actions. Two categories of positive parenting have been a particular object of inquiry: warmth and responsiveness to distress. MacDonald (1992) argued that these two features involve two different and distinct biological systems with different central emotions, separate evolutionary functions and biological bases, and different consequences for children's development. Thus responsiveness to distress is part of the attachment system that is activated when the child is in danger or in need of protection. Warmth, on the other hand, has more to do with the nurturing and affectionate aspect of parent–child interaction. Grusec, Goodnow, & Kuczynski (2000) have suggested that the two play different roles in the internalization of values, with responsiveness to distress promoting trust in the parent to make reasonable demands and warmth making children more likely to comply to please the parent.

In an attempt to demonstrate empirically that responsiveness to distress and warmth are antecedents of different forms of socioemotional behavior, Davidov & Grusec (2006a) assessed these separate features of parenting behavior. We hypothesized that responsiveness to distress would predict children's regulation of negative affect and their empathy and prosocial behavior, whereas warmth would be predictive of regulation of positive affect and social competence. Parents who comfort their children when they are distressed model and coach effective techniques for controlling negative affect, as well as helping the children to moderate underlying levels of physiological arousal. These opportunities for learning to cope with negative affect do not exist when the child is not upset or anxious. In a similar fashion, responsive parents model empathy and compassion, whereas similar opportunities do not exist when the child is not distressed. Parental comforting also assists children to read the negative emotions of others in an accurate way and therefore to be able to respond in a suitable fashion. Finally, parents who comfort facilitate children's ability not to be overwhelmed by the distress of others so that they are able to react to it in a sympathetic and helpful way.

On the other hand, parents who are warm, engaging in expressions of physical and verbal affection, allow their children to experience the pleasure associated with these kinds of interactions as well as modeling and coaching appropriate expressions of positive affect. Acceptance by peers should be facilitated for several reasons. Children of warm parents expect social exchanges to be pleasant and so they seek them out. They also have a balanced style of interaction that makes them pleasant partners in these exchanges. All of these are conditions that are not met when parents are responding to children's distress.

We tested these hypotheses in a study with children who ranged in age from six to eight years. Parental warmth and responsiveness to distress were assessed in a variety of ways, including self-report and observation. Children's regulation of emotion and behavior were also measured with self, maternal, and teacher report as well as observation and story telling. Regression analyses indicated that mothers' and fathers' responsiveness to distress predicted significant amounts of variance in regulation of negative affect as well as empathy and prosocial behavior. Mothers' and fathers' warmth was not predictive of these child outcomes, however. On the other hand, warmth did predict regulation of positive affect. For mothers and boys it also predicted peer acceptance. As expected, responsiveness to distress was not a predictor of these outcomes.

These results, then, provide a degree of support for the suggestion that links between features of the parent–child relationship and child outcomes are specific. It is important to distinguish between different aspects of the relationship as well as to distinguish between social and emotional outcomes that each promotes. We examined responsiveness to distress and warmth. There are many other aspects of the relationship, such as control, teaching, and playfulness. Each no doubt has its own special link with the child's functioning. Nor is there any reason to believe that a parent who operates well in one aspect or role necessarily operates well in all. Warm parents may not be good teachers. Good playmates may not be good providers of comfort and security. Indeed, Davidov & Grusec (2006a) found only moderate correlations between parental warmth and parental responsiveness to distress, empirical support for this contention.

Other studies have also demonstrated specific linkages between features of parenting and child behavior. Bornstein & Tamis-LeMonda (1997), for example, found that maternal responsiveness to infant nondistress activities at

5 months but not responsiveness to infant distress, uniquely predicted infant attention span and symbolic play at 13 months. They concluded that the effects of maternal responsiveness on infant mental development are specific and indirect rather than generic and direct. In a parallel fashion, Rodriguez *et al.* (2005) report that lack of maternal responsiveness when children were stressed, but not when they were not stressed, predicted children's later inability to delay gratification. They refer to the arguments of Mischel and his colleagues (e.g., Mischel & Shoda, 1995) for a contextualized approach in which assessments of individual differences in behavior are enhanced substantially by taking account of the specific situation in which the behavior occurs. These "if-then" assessments identify the stable contexts that give behavior its meaning. Thus maternal responsiveness appears to be effective in facilitating children's coping behaviors only when it involves responsiveness to distress—that is, when it takes its meaning from the context of child distress. Again, this finding supports the idea that a given parenting action has a desired impact only if it occurs in the appropriate domain.

In yet another demonstration of specificity between parenting actions and child outcomes, Davidov & Grusec (2006b) report that mothers' willingness to comply with children's wishes was a positive predictor of children's willingness to go along with a maternal request for compliance. When the children balked at the maternal request, however, it was the mothers' knowledge of how their children would react to different discipline techniques that predicted ultimate compliance. In contrast, maternal compliance did not predict compliance after protest, and maternal knowledge did not predict immediate compliance. The argument here is that children who protest move the dyadic interaction from a domain of mutual reciprocity into one of control and authority where different parental behavior is required.

Summary

The studies described here underline the fact that effective parenting depends on the child outcome that is being socialized. Different parent actions are linked to different child outcomes. For example, responsiveness to distress is implicated in the development of regulation of negative affect, empathy, and delay of gratification; warmth is important for regulation of positive affect; and responsiveness in the nondistress domain is important for cognitive development. However, there is still considerable work to be done in linking parent characteristics to child outcomes.

THE INTERACTION BETWEEN CHILD CHARACTERISTICS AND PARENTING STRATEGIES

Much research has indicated that many characteristics of children, as well as their actions, interact with specific parenting styles and strategies to produce different outcomes. Children's temperament, that is, their constitutionally situated characteristic emotional, motor, and attentional reactivity and self-regulation, has been a particular focus for those interested in these interactions. Kochanska (1997), for example, studied children who at an early age were fearful, displaying discomfort in strange situations, staying close to their mothers, and showing reluctance to explore. She found that maternal use of gentle discipline that deemphasized power assertion was a good predictor of these children's conscience development. For constitutionally fearless children, however, there was no such relation. Similarly, Colder, Lochman, & Wells (1997) found that boys who were temperamentally fearful and who had harsh mothers were more aggressive than either boys who were fearless with harsh mothers, or boys who were fearful but had gentle mothers. In a review of the relevant literature, Bates & Petit (2007) have summarized the outcomes of these and a large number of other studies and concluded that children with fearful temperaments internalize values better when gentle rather than harsh control is used, whereas those with fearless temperaments respond better when their relationship with the mother is warm. Children who are high in negative emotionality are more affected by the quality of parenting they receive than are those who are less irritable, with highly directive parenting reducing behavioral inhibition in irritable children and harsh parenting increasing the risk of externalizing problems in these same children. Children who are low in self-regulatory ability are also less likely to exhibit externalizing behaviors when their mothers are controlling.

In addition to temperament, other variables such as age and sex of child play a role in determining the effectiveness of parenting techniques. Young children, for example, are more likely to rate strong forms of parental intervention as appropriate and fair than are older children (Siegal & Cowen, 1984). As they grow older the number of behaviors that children consider to be personal issues and not subject to parental control increases (Smetana, 1988). Rothbaum & Weisz (1994), in a meta-analysis, found that the correlations between harsh parenting and externalizing problems were greater for older than for younger children: one good reason for this could be that older children are more likely to see harsh parenting as threatening their sense of autonomy or freedom from parental interference. In another demonstration of the importance of age in socialization, it has been argued that the effective employment of reinforcement contingencies has a significant role to play in minimizing antisocial behavior early in childhood, whereas monitoring of children's actions becomes a much more important approach during adolescence (Patterson, Crosby, & Vuchinich, 1992; Pettit, 1997). This is a shift that, again, could reflect a change with age in what is threatening to the child's autonomy, with the imposition of external contingencies less problematic for younger children who can tolerate greater restrictions on their autonomy. For older children, however, interventions may need to be less clearly signs of imposition of external controls. As a final example of the role of age, there are also age differences in the ability of children to understand complex reasoning

(Grusec & Goodnow, 1994) and to decipher messages whose content and manner of delivery are contradictory, for example, approval expressed in a neutral tone of voice (Bugental, Kaswan, & Love, 1970; Morton & Trehub, 2001).

In addition to age and temperament, the gender of the child is another variable that interacts with parenting actions. Thus boys appear to respond more negatively to control than do girls, being more likely, for example, to be caught up with their mothers in coercive cycles of increasing negative behavior (McFadyen-Ketchum *et al.*, 1996; Patterson, 1982). In their meta-analysis, Rothbaum & Weisz (1994) found maternal caregiving was more strongly linked to externalizing behavior problems in preadolescent boys than preadolescent girls. Another example of how boys are more negatively affected by control than girls comes from the results of a longitudinal study of teenage mothers and their 12-year-old children (Awong, Grusec, & Sorenson, in press). Very shortly after the birth of their children the mothers were assessed for their approval of "respect-based control", that is, control involving endorsement of absolute parental authority and unquestioning loyalty to parents and to their ideas, as well as the exclusion of outside influences. The children were assessed for externalizing problems 12 years later. We found that boys of mothers who endorsed authority-based control were more likely to have externalizing problems than those with mothers who did not endorse it. For girls, however, there was no impact of maternal control on externalizing problems. All of these studies, then, suggest there is something about boys that make them more resistant to maternal control than girls. This "something" may be related to levels of testosterone, although high levels of testosterone have been shown to predict aggression and destructive behavior only when the relationship between parent and child is a poor one (Booth *et al.*, 2003).

Summary

The list of variables that interact with parenting behavior is long and includes, in addition to temperament, age, and sex, such things as the child's mood, the nature of the behavior under consideration, the cultural context, the impact of sibling and peer comparisons, and the child's attachment status. Lengthier discussion of their impact can be found in Grusec (2002). For present purposes, they simply indicate again that the essence of effective parenting is not captured in a very easy manner.

WHAT MIGHT SOME OF THE FEATURES OF EFFECTIVE PARENTING BE?

Given all the caveats that have been placed on a description of effective parenting—it depends on parenting goals, it depends on the nature of the behavior being socialized, it depends on a variety of features of the child—is there in fact anything that can be said about the essence of effective parenting? Grusec, Goodnow, & Kuczynski (2000) have argued that effective parenting involves appraisal and flexible action in the face of constantly changing features of children and of situations. The most effective parents are those who engage in complex problem solving, matching actions appropriate to current conditions so as to achieve their desired goals, including the nature of the behavior being socialized. In essence, effective parents need to know their children, need to know how their children will respond to different kinds of interventions, and need to be willing or able to implement that knowledge in such a way as to achieve their child-rearing goals.

Researchers who underline the importance of monitoring children as a way of gaining knowledge of their activities and whereabouts and, thereby, making it easier to guide their behavior, have looked at knowledge in one particular way (see Crouter & Head, 2002, for a review of the relevant literature). Kerr and Stattin (2000; this volume) have oriented developmentalists to the importance of knowing about children's activities and whereabouts, emphasizing the important role played by children's volunteering of relevant information. In this case the argument is that positive parent–child relationships make children and adolescents more likely to volunteer information to their parents and, thereby, make it possible for parents to manage their children's environment more effectively. This conclusion, of course, suggests that it is not parental knowledge or monitoring that is responsible for prosocial behavior but, rather, a relationship that makes children more likely to confide in their parents. Not to be forgotten, as well, is the distinct possibility that children who volunteer information about their activities and whereabouts have less to hide than those who do not, and may therefore have fewer problems with respect to antisocial behavior.

Parents' Knowledge of Children's Perspectives as a Feature of Effective Parenting

In our research my colleagues and I have considered knowledge in a variety of somewhat different ways. We have operationalized it as (1) knowledge of a child's thoughts and feelings during conflict, (2) taking the perspective of the child, and (3) accurately predicting a child's reactions to different discipline interventions. In each case, we have found that knowledge was a good predictor of outcomes relevant to conflict resolution, conflict frequency and intensity, and/or child compliance.

In a first study, Hastings & Grusec (1998) interviewed mothers and fathers and their adolescent children individually about a recent disagreement that they had experienced with each other. Adolescents were asked to rate their anger, their evaluations of acceptability of their own and their parent's behavior, and their assignment of blame throughout the disagreement. Parents were asked to indicate their perceptions of their adolescent's answers to these same questions. A measure of parental accuracy was subsequently obtained by taking the difference between adolescent and parent ratings on the various questions. We found that the more accurate fathers were about their adolescent's thoughts and feelings, the fewer conflicts the dyad reported. For mothers, accuracy predicted their satisfaction with the outcome of the conflict. Moreover, use of power assertive or egalitarian (reasoning, negotiation) techniques by either parent was generally not predictive of conflict outcomes. There were two exceptions. Adolescent reports of egalitarian techniques for fathers positively predicted amount of conflict and mother reports of egalitarian techniques positively predicted their satisfaction with the outcome of the conflict. From these results it would appear that parental accuracy is certainly linked to outcomes, with these outcomes possibly a reflection of different goals that mothers and fathers have during disagreements with their children. Thus it could be that fathers are more oriented to avoiding conflict, whereas mothers are more concerned with maintaining mutual understanding and harmony (see Vuchinich, 1987), and that each parent uses his or her accurate knowledge to achieve a desired outcome.

Lundell *et al.* (in press) addressed the issue of parental knowledge from the point of view of perspective taking. In a study of mother-adolescent conflict, they observed that adolescents who were more likely to adopt confrontational goals during the disagreement (reporting that they had wished to show their mother how wrong she was, or to change her way of thinking) were involved in more intense and unpleasant conflict interactions. The link between adoption of negative goals and conflict intensity was mediated by mothers' reports of perspective taking, with low perspective taking part of the pathway between negative goals and intense conflict. The suggestion is that mothers use their ability to take the perspective of the adolescent to anticipate when the adolescent's goals are about to become confrontational and use their knowledge of the adolescent's perspective to head off difficulties. Finally, in a study referred to earlier in this chapter, Davidov & Grusec (2005) asked children to rate different discipline interventions (disapproval, reasoning, and acknowledgement of feelings) on a number of dimensions including fairness, impact on the parent–child relationship, and effectiveness in achieving compliance. Mothers were asked to say how their children would respond. The results indicated that mothers who were more accurate about their children's evaluations were better able to gain compliance from their children when the initial response to their request was one of protest. Again, the suggestion is that knowledge of how interventions are viewed by a child can provide valuable information to guide a mother's behavior when some sort of persuasive intervention is required in order to gain compliance.

Summary

Research indicates that many features of the child and situation interact to determine the effectiveness of a given parenting behavior. Yet again, then, it is not possible to say what the specific nature of effective parenting is. In this section, it has been suggested that effective parents are not those who engage in specific actions but, rather, those who have knowledge of their children's thoughts and feelings and are willing to put that knowledge into effect in order to achieve his or her goals.

CONCLUSION

An attempt has been made in this chapter to demonstrate that effective parenting cannot be characterized in any general way but is, instead, dependent on a wide range of variables. These variables include what it is that parents might be trying to achieve as they attempt to socialize their children, what behavior it is that they are trying to socialize, and what are the characteristics of the child who is being socialized. Not to acknowledge these multiple factors is to limit the usefulness of any attempt to define what it is that constitutes good parenting.

REFERENCES

Awong, T., Grusec, J. E., & Sorenson, A. (in press). Respect-based control and anger as determinants of children's socio-emotional development. *Social Development*.

Bates, J. E. & Pettit, G. S. (2007). Temperament, parenting, and socialization. In J. E. Grusec & P. D. Hastings (eds). *Handbook of Socialization* (pp. 153–177). New York: Guilford.

Baumrind, D. (1967). Child care practices anteceding three patterns of preschool behavior. *Genetic Psychology Monographs, 73*, 43–88.

Baumrind, D. (1971). Current patterns of parental authority. *Developmental Psychology, 4*, 1–103.

Booth, A., Johnson, D. R., Granger, D. A. *et al.* (2003). Testosterone and child and adolescent adjustment: The moderating role of parent-child relationships. *Developmental Psychology, 39*, 85–98.

Bornstein, M. & Tamis-LeMonda, C. (1997). Maternal responsiveness and infant mental abilities: Specific predictive relations. *Infant Behavior and Development, 20*, 283–296.

Bugental, D. B., Blue, J., & Cruzcosa, M. (1989). Perceived control over caregiving outcomes: Implications for child abuse. *Developmental Psychology, 25*, 532–539.

Bugental, D. B., Kaswan, J. W., & Love, L. R. (1970) Perception of contradictory meanings conveyed by verbal and nonverbal channels. *Journal of Personality and Social Psychology, 16*, 647–655.

Chao, R. (1994). Beyond parental control and authoritarian parenting style: understanding Chinese parenting through the cultural notion of training. *Child Development, 65*, 1111–1119.

Colder, C. R., Lochman, J. E., & Wells, K. C. (1997). The moderating effects of children's fear and activity level on relations between parenting practices and childhood symptomatology. *Journal of Abnormal Child Psychology, 25*, 251–263.

Crouter, A. C. & Head, M. R. (2002). Parental monitoring and knowledge of children. In M. H. Bornstein (ed.), *Handbook of Parenting: Vol. 3: Being and Becoming a Parent* (2nd edn, pp. 461–483). Mahwah, NJ: Erlbaum.

Darling, N. and Steinberg, L. (1993). Parenting style as context: An integrative model. *Psychological Bulletin, 113*, 487–496.

Davidov, M. & Grusec, J. E. (2006a). Untangling the links of parental responsiveness to distress and warmth to child outcomes. *Child Development, 77*, 44–58.

Davidov, M. & Grusec, J. E. (2006b). Multiple pathways to compliance: Mothers' willingness to cooperate and knowledge of their children's reactions to discipline. *Journal of Family Psychology, 20*, 705–708.

Deater-Deckard, K., Dodge, K. A., Bates, J. E., & Pettit, G. S. (1996). Physical discipline among African American and European American mothers: Links to children's externalizing behaviors. *Developmental Psychology, 32*, 1056–1072.

Deci, E. L. & Ryan, R. M. (1985). *Intrinsic Motivation and Self-determination in Human Behavior*. New York: Plenum Press.

Dix, T. (1992). Parenting on behalf of the child: Empathic goals in the regulation of responsive parenting. In I. E. Sigel, A. V. McGillicuddy-DeLisi, & J. J. Goodnow (eds), *Parental Belief Systems: The Psychological Consequences for Children* (2nd edn, pp. 319–346). Hillsdale, NJ: Erlbaum.

Dix, T., Reinhold, D. A., & Zambarano, R. J. (1990). Mothers' implicit theories of discipline: Child effects, parent effects, and the attribution process. *Child Development, 60*, 1373–1391.

Goodnow, J. J. (1992). Parents' ideas, children's ideas: the bases of congruence and divergence. In I. E. Sigel, A. V. McGillicuddy-DeLisi, & J. J. Goodnow (eds), *Parental Belief Systems: The Psychological Consequences for Children* (2nd edn, pp. 293–318). Hillsdale, NJ: Erlbaum.

Grolnick, W. S., Deci, E. L., & Ryan, R. M. (1997). Internalization within the family: The self-determination theory perspective. In J. E. Grusec & L. Kuczynski (eds), *Parenting and Children's Internalization of Values: A Handbook of Contemporary Theory* (pp. 135–161). New York: Wiley.

Grusec, J. E. (2002). Parenting and the socialization of values. In M. Bornstein (ed.), *Handbook of Parenting, Vol. 5* (pp. 143–168). Mahwah NJ: Erlbaum.

Grusec, J. E. (2005). *Spanking and Concern for Others in Different Cultural Contexts*. Unpublished manuscript, University of Toronto.

Grusec, J. E. & Goodnow, J. J. (1994). The impact of parental discipline methods on the child's internalization of values: a reconceptualization of current points of view. *Developmental Psychology, 30*, 4–19.

Grusec, J. E., Goodnow, J. J., & Kuczynski, L. (2000). New directions in analyses of parenting contributions to children's acquisition of values. *Child Development, 71*, 205–211.

Harwood, R. L., Miller, J. G., & Irizarry, N. L. (1995). *Culture and Human Development*. New York: Guilford Press.

Harwood, R. L., Schoelmerich, A., Ventura-Cook, E. *et al.* (1999). Culture and class influences on Anglo and Puerto Rican mothers' beliefs regarding long-term socialization goals and child behavior. *Child Development, 67*, 2446–2461.

Hastings, P. & Grusec, J. E. (1998). Parenting goals as organizers of responses to parent-child disagreement. *Developmental Psychology, 34*, 465–479.

Hoffman, M. L. (2000). *Empathy and Moral Development: Implications for Caring and Justice*. Cambridge: Cambridge University Press.

Kağiçıbası, Ç. (1996). *Family and Human Development Across Cultures: A View from the Other Side*. Hillsdale, NJ: Lawrence Erlbaum Associates, Inc.

Kerr, M. & Stattin, H. (2000). What parents know, how they know it, and several forms of adolescent adjustment: further support for a reinterpretation of monitoring. *Developmental Psychology, 36*, 366–380.

Kochanska, G. (1997). Multiple pathways to conscience for children with different temperaments: from toddlerhood to age 5. *Developmental Psychology, 33,* 228–240.

Kochanska, G., Kuczynski, L., & Radke-Yarrow, M. (1989). Correspondence between mothers' self-reported and observed child-rearing practices. *Child Development, 60,* 56–63.

Leung, K., Lau, S., & Lam, W. (1998). Parenting styles and academic achievement: A cross-cultural study. *Merrill-Palmer Quarterly, 44,* 157–172.

Lindahl, K. M. & Malik, N. M. (1999). Marital conflict, family processes, and boys' externalizing behavior in Hispanic American and European American families. *Journal of Clinical Child Psychology, 28,* 12–24.

Lundell, L., Grusec, J. E., McShane, K., & Davidov, M. (in press). Mother-adolescent conflict: Adolescent goals, maternal perspective-taking, and conflict intensity. *Journal of Research in Adolescence.*

MacDonald, K. (1992). Warmth as a developmental construct: An evolutionary analysis. *Child Development, 63,* 753–773.

McFadyen-Ketchum, S. A., Bates, J. E., Dodge, K. A., & Pettit, G. S. (1996). Patterns of change in early childhood aggressive-disruptive behavior: Gender differences in predictions from early coercive and affectionate mother-child interactions. *Child Development, 67,* 2417–2433.

Miller, J. G. (2002). Bringing culture to basic psychological theory: Beyond individualism and collectivism—Comment on Oyserman *et al.* (2002). *Psychological Bulletin, 128,* 97–109.

Miller, A. M., & Harwood, R. L. (2001). Long-term socialisation goals and the construction of infants' social networks among middle class Anglo and Puerto Rican mothers. *International Journal of Behavioural Development, 25,* 450–457.

Mischel, W., & Shoda, Y. (1995). A cognitive-affective system theory of personality: Reconceptualizing situations, dispositions, dynamics, and invariance in personality structure. *Psychological Review, 102,* 246–268.

Morton, J. B. & Trehub, S. E. (2001). Children's understanding of emotion in speech. *Child Development, 72,* 834–843.

Oyserman. D., Coon, H. M., & Kemmelmeier, M. (2002). Rethinking individualism and collectivism: Evaluation of theoretical assumptions and meta-analyses. *Psychological Bulletin, 128,* 3–72.

Parke, R. D. (1977). Some effects of punishment on children's behavior—revisited. In E. M. Hetherington & D. R. Parke (eds), *Contemporary Readings in Psychology.* New York: McGraw Hill.

Patterson, G. R. (1982). *Coercive Family Process.* Eugene, OR: Castalia.

Patterson, G. R., Crosby, L., & Vuchinich, S. (1992). Predicting risk for early police arrest. *Journal of Quantitative Criminology, 8,* 335–355.

Pettit, G. S., (1997). The developmental course of violence and aggression: Mechanisms of family and peer influence. *Psychiatric Clinics of North America, 20,* 283–299.

Rao, V. V. & Rao, V. M. (1979). An evaluation of the Bardis Familsm Scale in India. *Journal of Marriage and the Family, 41,* 417–421.

Rodriguez, M. L., Avduk, O., Aber, J. L. *et al.* (2005). A contextual approach to the development of self-regulatory competencies: The role of maternal unresponsivity and toddlers' negative affect in stressful situations. *Social Development, 14,* 136–157.

Rothbaum, F., Pott, M., Azuma, H. *et al.* (2000). The development of close relationships in Japan and the United States: Paths of symbiotic harmony and generative tension. *Child Development, 71,* 1121–1142.

Rothbaum, F. & Weisz, J. R. (1994). Parental caregiving and child externalizing behavior in nonclinical samples: A meta-analysis. *Psychological Bulletin, 116,* 55–74.

Rudy, D. & Grusec, J. E. (2001). Correlates of authoritarian parenting in individualist and collectivist cultures and implications for understanding the transmission of values. *Journal of Cross-Cultural Psychology, 32,* 202–212.

Rudy, D. & Grusec, J. E. (2006). Authoritarian parenting in individualist and collectivist groups: Associations with maternal emotion and cognition and children's self-esteem. *Journal of Family Psychology 20*, 68–78.
Siegal, M. & Cowen, J. (1984). Appraisals of intervention: The mother's versus the culprit's behavior as determinants of children's evaluations of discipline techniques. *Child Development, 55*, 176–1766.
Sinha, D. (1981). *Socialization of the Indian Child*. New Delhi: Naurang Rai.
Smetana, J. (1988). Adolescents' and parents' conceptions of parental authority. *Child Development, 59*, 321–335.
Smith, C. & Krohn, M. D. (1995). Delinquency and family life among male adolescents: The role of ethnicity. *Journal of Youth and Adolescence, 24*, 69–93.
Triandis, H. C. (1995). *Individualism and Collectivism*. Boulder, CO: Westview Press.
Trommsdorf, G. (1985). Some comparative aspects of socialization in Japan and Germany. In I. R. Lagunes & Y. H. Poortinga (eds), *From a Different Perspective: Studies of Behavior Across Cultures* (pp. 231–240). Lisse: Swets & Zeitlinger.
Vuchinich, S. (1987). Starting and stopping spontaneous family conflicts. *Journal of Marriage and the Family, 49*, 591–601.

CHAPTER 11

Positive Parenting and Positive Characteristics and Values in Children

Marc H. Bornstein
National Institute of Child Health and Human Development, Bethesda, USA

INTRODUCTION

What are the prominent features of adolescent development today? Too frequently it is problems that come to mind first—of aggression and bullying, prejudice and substance abuse, inferior intelligence and underachievement (Currie, 2005). Armed with the knowledge that things do not always go well in child development, policy makers, parent educators, and parents share the laudable and well-intentioned goal of developing interventions (prevention and remediation) in the service of children. The main modes of intervention have been to prevent or to remedy disrupted or broken childhoods. The helping professions attempt to understand individual functioning through the lens of a disease model, and they are preoccupied with "disorders, deficits, and disabilities" in development. Unfortunately, as professionals dispense this kind of negative language, society also comes to see children in those terms.

But, as Seligman & Csikszentmihalyi (2000) have underscored, pathologizing is not the only path to preventing or remedying disorders. An alternative is

This chapter summarizes selected aspects of my research, portions of the text have appeared in previous scientific publications cited in the references, and my research was supported by the Intramural Research Program of the NIH, NICHD. I thank M. Heslington and C. Varron for their assistance.

What Can Parents Do? New Insights into the Role of Parents in Adolescent Problem Behavior
Edited by Margaret Kerr, Håkan Stattin and Rutger C. M. E. Engels.

to promote things that are *positive*. Developmental success might be ensured by building individual competencies. Human strengths—optimism, courage, interpersonal skill, work ethic, hope, honesty, and perseverance—are not only desirable in themselves but they can also buffer against adversity and illness, and compensate for deficiency. Competencies promote resilience: for example, optimism broadens thought-action repertoires and serves as a powerful antidote to negativity, which narrows thought-action repertoires (Masten, 2001; Masten & Coatsworth, 1998). In lieu of a focus on "disorders, deficits, and disabilities," a positive developmental science fosters positive characteristics and values in children.

Such a strengths-based vision and vocabulary has been gaining momentum in developmental science and is beginning to supplant other long-held beliefs, such as the "storm and stress" view of adolescence, bequeathed to us by Goethe and Hall, Freud and Erikson, and perpetuated in today's daily newspapers. Problems beset children, of course, but youth is actually a sizeable and dynamic collection of strengths and assets. From this perspective, young people are not broken, in need of psychosocial repair, they are not problems to be managed, they are not immature adults who need to be re-educated (Roth *et al.*, 1998). Rather, young people are resources to be cultivated (Roth & Brooks-Gunn, 2003a,b), active and coequal participants in their development.

This chapter takes this "positive youth development" perspective as its starting point. In the first part, I look to the literature to identify and define desirable positive characteristics and values in children. In second part, I address the important goal of how we can best help children achieve those desirable positive characteristics and values.

POSITIVE CHARACTERISTICS AND VALUES IN YOUTH

In the "business plan" I develop here, it is critical first to have a clear idea of the goals that we are trying to attain, followed by an analysis of how best to achieve those goals. What are the positive characteristics and values we like to see and promote in children, and just how can parents and family, community and environment, foster their development?

The study of positive youth development is emerging fast but, to be fair, it is still critically in need of development: in terms of defining positive outcomes, enhancing the research base, undertaking longitudinal assessments of young people's evolution, and policing psychometric adequacy. However, several social commentators and scientific investigators have made a start. Diener & Lucas (2004) asked 10 175 respondents from 48 countries what they most wanted in terms of their children's emotions. People universally most desired high levels of happiness for their offspring. There are many individual and social indicators of positive child development in the interpersonal, intellectual, athletic, and artistic realms (Moore, 1997; Scales *et al.*, 2000). More specifically, Bennett (1993) asserted a set of "desired outcomes" for youth, which included perseverance, faith, friendship, courage, responsibility, and compassion. The Search Institute (Benson, 1993) likewise identified a set of key "internal assets," such as commitment to learning, positive values, social competencies, and positive identity. Lerner, Fisher, & Weinberg (2000) enumerated "5 Cs" of positive development: competence, confidence, connections, character, and caring. Recently, Peterson & Seligman (2004) listed "six strengths"—wisdom, courage, humanity, justice, temperance, and transcendence—that encompass 24 virtues like integrity, critical thinking, street smarts, love of beauty, and kindness.

In considering these positive developmental attributes, of course, we need to keep in mind that they are always "in the parental eye." Some parents may want to see control of emotionality in their children, whereas for others career success matters. More broadly, different ethnic groups and different cultures around the world espouse and promote some similar but some different values (Schwartz, 1994; Schwartz & Bardi, 2001; Schwartz & Sagiv, 1995).

Although there is diversity in specific vocabularies used to describe thriving on a more abstract level, there is also growing evidence for a consensual understanding of exemplary youth development. At the Center for Child Well-Being, in Atlanta, GA, my colleagues and I have identified three domains of positive youth development, each defined by a series of closely operationalized elements (Bornstein *et al.*, 2003). Positive development encompasses the physical, social and emotional, and cognitive domains. In developing this system, we avoided overly abstract or idealized strengths that we would have difficulty operationalizing. Furthermore, the elements in each domain may not be exhaustive, but they represent a core set of "essentials" that help to define that domain and positive development in children overall. I amplify each, before proceeding to explore how these specific positive characteristics and values can be promoted in children.

The Physical Domain of Childhood Positive Development

Positive development in the physical domain includes several requisites to a healthy life: good nutrition, health care, physical activity, safety and security, and reproductive health:

- Good nutrition is essential to growth and optimal development; healthy eating habits means avoiding excesses (obesity) as much as deficiencies (anorexia) (Leavitt, Tonniges, & Rogers, 2003).
- Health care is critical to positive development, which also includes maximizing desirable physical attributes (Tonniges & Leavitt, 2003).
- Physical activity and sleep—exercise as well as adequate rest—are fundamental to a healthy lifestyle (Connor, 2003).

- Children's feelings of safety and security not only in the home but at school, in their neighborhood, and in the surrounding community all exercise an impact over their positive development (Sleet & Mercy, 2003).
- In adolescence, reproductive health and sexuality become significant issues. We need to promote a positive constructive approach to sexual development, safe sexual practices, and accurate reproductive knowledge (Connor & Dewey, 2003).

The Social and Emotional Domain of Childhood Positive Development

This domain encompasses multiple elements related to self and social intercourse: temperament, emotion understanding and regulation, the ability to cope with stressors, trust, a self-system, character, and positive social relationships with parents, siblings, and peers:

- Possessing a positive temperament, including an approach orientation, an adaptive style, and in general having an "easy and winsome personality" is positive in development (Halle, 2003).
- Emotional intelligence, that is emotion expression, understanding, and regulation, is essential to social and emotional positive development in childhood and adolescence. Empathy is the emotional response to what another person is feeling, and sympathy is the emotional reaction to another's distress; positive social and emotional development means possessing both (Eisenberg, 2003; Graziano & Tobin, 2003).
- Coping implies the ability to interact with the environment positively, constructively, and adaptively (especially under conditions of stress, threat, or harm). Likewise, resilience implies the ability to recover and regain equilibrium in the face of negative environments and experiences (Bridges, 2003a).
- Trust in children is a hallmark of a secure attachment and the ability of the child to use the caregiver as a secure base from which to explore the environment (Bridges, 2003b).
- Near to the core of social and emotional positive development is children's sense of self, including a positive self-concept, identity, and regard as well as possessing self-efficacy, being able to self-regulate, and having a sense of self-determination (Zaff & Hair, 2003).
- Character includes values and moral behaviors—altruism, courage, honesty, duty, and responsibility—which constitute much admired human strengths and virtues.
- Social competencies encompass understanding one's place in the social world and navigating interpersonal dynamics well, so as to develop quality, warm, and trusting relationships with others, notably parents, siblings, and peers (Bukowski, 2003; Cox & Harter, 2003; Volling, 2003).

The Cognitive Domain of Childhood Positive Development

Thinking, communicating thought, and the products of thought in everyday life are essential to positive cognitive development. There are many specific elements within the cognitive domain, including information processing and memory, curiosity and exploration, mastery motivation, intelligence, problem solving, language and literacy, educational achievement, moral development, and talent:

- Cognitive science has identified two interrelated general mechanisms that are implicated in children's mental performance across a wide range of tasks. One is information processing (the execution of fundamental mental processes), and the other is working memory (the ongoing cognitive processing of that information) (Kail, 2003).
- Curiosity is the desire to learn more, and exploration the behavior that is energized and directed by curiosity (Wentworth & Witryol, 2003).
- Mastery motivation underlies the person's drive to learn; it is a psychological force that leads individuals to accomplish tasks for an intrinsic feeling of efficacy, rather than for extrinsic reward (Jennings & Dietz, 2003).
- Thinking involves basic processes, such as perceiving objects and events in the external environment, and high-level mental processes, such as reasoning, symbolizing, and planning. Traditional global measures of thinking are assessed by intelligence tests but a more encompassing contemporary view of intelligence embraces understanding oneself and others, logic, spatial relations, and even bodily kinesthetic adeptness (Siegler, 2003).
- Problem solving is the sequence of steps that attempt to identify and create alternate solutions for both cognitive and social problems, including the ability to plan, resourcefully seek help from others, and think critically, creatively, and reflectively (Smith, 2003).
- Language and literacy constitute a set of verbal achievements that are key to the child's entering the social community and to success through schooling (MacWhinney & Bornstein, 2003).
- Educational achievement is commonly measured by children's readiness to learn—that is the state in which the capacities and competencies of the child match the expectations and requirements of adults and school, by achievement test scores and by report card grades, which give direct assessments of children's mastery of specific skills (Plank & MacIver, 2003).
- Cognitive ability is strongly related to several components of morality: moral judgement, moral emotions, and moral action (Hart *et al.*, 2003).
- Finally, central elements of positive cognitive development are creativity and talent, whether intellectual, artistic, or other (Winner, 2003).

SOURCES OF POSITIVE CHARACTERISTICS AND VALUES

Following our "business plan," now that we have addressed the goals that we desire we need to define better how to attain those goals. There is no formula, unhappily, no "magic bullet," to promoting positive characteristics and values in children, the way the antibiotic agent penicillin treats against a broad spectrum of bacterial infections and diseases (Fleming, 1929).

However, developmental science points to three general origins of such psychological phenomena: children themselves, child effects, and parenting broadly conceived. First, of course, children can contribute directly to their own positive development. Stability describes consistency among individuals in a group with respect to the expression of a positive characteristic or value over time. A stable positive characteristic or value is one that some children possess in greater degree when they are very young and continue to possess when they are older. The notion of stability often entices developmentalists toward the belief that endogenous processes are at work, that stability is already *in* the child. Of course, this is not necessarily or always the case; a consistent environment can carry stability (Roberts & DelVecchio, 2000). Second, children contribute to their development indirectly by the influence they exert on others, notably their caregivers (Scarr & Kidd, 1983). Over and above stability, transaction means that children influence parents and reciprocally parents influence children through time (Sameroff, 1983). Stability and child effects place great weight on little shoulders. And realistically, we need to ask: how much can we intervene to change stable endogenous processes and even some child effects?

In the remainder of this chapter, I focus attention, rather, on the things we *can* affect and that make a difference. Beyond stability in children and child effects, environment and experience manifestly influence human development at all levels—from cells to cradle to culture.

To promote positive characteristics and values in children and to fathom their determinants we need to isolate and measure stabilities in the child and differentiate among different models of experience. This is difficult to do, and it has not been done enough. The unhappy truth is that we do not know as much as we would like scientifically about the threads that are woven into the fabric of development or about the weaving process itself. The discipline of developmental science is, after all, still quite young. Up until approximately the twentieth century, psychology was part of philosophy, and philosophers of different stripes simply asserted that human development was subject to one or another influence and followed one or another path. John Locke: the infant mind is a *tabula rasa*; Immanuel Kant: no, the infant is endowed with innate knowledge. J. J. Rousseau: young children are "noble savages, perfect in the state of nature." Thomas Hobbes: no, the life of man is "solitary, poor, nasty, brutish, and short." The question of "why we are who we are" is perhaps one of the most fundamental ever contemplated in human history. It was only with Charles Darwin that a developmental science began formally to supplant philosophy and that was only a little over a century ago. In 1877, Darwin published a "Biographical sketch of an infant," his son Doddy (Darwin had made his notes about Doddy before the publication of the *Origin of Species* in 1856, but did not publish his biographical sketch until 20 years later). Darwin instigated an essentially subjective tradition of "baby biographies" that itself was only replaced with systematic experimental and observational studies of child development in the middle of the twentieth century. As a consequence, the number of intellectual generations of developmental scientists is only about three. All previous work in this field, since at least Plato's *Laws*, had an anecdotal cast at worst, or some principled philosophical stance at best.

Furthermore, developmental understanding requires, at least in part, longitudinal research, and longitudinal study takes time; this is not a defensive statement so much as a factual one. The foregoing thumbnail history of developmental science does not so much complicate as explain the complexity that faces us in identifying and promoting elements of developmental wellbeing: the jejune nature of developmental science, the difficulty of identifying much less proving longitudinal effects (and distinguishing stability in individuals from the roles of experience), and the historical focus on negative outcomes.

What aspects of experience and environment can we manipulate in order to attain our goals for children? Here I turn to consider parents and parent programs.

PARENTS AND PARENTING PROGRAMS

Despite the fact that most people become parents, and all children who ever lived have had parents, parenting is a somewhat mystifying process, which almost everyone has opinions on but about which few people appear to agree. Yet, one thing is sure: it is the principal and continuing task of parents in each generation to prepare children of the next generation for the physical, economic, and psychosocial situations in which their children must survive and hopefully thrive. Bronfenbrenner (2005) has shown in the contextual ecological model of human development that many factors influence the growth and development of children—culture and social class, media and schools, family and peers—but in this nested system of distal to proximal influences parenthood is the "final common pathway" to childhood oversight and caregiving, development and stature, adjustment and success. Parents are children's primary advocates and their front-line defense. Parents are the corps available in the greatest number to lobby and labor for children. They are the ones who also have earliest and continuing access to children.

Not only is the sheer amount of interaction between parent and offspring greatest in childhood (Hill & Stafford, 1980), but childhood appears to be a time when human beings are particularly susceptible to external influences. Indeed, the opportunity for enhanced parental influence and prolonged learning is thought to be the evolutionary reason for neoteny—the extended duration of human childhood (Gould, 1977). It is a fact of biology that human children do not—and cannot—grow up as solitary individuals; infants, for example, are totally dependent on parents for survival. Childhood is the time when we first make sense of and understand objects in the world, forge our first social bonds, and first learn how to express and read basic human emotions. It is the time that individual personalities and social styles first develop. It is normally parents who escort children through all those dramatic "firsts." In the view of many social theorists, notably Freud and Bowlby, the influence of these developments then reverberates through time; the child's first relationships with parents set the tone and style for most or all of the child's later social relationships (Sroufe & Fleeson, 1986).

Thus, parenting constitutes an all-encompassing ecology of the child's development. Parenting is defined in terms of its propensity to move children toward those goals that the culture deems important. Mothers and fathers (as well as siblings, other family members, and even children's nonfamilial daycare providers) guide the development of children via many direct and indirect means. Direct effects of parents on children are of two kinds: genetics and experience. Of course, it is biological parents who endow a significant and pervasive genetic makeup to their children . . . with its beneficial, or other, consequences for the growth of children's proclivities and abilities. In this way, parents are ultimately, if passively, responsible for some childhood stability and for some child effects.

In addition to genes, however, all prominent theories of human development put experience in the world as either the principal source of individual growth or as a major contributing component. It falls to parents (and other caregivers) to shape most, if not all, of young children's experiences, and parents influence child development both by the cognitions they hold and by the practices they exhibit. These, then, are the logical targets of positive interventions: parents' cognitions and parents' practices.

Parenting cognitions include perceptions about, attitudes toward, and knowledge of all aspects of parenting and childhood; and each plays a telling part. How parents see themselves vis-à-vis children leads them to express one or another kind of affect, thinking, or behavior in childrearing. More extraverted mothers and fathers express more positive affect toward their children and are more sensitive and cognitively stimulating at home (Belsky, Crnic, & Woodworth, 1995). How parents see childhood functions in the same way: Parents who believe that they can or cannot affect a child's temperament, intelligence and so forth will modify their parenting accordingly. Unfortunately, one in four parents in the USA thinks that a baby is born with a certain level of intelligence that cannot be increased or decreased by the parent's interactions with the baby (Zero-to-Three, 1997). Finally, how parents see their own children has its special consequences. Parents who regard their children as being difficult are less likely to pay attention or respond positively to their children's overtures. Their inattentiveness and nonresponsiveness can, in turn, foster further temperamental difficulties and cognitive shortcomings (Putnam, Sanson, & Rothbart, 2002).

Perhaps more salient in the phenomenology of childhood are parents' practices, the tangible experiences parents provide for children. The contents of parent–child interactions are varied, of course; some are compulsory, and some discretionary (Bornstein, 2006). A prominent and perhaps universal core of central domains of the childcare repertoire meets the tasks of child development and is geared to promote positive characteristics and values in children in the three domains of development identified earlier (Bornstein *et al.*, 2003). Nurturant caregiving meets the biological and health requirements of children, the physical domain of positive development. Nurturance in prerequisite to children's survival and wellbeing. Children's fruit and vegetable consumption is shaped not just by children's taste preferences but also by their mother's nutritional knowledge, her attitudes about the health benefits of eating more produce, and by her own consumption of fruit and vegetables (Galloway *et al.*, 2005). Social caregiving includes the variety of visual, verbal, affective, and physical behaviors parents use to engage children emotionally and manage their interpersonal exchanges, the social–emotional domain. Through sensitivity and responsiveness, positive feedback, openness and negotiation, listening, and emotional closeness, parents make their children feel valued, accepted, and approved of. Early parental support—acts of caring, acceptance, and assistance—constitute important long-term influences on adult mental health. A representative sample of 3000 adults, ages 25–74, from the National Survey of Midlife Development in the USA, 1995–1996, reported that parental support during early childhood was a principal factor associated with reduced levels of depressive symptoms and reduced levels of chronic illnesses in adulthood (Brim *et al.*, 1996); furthermore, the associations between early parental support and adult health persisted beyond the age of 70 (Shaw *et al.*, 2004). Didactic caregiving consists of the variety of strategies parents use to stimulate children to engage and understand the environment and to enter the world of learning, the cognitive domain. Didactics means introducing, mediating, and interpreting the external world to the child; teaching, describing, and demonstrating; as well as provoking or providing opportunities to observe, to imitate, and to learn. Activities as simple as reading books to children, for example, promote the development of language skills as well as later literacy (Arnold & Doctoroff, 2003; MacWhinney & Bornstein, 2003).

Nurturing, social, and didactic behaviors constitute direct parenting. Mothers and fathers indirectly influence their children's positive development in several ways as well. First, by virtue of their influence on one another, for example by marital support and communication. Women who report having supportive relationships with husbands (or grandparents or lovers) feel less harried and overwhelmed, have fewer competing demands on their time, and as a consequence can be more attentive, sensitive, and responsive to their children (Crockenberg, 1981).

Second, parents co-construct their child's environment; material caregiving includes the ways in which parents provision, organize, and arrange their child's home and local environments. Adults are responsible for the number and variety of inanimate objects (toys, books, tools) available to the child, the level of ambient stimulation, and overall safety and physical dimensions of children's experiences. Parents who provide their child with new toys and changes in room decorations are also likely to name those objects for the child, but physical parameters of the environment exert an influence on child language acquisition in and of themselves and not simply as a function of parental naming (Wachs & Chan, 1986). It is important that parents keep in mind that the amount of time children spend interacting with their inanimate surroundings rivals or exceeds the time children spend in direct social interaction with parents or others.

Third, parents are citizens. Through their politics, parents influence the social health or social toxicity of the environments their children inhabit (Garbarino, Vorrasi, & Kostelny, 2002). In turn, the contexts and environments parents make contribute in critical ways to augment or depreciate children's positive characteristics and values. Children need adult mentors in their homes, schools, and communities who live what they preach. As the novelist James Baldwin observed, children do not always do what we say but they almost always do what we do. If we lie, children will. If we give nothing to the poor, they won't. If we do not vote, they will not fulfill their civic responsibilities as adults. If we are violent and tolerate the glorification of violence, we should expect they will also. Ultimately, citizens shape the quality of daycare, the adequacy of schools, and the availability of opportunities in their community. Of course, economic security is also crucial. Poverty puts children at tremendous and pervasive disadvantage (McLoyd, 1998).

All these citizenship efforts begin and end around the dinner table and with grassroots institutions that labor in the good cause of children. In the USA, for example, Early Head Start funds community agencies to provide parenting support and child care/child development services as well as to help meet other family needs, including those for health care and assistance in moving toward "self-sufficiency." The Labour government in the UK has likewise supported parenting with the establishment of the Ministerial Group on the Family, chaired by the Home Secretary, the publication of the Consultation Document Support Families, the expansion of the telephone helpline, Parentline Plus, and the organization of the National Family and Parenting Institute as well as the Family Policy Unit in the Home Office, which has both grant-giving and policy-formulation roles (Coleman & Roker, 2001).

NATURE, NURTURE AND POSITIVE CHARACTERISTICS AND VALUES IN CHILDREN

With the idea of effective positive interventions in mind, it is important to recognize that adult influences on children are not straightforward but operate according to several complicating principles. Sorrowfully, it is not the case that overall level of stimulation directly affects children's overall level of functioning and compensates for selective deficiencies: Simply providing an adequate financial base, a big house, or the like does not guarantee a child's development of healthy eating habits, an empathic personality, verbal competence, or other positive characteristics and values. The *specificity principle* asserts that "specific experiences specific parents provide specific children at specific times exert effects in specific ways over specific aspects of child development" (Bornstein, 1989, 2006). This principle needs to be parsed attentively. For example, the extant literature suggests that maternal responsiveness, a parental behavior, is not global in its efficacy. When maternal responsiveness is decomposed into different dimensions (e.g., mothers' responding to their children's play versus responding to their children's language), for example, different components of responsiveness show domain-specific relations with specific child abilities. The responses of mothers to children's language (with expansions or imitations) are associated with advances in children's language, not play sophistication, just as responsiveness to play is related to advances in play not language (Paavola *et al.*, 2005; Tamis-LeMonda *et al.*, 1996). Parental responsiveness to distress, but not warmth, predicts better regulation of negative affect and greater empathy and prosocial responding; reciprocally, parental warmth, but not responsiveness to distress, predicts positive affect regulation (Davidov & Grusec, 2006; see also Del Carmen *et al.*, 1993; Roberts & Strayer, 1987). This mechanism specificity suggests that maternal responsiveness is more profitably conceived of as a multidimensional, modular, and specific construct (Bornstein, Tamis-LeMonda, & Hahn, 2005).

The specificity principle is apparently counterintuitive because a majority of new parents in the USA, for example, simplistically think that the more stimulation a baby receives, the better off the baby is (Zero-to-Three, 1997). In fact, parents and caregivers need to match carefully the amounts and kinds of stimulation they offer to their child's level of development, special interests, temperament, mood at the moment, and so forth. It is not, simplistically, that more or positive is best, but the fit must be right: between temperament and environment, for example (inhibited children do less well by some social criteria but they may also get into fewer dangerous scrapes). Developmental researchers and theoreticians today do not ask whether caregiving affects development but which caregiving experiences affect what aspects of child development when and how, and they are also interested to learn the ways in which individual children are so affected, as well as the ways individual children affect their own development.

These questions lead to the *transaction principle*, which asserts that experiences shape the characteristics and values of the child through time but, on the other hand, the characteristics and values of children shape their experiences (Sameroff, 1983). The transactional effects model postulates reciprocal and recurrent interactions over time between the organism and the environment. Children often influence which experiences they will be exposed to; children always interpret their experiences, and therefore ultimately how those experiences affect them (Roberts & DelVecchio, 2000; Scarr & Kidd, 1983). Child and parent bring distinctive characteristics and values to their mutual interactions, and child and parent alike change as a result of those interactions; both parent and child then enter future interactions as somewhat "different" individuals.

The intersection of the transaction principle and the specificity principle is a degree of uncertainty about how to intervene, and what can be safely predicted, about positive characteristics and values in children. There are many pathways to success. We expect some populations to fail miserably, just as those we think should have it made almost always show a surprising diversity of outcomes. Examples are teen parents or children born to crack-cocaine mothers or in other risky contexts who nevertheless succeed (Garmezy, 1993). Upper class suburban children sometimes manifest elevated levels of substance use, anxiety, and depression. Two sets of factors seem to be implicated: excessive pressures to achieve and isolation from parents—both literal and emotional (Currie, 2005; Luthar & Becker, 2002). As stated earlier, family wealth does not automatically confer either wisdom in parenting or equanimity of spirit. Mayer (1997) found large reductions in the estimated impact of parental income on achievement and behavior problems, leading her to conclude that much of the effect of parental income on children is spurious. Blau (1999) used data from the National Longitudinal Survey of Youth (NLSY) to estimate a number of models relating income and other aspects of parental family background to children's ability, achievement test scores, and behavior problems. In general, he found small and insignificant effects for current income and larger (though still modest) effects for long-term income. Of course, this is not to argue that household income has no effect; it may be especially meaningful at low socioeconomic status. If estimates by Duncan *et al.* (1998) are accurate, a $5 000 increment to income averaged over the first five years of a low-income child's life would produce nearly a half-year increase in completed schooling and a 70 % increase in the odds of finishing high school.

To detect regular relations between experience and environment as parenting antecedents, and positive characteristics and values as outcomes, we need to seek and to find the right combinations of independent and dependent variables. As a result, we don't want to throw parents out with the bath water.

Yet parenting is under "friendly fire" today on account of strong secular and historical trends operating in modern society. The litany is familiar: dual parental employment, the emergence of striking permutations in parenthood and the constellation of the family structure, in the rise of single-parent headed households, divorced and blended families, and teenage first-time parents. All reflect centrifugal forces on children, parents, and the family. This circumstance had led, unremarkably, to the argument that parents might matter very little in their child's development; rather peers, for example, make all the difference (Harris, 1998). This argument distorts a substantial amount of well-grounded research, is terribly myopic, and flies in the face of logic (Collins *et al.*, 2000). Few sentient parents want to abrogate their childrearing responsibilities. Quite the opposite, virtually all parents want only the best for their children. Against modern trends, we want to engage centripetal forces for children, parents, and family. Insofar as parents can be enlisted and empowered to provide children with experiences and environments that optimize child development, society can obviate after-the-fact remediation with "an ounce of proper parenting" so to speak.

PARENTING SUPPORTS FOR POSITIVE CHARACTERISTICS IN CHILDREN

About one month after giving birth, 79% of mothers are proud of their newfound status, and 72% have no disappointments about motherhood (Green & Kafetsios, 1997). So, parents start off pretty high. However, to parent effectively means not only being attitudinally predisposed to being a parent—it means knowing how children develop, and understanding and effecting appropriate parenting practices (Ginnott, 2003). Benjamin Spock (Spock & Needlman, 2004, p. 3) once assured the postwar generation of new parents "You know more than you think you do." Just as the baby is not a *tabula rasa*, the parent is not a *tabula rasa* either. Many parents today still need help, however. How can we best support positive parenting?

First, we apparently suffer a chronic undersupply of family time. Data from two US national surveys show that nearly half of parents report feeling they have too little time with their children (Nock & Kingston, 1988; Zick & Bryant, 1996). Longer work hours translate into fewer family hours. According to the Bureau of Labor Statistics (2004), that's two hours per day for mothers with children under six, and about one hour for fathers. Time with children is a precious commodity to parents, who rate talking with, caring for, taking trips, and playing games with their children as their four most enjoyable activities—higher than paid work, talking with friends, and many leisure pastimes (Juster & Stafford, 1985).

No one factor is determinative and trumps all others in support of parenting, however; in the "systems view" many factors—environment, experience, genetics, and biology as well as their dynamic transaction—influence outcome. Understanding the role of each improves explanatory power. Systems theories are also "nonblaming," but they are also less linear and less cause-and-effect oriented than are traditional linear models in developmental science.

Beyond family time, over which many may have little control, there are abundant avenues for more feasible interventions aimed at promoting positive parenting and children's wellbeing. Some programs promote child development directly (such as those that target early reading); others focus on activities that influence child development indirectly through improving parents' lives or actions. The goals of most parent-based strategies are to enhance either parenting skills or resources in hopes that parents will be better positioned to nurture, teach, or in other ways provide for their children, and in so doing enhance their children's positive growth and development. There are generally two types of parenting programs—parenting education and parenting management training. Management training programs are usually designed for parents of children with problem behaviors. A successful example of parenting management training is Webster-Stratton's group discussion videotape program (Webster-Stratton, Kolpacoff, & Hollinsworth, 1988).

Parent support and education interventions grew out of the belief that early experience influences later ability and that "0 to 3" is critical in child development. Often, parents do not adequately stimulate, model, and support their children's development, and therefore prepare their children inadequately for school. Many parenting education programs seek to improve parents' general knowledge about parenting and child development. They consist of a range of activities, including the provision of information, prevention strategies, empowerment initiatives, and training. Parent support and education is now an established branch of social services. Some programs are universal; others target groups defined as being in special need. In the final analysis, parent intervention decisions are best made according to local circumstances, specific needs, and the opportunities available. It may be ideal to use both targeted and universal approaches simultaneously. Some approaches to parent support and education affect parenting, but research designs, analytic strategies, and/or measures used also often obscure effects (Halpern, 2004). For example, programs vary in their theories about parenting and therefore which dimensions of parenting they target and how they assess those dimensions. Parenting is difficult to define and to alter, and so parent support and education programs have had only modest effects. Furthermore, these programs serve mothers who are multiply disadvantaged by youth, poverty, and the lack of basic education. Services themselves are often low in quality. Sometimes parenting is a shared responsibility, raising questions about who constitutes the most appropriate focus of intervention efforts. Parenting education and training programs make demands on the time and effort of parents. All that said, a review of 24 parent-focused home interventions (for low-SES children) showed that 19 produced favorable effects on parenting, including more sensitive parenting and a higher-quality home environment (Brooks-Gunn, Berlin, & Fuligni, 2000).

More child-focused programs show better parenting outcomes and children show more optimal growth and development. Two studies have compared the benefits of combined parent and child programs with the benefits of child- and parent-only programs (Kazdin, Siegal, & Bass, 1992; Webster-Stratton & Hammond, 1997). Parent-only and child-only programs benefit children, but the benefits of the combined approach exceed both. What appears to succeed best, however, is a "process" approach that attempts to focus on the complexity of parenting, particular programs, particular program staff, or particular families, all in a particular community context. It assumes that families respond to a program and its staff in specific ways based on their specific characteristics, motives, and needs.

To fathom the nature of effective interventions and parent–child relationships requires a multivariate and dynamic stance. It is only by taking multiple factors into consideration that we can appreciate individual, dyadic, and family level contributions to child development and accurately reflect the embeddedness of the family within its many relevant extrafamilial systems. Some positive characteristics and values possess a partly biological basis. At the same time, children are susceptible to influences from outside the family, such as peer dynamics, and from inside the family—their own parents.

The dynamic aspect involves the different developmental trajectories of individuals in the family. As all parents know, childrearing is akin to trying to "hit a moving target", the ever-changing child developing in fits and starts at his or her own pace. Parents cannot use the same behaviors to reach particular goals for their children at different points in childhood: "Keeping an eye on" a toddler is appropriate when the child is beginning to walk, but parents may need to share notes with the parents of their teen's friends to maintain equivalent monitoring. In order to exert appropriate influence and guidance, parents must constantly and effectively adjust their interactions, cognitions, emotions, affections, and strategies to the age-graded activities, abilities, and experiences of their children. Parenting is time consuming and challenging. From the start, parenthood is a 168-hour-a-week job. Sigmund Freud listed bringing up children as one of the three "impossible professions"—the other two being governing nations and psychoanalysis.

The multiple pathways and dynamic systems of parenting and child development also make for quite a messy situation. Practitioners and researchers, for their part, have to develop paradigms and methodologies to accommodate this chaos; this perspective makes the development and implementation of prevention and intervention programs and policy "nightmarish." Some will fail. Yet, it is only by addressing this complexity and chaos in process research that we can hope to understand more that is valid about families and parenting, children and development.

The good news is that there is ample evidence that we can improve *all* of the positive characteristics and values listed at the start of this chapter. Contemporary research in lifespan developmental science (Baltes, Lindenberger, & Staudinger, 1998), bioecological development (Bronfenbrenner, 2005), and life-course sociology (Elder, 1998) demonstrates that we can optimize individual and group change by altering bidirectional relations between individuals and their ecologies to capitalize on developmental plasticity. Contemporary models of human development eschew the reduction of individual and social behavior to fixed genetic influences, and instead stress plasticity of human beings and the adaptibility of human development. They argue that the potential for systematic change in behavior exists as a consequence of mutually influential relations between the developing person and his or her biology, psychological characteristics, family, community, culture, physical and designed ecology, and historical niche.

To be concrete, intelligence is inherited in part, but to be inherited does not mean to be immutable or nonchangeable. Longitudinal studies of intelligence show that individuals definitely change over time (Neisser *et al.*, 1996). Even heritable traits depend on learning for their expression, and they are subject to environmental effects. Moreover, even small changes in IQ can result in substantial changes for the individual as, for example, in lifetime earnings. Krueger (2003) estimated that one-fifth of a standard deviation increase in tests scores from the Tennessee STAR class-size experiment increased future earnings by between $5 000 and $50 000.

Fatalists accept the environment they live in. Others take the personal, social, and political steps to construct environments with appropriate stimulation for children, to organize children's daycare, to promote children's associations with positive peers, to make sure their community affords good schooling and to enroll children in growth promoting extracurricular activities (church or temple, boy or girl scouts, little league or soccer).

Consider homework (Pomerantz, Wang, & Ng, 2005). Parenting is a strong predictor of children's academic performance and, when parents bridge the gap between home and school, children experience benefits in their psychological functioning as well as achievement (Epstein & Sanders, 2002). Parenting is an inherently affective endeavor, and homework is affective and (usually negative) emotion-laden as well (Fuligni, Yip, & Tseng, 2002; Leone & Richards, 1989). Mothers, too, report increased negative affect on days their children have homework, and parents' negativity can have detrimental effects for children: It can undermine their children's motivation and their intrinsic interest in school (see Estrada *et al.*, 1987; Hokoda & Fincham, 1995; Nolen-Hoeksema *et al.*, 1995) and convey that the challenges of schoolwork are distressing (Nolen-Hoeksema *et al.*, 1995) and that their children are insignificant. However, mothers helping with homework do not report decreased positive affect—positive and negative affect are independent.

Rather, parents' positive involvement in their children's homework can afford a structured context in which to spend time with children and gain knowledge about a significant area of children's lives, and work together with children to overcome obstacles, enjoy the gratifying process, and strengthen the bond between them and their children (Levin *et al.*, 1997). They can convey to children that, although schoolwork can be frustrating, it is also a positive endeavor, and they can signal that they are available to support their children during times of difficulty. In short, so long as parents stay positive on days they provide homework assistance, their irritation and frustration is not problematic for children. When parents get involved in their children's homework, a key goal is to keep the interaction fun, loving, and positive, despite any irritation and annoyance both parent and child may feel.

SCIENCE, POLICY, AND VALUES

Social science can be a positive force for understanding and promoting the highest qualities of personal and civic life. The Positive Youth Development movement is geared to making young people stronger and more productive as well as actualizing latent human potential (Peterson & Seligman, 2004).

Human development is influenced by genetic endowment, by early experiences, and by the current contexts in which individuals adapt. To explain development and to intervene effectively with children require conceptualizing development appropriately as a function of past and current influences and efforts to adapt to them. Policy needs to focus on interventions that attempt to cure sick individuals, of course; but policy also needs to provide for experiences that are valuable in their own right because they improve current conditions and optimize strengths. In short, "models of care" are just as important as "models of cure."

Are these views of positive parenting and positive development new? Are they parochial? I think not. We all readily recognize the *tipi* of the North American Plains Indians—a portable, conical structure, the *tipi* is covered with buffalo hides sewn together with animal sinew around a set of leaning poles. However, the meaning of the *tipi*'s architectural symbolism is less well known. The Plains Indians' everyday dwellings instantiated a system of positive developmental science. Each of the 14 poles of the traditional *tipi* represented a positive characteristic or value: obedience, respect, humility, happiness, love, faith, kinship, cleanliness, thankfulness, sharing, strength, good childrearing, hope, and ultimate protection. In other words, Plains Indian parents of that era enveloped their children with positive messages. The *tipi* structure was an ever present teaching tool and reminder in their lives. Similarly, parents in Korea try to promote 12 virtues of "filial piety" or *Hyo* 효 in their children. These cultural factors set the frame for Korean behavior and life styles, and *Hyo* is the most essential element, which shapes parent–child relationships and parenting. The history of this concept goes back more than 1500 years. *Hyo* reflects bidirectional, interpersonal responsibility between parents and children, and traditionally in Korea *Hyo* has been the basis of children's education. It is "the foundation of all virtues, and all lessons come from it." Some of the virtues of children's filial piety include *Gam-sa* (gratitude/appreciation), *Soo-shin* (self-cultivation), and *Jull-ze* (moderation/controlling of desire). In short, historically and across cultures, people have felt the need to identify and promote positive characteristics and values in children.

Becoming a parent is a time of joy, and presents people with a developmental opportunity for significant personal growth. Several international surveys show that interactions with one's children top the list of enjoyable activities among parents, followed by going on trips, being with friends, and working at one's job (Flood, 1997; Juster, 1985). (Grocery shopping and cleaning the house are rated lowest among 28 household activities.) Feelings of competence as a parent constitute a highly common aspect of the "self" desired by adults (Markus, Cross, & Wurf, 1990). But, rearing a child with positive characteristics and values is a challenging human activity, and it will be as complex, demanding, and fulfilling tomorrow as it is today. This mystical process cannot be reduced to a single essential ingredient. However, we know of at least one crucial factor that determines whether a child succeeds or fails in life: It is the presence of caring adults, usually parents.

CONCLUSIONS

As adolescents are "launched" from the nest, what do we most want for them? Parenthood ultimately means facilitating a child's optimism and happiness, self-confidence and purpose, capacity for intimacy and friendships with peers, adaptive choices and achievement motivation, pleasure in play and work and continuing academic success and fulfillment—all positive characteristics and values. Take the importance of optimism. Optimists tend to do better in school than pessimists; optimists also perform well at work and in sports. Their physical and mental health tends to be better, and they may even live longer than pessimists (Seligman, 1991). Positive affective states are protective, and optimists tend to cope with adverse situations in more adaptive ways (Scheier & Carver, 1993). The rate of cardiovascular recovery after stress is more rapid in individuals who express such positive emotionality (Tugade & Fridrickson, 2004). Research in positive psychology documents the significance of positive wellbeing to creativity, leadership, and the realization of potential (Baylis, Huppert, & Kaverne, 2004; Ryan & Deci, 2001). Adolescents who are optimistic tend to be less angry (Puskar *et al.*, 1999) and abuse substances less often (Carvajal *et al.*, 1998). Conceptualization and measurement of positive characteristics and values in children has lagged behind that of adults (Spieth & Harris, 1996). Yet, childhood may be the optimal time to promote healthy attitudes, behavior, adjustment, and to prevent problems (Roberts & Peterson, 1984). Research is needed to determine more precisely the sequence of development and what types of experiences promote optimism or other positive characteristics and values in children. It is only through complex, responsive, and sophisticated parenting and interventions that parent and family, community and environment can be brought to bear on the route and terminus of a child's acquisition of positive characteristics and values, like optimism. That they challenge us does not mean we should shrink from them. Effects have causes.

Positive social science in this century will have the prevention of illness as a salutatory indirect effect, for there are many human strengths that most likely buffer against, and compensate for, "disorder, deficit, and disability": optimism, courage, interpersonal skill, hope, responsibility, future-mindedness, honesty, and perseverance, to name several. But positive social science will have as its direct effect promoting those positive characteristics and values we most desire to see in the next generation.

REFERENCES

Arnold, D. H. & Doctoroff, G. L. (2003). The early education of socioeconomically disadvantaged children. *Annual Review of Psychology, 54*, 517–545.

Baltes, P. B., Lindenberger, U., & Staudinger, U. M. (1998). Life-span theory in developmental psychology. In W. Damon (series ed.) & R. M. Lerner (vol. ed.), *Handbook of Child Psychology: Vol. 1. Theoretical Models of Human Development* (5th edn, pp. 1029–1144). New York: John Wiley.

Baylis, N., Huppert, F. A., & Kaverne, B. (2004). *The Science of Well-being*. London: Royal Society.

Belsky, J., Crnic, K., & Woodworth, S. (1995). Personality and parenting: Exploring the mediating role of transient mood and daily hassles. *Journal of Personality, 63*, 905–929.

Bennett, W. J. (1993). *The Book of Virtues*. New York: Simon & Schuster.

Benson, P. L. (1993). *The Troubled Journey: A Portrait of Sixth–Twelfth Grade Youth*. Minneapolis: Search Institute.

Blau, D. M. (1999). The effect of income on child development. *The Review of Economics and Statistics, 81(2)*, 261–276.

Bornstein, M. H. (1989). Between caretakers and their young: Two modes of interaction and their consequences for cognitive growth. In M. H. Bornstein & J. S. Bruner (eds), *Interaction in Human Development* (pp. 197–214). Hillsdale, NJ: Lawrence Erlbaum Associates.

Bornstein, M. H. (2006). Parenting science and practice. In I. E. Sigel & K. A. Renninger (eds), W. Damon & R. M. Lerner (series eds), *Handbook of Child Psychology: Vol. 4. Child Psychology and Practice* (6th edn, pp. 893–949). New York: Wiley.

Bornstein, M. H., Davidson, L., Keyes, C. M. *et al.* (2003). *Well-being: Positive Development Across the Life Course*. Mahwah, NJ: Lawrence Erlbaum Associates.

Bornstein, M. H., Tamis-LeMonda, C. S., & Hahn, C.-H. (2005). *Maternal Responsiveness to Very Young Children of Three Ages: Longitudinal Analysis of a Multidimensional, Modular, and Specific Parenting Construct*. Unpublished manuscript, National Institute of Child Health and Human Development.

Bridges, L. J. (2003a). Coping as an element of developmental well-being. In M. H. Bornstein, L. Davidson, C. M. Keyes *et al.* (eds), *Well-being: Positive Development Across the Life Course* (pp. 155–166). Mahwah, NJ: Lawrence Erlbaum Associates.

Bridges, L. J. (2003b). Autonomy as an element of developmental well-being. In M. H. Bornstein, L. Davidson, C. M. Keyes *et al.* (eds), *Well-being: Positive Development Across the Life Course* (pp. 167–175). Mahwah, NJ: Lawrence Erlbaum Associates.

Brim, O. G., Baltes, P. B., Bumpass, L. L. *et al.* (1996). *National Survey of Midlife Development in the United States (MIDUS), 1995–1996*. Boston: Harvard Medical School, Department of Health Care Policy.

Bronfenbrenner, U. (ed.) (2005). *Making Human Beings Human: Bioecological Perspectives on Human Development*. Thousand Oaks, CA: Sage.

Brooks-Gunn, J., Berlin, L. J., & Fuligni, A. S. (2000). Early childhood intervention programs: What about the family? In J. P. Shonkoff & S. J. Meisels (eds), *Handbook of Early Childhood Intervention* (2nd edn, pp. 549–588). Cambridge: Cambridge University Press.

Bukowski, W. M. (2003). Peer relationships In M. H. Bornstein, L. Davidson, C. M. Keyes *et al.* (eds), *Well-being: Positive Development Across the Life Course* (pp. 221–233). Mahwah, NJ: Lawrence Erlbaum Associates.

Bureau of Labor Statistics (2004). Time use survey. Washington, DC: United States Department of Labor. Available from http://www.bls.gov/tus/, accessed 27 September 2007.

Carvajal, S. C., Clair, S. D., Nash, S. G., & Evans, R. I. (1998). Relating optimism, hope, and self-esteem to social influences in deterring substance use in adolescence. *Journal of Social and Clinical Psychology, 17*, 443–465.

Coleman, J. & Roker, D. (2001). Setting the scene: Parenting and public policy. In J. Coleman & D. Roker (eds), *Supporting Parents of Teenagers: A Handbook for Professionals* (pp. 7–21). London: Jessica Kingsley.

Collins, W. A., Maccoby, E. E., Steinberg, L. *et al.* (2000). Contemporary research on parenting: The case for nature and nurture. *American Psychologist, 55*, 218–232.

Connor, J. M. (2003). Physical activity and well-being. In M. H. Bornstein, L. Davidson, C. M. Keyes *et al.* (eds), *Well-being: Positive Development Across the Life Course* (pp. 65–79). Mahwah, NJ: Lawrence Erlbaum Associates.

Connor, J. M. & Dewey, J. E. (2003). Reproductive health. In M. H. Bornstein, L. Davidson, C. M. Keyes *et al.* (eds), *Well-being: Positive Development across the Life Course* (pp. 99–107). Mahwah, NJ: Lawrence Erlbaum Associates.

Cox, M. J. & Harter, K. S. M. (2003). Parent-child relationships. In M. H. Bornstein, L. Davidson, C. M. Keyes *et al.* (Eds.), *Well-being: Positive Development Across the Life Course* (pp. 191–204). Mahwah, NJ: Lawrence Erlbaum Associates.

Crockenberg, S. B. (1981). Infant irritability, mother responsiveness, and social support influences on the security of infant-mother attachment. *Child Development, 52*, 857–865.

Currie, E. (2005). *The Road to Whatever: Middle-class Culture and the Crisis of Adolescence.* New York: Metropolitan Books, Henry Holt.

Davidov, M. & Grusec, J. E. (2006). Untangling the effects of parental responsiveness to distress and warmth on child outcomes. *Child Development, 77*(1), 44–58.

Del Carmen, R., Pedersen, F. A., Huffman, L. C., & Bryan, Y. E. (1993). Dyadic distress management predicts subsequent security of attachment. *Infant Behavior and Development, 16*, 131–147.

Diener, M. L. & Lucas, R. E. (2004). Adults' desires for children's emotion across 48 countries: Associations with individual and national characteristics. *Journal of Cross-Cultural Psychology, 35*, 525–547.

Duncan, G. J., Yeung, W. J., Brooks-Gunn, J., & Smith, J. R. (1998). How much does childhood poverty affect the life chances of children? *American Sociological Review, 63*, 406–423.

Eisenberg, N. (2003). Prosocial behavior, empathy, and sympathy. In M. H. Bornstein, L. Davidson, C. M. Keyes *et al.* (eds), *Well-being: Positive Development Across the Life Course* (pp. 253–265). Mahwah, NJ: Lawrence Erlbaum Associates.

Elder, G. H., Jr. (1998). The life course and human development. In W. Damon (series ed.) & R. M. Lerner (vol. ed.), *Handbook of Child Psychology: Vol. 1. Theoretical Models of Human Development* (5th edn, pp. 939–991). New York: John Wiley.

Epstein, J. L. & Sanders, M. G. (2002). Family, school, and community partnerships. In M. H. Bornstein (ed.), *Handbook of Parenting Vol. 5 Practical Parenting* (2nd edn, pp. 407–437). Mahwah, NJ: Lawrence Erlbaum Associates.

Estrada, P., Arsenio, W. F., Hess, R. D., & Holloway, S. D. (1987). Affective quality of the mother-child relationship: Longitudinal consequences for children's school-relevant cognitive functioning. *Developmental Psychology, 23*, 210–215.

Fleming, A. (1929). On the antibacterial action of cultures of a penicillium, with special reference to their use in the isolation of B. influenzae. *British Journal of Experimental Pathology, 10*, 226–236.

Flood, L. (1997). *Household, Market, and Nonmarket Activities: Procedures and Codes for the 1993 Time-use Survey*. Uppsala, Sweden: Uppsala University Department of Economics.

Fuligni, A. J., Yip, T., & Tseng, V. (2002). The impact of family obligation on the daily activities and psychological well-being of Chinese American adolescents. *Child Development, 73*, 302–314.

Galloway, A. T., Fiorito, L., Lee, Y., & Birch, L. L. (2005). Parental pressure, dietary patterns, and weight status among girls who are 'picky eaters'. *Journal of the American Dietetic Association, 105*, 541–548.

Garbarino, J., Vorrasi, J. A., & Kostelny, K. (2002). Parenting and public policy. In M. H. Bornstein (ed.), *Handbook of Parenting Vol. 5 Practical Parenting* (2 edn, pp. 487–507). Mahwah, NJ: Lawrence Erlbaum Associates.

Garmezy, N. (1993). Vulnerability and resilience. In D. C. Funder, R. D. Parke, C. Tomlinson-Keasey, & K. Widaman (eds), *Studying Lives through Time: Personality and Development* (pp. 377–398). Washington, DC, US: American Psychological Association.

Ginnott, H. (with A. Ginott & H. W. Goddard, eds) (2003). *Between Parent and Child*. New York: Three Rivers Press.

Gould S. J. (1977). *Ontogeny and Phylogeny*. Cambridge, MA: Harvard University Press.

Graziano, W. G. & Tobin, R. M. (2003). Emotion regulation from infancy through adolescence. In M. H. Bornstein, L. Davidson, C. M. Keyes *et al.* (eds), *Well-being: Positive Development across the Life Course* (pp. 139–154). Mahwah, NJ: Lawrence Erlbaum Associates.

Green, J. M. & Kafetsios, K. (1997). Positive experiences of early motherhood: predictive variables from a longitudinal study. *Journal of Reproductive and Infant Psychology, 15*, 141–157.

Halle, T. G. (2003). Emotional development and well-being. In M. H. Bornstein, L. Davidson, C. M. Keyes *et al.* (eds), *Well-being: Positive Development Across the Life Course* (pp. 125–138). Mahwah, NJ: Lawrence Erlbaum Associates.

Halpern, R. (2004). Parent support and education: Past history, future prospects. *Applied Research in Child Development, 6*, 1–12.

Harris, J. R. (1998). *The Nurture Assumption*. New York: Free Press.

Hart, D., Burock, D., London, B., & Miraglia, A. (2003). Moral development in childhood. In M. H. Bornstein, L. Davidson, C. M. Keyes *et al.* (eds), *Well-being: Positive Development Across the Life Course* (pp. 355–370). Mahwah, NJ: Lawrence Erlbaum Associates.

Hill, C. R. & Stafford, F. P. (1980). Parental care of children: Time diary estimates of quantity, predictability, and variety. *Journal of Human Resources, 15*, 219–239.

Hokoda, A. & Fincham, F. D. (1995). Origins of children's helpless and mastery achievement patterns in the family. *Journal of Educational Psychology, 87*, 375–385.

Jennings, K. D. & Dietz, L. J. (2003). Mastery motivation and goal persistence in young children. In M. H. Bornstein, L. Davidson, C. M. Keyes *et al.* (eds), *Well-being: Positive Development Across the Life Course* (pp. 295–309). Mahwah, NJ: Lawrence Erlbaum Associates.

Juster, F. T. (1985). In F. T. Juster, & F. Stafford (eds), *Time, Goods and Well-being* (pp. 397–414). Ann Arbor, MI: Institute for Social Research.

Juster, F. T. & Stafford, F. P. (1985). Preferences for work and leisure. In F. T. Juster & F. P. Stafford (eds), *Time, Goods and Well-being* (pp. 333–351). Ann Arbor, MI: Institute for Social Research.

Kail, R. V. (2003). Information processing and memory. In M. H. Bornstein, L. Davidson, C. M. Keyes *et al.* (eds), *Well-being: Positive Development across the Life Course* (pp. 269–279). Mahwah, NJ: Lawrence Erlbaum Associates.

Kazdin, A. E., Siegal, T. C., & Bass, D. (1992). Cognitive problem-solving skills training and parent management training in the treatment of anti-social behavior in children. *Journal of Consulting and Clinical Psychology, 60*, 733–747.

Krueger, A. B. (2003). Economic considerations and class size. *The Economic Journal, 113*, 34–63.

Leavitt, C. H., Tonniges, T. F., & Rogers, M. F. (2003). Good nutrition—the imperative for positive development. In M. H. Bornstein, L. Davidson, C. M. Keyes *et al.* (eds), *Well-being: Positive Development across the Life Course* (pp. 35–49). Mahwah, NJ: Lawrence Erlbaum Associates.

Leone, C. M. & Richards, M. H. (1989). Classwork and homework in early adolescence: the ecology of achievement. *Journal of Youth and Adolescence, 18*, 531–548.

Lerner, R. M., Fisher, C. B., & Weinberg, R. A. (2000). Toward a science for and of the people: promoting civil society through the application of developmental science. *Child Development, 71*, 11–20.

Levin, I., Levy-Shiff, R., Appelbaum-Peled, T. *et al.* (1997). Antecedents and consequences of maternal involvement in children's homework: A longitudinal analysis. *Journal of Applied Developmental Psychology, 18*, 207–227.

Luthar, S. S. & Becker, B. E. (2002). Privileged but pressured: A study of affluent youth. *Child Development, 73*, 1593–1610.

MacWhinney, B. & Bornstein, M. H. (2003). Language and literacy. In M. H. Bornstein, L. Davidson, C. M. Keyes *et al.* (eds), *Well-being: Positive Development across the Life Course* (pp. 331–339). Mahwah, NJ: Lawrence Erlbaum Associates.

Markus, H., Cross, S., & Wurf, E. (1990). The role of the self-system in competence. In R. J. Sternberg & J. J. Kolligian (eds), *Competence Considered* (pp. 205–225). New Haven, CT: Yale University Press.

Masten, A. S. (2001). Ordinary magic: Resilience processes in development. *American Psychologist, 56*, 227–238.

Masten, A. S. & Coatsworth, J. D. (1998). The development of competence in favorable and unfavorable environments: Lessons from research on successful children. *American Psychologist, 53*, 205–220.

Mayer, S. (1997). *What Money Can't Buy: The Effects of Parental Income on Children's Outcomes.* Cambridge, MA: Harvard University Press.

McLoyd, V. C. (1998). Children in poverty: Development, public policy, and practice. In I. E. Sigel & K. A. Renninger (eds), W. Damon (series ed.), *Handbook of Child Psychology: Vol. 4. Child Psychology in Practice* (5th edn, pp. 135–208). New York: Wiley.

Moore, K. A. (1997). Criteria for indicators of child well-being. In R. M. Hauser, B. V. Brown, & W. R. Prosser (eds), *Indicators of Children's Well-being* (pp. 36–44). New York: Russell Sage Foundation.

Neisser, U., Boodoo, G., Bourchard, T. J. *et al.* (1996). Intelligence: knowns and unknowns. *American Psychologist, 51*, 77–101.

Nock, S. L. & Kingston, P. W. (1988). Time with children: The impact of couples' work-time commitments. *Social Forces, 67*, 59–85.

Nolen-Hoeksema, S., Wolfson, A., Mumme, D., & Guskin, K. (1995). Helplessness in children of depressed and nondepressed mothers. *Developmental Psychology, 31*, 377–387.

Paavola, L., Kunnair, S., Moilanen, I., & Lehtihalmes, M. (2005). The functions of maternal verbal responses to prelinguistic infants as predictors of early communicative and linguistic development. *First Language, 25,* 173–195.

Peterson, C. & Seligman, M. E. P. (2004). *Character Strengths and Virtues: A Handbook and Classification.* Washington, DC: American Psychological Association.

Plank, S. B. & MacIver, D. J. (2003). Educational achievement. In M. H. Bornstein, L. Davidson, C. M. Keyes *et al.* (eds), *Well-being: Positive Development across the Life Course* (pp. 341–354). Mahwah, NJ: Lawrence Erlbaum Associates.

Pomerantz, E. M., Wang, Q., & Ng. F. F-Y. (2005). Mothers' affect in the homework context: The importance of staying positive. *Developmental Psychology, 41,* 414–427.

Puskar, K. R., Sereika, S. M., Lamb, J. *et al.* (1999). Optimism and its relationship to depression, coping, anger, and life events in rural adolescents. *Issues in Mental Health Nursing, 20,* 115–130.

Putnam, S. P., Sanson, A. V., & Rothbart, M. K. (2002). Child temperament and parenting. In M. H. Bornstein (Ed.), *Handbook of Parenting Vol. 1 Children and Parenting* (2nd edn, pp. 255–277). Mahwah, NJ: Lawrence Erlbaum Associates.

Roberts, B. W. & DelVecchio, W. F. (2000). The rank-order consistency of personality traits from childhood to old age: A quantitative review of longitudinal studies. *Psychological Bulletin, 126,* 3–25.

Roberts, M. C. & Peterson, L. (1984). Prevention models: Theoretical and practical implications. In M. C. Roberts & L. Peterson (eds), *Prevention of Problems in Childhood: Psychological Research and Applications* (pp. 1–39). New York: Wiley-Interscience.

Roberts, W. & Strayer, J. (1987). Parents' responses to the emotional distress of their children: relations with children's competence. *Developmental Psychology, 23,* 415–422.

Roth, J. L. & Brooks-Gunn, J. (2003a). What is a youth development program? Identification and defining principles. In F. Jacobs, D. Wertlieb, & R. M. Lerner (vol. eds), *Enhancing the Life Chances of Youth and Families: Public Service Systems and Public Policy Perspectives: Vol. 2. Handbook of Applied Developmental Science: Promoting Positive Child, Adolescent, and Family Development through Research, Policies, and Programs* (pp. 197–223). Thousand Oaks, CA: Sage.

Roth, J. L. & Brooks-Gunn, J. (2003b). What exactly is a youth development program? Answers from research and practice. *Applied Developmental Science, 7,* 94–111.

Roth, J. L., Brooks-Gunn, J., Murray, L., & Foster, W. (1998). Promoting healthy adolescents: Synthesis of youth development program evaluations. *Journal of Research on Adolescence, 8,* 423–459.

Ryan, R. M. & Deci, E. L. (2001). On happiness and human potentials: A review of research on hedonic and eudaimonic well-being. *Annual Review of Psychology, 52,* 141–166.

Sameroff, A. J. (1983). Developmental systems: Contexts and evolution. In W. Kessen (ed.), P. H. Mussen (series ed.), *Handbook of Child Psychology: Vol. 1. History, Theory, and Methods* (pp. 237–294). New York: Wiley.

Scales, P. C., Benson, P. L., Leffert, N., & Blyth, D. A. (2000). The contribution of developmental assets to the prediction of thriving among adolescents. *Applied Developmental Science, 4,* 27–46.

Scarr, S. & Kidd, K. K. (1983). Developmental behavior genetics. In M. M. Haith & J. J. Campos (eds), P. H. Mussen (series ed.), *Handbook of Child Psychology: Vol. 2. Infancy and Developmental Psychobiology* (pp. 345–433). New York: Wiley.

Scheier, M. F. & Carver, C. S. (1993). On the power of positive thinking: The benefits of being optimistic. *Current Directions in Psychological Science, 2,* 26–30.

Schwartz, S. H. (1994). Are there universal aspects in the structure and contents of human values? *Journal of Social Issues, 50,* 19–45.

Schwartz, S. H. & Bardi, A. (2001). Value hierarchies across cultures: Taking a similarities perspective. *Journal of Cross-Cultural Psychology, 32,* 268–290.

Schwartz, S. H. & Sagiv, L. (1995). Identifying culture-specifics in the content and structure of values. *Journal of Cross-Cultural Psychology, 26*, 92–116.

Seligman, M. E. P. (1991). *Learned Optimism*. New York: Knopf.

Seligman, M. E. P. & Csikszentmihalyi, M. (2000). Positive psychology: An introduction. *American Psychologist, 55*, 5–14.

Shaw, B. A., Krause, N., Chatters, L. M. *et al.* (2004). Emotional support from parents early in life, aging, and health. *Psychology and Aging, 19*, 4–12.

Siegler, R. S. (2003). Thinking and intelligence. In M. H. Bornstein, L. Davidson, C. M. Keyes *et al.* (eds), *Well-being: Positive Development across the Life Course* (pp. 311–320). Mahwah, NJ: Lawrence Erlbaum Associates.

Sleet, D. A. & Mercy, J. A. (2003). Promotion of safety, security, and well-being. In M. H. Bornstein, L. Davidson, C. M. Keyes *et al.* (eds), *Well-being: Positive Development across the Life Course* (pp. 81–97). Mahwah, NJ: Lawrence Erlbaum Associates.

Smith, D. C. (2003). Problem solving as an element of developmental well-being. In M. H. Bornstein, L. Davidson, C. M. Keyes *et al.* (eds), *Well-being: Positive Development across the Life Course* (pp. 321–330). Mahwah, NJ: Lawrence Erlbaum Associates.

Spieth, L. E. & Harris, C. V. (1996). Assessment of quality-of-life outcomes in children and adolescents: An integrative review. *Journal of Pediatric Psychology, 21*, 175–193.

Spock, B. & Needlman, R. (2004). *Dr Spock's Baby and Child Care* (8th edition). New York: Simon & Schuster.

Sroufe, L. A. & Fleeson, J. (1986). Attachment and the construction of relationships. In W. Hartup & Z. Rubin (eds), *Relationships and Development* (pp. 51–71). Hillsdale, NJ: Erlbaum.

Tamis-LeMonda, C. S., Bornstein, M. H., Baumwell, L., & Damast, A. M. (1996). Responsive parenting in the second year: specific influences on children's language and play. *Early Development and Parenting, 5*, 173–183.

Tonniges, T. F. & Leavitt, C. H. (2003). Preventive health care in early childhood and through the life span. In M. H. Bornstein, L. Davidson, C. M. Keyes *et al.* (eds), *Well-being: Positive Development across the Life Course* (pp. 51–64). Mahwah, NJ: Lawrence Erlbaum Associates.

Tugade, M. M. & Fridrickson, B. L. (2004). Resilient individuals use positive emotions to bounce back from negative emotional experiences. *Journal of Personality and Social Psychology, 86*, 320–333.

Volling, B. L. (2003). Sibling relationships. In M. H. Bornstein, L. Davidson, C. M. Keyes *et al.* (eds) *Well-being: Positive Development across the Life Course* (pp. 205–220). Mahwah, NJ: Lawrence Erlbaum Associates.

Wachs, T. D. & Chan, A. (1986). Specificity of environmental action, as seen in environmental correlates of infants' communication performance. *Child Development, 57*, 1464–1474.

Webster-Stratton, C. & Hammond, M. (1997). Treating children with early onset conduct problems: a comparison of child and parent training interventions. *Journal of Consulting and Clinical Psychology, 65*, 93–109.

Webster-Stratton, C., Kolpacoff, M., & Hollinsworth, T. (1988). Self-administered videotape therapy for families with conduct problem children: comparison with two cost-effective treatments and a control group. *Journal of Consulting and Clinical Psychology, 56*, 558–566.

Wentworth, N. & Witryol, S. L. (2003). Curiosity, exploration, and novelty-seeking. In M. H. Bornstein, L. Davidson, C. M. Keyes *et al.* (eds), *Well-being: Positive Development across the Life Course* (pp. 281–294). Mahwah, NJ: Lawrence Erlbaum Associates.

Winner, E. (2003). Creativity and talent. In M. H. Bornstein, L. Davidson, C. M. Keyes *et al.* (eds), *Well-being: Positive Development across the Life Course* (pp. 371–380). Mahwah, NJ: Lawrence Erlbaum Associates.

Zaff, J. F. & Hair, E. C. (2003). Positive development of the self: self-concept, self-esteem, and identity. In M. H. Bornstein, L. Davidson, C. M. Keyes *et al.* (eds), *Well-being: Positive development across the Life Course* (pp. 235–251). Mahwah, NJ: Lawrence Erlbaum Associates.
Zero-to-Three (1997). *Key Findings for a Nationwide Survey among Parents of Zero to Three Year Olds*. Washington, DC: Peter D. Hart Research Associates.
Zick, C. D. & Bryant, W. K. (1996). A new look at parents' time spent in child care: primary and secondary time use. *Social Science Research*, *25*, 260–280.